Human Rights and Subjectivity

This book draws on a range of theoretical frameworks to challenge the limited conception of subjectivity upon which human rights are based.

The book focuses on some of the ways in which dominant discourses are in tension with human rights' fundamental claim to universality by ignoring multiple ways of being. Different theoretical and methodological approaches are used to analyse this creation of exclusions. These include Hannah Arendt's figure of the refugee, posthumanist critiques and non-Western critical theories such as Black, Indigenous and decolonial approaches. Often these approaches are used in isolation, but together they reveal how the dominant concept of subjectivity has always needed an 'Other' and that the 'human' at the heart of human rights is not a universal concept. The book also pursues an analysis of visual discourses in the field of international human rights, with a focus on the ways in which exclusions are represented and entrenched through the visual. It argues that international human rights are based on a vision-centred sensorium and certain processes of reasoning that exclude emotions. Finally, the book considers how international human rights could embrace other forms of thinking and being in the world and recognize different sensory experiences.

This original perspective on the limits of human rights will appeal to legal theorists, socio-legal scholars, and others working in politics, sociology, anthropology and cultural studies with an interest in contemporary approaches to social justice and critical approaches.

Elisabeth Roy-Trudel is a member of the Centre for Sensory Studies at Concordia University, Montreal, Canada.

Human Rights and Subjectivity

Imagining a Sensing and Feeling Human

Elisabeth Roy-Trudel

Routledge
Taylor & Francis Group
a GlassHouse Book

First published 2025
by Routledge
4 Park Square, Milton Park, Abingdon, Oxon OX14 4RN

and by Routledge
605 Third Avenue, New York, NY 10158

Routledge is an imprint of the Taylor & Francis Group, an informa business

A GlassHouse book

British Library Cataloguing-in-Publication Data
A catalogue record for this book is available from the British Library

Library of Congress Cataloging-in-Publication Data
Names: Roy-Trudel, Elisabeth, 1980– author.
Title: Human rights and subjectivity : imagining a sensing and feeling human / Elisabeth Roy-Trudel.
Description: Abingdon, Oxon [UK] ; New York, NY : Routledge, 2025. | Includes bibliographical references and index.
Identifiers: LCCN 2024029299 (print) | LCCN 2024029300 (ebook) | ISBN 9781032548890 (hardback) | ISBN 9781032548913 (paperback) | ISBN 9781003427957 (ebook)
Subjects: LCSH: Human rights. | International law and human rights. | Subjectivity | Knowledge, Theory of. | Posthumanism—Philosophy.
Classification: LCC K3240 .R85 2025 (print) | LCC K3240 (ebook) | DDC 323.01—dc23/eng/20240625
LC record available at https://lccn.loc.gov/2024029299
LC ebook record available at https://lccn.loc.gov/2024029300

ISBN: 978-1-032-54889-0 (hbk)
ISBN: 978-1-032-54891-3 (pbk)
ISBN: 978-1-003-42795-7 (ebk)

DOI: 10.4324/9781003427957

Typeset in Sabon
by Apex CoVantage, LLC

Contents

Figures

Acknowledgments

This book could not have been completed without the continuous support of and praise from Philipp Kastner. The countless hours Philipp has spent in conversations with me about pretty much every aspect of my research have been very fruitful and rewarding.

I would like to show my gratitude to Amy Swiffen for her thorough engagement with my work. Her insightful feedback has broadened my horizon and pushed me to strengthen my argument even more than I expected. I also express my thanks to David Howes, Nayrouz Abu Hatoum and Sheryl N. Hamilton for their enthusiasm and useful comments made on earlier versions of some of this work; to Colin Perrin and Naomi Round Cahalin from Routledge for their support; and to the anonymous reviewers of the book proposal for their helpful suggestions. While I would never consider this kind of research as being finished, I am glad I completed this manuscript, and I hope it will be an interesting read for others.

Finally, I wish to acknowledge the financial support I have received from the Social Sciences and Humanities Research Council of Canada through a doctoral fellowship; the Social Justice Center of Concordia University; the Centre for Interdisciplinary Studies in Society and Culture of Concordia University; and the Ministère de l'Éducation du Québec. I also thank the Law School at the University of Western Australia for welcoming me, first from 2015 to 2018 as an honorary fellow and subsequently as a visiting research fellow in 2018.

Introduction

There is an apparent contradiction between the professed universal ambition of international human rights law to apply to and protect all individuals and groups and the numerous and varied violations of human rights carried out by states and other actors. Indeed, the list of those who cannot effectively claim their rights is long. Refugees and migrants are particularly evident examples, but there are many individuals and groups for whom rights remain abstract concepts and largely inaccessible in practice.[1] Despite numerous and different kinds of critiques, human rights are still ambiguous and often illusive. It is therefore imperative to try to better understand why, although human rights developed into one of the main global ethical discourses during the second half of the 20th century,[2] the international human rights system continues to fail many people today.

I argue in this book that the dominant subject of human rights needs to be challenged. I focus on the problematic construction of an ideal, or idealized, and normalizing[3] legal subject, and on the related paradoxical tendencies to produce exclusions in international human rights law and practice, notably because of the lack of recognition of the multiple ways of being. Without denying that human rights can have a positive impact, I analyse some of the ways in which dominant human rights discourses afford limited expression and hence perpetuate social exclusions. The international human rights system certainly seeks to include and even to empower everyone, in particular those who are considered vulnerable and who would need the protection of human rights the most; at the same time, and in tension with its fundamental claim to universality, it often denies many individuals and groups their agency. As Boaventura de Sousa Santos and Bruno Sena Martins have

---

1 On the extent of ongoing violations of human rights, see for instance the work of the UN Office of the High Commissioner for Human Rights and specialized non-governmental organizations like Amnesty International and Human Rights Watch.
2 Dembour, 4.
3 Thanks to Sheryl H. Hamilton for pointing out the normalizing aspect of the exclusionary figure of the human.

DOI: 10.4324/9781003427957-1

argued, "most of the world's population is not the subject of human rights, but the object of its discourse".[4] Crucially, inclusion is always conditional and limited, since a complete inclusion – and effective protection – would necessitate embracing the language and logic projected by dominant discourses. This does not imply that international human rights are applied in the same way everywhere or mean the same to everyone;[5] yet there is a dominant approach that, despite multifaceted efforts to render the human rights system more effective, continues to have important shortcomings.

I maintain that the concept of human rights itself is not genuinely inclusive, precisely because it relies on the idea of a certain human as its subject. While the concept of the human is far from clearly defined in relevant human rights texts and other discourses – in fact, "there is nothing simple or straightforward about the human that is said to be the bearer of human rights", as Ben Golder has noted[6] – there is still a tacit understanding of what this human is. For one thing, terms like 'human', 'humanity' and 'humanness' usually have a positive connotation in both everyday and theoretical discourses, as if what they refer to was indubitably admirable and worth protecting, as in the case of human rights.[7] Indeed, the *raison d'être* of the 'human'[8] is rarely questioned, and the implicit assumption is that this concept is useful and ought to be preserved. However, and fundamentally, this 'human' – and idealized subject of human rights – remains embodied by the rational, heterosexual white man of European descent and his sensuous preferences against which other experiences are measured and compared.[9] This means that even though the 'human' lies at the heart of human rights, not all human beings equally fall within their protection. While not arguing "against humanity",[10] I hence interrogate the functions of the dominant and ideological concept of the human, and I do this in three moves. First, I demonstrate by bringing together different critical theories that the 'human' has always been constructed through exclusions, and I develop the figure of *migrating 'Others'* to challenge the dominant subject of human rights and to propose a reconceptualization. Images used in the field illustrate and exacerbate the exclusions underlying this dominant subject, as I then argue by engaging in a critical analysis of visual discourses. Yet the problem is not only what is (or is

---

4 Santos & Sena Martins, 3.
5 On a cross-cultural understanding of human rights, see for instance An-Na'im.
6 Golder, 149.
7 Since the term humanity is often used in a general sense, I believe it is useful to make the following distinction: I tend to associate 'humanity' with the (alleged) community of human beings and 'humanness' with the (alleged) attributes ascribed to being human. This distinction obviously does not always apply when other authors are cited.
8 The 'human' between inverted commas is used to denote the *concept* of the human.
9 Bryans.
10 Dubal.

not) represented but that the international human rights system, in contradiction with its claim to universality, operates with a vision-centred sensorium that overlooks the multiplicity of sensing and being in the world.

Fundamentally, the exclusions that are created through the construction of an idealized subject, and related multiple modes of 'othering' at work in international human rights discourses, are made possible because human rights are built on Western epistemology and ontology.[11] Although claiming to be universal in form and applicability, human rights are a particular moral and legal project stemming largely from Western liberal-legal thought,[12] which explains the tacit assumption of an ideal subject. Due to these cultural – arguably monocultural[13] – and historical origins, the international human rights system is geared to recognize certain subjects as genuine rights bearers and to provide remedies for certain forms of violations, while ignoring others. As an example, the rights of Indigenous peoples and of refugees and migrants have historically been and are still often violated, because these peoples are not considered to be genuine subjects. The United Nations Special Rapporteur on contemporary forms of racism, racial discrimination, xenophobia and related intolerance has highlighted some of the ongoing forms of global exploitation that are related to inherent biases within the international human rights system:

> [t]oo often within the United Nations human rights system, global structural inequality rooted in the histories and political economies of colonial and other forms of imperial subordination receives limited attention. . . . To neglect the global structures of inequality and the global systems that promote or permit the consistent exploitation of certain nations and geographic regions at the expense of others is to endorse an "international" system that exists largely for the benefit of powerful nations and their transnational corporations.[14]

The concept of the human that underlies international human rights law as well as the idea of an 'Other'[15] – and stereotypes associated with this

---

11 The terms 'Western' and the 'West' are often used as a shorthand for a number of complex, interrelated dynamics of domination and exploitation. I engage in more detail with these concepts below and in Chapter 3.

12 International human rights are one of several areas that are governed by Western-derived international law, such as commercial exchanges, labour relations, the environment and finance.

13 Santos & Sena Martins, 1.

14 *Report of the Special Rapporteur on Contemporary Forms of Racism, Racial Discrimination, Xenophobia and Related Intolerance: Global Extractivism and Racial Equality*, para 17.

15 The 'Other' is capitalized to emphasize the creation of an ontological position and to highlight the existence of a genuine subject behind what is usually constructed only in opposition to the dominant subject.

'Other' – are not new; they arguably go back to the origins of Western civilization and the very idea of such a 'civilization'.[16] Indeed, these ideas were already present in ancient Greece and were further entrenched with Christianity. These two traditions assumed the belief in the supposedly unique dignity and worth of human beings,[17] and to be more precise, of certain human beings who were considered 'civilized'. The civilized were defined in opposition to 'non-civilized' people like so-called barbarians, savages or simply foreigners.[18] In fact, in ancient Greece, everything that was "considered alien, exotic, and strange" actually helped define who the Greeks were as a 'civilized' people, which is perceptible in the literature, art and philosophy of the time.[19] From the monsters encountered by civilization in Homer's epic poems to the writings of Socrates, Plato and Aristotle, the idea of an uncivilized 'Other' and stereotypes associated with it have been used since then to describe the relationship between the presumably civilized West and everyone else.[20] The Romans subsequently even entrenched this distinction in law: the *homo humanus*, the educated, civilized Roman citizen, was subjected to the *jus civile* and clearly distinguished from all others living in the Empire, referred to as barbarians.[21] As Costas Douzinas has pointed out, "[t]he concept 'humanity' has been consistently used to separate, distribute, and classify people into rulers, ruled, and excluded. 'Humanity' acts as a normative source for politics and law against a background of variable inhumanity".[22] This trend still underpins contemporary social and political life in various contexts. For instance, Sam Dubal argues in an ethnographic study of the Lord's Resistance Army, a Ugandan armed opposition group, that "under some of the most innocent and well-meaning uses of humanity lie moralizing agendas that obfuscate the experiences and social relations of life on the ground".[23] Yet, social life is more complex than the oftentimes "limiting, simplistic, and moralizing" claims to humanity.[24] In sum, deploying the concepts of humanity and the 'human' to distinguish and to define the Western

---

16 Williams, 4.
17 Anderson, *Race*, 35. On the complex notion of human dignity, see for instance McCrudden. Hannah Arendt also expressed doubts in regard to the concept of dignity because of its ambiguity. Arendt, *The Origins of Totalitarianism*, 298. For a discussion of dignity beyond the Eurocentric understanding and various examples from the Global South, see the contributions in Santos & Sena Martins, eds.
18 Douzinas, 52.
19 Williams, 4.
20 Williams, 5–7. This idea of an 'Other' is, for instance, present in Aristotle's writings on the *polis* and its inhabitant, the *zoon politikon*, which are both marked by exclusion. Glendinning, 26.
21 Douzinas, 53.
22 Douzinas, 53.
23 Dubal, 12.
24 Dubal, 9.

subject has a long tradition that continues to create forms of domination and exclusions, including in the context of international human rights.

A key question raised by some scholars in the social sciences and humanities hence is who is or can be a genuine subject. As Alexander Nékám wrote already in the 1930s, the concept of the legal subject has no essence; the subject is always a subjective construction or, said differently, a result of emotional judgment. Whenever one tries to define who the subject of rights is, one merely ends up asserting "the answers dictated by the system in which we ourselves were brought up and which, therefore, seem natural and reasonable to us".[25] One has the tendency to "regard the values he [sic] accepts, the set of conditions he is familiar with, as absolute and the only natural ones"; what one considers lawful and just is always a result of "certain emotions" learned through a specific upbringing in a specific community, the result of "the structure and outlook of the society in which they lived".[26] Because of the structure and parameters of Western modern thought, it is also unclear if any beings other than humans could ever be considered real subjects. As Matthew Calarco has argued from a posthumanist approach, "[t]he subject is not just the *fundamentum inconcussum* of modernity but is the avowedly *human* locus of this foundation".[27] It is as if human beings have built a mirror in which they can recognize only themselves;[28] a mirror in which nonhuman beings could appreciate themselves – or in which humans could appreciate non-human beings on the latter's terms – appears to be a conceptual impossibility. Within the anthropocentric model, no being could receive attention without adopting that model's language and codes.[29] Moreover, while the Western modern perspective puts forth the idea that it is the individual subject that has rights and produces knowledge by itself, from a decolonial perspective, the subject needs other beings to exist and forms itself precisely in relation with other subjects. In the words of Aníbal Quijano, "[e]very individual discourse, or reflection, remits to a structure of intersubjectivity. The former is constituted in and vis a vis the latter".[30] In other words, the concept of subjectivity is not an envelope that could easily be filled with whatever forms of life; it has never been a neutral concept, but rather a loaded and problematic one.

The focus in dominant Western thought on rationality and the sidelining of emotions and the senses (aside from vision) is a form of 'othering'

---

25 Nékám, 21.

26 Nékám, 6–7, 14.

27 Calarco, 10.

28 In fact, Agamben maintains that the human "has no specific identity other than the *ability* to recognize himself . . . *man is the animal that must recognize itself as human to be human*". Agamben, *The Open*, 26.

29 Calarco, 9.

30 Quijano, 173.

that creates particular ethical and practical challenges in the context of presumably universal international human rights. The concept of rights, for instance, at the core of the international human rights system, and the idea of conceiving individuals as "interchangeable units"[31] originated from Western rational thought and were foreign to many other legal traditions.[32] The Western world, in what can only be described as a continuous form of imperialism, imposed its worldview and way of reasoning on other traditions and considered other forms of thinking to be irrational. As Martha Nussbaum has argued,

> a colonial form of "argument" holds the people of developing countries to be, in general, excessively emotional and unfit for self-government. Stereotypes of the people of India, or of Africa, as "intuitive", "irrational", "emotional" are too common to require illustration – and one can add that this simple portrait is all too often produced by alleged admirers of these societies as well as by detractors.[33]

Alternative perspectives are often dismissed not only as irrational but also as utopian and unrealistic. Santos, who is an important source of inspiration for this book and who persuasively calls for the recognition of alternative epistemologies, explains that the West cannot imagine real alternatives:

> [t]he oppressors tend to experience the world in which they live as the best possible world. The same is true for all those who, not being directly oppressors, benefit from oppressive practices. As far as they are concerned, it is rational to wager on the impossibility of a better world.[34]

I claim that a related form of 'othering' occurs because visuality and understanding the world primarily through the sense of vision are a privileged way of thinking and being in international human rights law. This visiocracy, which is grounded in the Western predilection for rationality, sidelines other ways of thinking and being in the world and, as a result, generates certain exclusions in the international human rights system. The omnipresence of images in the context of human rights may appear natural, particularly to those raised in a Western context; yet the use of certain images and the heavy reliance on images and vision itself are not neutral endeavours.

I challenge this visiocracy based on the argument that all the senses, and not only vision, contribute to defining human beings as individuals and as groups,

---

31 Nedelsky, 97.
32 Rights are, of course, tied to the construct of the state, itself a product of Western rational thought. Glenn, 276.
33 Nussbaum, "Emotions and Women's Capabilities", 365.
34 Santos, "A Non-Occidentalist West?", 120.

and that it is these individuals and groups that make law and give meaning to human rights. This is especially relevant considering both international human rights' notorious claim to universal application and the possibility that not everyone expresses oneself – including one's legal subjectivity – in terms of rationality and vision, or through the five senses commonly recognized in the West. My research therefore highlights the importance of other senses, including but also going beyond the four other senses that are, in addition to vision, part of the Western sensorium, for the construction and expression of the self and its legal subjectivity. Different ways of sensing and being, such as those in the tradition of Indigenous peoples, are insightful here and illustrate the currently limited reach of international human rights. Allowing Indigenous peoples to give evidence in alternative ways, for instance through songs and dances, before tribunals in settler colonial states and international human rights bodies,[35] can be considered an interesting and welcome, yet only superficial, recognition of the relevance of different sensoria and associated forms of knowledge. A more substantial appreciation – beyond such specific procedural issues – of different epistemologies and ontologies could arguably go to the roots of the problem. Fundamentally, this book therefore asks whether and how it would be possible to embrace other ways of thinking and being in the world and to recognize different sensory experiences and lexicons within the international human rights framework.

Theoretical and methodological framework

In order to analyse and challenge the problematic, tacit assumption that there is a certain, ideal subject underpinning international human rights, I build on different theoretical and methodological approaches stemming from several disciplines. First, my research is inspired by socio-legal and legal-pluralist approaches that highlight the legal agency of subjects and their role in legal meaning-making and, as I understand these approaches, also the multiplicity of ways of being.[36] This means that in international human rights law, as in other legal systems, law – here understood in a non-prescriptivist sense as interaction governed by rules[37] – not only assumes but also constitutes legal subjectivity. The constitution of legal subjectivity is important and powerful since this subjectivity embodies and signals social values and aspirations and transforms desires into rights.[38] The way legal subjectivity is conceptualized hence determines not only who is a legal subject that has rights and duties but affects the very meaning of law and rights. This is the case even if, as in

35 E.g. Koch & Grace.
36 E.g. Macdonald, "Metaphors of Multiplicity"; Kleinhans & Macdonald; Merry; Griffiths; Wilson.
37 This definition draws on Macdonald. See e.g. Macdonald & Sandomierski, 616.
38 E.g. Grear; Fagundes.

international human rights, the subject often remains ambiguous or implicit. Relying on critical legal pluralism[39] helps to realize that the legal subject is often disempowered and that it is only an abstract individual "subsumed under one (or even several) homogenous labels, instead of being allowed to persist as heterogeneous, multiple creatures".[40] This also sheds light on the exclusion of non-dominant subjects and on the existence of silenced normative orders and discourses. An understanding of law and legal subjects that is infused by critical legal pluralism and that is, as I believe, compatible with other critical approaches relied upon in this book is therefore useful to grasp and address structural inequalities and power dynamics that affect legal subjects.

To explore the necessity and possibilities of reconceptualizing the dominant subject of international human rights and to highlight fundamental gaps in the theorization of human rights, I develop the figure of *migrating 'Others'*. To do this I draw, more specifically, on several critical theories from the social sciences and the humanities. As I show by relying on Hannah Arendt's theory, the main issue does not revolve around the practical application of human rights, but rather around the deeper question of who has the "right to have rights".[41] Arendt, who proposed one of the most powerful early critiques of human rights, highlighted that one of the fundamental shortcomings of the modern system is that the individual needs to be a citizen to be a genuine subject of international human rights.[42] She argued that because of the state-based structure of the human rights system, which presupposes the sovereignty of states and designates them as the primary duty-bearers, the 'proper' subject needs to be not only human in the generic sense but also a citizen of a state. Even if human rights – at least in their international form – purport to apply to all, it has always been the citizen that supposedly lives the appropriate life. Rights are granted to the human being by the state only to the extent to which this person is assumed to be a citizen. In other words, the exclusions built into the category of citizenship are implicitly translated into the international human rights system. Because there is no space within this state for a human being to exist autonomously, Arendt profoundly questioned human rights. Her figure of the refugee is particularly insightful in this context. The idea that refugees are not an exception of the political system but "the most symptomatic group in contemporary politics"[43] brings to light a threat that could potentially affect everyone. It reveals structural problems challenging the foundational claim to universality of human rights, and it points to deep tensions within liberal democratic

---

39 E.g. Kleinhans & Macdonald; Macdonald & Sandomierski; Melissaris.
40 Kleinhans & Macdonald, 36.
41 Arendt, *The Origins of Totalitarianism*, 296.
42 Arendt, *The Origins of Totalitarianism*; Arendt, "We Refugees".
43 Arendt, *The Origins of Totalitarianism*, 277.

states and to real exclusions that exist because of the way the system works. Her thinking, as well as more contemporary perspectives on refugees and migrants that build on her critique, such as those of Giorgio Agamben[44] and Seyla Benhabib,[45] are particularly useful to explore the argument that the traditional concept of the citizen-subject of international human rights is problematic.

I also work with posthumanism and several theories from the margins, namely Black, Indigenous and decoloniality approaches, which challenge the dominant Western epistemology and ontology and deconstruct dominant categorizations and assumptions, including with respect to human rights and its subject. While these critical theories put forward various reasons and deploy different strategies, they all help understand that Western claims are not objective but, like all claims, situated and hence biased.[46] From this, it follows that the 'human', to take a concept at the heart of human rights, is not a universal concept but is historically determined. Posthumanist critiques[47] point out that the concept of the human has always had flaws and negative consequences. They highlight, in particular, the false assumption of a necessary and inherent difference between human and nonhuman beings, the resulting alleged superiority of the former, as well as the related essentialization of groups of beings. As for Black,[48] Indigenous[49] and decoloniality[50] approaches, they arguably make even more profound critiques about modernity and the modern ontology than posthumanism could offer, including at the level of knowledge and knowledge production. These theories from the margins, indeed, reveal some of the inherent biases and shortcomings of Eurocentric concepts.

It should be noted that these theories from the margins, which are sometimes referred to as theories from the Global South, are not limited to the geographical localization but can be considered "a metaphor for the systematic suffering inflicted upon large bodies of population by Western-centric colonialism, capitalism, and patriarchy"; as argued by Santos, the Global South is found both outside and inside Europe, North America and other dominant societies.[51] It should also be stressed that the Western world – or

---

44 E.g. Agamben, "We Refugees"; Agamben, "Beyond Human Rights".
45 E.g. Benhabib, *The Reluctant Modernism of Hannah Arendt*; Benhabib, *The Rights of Others*.
46 See e.g. Barreto, "Decolonial Thinking", 490–1.
47 E.g. Z. I. Jackson, "Animal"; Whatmore, "Humanism's Excess"; Wolfe, *Animal Rights*; Wolfe, "What Is Posthumanism?".
48 E.g. Anderson, *Race*; Z. I. Jackson, "Outer Worlds"; Walcott.
49 E.g. Blaser, "Ontology and Indigeneity"; Cameron, de Leeuw & Desbiens; Hunt; Radcliffe, "Geography and Indigeneity I"; Radcliffe, "Geography and Indigeneity II".
50 E.g. Maldonado-Torres; Mignolo, "Introduction – Coloniality of Power and De-Colonial Thinking"; Quijano.
51 Santos, "Epilogue", 175–6.

the Global North, as it is also called – is not to be understood as a monolithic entity, as there has always been some diversity in approaches, and the Western world has also undergone significant changes over time and continues to evolve.[52] However, while there are of course cultural differences between so-called Western countries or cultures, there are also similarities, notably due to a shared Judeo-Christian heritage. A dominant, and arguably hegemonic, worldview does exist and is palpable in the field of international human rights, having its roots in Eurocentric thought. Using the term 'the West', or the 'Western world', as I do in these pages, also recognizes the lingering effect of colonialism stemming from Europe, as will be explored in more detail in Chapter 3. Finally, while I believe that drawing on different critical theories and their combined insights allows questioning the prevailing privilege of Western thought in a powerful way, I also seek to respect and highlight the particularities of each approach.

Building on these critical theories and their insights, I then turn to ways in which exclusions are exemplified and entrenched through visual discourses in international human rights, which are a result of the vision-centredness of human rights. First, to lay the groundwork for this analysis, I explore the idea that in international human rights, like in Western law and culture more generally,[53] the visual – mainly in the form of photographs and videos – is omnipresent and has important effects. The images used by various actors in the field of international human rights, for instance to attract potential donors and justify certain forms of intervention, often rely on and reinforce preconceived ideas about who deserves rights and, by extension, they make fundamental assertions on legal subjectivity. In that sense, images are not only omnipresent in human rights; as I argue, they are also tools to define, categorize and delineate legal subjectivity. The importance and the role of the visual discourse are, however, rarely discussed in this context.

Relying on a combination of iconography, iconology and semiotics,[54] which are methods that are commonly used in the social sciences and the humanities to analyse different visual materials and which can usefully inform each other in the study of both historical and contemporary images,[55] I subsequently pursue a critical analysis of visual discourses[56] of human rights. I consider iconic images in the history of human rights as well as contemporary

---

52 The term Global South is of course not without its problems either, among other reasons because it does not capture the great diversity of perspectives in the South. Comaroff & Comaroff.

53 E.g. Dahlberg; Douzinas & Nead; Flynn; Goodrich, "Visiocracy: On the Futures of the Fingerpost"; Sherwin.

54 E.g. D'Alleva; Barthes.

55 van Leeuwen.

56 E.g. Stuart Hall; van Leeuwen & Jewitt; Rose. On critical discourse analysis more generally, including iconography as part of a multimodal analysis, see Machin & Mayr.

examples of images used in the field. The purpose of such a critical visual discourse analysis does not only consist in understanding how meaning, including legal meaning, is expressed through images; it also entails exploring how images shape legal ideology, consciousness and subjectivities. In other words, I seek to show how the exclusions and forms of 'othering' that I identify in the theoretical discussion structure how these images, as well as their meanings and influence, are used in this context. I ask what type of subject of human rights these images portray and what this suggests about human rights discourses more broadly. The analysis of such images is pursued at a formal and a contextual level in search for meaning: I study visual elements, consider signs and meanings associated with them and draw on knowledge about the context and cultural background of the image. I am particularly interested in understanding who and what is represented, in which ways and for which reasons, whose voices are expressed and whose are ignored, and who can potentially benefit from the representation in question. I believe this analysis reflects the important power dynamics that I identify as being at play in international human rights, notably in terms of representing certain subjects in certain ways. This also takes up the call made by critical theories from the margins to seriously consider the diversity of sites and modes of knowledge and knowledge production. Such an exploratory, qualitative methodological approach is useful to test and illustrate my theoretical arguments, and to study the meaning and meaning-making of law and subjectivities.

Then, with respect to a perhaps even more fundamental aspect of my analysis, I discuss the idea that it is not only the kind of visual discourse that may be problematic and lead to exclusions, but the very fact that visuality dominates and precludes other ways of expressing oneself in and through international human rights. To explore the shortcomings and implications of the visiocracy of international human rights for the construction and expression of subjectivity, it seems important to attend to the possibility of a fuller sensorium and to consider the role of emotions in the context of human rights. Indeed, while law sees itself as rational and objective, which explains and reinforces its heavy reliance on the allegedly most rational sense of vision, law and emotions scholarship,[57] has shown that emotions are entangled with all things related to law. In fact, recent research in the humanities, social sciences and neuroscience has revealed that emotions are involved in cognitive thinking. Rationality, in other words, is not detached from emotions, which suggests that Western law is not as objective as it tends to portray itself. Emotions are part of legal reasoning and are involved in determining legal subjectivity, with important consequences for the protection and promotion of human rights. Moreover, the Western world might privilege the

---

57 E.g. Bandes, "Introduction"; Makdisi, "Legal Logic"; Maroney; Nedelsky; Nussbaum, "Secret Sewers of Vice"; Sanger; West, "Disciplines, Subjectivity, and Law".

sense of vision – admittedly often unconsciously – and consider it to be the most rational and hence legitimate sense; yet, as I argue, this is not a truly universal understanding. Anthropological scholarship on the senses, including ethnographies that study the roles and meanings of different senses in specific contexts, supports this analysis.[58] The senses as a means of inquiry reveal the variety of ways in which different sensory experiences and their meanings, often as part of everyday life, construct identities of both individuals and groups, and even define the 'human'. Such an approach can also expose hierarchies, stereotypes, hegemonic influences and other biases that are significant – but often concealed – for the construction and expression of identities of both dominant and dominated groups and that are responsible for various forms of privilege and disadvantage, inclusion and exclusion. These insights allow me to explore the idea that the international human rights system, because of its visiocracy and alleged rationality, does not grasp such complexities and the importance of the senses and of emotions in constituting identities and subjectivities. This failure appears to be one of the reasons why the system creates and sustains paradoxical exclusions of many individuals and groups, and why it is therefore deeply problematic to work with a model of human rights that is heavily based on one sense.

Contributions and objectives

My research aims to identify one of the fundamental reasons why international human rights, despite an increasingly sophisticated institutional architecture, continue to fail many people. Admittedly, international human rights have been criticized from various angles and through various approaches since their emergence in the middle of the 20th century. Important critiques have focused, among others, on the alleged basis on shared values and fundamental claim to universality and on the colonial and (neo)imperial tendencies of the international human rights system; on the sovereignty of states and the lack of effective enforcement mechanisms; and on the gendered nature that infuses international human rights.[59] Unlike these more established approaches, the critical theories that I discuss in this book have not been relied upon in any systematic manner to inform critiques vis-à-vis international human rights and its dominant subject. Moreover, if scholars have started to consider the relationships between law and images, law and emotions, and law and the senses, as I discuss in detail in the following chapters, very little

---

58 E.g. Bently; Classen, "Foundations"; Howes, "Introduction: 'To Summon All the Senses'"; Howes, "Introduction: Empire of the Senses"; Howes & Classen; Hsu; Ong. For ethnographies specifically, see for instance, Geurts; McHugh; Newcomb; Potter; Seremetakis; Stroeken.

59 E.g. Douzinas; Kennedy, "International Human Rights Movement"; Rajagopal; Charlesworth, Chinkin & Wright; Engle.

attention has been given to international human rights in this literature. In other words, there exists a robust body of literature on international human rights and their critiques, but the exclusions related to the visual in the context of international human rights have not yet been discussed in any depth, which is what I do here. More specifically, through an analysis of the role of visual discourses and of the possibility of a fuller sensorium in international human rights, I try to understand whether and in which ways subjects construct – or deconstruct – law, rights and subjectivity. This seems particularly relevant because critical analyses of human rights have often focused on the concept of rights and its implications, which can be seen as part of a larger trend of scholarly focus on objectivity, such as the objectivity of legal interpretation, and not on legal subjectivity.[60] However, the concepts of the human and of legal subjectivity also lie at the root of numerous problems related to human rights, and analysing these concepts in the context of human rights allows uncovering many factors that have long been overlooked.[61] It also prompts the somewhat paradoxical question as to who is, in fact, a subject in the international human rights system – and, more generally, who counts as a human being – and the question as to how this subject lives and constructs its subjectivity. In this sense, my focus does not lie on identifying and suggest-ing remedies for specific rights violations that occur because of the sensuous preferences, or biases, built into the international human rights system; I am concerned with the historical and ongoing construction of the concept of the human that prevents many individuals and groups, who are supposed to be bearers of human rights, from accessing these rights. In other words, while it is, of course, important to denounce specific rights violations, such as illegal pushback operations, the arbitrary detention and ill-treatment of migrants, I try to put the finger on the underlying conceptual factors that enable such dynamics in the first place.

In sum, this book aims to contribute to the existing critical literature by offering a new story about human rights. It challenges the idealized subject of international human rights through the figure of *migrating 'Others'* and, by relying on an innovative combination of theoretical and methodologi-cal approaches from the social sciences and the humanities, it deconstructs the visual discourses in international human rights and the normalization of its subject through the senses. These approaches are often used in isolation but, as I submit, they can usefully inform each other, including in a critical discussion of the subject of international human rights. Through such a com-bination of approaches, I therefore seek to comprehend and explain some of

---

60 Balkin, 107; Boyle, 489.
61 Trying to reveal such root causes that may explain why the human rights system fails many individuals and groups does not, of course, imply that flaws in policies and procedures – what Susan Marks has provocatively called "planned misery" – are not relevant. See Marks.

the implicit and rarely exposed biases and sources of exclusion inherent in international human rights, which, despite professing universality, remain dominated by Western-sourced thought and its conception of the senses.

Outline of the book

Part I lays the groundwork for and informs my critique of the dominant subject of the international human rights system. In the three chapters that compose this Part, I draw on Hannah Arendt's figure of the refugee, posthumanist critiques and several non-Western critical theories to expose one of the central weaknesses of the international human rights system, namely its concept of the human. I argue that the dominant ways of conceiving legal subjectivity are problematic and that more attention needs to be paid to this concept. My discussion also points to the inherently fragmented and plural nature of legal subjectivity as well as the capacity of legal subjects to create law and their normative universe.

More specifically, in the first chapter I explain and build on Arendt's figure of the refugee. I also rely on contemporary scholars theorizing human rights, such as Giorgio Agamben and Seyla Benhabib, who have been highly influenced by Arendt's thinking, to further develop and actualize the figure of the refugee: as I argue, the figure of the *migrant* represents a particular challenge to – but also possibility for – the current human rights paradigm. The figure of the *migrant*, as opposed to the narrower figure of the refugee, is not dependent on and goes beyond the specific criteria of being a refugee under international law. I also suggest that the subject of human rights can and should be reconceptualized beyond state sovereignty and citizenship. While not directly dealing with practical problems encountered by refugees, migrants and others whose human rights are often not protected, this analysis is nevertheless inspired by their lived and concrete realities of exclusion, discrimination and dehumanization.

In the second chapter I explore an important way, namely posthumanism, in which critical scholars in the West have attempted to decentre and critique the human, which helps reveal the construction of a certain type of subject of international human rights. While the human being is the only recognized subject of humanism, and therefore also of human rights, the construction of the human as a concept is, as posthumanist authors suggest, a result of processes that have discriminated against nonhuman beings and some, or rather many, human beings. This is particularly relevant for my discussion of the dominant subject of international human rights. I rely on posthumanism to demonstrate that both non-human animals and, perhaps somewhat surprisingly, many human beings are excluded or kept far away from humanity and precluded from enjoying protections, such as human rights guarantees, and that these exclusions are made possible by processes of dehumanization and animalization. So-called irregular migrants, who do not match the current definition of an ideal subject, illustrate this particularly well. This is why posthumanist authors that I discuss advocate for a fundamental change in the nature of thought, which implies resisting hegemonic discourses and rethinking the relationships between beings in non-anthropocentric terms. While this might challenge the very idea of human rights, it could also usefully inform the reconceptualization of the human in human rights, as I suggest through the refined figure of the *migrating 'Other'*.

The third chapter focuses on the ways in which Black, Indigenous and de-coloniality approaches all suggest a pressing need to go beyond Eurocentric critiques of Eurocentrism. These theories from the margins bring to light the fact that Western theory has always needed an 'Other' to define a subject and that the concept of subjectivity has remained indebted to what has been persistently ignored or rejected. This is also true in regard to the concept of the human, including as the subject of international human rights. In the words of Santos, the Western "concept of humanity is unthinkable without the concept of subhumanity".[62] This historical bias arguably continues to affect the conceptualization and application of international human rights today. These theories from the margins are hence useful to understand the ongoing debates concerning the concept of the human and the plurality of ways of being, as I highlight through a final refinement of the figure that I propose, namely the figure of *migrating 'Others'*.

Building on these theoretical discussions, Part II turns to the sensuous aspects of international human rights. It starts by highlighting the omnipresence and great influence of vision and the visual in the Western-rooted field of human rights and then offers a challenge to this omnipresence that has problematically sidelined the other senses.

I therefore embark in Chapter 4 on an analysis of visual discourses in the field of international human rights. I rely on iconography, iconology and semiotics to ask, in particular: how are subjects represented in the context of international human rights? To situate this analysis, I start the chapter by recalling the great power of images, which is too rarely recognized in the context of modern law, including international human rights law, although the visual is omnipresent in the legal sphere. Having in mind the idea that the professed universality of international human rights should concern their applicability *and* their form, I argue that more attention needs to be paid to the visual discourse, although – or rather because – not everyone would naturally or primarily rely on this mode of expression. International human rights law, precisely because of its claim to universality, should be aware of its visual biases that create and entrench certain forms of domination and exclusion. The visual discourse used in international human rights law may be conceived as a universal language; in fact, it prevents large sections of society

---

62 Santos, "Human Rights, Democracy and Development", 25.

from creating their own legal subjectivity and from accessing rights. By addressing questions of cultural meaning, agency and power of the creators, subjects and consumers of images, the critical discourse analysis in this chapter therefore seeks to understand some of the complex connections between images and human rights, and society more generally.

I consider some of the key moments in the history of human rights that have been depicted visually, namely the adoption of the 1789 *Déclaration des droits de l'homme et du citoyen* and the adoption of the *Universal Declaration of Human Rights* in 1948. The drafting of these declarations obviously occurred within a particular context, but, as I maintain, looking at the images produced at such decisive moments can nonetheless reveal much about the crystallization of certain concepts and norms that are still relevant. I also analyse several pictures used by major United Nations bodies concerned with human rights, such as in reports published and distributed by the Office of the High Commissioner for Human Rights and the High Commissioner for Refugees. Moreover, to show the gaps between the perception of those working in the human rights system and those 'subjected' to it, my analysis not only includes 'official' visual discourses, like images produced by the United Nations, one of the main actors in the international human rights system; it also studies ways in which persons who experience human rights violations present themselves. Self-representation, for instance how refugees and migrants visually represent themselves, can arguably be a meaningful, if inherently limited, way to resist dominant forms of defining and categorizing individuals and groups and, therefore, represents an insightful source of alternative discourses.[63] Moreover, to contextualize the supremacy of Western thought and visual discourse in human rights, my analysis considers non-Western approaches, as for example the ways in which some Indigenous artists conceive and represent (or not) the human in their work.

Informed by the insights of the visual discourse analysis, I demonstrate in Chapter 5 that the international human rights system, which is based on a vision-centred sensorium and, as a field of law more generally, on allegedly rational processes of reasoning devoid of emotions, makes problematic assumptions about its subjects. More specifically, I argue that the currently dominant system largely ignores the multiple ways in which legal subjectivity and humanness are constructed and expressed through the senses as well as through emotions. This, in turn, discriminates against many, if not most, people: with some ways of sensing the world conceived as natural, and others overlooked and discredited, arbitrary categorizations of people, for instance along ability/disability, gender and ethnicity, are considered natural.[64] The denial of human rights and the objectivization of certain bodies, such as

63 See e.g. Schwartz.
64 Davis, 75–6.

those of refugees and migrants, as I discuss, are dramatic examples of such processes of sidelining or 'othering' through the senses.

In the first section of this chapter, I challenge the long-standing claim in Western legal thought that law is intertwined with both rationality and vision, and that emotions and the senses other than vision can only be part of extra-legal processes. I turn to law and emotions scholarship to demonstrate that emotions are omnipresent in the legal realm, including in the field of international human rights law, and cannot be separated from the kind of reasoning promoted by dominant legal thought. Based on these insights, I argue that the relationship between law and the emotions should be acknowledged, notably to give more space and agency to individuals and groups that have been marginalized by the currently dominant model that seeks to keep international human rights and its subject away from emotions. In the next sections of this chapter, I rely on anthropological scholarship on the senses and ethnographies to explore the relevance of the senses for the construction of legal subjectivity in the field of international human rights law. Ethnographic studies concerned with the senses inform the discussion and highlight that, in addition to cultures having different sensoria – that is different from the Western 'classic five' model – there is also great variation in the ways in which the senses are categorized and hierarchized. Moreover, there can be several sensoria within a given culture, and sensoria can be influenced by the specific social context and the type of social interaction. Building on this anthropological scholarship, I also demonstrate that the senses play a crucial part in the construction of the self, but that they do so in different ways for different individuals and groups. This analysis supports my argument that identities and subjectivities, and different forms of inclusion and exclusion, are constructed and expressed through the senses in ways that cannot be captured by the largely vision-centred international human rights system. Indeed, the continued reliance on Western rational-legal thought and its biased sensorium, although rarely recognized and discussed, constitutes an important obstacle to fulfilling the emancipatory and counter-hegemonic potential of human rights. This is why, as I maintain, it would be important that the human rights system recognize the fundamental role played by the senses and seek to be more inclusive, in particular by embracing sensory experiences beyond the dominant Western tradition. Indeed, international human rights law could and should be more attentive to other ways of sensing, feeling and understanding the world, as lived and expressed by different individuals and groups. Contemporary political and social life is shaped by a diversity of political and legal cultures, and their respective sensoria and relationships with emotions, that determine which experiences and motivations are considered valid. There are different ways of being human and of being a subject of human rights: beyond citizenship, beyond vision, and beyond rationality.

In conclusion, I argue that this diversity should not only be acknowledged but also embraced by the international human rights system, especially if it wants to honour its own ambition to be universal (even if this goal might not be achievable). This could also be an avenue to break with the enduring tendency to create 'Others' and associated hierarchies and exclusions, and hence to strengthen the emancipatory potential of human rights. Liberating itself from Western thought and its dominant sensorium would, among others, imply for the international human rights system trying to do justice to different relationships with the senses and with emotions. Inspiration could come from non-Western experiences, knowledges and scholarship, as expressed, for instance, by Santos' invitation to learn from the South.[65] I therefore suggest that international human rights law, to become more inclusive and legitimate, should be open to alternative discourses, knowledges and approaches, even if they may challenge some of its own ontological and epistemological foundations.

Bibliography

Agamben, Giorgio. "We Refugees" (1995) 49:2 *Symposium: A Quarterly Journal in Modern Literatures* 114.
———. *The Open: Man and Animal* (Stanford: Stanford University Press, 2004).
———. "Beyond Human Rights" (2008) 15 *Social Engineering* 90.
Anderson, Kay. *Race and the Crisis of Humanism* (London: Routledge, 2007).
An-Na'im, Abdullahi A. "Toward a Cross-Cultural Approach to Defining International Standards of Human Rights: The Meaning of Cruel, Inhuman, or Degrading Treatment or Punishment" in Abdullahi A. An-Na'im, ed, *Human Rights in Cross-Cultural Perspectives: A Quest for Consensus* (Philadelphia: University of Pennsylvania Press, 1992).
Arendt, Hannah. *The Origins of Totalitarianism* (Cleveland: Meridian Books, 1958).
———. "We Refugees" in Marc Robinson, ed, *Altogether Elsewhere* (London: Faber and Faber, 1994) 111.
Balkin, J.M. "Understanding Legal Understanding: The Legal Subject and the Problem of Legal Coherence" (1993) 103:1 *Yale Law Journal* 105.
Bandes, Susan A. "Introduction" in Susan A Bandes, ed, *The Passions of Law* (New York: New York University Press, 1999) 1.
Barreto, José Manuel. "Decolonial Thinking and the Quest for Decolonising Human Rights" (2018) 46 *Asian Journal of Social Science* 484.
Barthes, Roland. *Éléments de sémiologie* (Paris: Éditions du Seuil, 1964).
Benhabib, Seyla. *The Reluctant Modernism of Hannah Arendt* (London: Sage, 1996).
———. *The Rights of Others: Aliens, Residents, and Citizens* (Cambridge: Cambridge University Press, 2004).
Bently, Lionel. "Introduction" in L. Bently and L. Flynn, eds, *Law and the Senses: Sensational Jurisprudence* (London: Pluto Press, 1996) 1.
Blaser, Mario. "Ontology and Indigeneity: On the Political Ontology of Heterogeneous Assemblages" (2014) 21:1 *Cultural Geographies* 49.
Boyle, James. "Is Subjectivity Possible? The Postmodern Subject in Legal Theory" (1991) 62 *University of Colorado Law Review* 489.
Bryans, John. "Masculinity Studies and the Senses", <www.lawandthesenses.org>.

---

65 Santos, *Epistemologies of the South*.

Calarco, Matthew. *Zoographies: The Question of the Animal from Heidegger to Derrida* (New York: Columbia University Press, 2008).

Cameron, Emilie, Sarah de Leeuw & Caroline Desbiens. "Indigeneity and Ontology" (2014) 21:1 *Cultural Geographies* 19.

Charlesworth, Hilary, Christine Chinkin & Shelley Wright. "Feminist Approaches to International Law" (1991) 85:4 *American Journal of International Law* 613.

Classen, Constance. "Foundations of an Anthropology of the Senses" (1997) 49:153 *International Social Science Journal* 401.

Comaroff, Jean & John L. Comaroff. *Theories from the South: Or, How Euro-America Is Evolving toward Africa* (Boulder, CO: Paradigm Publishers, 2012).

Dahlberg, Leif. "Introduction: Visualising Law and Authority" in Leif Dahlberg, ed, *Visualizing Law and Authority: Essays on Legal Aesthetics* (Berlin: Walter de Gruyter 2012) 4.

D'Alleva, Anne. *How to Write Art History* (London: Laurence King, 2006).

Davis, Elizabeth. "Structures of Seeing: Blindness, Race, and Gender in Visual Culture" (2019) 14:1 *The Senses and Society* 63.

Dembour, Marie-Bénédicte. "What are Human Rights? Four Schools of Thought" (2010) 32 *Human Rights Quarterly* 1.

Douzinas, Costas. "The Paradoxes of Human Rights" (2013) 20:1 *Constellations* 51.

Douzinas, Costas & Lynda Nead. "Introduction" in Costas Douzinas & Lynda Nead, eds, *Law and the Image: The Authority of Art and the Aesthetics of Law* (Chicago: University of Chicago Press, 1999).

Dubal, Sam. *Against Humanity: Lessons from the Lord's Resistance Army* (Oakland, CA: University of California Press, 2018).

Engle, Karen. "Female Subjects of Public International Law: Human Rights and the Exotic Other Female" (1991) 26 *New England Law Review* 1509.

Fagundes, David. "What We Talk about When We Talk about Persons: The Language of Legal Fiction" (2001) 114:6 *Harvard Law Review* 1745.

Flynn, Leo. "See What I Mean: The Authority of Law and Visions of Women" in L. Bently & L. Flynn, eds, *Law and the Senses: Sensational Jurisprudence* (London: Pluto Press, 1996) 139.

Geurts, Kathryn Linn. *Culture and the Senses – Bodily Ways of Knowing in an African Community* (Berkeley: University of California Press, 2002).

Glendinning, Simon. "From Animal Life to City Life" (2000) 5:3 *Angelaki: Journal of the Theoretical Humanities* 19.

Glenn, H. Patrick. *Legal Traditions of the World: Sustainable Diversity in Law*, 5th ed (Oxford: Oxford University Press, 2014).

Golder, Ben. "Critical Humanities and the Human of International Human Rights Law" in Shane Chalmers & Sundhya Pahuja, eds, *Routledge Handbook of International Law and the Humanities* (New York: Routledge, 2023) 148.

Goodrich, Peter. "Visiocracy: On the Futures of the Fingerpost" (2013) 39:3 *Critical Inquiry* 498.

Grear, Anna. "Human Rights – Human Bodies? Some Reflections on Corporate Human Rights Distortion, The Legal Subject, Embodiment and Human Rights Theory" (2006) 17:2 *Law and Critique* 171.

Griffiths, John. "What Is Legal Pluralism?" (1986) 24 *Journal of Legal Pluralism* 1.

Hall, Stuart. "The Spectacle of the 'Other'" in Stuart Hall, ed, *Representation: Cultural Representations and Signifying Practices* (London: Sage, 1997) 223.

Howes, David. "Introduction: 'To Summon All the Senses'" in David Howes, ed, *The Varieties of Sensory Experience: A Sourcebook in the Anthropology of the Senses* (Toronto: University of Toronto Press, 1991) 3.

———. "Introduction: Empire of the Senses" in David Howes, ed, *Empire of the Senses – The Sensual Culture Reader* (New York: Berg, 2005) 1.

Howes, David & Constance Classen. *Ways of Sensing: Understanding the Senses in Society* (New York: Routledge, 2014).

Hsu, Elisabeth. "The Senses and the Social: An Introduction" (2008) 73:4 *Ethnos* 433.

Hunt, Sarah. "Ontologies of Indigeneity: The Politics of Embodying a Concept" (2014) 21:1 *Cultural Geographies* 27.

Jackson, Zakiyyah Iman. "Animal: New Directions in the Theorization of Race and Posthumanism" (2013) 39:3 *Feminist Studies* 669.

———. "Outer Worlds: The Persistence of Race in Movement 'Beyond the Human'" (2015) 21:2–3 *Gay and Lesbian Quarterly* 215.

Kennedy, David. "International Human Rights Movement: Part of the Problem?" (2002) 15 *Harvard Human Rights Journal* 101.

Kleinhans, Martha-Marie & Roderick A. Macdonald. "What Is a Critical Legal Pluralism?" (1997) 12 *Canadian Journal of Law and Society* 25.

Koch, Grace & Alexandra Crowe. "Song, Land and Ceremony: Interpreting the Place of Songs as Evidence for Australian Aboriginal and Torres Strait Islander Land Claims" (2013) 6 *Collaborative Anthropologies* 373.

Macdonald, Roderick A. "Metaphors of Multiplicity" (1998) 15:1 *Arizona Journal of International and Comparative Law* 69.

Macdonald, Roderick A. & David Sandomierski. "Against Nomopolies" (2006) 57 *Northern Ireland Legal Quarterly* 610.

Makdisi, John. "Legal Logic and Equity in Islamic Law" (1985) 33:1 *American Journal of Comparative Law* 63.

Maldonado-Torres, Nelson. "On the Coloniality of Being – Contributions to the Development of a Concept" (2007) 21:2–3 *Cultural Studies* 240.

Marks, Susan. "Human Rights and Root Causes" (2011) 74:1 *Modern Law Review* 57.

Maroney, Terry A. "Law and Emotion: A Proposed Taxonomy of an Emerging Field" (2006) 30:2 *Law and Human Behavior* 119.

McCrudden, Christopher, ed. *Understanding Human Dignity* (Oxford: Oxford University Press, 2013).

McHugh, James. "The Classification of Smells and the Order of the Senses in Indian Religious Traditions" (2007) 54:4 *Religion through the Senses* 374.

Melissaris, Emmanuel. "The More the Merrier? A New Take on Legal Pluralism" (2004) 13:1 *Social and Legal Studies* 57.

Merry, Sally Engle. "Legal Pluralism" (1988) 22 *Law & Society Review* 869.

Mignolo, Walter D. "Introduction – Coloniality of Power and De-Colonial Thinking" (2007) 21:2–3 *Cultural Studies* 155.

Nedelsky, Jennifer. "Embodied Diversity and the Challenges to Law" (1997) 42 *McGill Law Journal* 91.

Nékám, Alexander. *The Personality Conception of the Legal Entity* (Cambridge: Harvard University Press, 1938).

Newcomb, Rachel. "Modern Citizens, Modern Food: Taste and the Rise of the Moroccan Citizen-Consumer" in S. Trnka, C. Dureau & J. Park, eds, *Senses and Citizenships: Embodying Political Life* (New York: Routledge, 2013) 147.

Nussbaum, Martha. "Emotions and Women's Capabilities" in Martha Nussbaum & Jonathan Glover, eds, *Women, Culture and Development: A Study of Human Capabilities* (Oxford: Clarendon Press, 1995) 360.

———. "Secret Sewers of Vice: Disgust, Bodies, and the Law" in Susan A Bandes, ed, *The Passions of Law* (New York: New York University Press, 1999) 19.

Ong, Walter J. "The Shifting Sensorium" in David Howes, ed, *The Varieties of Sensory Experience* (Toronto: University of Toronto Press, 1991) 25.

Potter, Caroline. "Sense of Motion, Senses of Self: Becoming a Dancer" (2008) 73:4 *Ethnos* 444.

Quijano, Aníbal. "Coloniality and Modernity/Rationality" (2007) 21:2–3 *Cultural Studies* 168.

Radcliffe, Sarah A. "Geography and Indigeneity I: Indigeneity, Coloniality and Knowledge" (2017) 41:2 *Progress in Human Geography* 220.

———. "Geography and Indigeneity II: Critical Geographies of Indigenous Bodily Politics" (2017) 42:3 *Progress in Human Geography* 436.

Rajagopal, Balakrishnan. "Counter-Hegemonic International Law: Rethinking Human Rights and Development as a Third World Strategy" (2006) 27 *Third World Quarterly* 767.

Report of the Special Rapporteur on Contemporary Forms of Racism, Racial Discrimination, Xenophobia and Related Intolerance: Global Extractivism and Racial Equality, UN Doc A/HRC/41/54 (14 May 2019).

Rose, Gillian. *Visual Methodologist: An Introduction to Researching with Visual Materials*, 3rd ed (London: Sage, 2012).

Sanger, Carol. "Legislation with Affect: Emotion and Legislative Law Making" in James E. Fleming, ed, *Passions and Emotions* (New York: New York University Press, 2013) 38.

Santos, Boaventura de Sousa. "A Non-Occidentalist West? Learned Ignorance and Ecology of Knowledge" (2009) 26:7–8 *Theory, Culture & Society* 103.

———. *Epistemologies of the South – Justice against Epistemicide* (Boulder, CO: Paradigm Publishers, 2014).

———. "Epilogue: A New Vision of Europe: Learning from the South" in G. Bhambra & J. Narayan, eds, *European Cosmopolitanism: Colonial Histories and Postcolonial Societies* (New York: Routledge, 2017) 172.

———. "Human Rights, Democracy and Development" in Boaventura de Sousa Santos & Bruno Sena Martins, eds, *The Pluriverse of Human Rights: The Diversity of Struggles for Dignity* (New York: Routledge, 2021) 21.

Santos, Boaventura de Sousa & Bruno Sena Martins. "Introduction" in Boaventura de Sousa Santos & Bruno Sena Martins, eds, *The Pluriverse of Human Rights: The Diversity of Struggles for Dignity* (New York: Routledge, 2021) 1.

Schwartz, Andi. "Radical Vulnerability: Selfies as a Femme-Inine Mode of Resistance" (2022) 13:1 *Psychology and Sexuality* 43.

Seremetakis, C. Nadia. "The Memory of the Senses: Historical Perception, Commensal Exchange and Modernity" (1993) 9:2 *Visual Anthropology Review* 2.

Sherwin, Richard K. *Visualizing Law in the Age of the Digital Baroque – Arabesques and Entanglements* (New York: Routledge, 2011).

Stroeken, Koen. "Sensory Shifts and 'Synaesthetics' in Sukuma Healing" (2008) 73:4 *Ethnos* 466.

van Leeuwen, Theo. "Semiotics and Iconography" in Theo van Leeuwen & Carey Jewitt, eds, *The Handbook of Visual Analysis* (London: Sage, 2001) 92.

van Leeuwen, Theo & Carey Jewitt, eds. *The Handbook of Visual Analysis* (London: Sage, 2020).

Walcott, Rinaldo. "The Problem of the Human: Black Ontologies and 'the Coloniality of Our Being'" in Sabine Broeck & Carsten Junker, eds, *Postcoloniality–Decoloniality–Black Critique – Joints and Fissures* (Frankfurt: Campus Verlag, 2014) 93.

West, Robin. "Disciplines, Subjectivity, and Law" in Austin Sarat & Thomas Kearns, eds., *The Fate of Law* (Ann Arbour: University of Michigan Press, 1991) 119.

Whatmore, Sarah. "Humanism's Excess: Some Thoughts on the 'Post-Human/ist' Agenda" (2006) 7:4 *Social & Cultural Geography* 1360.

Williams, Robert A. *Savage Anxieties: The Invention of Western Civilization* (New York: Palgrave Macmillan, 2012).

Wilson, Richard A. *The Politics of Truth and Reconciliation in South Africa: Legitimizing the Post-Apartheid State* (Cambridge: Cambridge University Press, 2001).

Wolfe, Cary. *Animal Rites – American Culture, the Discourse of Species, and Posthumanist Theory* (Chicago: University of Chicago Press, 2003).

———. *What is Posthumanism?* (Minneapolis: University of Minnesota Press, 2010).

Part I

A challenge to the 'human' of human rights

Part I argues that the dominant ways of conceiving legal subjectivity in international human rights are problematic, and it exposes the shortcomings of the core concept of the human. To achieve this, I draw on different theoretical approaches that highlight fundamental shortcomings in the conceptualization of human rights. My discussion is based on the insight that the concept of the human is rarely engaged with in human rights texts and discourses but rather taken for granted. Yet the 'human' is a powerful notion that pervades human rights thinking. As I will discuss, the way in which this 'human' has been conceptualized in Western modern, humanist thought greatly influences, and limits, the application and enforcement of rights in practice. Indeed, even if human rights, especially in their international form, claim to be universal in application, they are inherently limited and biased, notably because they depend on a subject that has been defined – even if largely implicitly – in opposition to an 'Other'.

   In the first chapter, I demonstrate that international human rights have, since their inception, and despite claims to universality, greatly favoured the human being that also has the status of a citizen, which implies that the full protection of rights is afforded only to the citizen. This also means that the subject of human rights is defined in opposition to the non-citizen, that is the refugee or migrant. The main reason for this is that international human rights law is an offspring of the inherently state-centred international legal system and has always relied on states for the conceptualization and also enforcement of human rights. As Hannah Arendt noted, this state-centredness obviously affects those who do not have the legal status of a citizen by preventing them from accessing human rights. Because of this limitation, it can be argued that everyone's human rights can be taken away: since citizenship is not absolute or inalienable, as history has shown, neither are human rights. Throughout the chapter, I therefore draw on Hannah Arendt's figure of the refugee and contemporary scholars theorizing human rights to suggest that the dominant subject can and should be reconceptualized beyond state sovereignty and citizenship.

DOI: 10.4324/9781003427957-2

Moreover, as I highlight by drawing on further critical approaches, it is useful to consider other inherent limitations of the subject of human rights. Indeed, the subject is defined not only in opposition to the non-citizen, who is arguably the most obvious 'Other' in this context, but also against an 'Other' in additional forms. In the second chapter, I turn to posthumanist critiques to argue that the 'human' of human rights is also conceived, perhaps more implicitly but not with lesser consequences, against the non-human animal and against humans that are animalized to deny their humanness. It is because of this conception and resulting processes of dehumanization and animalization that many beings are excluded from humanity and precluded from human rights guarantees. Then, in the third and final chapter of Part I, a discussion of several theories from the margins reveals that the 'human' has always been defined against yet another 'Other', namely the non-European or non-white body, and that this restricts the application of human rights. Indeed, Black, Indigenous and decoloniality approaches offer powerful insights about the Eurocentric and humanist construction of the 'human' and resulting exclusions that continue to pervade the contemporary international human rights system. These insights will also inform my arguments about the vision-centredness and sensuous preferences of the international human rights system in Part II, such as with respect to the creation of exclusions through certain depictions of victims of human rights violations.

Throughout Part I, and building on these critiques, the figure of *migrating 'Others'* will be proposed as a better way to capture the plurality of ways of being in the world and to possibly render international human rights more effective. I actualize Arendt's figure of the refugee, which remains highly relevant and useful to grasp contemporary forms of exclusion, including through the senses, in the context of international human rights. Considering migrants in a more general sense – in other words beyond the specific legal category of the refugee – and the rightlessness they often experience, as I do here, can inform an analysis of the dominant subject of international human rights in a system greatly focused on states and citizenship. Yet, as the discussion based on various theoretical approaches exposes, citizenship is not the only source of exclusion, which is why I adapt the figure of the refugee in several steps. I first propose that it is the figure of the *migrant*, instead of the *refugee*, that captures ongoing dynamics of exclusion in relation to the dominant citizen-subject; as the discussion progresses to further critical approaches, the figure evolves to the *migrating 'Other'*, and then even *migrating 'Others'*, which, I argue, reveals additional biases and limitations in the conceptualization of the subject of human rights.

Foreshadowing some of the arguments made in Part II, the figure of *migrating 'Others'* also allows imagining different ways of thinking and being, beyond the current framework. Based on the insight that Western claims to universality in the context of human rights and its subject are not objective but, like all claims, situated and historically determined, I suggest that it is necessary to question the dominant ontology and epistemology and to reconceptualize the 'human' of human rights by recognizing and embracing different ways of being, thinking and experiencing the world, notably beyond rationality and vision as conceived and promoted by Western modern thought.

Chapter 1

Actualizing the figure of the refugee to challenge a system based on the citizen-subject

Despite its claim to universal application, the international human rights system remains heavily based on citizen's rights, which is why considering the condition of refugees and migrants, who experience rightlessness to an important extent, reveals some of the inherent shortcomings of this system. While migration has always been part of human history, there has been a dramatic increase of people who leave their home country throughout the 20th and 21st centuries, often because they are forced or feel compelled to do so. In 2020, there were 281 million people, or 3.6% of the world population, living in a country other than the one they were born in; this number is three times higher than in 1970.[1] Armed conflicts, from World War II to Syria in the 21st century, and socio-economic causes have intensified a phenomenon that increasingly shapes global politics and also questions the limits of the international human rights system. The recent rise of migration to Europe, especially via the Mediterranean Sea, is only one of the latest instantiations of what is often seen as a challenge to established democracies.[2]

If migration is not a new phenomenon, the political context in which migration occurs today and the contemporary challenges that refugees and migrants face are different from the ones that prevailed when the landmark 1951 *Convention relating to the Status of Refugees* (*Refugee Convention*) was adopted. Refugees in the classical understanding of this convention still exist,[3] but often those who fulfill the criteria of the *Refugee Convention* are

---

1 International Organization for Migration, *World Migration Report 2020*. These numbers do not take into account internal migration, that is people displaced within their own country.
2 In this context, it is important to recall that it is states in the Global South that receive most refugees: two thirds of those whom the United Nations High Commissioner for Refugees is concerned with are in Asia, Africa and Latin America (Brown, 159). Nevertheless, it is in the Global North that refugees (and migrants more generally) seem to be a greater source of anxiety and that policies are increasingly centred on extraterritorial policing and the militarization of borders as well as on incarceration and deportation (Hayden, 258, 261).
3 Article 1(A)(2) of the *Convention relating to the Status of Refugees* stipulates that protection must be accorded to those who can demonstrate a "well-founded fear of being persecuted

DOI: 10.4324/9781003427957-3

forced to cross borders illegally to eventually have a chance of being recognized legally as refugees by another state. Moreover, many others leave their country of origin without meeting the criteria of the legal definition of a refugee and may be obliged to pretend that they do. Some flee unsafe situations without a particular threat of persecution; for others, it is primarily socio-economic reasons that make them leave their home. Climate change is an additional factor that has already started to push more and more persons to leave their homes and seek refuge elsewhere, a phenomenon that is likely to intensify over the next decades. Whatever the underlying reasons for leaving, and often as a result of having had to cross one or several borders without the approval of the respective state authorities, migrants typically find themselves, at least for certain periods of time, in a condition of rightlessness. In that sense, the consequences of migration, especially the difficulty to access rights, have not changed significantly over time, and the conceptual differences between movements of refugees and migrants in the 20th and 21st centuries appear minimal.[4]

To analyse the focus on the citizen-subject of the international human rights system and to explore whether the subject of international human rights can and should be reconceptualized beyond state sovereignty and citizenship, I suggest in this chapter that it is useful to seek inspiration from Arendt's theorization of the refugee. Arendt was a major political thinker of the 20th century and one of the first political theorists to write on the figure of the refugee and on statelessness. While authors such as Edmund Burke, Jeremy Bentham and Karl Marx noted some paradoxes of rights more generally, Arendt developed one of the most powerful critiques of human rights.[5] Most notably, her treatment of the figure of the refugee reveals structural problems in international human rights law and brings to light a threat that could potentially affect everyone. This points to deep tensions within liberal democratic states and to real exclusions that exist in the international human rights regime. Arendt's argument that refugees, who are forced to flee their home country because of politically motivated persecution, are not an exception of the political system but "the most symptomatic group in contemporary politics",[6] which she made in the early 1950s, is still relevant today. She was, in particular, critical of the fact that humans are supposed to have human rights as declared in legal instruments, but that these rights are, in practice, not accessible to everyone in a system where the protection of rights

---

for reasons of race, religion, nationality, membership of a particular social group or political opinion". *Convention relating to the Status of Refugees.*
4 Haddad, 4. As Haddad notes, "[w]hat has evolved and continues to evolve would seem to be the normative understanding of the refugees". Ibid, 5. For a brief history of the definition of the refugee, see ibid, 30–1.
5 Gündoğdu, 25–7.
6 Arendt, *The Origins of Totalitarianism*, 277.

is based on states and hence dependent on citizenship. Arendt's thinking also had a profound influence on many other scholars,[7] and it is frequently referred to in discussions on refugees and so-called illegal or undocumented migrants[8] and on the ways in which modern democracies deal with them. While Arendt's work has been criticized and, as I discuss, sometimes read quite narrowly, a creative understanding of her work allows to further develop and actualize her analysis of the refugee. I argue that refugees and migrants represent a particular challenge – but, crucially, also a possibility for change – to the current human rights paradigm. These challenges and possibilities are well captured by the figure of the *migrant* which builds on but goes beyond Arendt's figure of the refugee.

While not directly dealing with practical problems encountered by refugees, migrants and others whose human rights are often not protected, my analysis is nevertheless inspired by their lived and concrete realities of exclusion, discrimination and dehumanization. It should also be noted that although the main focus lies on the international human rights system, this system rests on the original idea of rights as it emerged and crystallized at the national level through, among others, the American *Declaration of Independence* and the French *Déclaration des droits de l'homme et du citoyen*.

1.1 Arendt's figure of the refugee: exposing the fundamental problem of human rights as citizen's rights

Revisiting the development of the international human rights system and its relations to the nation-state, Arendt argued that human rights, as they were conceived, are in fact not that different from national rights guarantees granted to citizens. She pointed out that even if the idea of natural rights applying universally, and without a link to the state, is older than the modern international human rights system, the latter clearly builds on the rights declared during the American and French Revolutions.[9] These declarations proclaimed to emancipate man and made him both the source and goal of these rights.[10] As the 1776 American *Declaration of Independence* states, "[w]e hold these Truths to be self-evident, that all Men are created equal, that they are endowed by their Creator with certain unalienable Rights, that among these are Life, Liberty, and the pursuit of happiness".[11] Similarly, the French 1789 *Déclaration des droits de l'homme et du citoyen* refers to natural, inalienable and sacred

---

7 Benhabib, *The Reluctant Modernism*, xxxvii–xxxxviii.
8 As will be explained below, the status or name given to these different groups is not considered relevant for the analysis made in this book. Crossing borders can also be viewed not as criminal but as "an expression of human freedom". Benhabib, *The Rights of Others*, 177.
9 See for instance Pavlich.
10 Arendt, *The Origins of Totalitarianism*, 291.
11 *American Declaration of Independence*.

rights of Man and stipulates, in its first article, that "[l]es hommes naissent et demeurent libres et égaux en droits".[12] Rights were hence declared to exist naturally and independently of national membership, as being pre-national.[13] At the same time, as Arendt noted, the declarations were made in the context of national struggles: while the state, as the ultimate legal institution, was meant to protect all inhabitants regardless of origin, it was monopolized by the increasing awareness and importance of national affiliation and turned rights discourse into "an instrument of the nation".[14]

Arendt hence demonstrated that the coupling of the declaration of the rights of Man with the affirmation of the sovereignty of the nation in the French *Déclaration* engraved the tension between the state and the nation as well as the contradiction in declaring rights as being both inherent in human beings and based on citizenship in specific nations. As article 3 states, "[l]e principe de toute souveraineté réside essentiellement dans la Nation. Nul corps, nul individu ne peut exercer d'autorité qui n'en émane expressément". Although the rights of Man were supposed to provide protection against the power of the newly created sovereign states, the fact that they were implemented in the form of political rights made them dependent on the state and also contributed to reinforcing the supremacy of the nation-state as the highest political actor. As Arendt wrote, in the history of political thought "man had hardly appeared as a completely emancipated, completely isolated being who carried his dignity within himself without reference to some larger encompassing order, when he disappeared again into a member of a people".[15] Since "a nonnational guarantee"[16] of rights always seemed inconceivable, whole nations, or peoples, became the actual bearers of rights in the newly secularized society. In other words, and as I explain in more detail below, Arendt noted that one had to belong to a political community to have and claim rights, and that this community was conceived as a nation, constituted within the territory of a nation-state and united through its shared origins. This was highly problematic according to Arendt, who was cautious of nationalism in all its forms, for it tends to suppress what makes individuals different and therefore to repress human plurality, which is a core element of being human for her. The focus on the state and its sovereignty implied that rights would only apply to its citizens and be protected within its borders, and it entailed the state's power to deny citizenship and concomitant rights to those who were not considered

---

12 *Déclaration des droits de l'homme et du citoyen.*
13 Menke, Kaiser & Thiele, 744.
14 Arendt, *The Origins of Totalitarianism*, 230. See also Cotter, 96.
15 Arendt, *The Origins of Totalitarianism*, 291. It is worth noting that Arendt also expressed doubts in regard to the inherently ambiguous concept of dignity, which is foundational for human rights. Ibid, 298.
16 Arendt, *The Origins of Totalitarianism*, 292.

fit to be part of the nation.[17] Privileging the nation, instead of the individual, also implied from the outset that the full realization of human rights, as they would eventually be called, could never be achieved.

For Arendt, refugees, or stateless, reveal many of the shortcomings of the international human rights system. She argued that they are not an exception to be disregarded as irrelevant for understanding the concepts of citizenship and rights, although they are often presented as such; rather, because of their statelessness, they pose a challenge to the system of state sovereignty and human rights, and they point to an issue that, perhaps, cannot be fixed within that system. In Arendt's theory, refugees are even "the most symptomatic group in contemporary politics", as they highlight fundamental weaknesses that can affect everyone, notably because they show that human rights are not inalienable, that is anyone could lose their rights.[18] Arendt claimed that the main problem does not consist in the fact that there are more and more refugees, but that the very nature of the state system inevitably produces refugees. The existence and precarious condition of refugees shed light on some of the fundamental tensions and "perplexities" within the modern, rights-based democratic system.[19] It is hence through the refugee or the stateless person – note that Arendt said that "the core of statelessness . . . is identical with the refugee question"[20] – that she critically analysed fundamental concepts, such as sovereignty, the nation-state and human rights.

In particular, as Arendt maintained, because refugees are without an effective citizenship and because it is only membership in a political community that can guarantee rights, including at an international level, they cannot access human rights.[21] Refugees appear in a kind of nakedness, as they are stripped of legal and political existence except for the fact they exist, and would be in dire need of the protection of human rights, but they are non-nationals, excluded from a political community that could give force to these rights.[22] In other words, every human being might be entitled to international human rights in the abstract, as promulgated in legal instruments like the *Universal Declaration of Human Rights*, but not everyone can access these rights in practice in a system that is premised on state sovereignty and the protection of human rights via states. This, in turn, reveals the inherent tension in the relation between national sovereignty and the idea of natural, abstract and universal human rights.[23] As such, refugees are indicative or, as

---

17 For a discussion of the two meanings of "national sovereignty" that can be distinguished in Arendt's writings, namely people's sovereignty and state sovereignty, see Cotter, 97–101.
18 Arendt, *The Origins of Totalitarianism*, 277.
19 Cotter, 95–6.
20 Arendt, *The Origins of Totalitarianism*, 279.
21 Gündoğdu, 2–3.
22 Gündoğdu, 40.
23 Benhabib, *The Rights of Others*, 61.

Arendt said, "symptomatic" of many of the historical and ongoing short-comings of the international human rights system.[24]

The fiction of inalienable and inherent rights

A fundamental problem exposed by Arendt in regard to human rights is that declarations of rights are founded explicitly not on a social contract but on the idea that there is such a thing as a human nature.[25] She rejected the alleged abstractness of human life and put forward the argument that no one lives in a pure natural state but always and necessarily within some form of social context.[26] She hence questioned the logic of grounding human rights in an assumed essence of humanity, in an abstract human or a "Mensch überhaupt",[27] when they are in fact a form of political rights. Her understanding was that human rights are neither inherent to human beings nor inalienable. She rather maintained that the very notion of rights is dependent on their enforcement: despite declarations of the inalienability of human rights or of rights being inherent attributes of humans, concrete political institutions that protect and enforce rights are always needed.[28] Rights, in her perspective, can only exist through positive law, and importantly, laws only through states that are willing and able to enforce these rights and laws.[29] Moreover, it is individuals coming together in a given political context that agree to grant each other rights, as it is the case in most democracies in the form of charters, bills of rights and other constitutional guarantees. This is why belonging to a political community was so fundamental for Arendt.

It is especially because of totalitarian regimes and their attempts at making subjects superfluous that it became clear for Arendt that the proclaimed inalienability of human rights and of humanness presented as a guarantee of rights are an illusion: if human rights were genuinely inalienable, then totalitarian regimes would not be able to make human beings and their individuality redundant and disposable.[30] The phenomenon of mass statelessness in the 20th century, which left millions of people unprotected by the law, also revealed the deceptive idea of abstract and inalienable rights and that the human, when removed from the context of the nation, had little meaning. Those that are not recognized as citizens are particularly vulnerable and would, as a result, need protection in the form of human rights, such as refugees (and

---

24 This is the case even if the sources of the international human rights law can be considered to include not only treaties but also customary international law and so-called soft law. Benhabib, *The Rights of Others*, 7.
25 Arendt, *The Origins of Totalitarianism*, 298.
26 Arendt, *The Origins of Totalitarianism*, 291.
27 Arendt, *Elemente und Ursprünge*, 604.
28 Bernstein, 85.
29 Menke, Kaiser & Thiele, 742.
30 Arendt, *The Origins of Totalitarianism*, 456–7.

also many other individuals and groups excluded in contemporary societies, as theories from the margins usefully point out[31]), are left aside; their rights are ill-defined and seemingly unenforceable:

> The conception of human rights, based upon the assumed existence of a human being as such, broke down at the very moment when those who professed to believe in it were for the first time confronted with people who had indeed lost all other qualities and specific relationships – except that they were still human. The world found nothing sacred in the abstract nakedness of being human.[32]

As Arendt noted, it is not clear which rights exactly these people have lost, but what was obvious for her – and this emerges as a key point in her thinking – is that the loss of citizen's rights automatically entailed the withdrawal of human rights,[33] which therefore must be considered alienable. To illustrate this point, she turned to the lack of legal protection experienced by national minorities in Europe in the 20th century and their attempts to gain access to some rights by insisting on their affiliation with a nation with which they shared cultural and linguistic origins. Minorities and refugees, she said, did not claim rights in the form of abstract human rights; rather, they claimed to have rights as Poles, or Jews or Germans, and so on. Since the "loss of national rights was identical with loss of human rights", minorities looked to their "mother country" that would protect them.[34]

Furthermore, given the importance attached to a form of citizenship that was equated with affiliation to a nation-state, it was not the individual but the people that was considered "the image of man",[35] and that ended up filling in the alleged abstractness of the human and human rights. What declarations like the 1789 *Déclaration des droits de l'homme et du citoyen* and the 1948 *Universal Declaration of Human Rights* proclaim, namely that the "naked" human is the source and subject of human rights, is a fiction.[36] It follows that if human rights are nothing more than the rights of citizens translated to the international level, human beings always need a state for recognition and enforcement of their rights:

> The Rights of Man, after all, had been defined as "inalienable" because they were supposed to be independent of all governments; but it turned

---

31 See section 2.3 below.
32 Arendt, The *Origins of Totalitarianism*, 299.
33 Arendt, *The Origins of Totalitarianism*, 293, 299.
34 Arendt, *The Origins of Totalitarianism*, 292.
35 Arendt, *The Origins of Totalitarianism*, 291. Arendt spoke of 'man' with reference to the declarations of the rights of Man.
36 Arendt, *The Human Condition*, 97. The fundamental (in)distinction between biological and political life, explored and developed subsequently by Agamben, as discussed below, was hence already part of Arendt's reasoning.

out that the moment human beings lacked their own government and had to fall back upon their minimum rights, no authority was left to protect them and no institution was willing to guarantee them.[37]

In sum, an important problem identified by Arendt, and that continues to haunt human rights, is that to effectively possess rights, humans must be citizens; that citizenship is more important than the abstract notions of humanity and humanness; and that rights can only exist in practice when there is a state that protects and enforces them. While human rights discourses explicitly cite the inherent value of the human as the source of rights,[38] the real source is implicitly citizenship underpinned by state sovereignty.

Arendt's "right to have rights": the right to have a place in the world and to be human

According to Arendt, human rights cannot be truly universal or inalienable, since they are based on an inherently exclusive and limited membership in a political community. So-called human rights contained in declarations can be denied, yet without taking away a human's essential quality as human; it is only the lack of the possibility for meaningful action, which she considered crucial for being human and which is enabled through membership in a political community, that constitutes an expulsion from humanity.[39] In other words, Arendt's understanding of human beings as political animals means that exclusion from politics implies a denial of what makes such beings human, a denial of their humanness. She argued that human beings are thus not born equal, unlike what major international human rights instruments claim,[40] but that they become equal as part of a group that decides to protect its members' rights: "Our political life rests on the assumption that we can produce equality through organization, because man can act in and change and build a common world, together with his equals and only with his equals".[41] For Arendt, the chief purpose of political life is to engage in this activity of building a common world and securing equality.

Refugees, because they are without an effective connection to a state, are deprived of the right to belong to an organized political community, what Arendt called "the right to have rights", and can therefore be made

---

37 Arendt, *The Origins of Totalitarianism*, 291–2.
38 This is explored in more detail in the next section below.
39 Arendt, *The Origins of Totalitarianism*, 297.
40 See for instance the *Universal Declaration of Human Rights*, article 1.
41 Arendt, *The Origins of Totalitarianism*, 301. This kind of equality implies freedom, in the sense of not being under the command of others or commanding others, but it does not have a necessary connection with justice. Arendt, *The Human Condition*, 32.

superfluous.[42] Arendt considered this right to have rights as the most fundamental right, since rights need institutional guarantees established by a
community to be realized. Refugees, and arguably other migrants as well,
are similar to subjects made superfluous by totalitarianism in that they have
no right to have rights, thus revealing the inherent shortcomings of the human rights system.[43] Importantly, it can be argued that making refugees and
migrants superfluous shows that a human being, and hence in principle any
human being, can be made superfluous and excluded from humanity. Arendt
argued that refugees not only lost a home but, more importantly, were denied
the possibility of a new community that could guarantee protection in the
form of rights. As she wrote with reference to the refugees of World War I,
"[o]nce they had left their homeland they remained homeless, once they had
left their state they became stateless; once they had been deprived of their
human rights they were rightless, the scum of the earth".[44] These refugees
had been made superfluous and were expelled from humanity in the sense
of being denied a political existence. Since they could not rely on a political
community, they lost all other rights and even the right to claim the rights
they were deprived of.[45] Like subjects of totalitarian regimes, refugees lose
their legal personality and must endure a world subjected to the force of law
but without access to its protection.[46] They might keep certain liberties, but
there are no guarantees for these liberties without membership in a political community.[47] As Arendt wrote, the "fundamental deprivation of human
rights is manifested first and above all in the deprivation of a place in the
world which makes opinions significant and actions effective", and people
deprived of human rights "are deprived not of the right to freedom, but of
the right to action; not of the right to think, whatever they please, but of the
right to opinion".[48] Arendt considered the phenomenon of mass statelessness
in the 20th century as unprecedented in history and particularly problematic because of the increasing unavailability of uninhabited places on earth,
where refugees could resettle and (re-)create a community of their own.[49]
The impossibility of finding a place in the world where meaningful action is
possible (i.e. precisely what refugees experience) is equivalent to being made

42 Arendt, *The Origins of Totalitarianism*, 296.
43 Gündoğdu, 2–3.
44 Arendt, *The Origins of Totalitarianism*, 267.
45 Balibar, "(De)Constructing the Human", 733.
46 Krause, 333–5.
47 Cotter, 109. It is worth noting that even human rights declarations take it as a given and
    build on the idea that human beings always already belong to a political community. Menke,
    Kaiser & Thiele, 744.
48 Arendt, *The Origins of Totalitarianism*, 296.
49 Arendt, *The Origins of Totalitarianism*, 293.

superfluous and being constantly endangered.[50] Refugees do not have a genuine right to action and to opinion in their host state, or any other political and civil rights (and, arguably, other rights as well, such as economic, social and cultural rights), at least not to the same extent as citizens. This is highly problematic for Arendt, since she understood human beings as inherently political beings, which is why she argued that refugees should be reintegrated into a political community.

Arendt's critique of the way in which human rights were conceived is hence closely related to her understanding of human nature and, more precisely, the importance of meaningful action in a political sense. Action is, indeed, a key concept for Arendt that allowed her to theorize the human condition and its plurality.[51] It is a fundamental activity that occurs directly between humans and can therefore be understood as inter-action.[52] Action, Arendt wrote, is "the political activity par excellence" and has the potential to create something new.[53] It is in this sense that refugees are like subjects in totalitarian regimes, with both categories of individuals being deprived of action and of supposedly inalienable rights as a result of being made superfluous. Arendt showed that totalitarianism simply does not need human beings in their individuality: "[t]otalitarianism strives not toward despotic rule over men, but toward a system in which men are superfluous. Total power can be achieved and safeguarded only in a world of conditioned reflexes, or marionettes without the slightest trace of spontaneity".[54] Totalitarianism aims to control every aspect of the life of human beings, with the goal of erasing individuality: "character is a threat and . . . individuality, anything indeed that distinguishes one man from another, is intolerable".[55] In other words, the suspicion that Arendt expressed towards abstractness and the denial of individuality in totalitarian regimes can be understood not only because this abstractness hinders the enforcement of concrete rights, but also because abstractness – with respect to the universal human nature and the individual – bears the threat to further anonymity and to erase differences.[56] These differences, however, are essential.

Indeed, Arendt saw differences and the plurality of individuals, and not inherent human rights or human reason, as humanity's most fundamental – or even the only common – feature: "[p]lurality is the condition of human action because we are all the same, that is, human, in such a way that nobody

---

50 Hayden, 257.
51 Arendt, *The Human Condition*, 7.
52 This idea can already be found in Aristotle's thought. Benhabib, *The Reluctant Modernism*, 105.
53 Arendt, *The Human Condition*, 104.
54 Arendt, *The Origins of Totalitarianism*, 457.
55 Arendt, *The Origins of Totalitarianism*, 457.
56 Bernstein, 44.

is ever the same as anyone else who ever lived, lives or will live".[57] In Arendt's perspective, it is through plurality that human beings are both distinct and equal and can hence strive as a species.[58] Because it is via speech that plurality is expressed and that everything humans do and experience becomes meaningful, Arendt argued that speech makes political beings and hence human subjects.[59] The plurality voiced through speech is fundamental in revealing who human beings are as individuals and how their personalities are distinct; it allows the human to live "as a distinct and unique being among equals".[60] Therefore, any human action without speech does not amount to action in an Arendtian sense; without speech, there is no actor. Losing relevant political speech and relationships, that is losing the possibility for action, equals losing some of the most important features of what it means to be human.[61]

While the exclusion of refugees – and other migrants – from a political community means they are denied the right to have rights and are hence unable to access human rights, it can be argued that if refugees do not compromise their identity and resist society's attempt to silence them, they remain members through their affirmed 'Otherness', and can indeed be the

---

57 Arendt, *The Human Condition*, 8. See also Williams & Lang, 9, 11. Interestingly, although Arendt drew on Heidegger, she transformed his category of "being-in-the-world" into plurality as the fundamental human condition. For Arendt, as Benhabib says, "being-with-others in the world who are like one and yet different than one is the human condition par excellence". Benhabib, *The Reluctant Modernism*, xliii.

58 Arendt, *The Human Condition*, 175.

59 Arendt, *The Human Condition*, 4. It may be worth noting that animals too have languages and that these can be very complex. See the discussion in section 2.2.

60 Arendt, *The Human Condition*, 178–9.

61 Arendt, *The Origins of Totalitarianism*, 297–8. Arendt's method of relying on storytelling interestingly illustrates her belief in the plurality of humanity and allowed her to make this point more persuasively. Convinced that politics and philosophy concern everyone (for this point, see Young-Bruehl, 185), she told stories of people she knew and of people who had already passed away when she was born, as well as her own story as a refugee (see Bernstein, *Hannah Arendt and the Jewish Question*, ix). In doing so, she put in practice an idea of impartiality that is different to the more common one that relies on reasoning; her storytelling is impartial in the sense that it tells the story of an event from different and sometimes competing perspectives. It is also this plurality of narratives that turns an event into a public one. Arendt consciously tried to resist the commonly held opinion that in order to conduct insightful analyses about politics and power, one would have to detach oneself as much as possible from the actual social context (see Disch, 666–8). Instead, having become stateless and a refugee herself in 1933 after having had to escape Germany because of her Jewishness, she was greatly influenced by and built on what she and other refugees experienced and had to tolerate. Consequently, Arendt's right to have rights is not an abstract right, but, as it has been argued, "a claim rooted in the concrete plurality of human beings – the fundamental human condition that we share the world with others who are both like and unlike ourselves. It is the right to participate in the discourse of plural human beings" (see Krause, 340). For a detailed account of storytelling as part of Arendt's methods, see Disch. Arendt did not, however, speak much of her identity or condition as a woman. See for instance Benhabib, *The Reluctant Modernism*, 1–2.

"vanguards" of the whole political community. In fact, Arendt herself exhorted refugees, and specifically Jewish refugees, to remain faithful to their identity and values in spite of the ways dominant society treats them and limits their capacity for action.[62] In spite of being marginalized on the basis of their 'Otherness',[63] Arendt claimed that they should not repudiate their identity but persist and resist; it is possible to remain faithful to oneself and one's "humane attitude".[64] Importantly, refugees, as in the case of the Jewish refugees in the 1930s, know that their outlawing is part of a dangerous trend that risks affecting many others.[65] It can therefore be concluded with Arendt that if the rights of refugees, including the fundamental right to have rights, can be taken away and their humanness denied, then there is no reason to believe that others could not experience the same. This danger threatens everyone. In this sense, the experience of refugees reveals the inherent vulnerability of all human beings and the shortcomings of human rights, both conceptually and in practice.

1.2 The ongoing relevance of questioning human rights as the rights of citizens

Arendt was a groundbreaking and controversial thinker, and her analysis of human rights was visionary: the contradictions and paradoxes of human rights still exist today, and some have even become more prominent,[66] with the question of refugees and migrants becoming one of the most pressing global issues.[67] It is also worth noting that although Arendt's thinking emerged in the context of analysing 20th-century totalitarian regimes, her point about sovereignty and the nation applies to democracies, too, since they also curtail and even remove individual rights, for instance out of national security concerns.[68] Moreover, and this is at least equally fundamental, states retain the authority to grant or deny citizenship and hence the right to have rights. In fact, her critique not only exposes logical inconsistencies and conceptual limitations of the human rights system as well as resulting

---

62 Arendt, "We Refugees", 116–17. For an in-depth discussion on the omnipresence of the Jewish question in Arendt's work, see Bernstein. Bernstein argues that this question is much more present and profound in her work than what is usually acknowledged. For instance, it is Arendt's concern with this question that led her to expose the link between the state and the nation. Bernstein, 64.
63 Benhabib, *The Reluctant Modernism*, xl.
64 Arendt, "We Refugees", 119.
65 Arendt, "We Refugees", 119.
66 Bernstein, 79–80.
67 Benhabib, *The Reluctant Modernism*, 81.
68 Cotter, 100.

exclusions; it also questions whether the paradox at the core of human rights even precludes the possibility of them being truly actualized.[69]

In this section, I explore the influence and ongoing relevance of Arendt's thinking, in particular of her analysis of the position of the refugee, through the ways in which several more contemporary authors have relied on and built on her writings. In fact, her insights have been analysed in quite different ways. It is possible and useful, as I discuss, to focus on the negative consequences of her assessment of human rights being aporetic, or without a solution. Yet it is also possible, and as I would argue ultimately more constructive, to adopt a more optimistic reading and to highlight that identifying the perplexities of human rights, as Arendt did, can lead to a better understanding of the shortcomings of the system and lay the groundwork for conceptual change to render human rights more meaningful and effective.

Agamben's exposure of the problematic exercise of modern power

Giorgio Agamben, who is one of Arendt's most prominent contemporary readers and a crucial voice in political theory,[70] also sees refugees as a key figure of modern politics. His arguments in this context are highly relevant to understand the dominant subject of human rights and some of the inherent limitations of the current system. Agamben's analysis proceeds from the paradox revealed by Arendt that human rights are tied to citizenship and unavailable to those who need them most:

> precisely the figure that should have embodied human rights more than any other – namely, the refugee – marked instead the radical crisis of the concept . . . so-called sacred and inalienable human rights are revealed to be without any protection precisely when it is no longer possible to conceive of them as rights of the citizens of a state.[71]

Agamben argues that prioritizing natural life over political life has led to the "transformation and decadence of the political" and that today, national sovereignty is founded on an inclusion – but through exclusion. What he terms "bare life"[72] is a form of life that is included in the realm of law by being excluded from it; it is "humanity stripped of nearly all of its defining characteristics".[73] Refugees, who are created by sovereignty, are not really

---

69 Gündoğdu, 26–7.
70 As Owens says, "in the past decade, Agamben has challenged Hannah Arendt's place as *the* 'charismatic legitimator' within critical refugee studies". Owens, "Beyond 'Bare Life'", 134.
71 Agamben, "Beyond Human Rights", 92.
72 Agamben, *Homo Sacer*, 3–4.
73 Hegarty, 20.

outside the system; rather, they are included in the system by being excluded. In other words, developing an argument that starts with Arendt but departs significantly from her, Agamben ends up calling for the abandonment of human rights. The reason is because, far from protecting human life, sovereignty instead creates a state of exception where forms of life – like the refugee – exist that are wholly subject to the power of sovereign states yet excluded from its legal protection.

For Agamben, modern sovereignty consists in the power to decide on the exception, that is to decide when the law can be suspended or not applied.[74] Sovereignty is manifest in the state of exception, often precipitated by an emergency, when the juridical order, with its laws and rights, is (at least partly) suspended, and the executive power governs without legislative and judicial oversight. This suspension creates a space where law is not absent, although its true meaning is lost; law ends up only exercising force, without offering protection, as exemplified by the concentration camps and "bare life". While the state of exception used to be an exception limited in time, for instance in countries at war during World War I,[75] Agamben claims that it has become the norm in modern politics, including in democracies. Nowadays, the state of exception is even becoming the prevailing "paradigm of government".[76] Said differently, the state of exception is no longer an exceptional measure; it has become a regular practice and technique to govern in many states. In this new permanent state of exception, the sovereign can act without restraint, as neither the separation of powers nor the rule of law is respected. Individuals have no rights but are still under the force of the law and are exposed to violence exerted by the state.[77] Jews experienced this state of exception in Nazi camps, as did the detainees in post-9/11 Guantanamo.[78] What this means is that the polity is, paradoxically, founded on people like refugees who can be turned into exceptions and hence be excluded; such exclusions are not an accidental byproduct but a necessary feature of sovereignty. Sovereignty is, in fact, based on a relation to bare life, which, rather than a natural state, is a political operation.

Agamben, in addition to building on Arendt's figure of the refugee, draws on biopolitical theories to discuss in more depth how modern sovereign power is "exercised at the level of life",[79] with political strategies focusing on the living bodies that make up the population. From Michel Foucault, Agamben takes the idea that sovereignty is expressed in the power over life

74 Agamben heavily draws on Carl Schmitt's theory of the state of exception. Agamben, *State of Exception*, 32–36.
75 Agamben, *State of Exception*, 12.
76 Agamben, *State of Exception*, 2.
77 Swiffen, "Giorgio Agamben", 168.
78 Agamben, *State of Exception*, 3–4.
79 Swiffen, "Derrida Contra Agamben", 352 (citing Foucault).

and control of the life and health of a population.[80] This governance through biopolitical control is based on defining and categorizing forms of life and constitutes a departure from the traditional understanding of sovereignty based on territorial control.[81] While the production of biopolitical bodies can be considered "the original activity of sovereign power" throughout history, it has arguably become a common and central practice of the modern state.[82] At the basis of Agamben's linking of Arendt and Foucault is a distinction he claims is already present in Aristotle's concept of politics, and taken up by Arendt. This distinction is between two concepts to designate life that still reflect the fundamental tension between human beings and citizens: *zoe*, which denotes life in its simple form of all beings, who can be humans, animals and gods, outside the polis; and *bios*, which is a specific form of life or qualified life that is linked to political life.[83] In classical thought, according to Agamben, the two remained strictly separate, and natural life was excluded from the political sphere,[84] although the process of including *zoe* in political life already occurred.[85] The inclusion of *zoe* or natural life into the political sphere is constitutive of sovereign power, which actually predates modernity. The prime example today are refugees, whose natural life is governed by the law, including through immigration and citizenship laws, yet who remain excluded from its protection.

What is new in modern sovereignty, according to Agamben, is that the exception becomes the norm, and that natural life begins to move from the margins to the very centre of the political order, with natural and political lives becoming indistinguishable: "exclusion and inclusion, outside and inside, *bios* and *zoe*, right and fact, enter a zone of irreducible indistinction".[86] This is Agamben's concept of "bare life", which, mirroring the concept of *homo sacer* in Roman law, refers to life that is constituted by "inclusive exclusion".[87] In the ancient world, excluded from the laws of humans and of gods, *homo sacer* cannot be sacrificed but can be killed without sanctions. It is related to law only in being excluded from it. As Agamben claims,

---

80 These arguments were obviously developed well before the outbreak of the global COVID-19 pandemic, which forcefully rendered concrete the already existing capacity of states to exercise biopolitical control and their readiness to curb human rights. See for instance Zouev. For a comparative study of restrictions of human rights and freedoms around the world related to the pandemic, see Human Rights Watch, "Covid-19 Triggers Wave of Free Speech Abuse"; see also Guterres.

81 Owens, "Beyond 'Bare Life'", 139.

82 Agamben, *Homo Sacer*, 6.

83 Agamben, *Homo Sacer*, 1.

84 Agamben, *Homo Sacer*, 2. For a criticism of the validity of this claim according to Derrida, see Swiffen, "Derrida Contra Agamben", 353–4.

85 Agamben, *Homo Sacer*, 9.

86 Agamben, *Homo Sacer*, 9.

87 Swiffen, "Derrida Contra Agamben", 351.

"[n]either political *bios* nor natural *zoe*, sacred life is the zone of indistinction in which *zoe* and *bios* constitute each other in including and excluding each other".[88] He argues modern sovereignty is dependent on this form of life – bare life – that cannot benefit from law's protection, but that at the same time is still governed by law in the sense that it is subjected to the force of law. It is a form of life that matters from a legal point of view "only as a living organism, not as a political subject".[89] Because the state of exception has become the centre of political life, today's prevalent form of sovereignty is radically different than in antiquity and the Middle Ages. Modern sovereignty must maintain a perpetual relation to bare life to constitute and maintain itself, which it must produce through exclusive inclusions (i.e. the creation of *homines sacri*).[90] These dynamics explain why the humanness of refugees and migrants is routinely denied in contemporary societies, including in Western democracies. Human rights, as I will now discuss, can only offer a limited remedy and are, in fact, enmeshed in these dynamics.

The inherent link between human rights and bare life

This analysis of modern power leads Agamben to highlight a fundamental paradox in regard to human rights and the political system they are built on. For him, human rights are intimately linked to the exercise of modern sovereignty, and modern democracies are characterized by an inherent contradiction. Democracies, which are supposed to be champions of the protection and empowerment of individuals through rights, claim to liberate the natural life and emancipate it from state power by seeking to transform it into a subject, into a political being; yet the simple fact of living is the continued object of biopolitical power, with bare life being the necessary foundation of sovereignty, including in democracies.[91] To recall, exercising sovereignty, at its core, means deciding on the exception and hence on constituting a relation to bare life through law. Human rights, as Agamben claims, are part of and reinforce this dynamic, because, notwithstanding their discourse of emancipation, they inclusively exclude natural life from the political sphere of the state.[92] Like Arendt, Agamben notes that human rights assert that humans have rights because they are humans, that is rights are supposed to be innate, but they are inherently tied to the notion of citizenship. This is best illustrated

88 Agamben, *Homo Sacer*, 90.
89 Swiffen, *Law, Ethics, and the Biopolitical*, 13.
90 Swiffen, "Giorgio Agamben", 169.
91 Agamben, *Homo Sacer*, 9.
92 Agamben, "Beyond Human Rights", 92–3.

by the ambiguous title of the 1789 *Déclaration des droits de l'homme et du citoyen*. Moreover, the declaration also shows that

> bare natural life . . . appears here as the source and bearer of rights. . . . At the same time, however, the very natural life that . . . is placed at the foundation of the order vanishes into the figure of the citizen in whom rights are "preserved".[93]

Since rights do not really exist outside the state system and always rely on states for their enforcement, being human as recognized in human rights law is inherently tied to the exercise of sovereignty, which in turn creates the very forms of bare life that are the proper subjects of human rights.[94] Moreover, because the protection of human rights falls upon states that need natural life to exist and exercise power, the very concept of human rights contributes to strengthening state power and introduces new forms of domination.[95] The rise of human rights is hence one of the modern processes that have turned humans increasingly into objects subjected to law and biopolitical governance, instead of legal subjects that hold rights and have agency. Strengthening rights hence implies strengthening sovereign power and its increasingly comprehensive control over everyday life. Importantly, this means that the contemporary situation concerning refugees and migrants cannot be improved by expanding and trying to ensure the right to asylum, for instance, or by claiming that all humans are legal subjects. All these concepts are inherently problematic for they depend on enforcement by some sovereign order and thus require divisions between outsiders and insiders to be continually produced.[96]

Relying on Arendt's idea that rights are tied to the notion of citizenship and ultimately need a state to be enforced, Agamben calls for the abandonment of human rights. He ends up rejecting the very concept of rights as well as other traditional political concepts, such as the citizen,[97] since rights could only be made more robust if sovereignty was also strengthened. While Arendt foresaw the fate of the modern state, according to Agamben, she remained unduly committed to the idea of the right to have rights, or the right

---

93 Agamben, *Homo Sacer*, 127.
94 Gündoğdu, 105.
95 Agamben, *Homo Sacer*, 126–8; Gündoğdu, 88.
96 Owens, "Beyond 'Bare Life'", 141. It can also be argued that human rights reduce the possible agency of refugees by assigning them the role of helpless victims in need of humanitarian assistance. Lechte & Newman, 531–2. For a discussion on human rights and humanitarian intervention, see Rancière, 308–9.
97 Agamben, "Beyond Human Rights", 94; Swiffen, "Giorgio Agamben", 166.

to be a member of a political community, which has become impossible, both practically and theoretically because it depends on sovereignty:[98]

> we will have to abandon decidedly, without reservation, the fundamental concepts through which we have so far represented the subjects of the political (Man, the Citizen and its rights, but also the sovereign people, the worker, and so forth) and build our political philosophy anew starting from the one and only figure of the refugee.[99]

Refugees are examples of biopolitical subjects par excellence for Agamben: like Arendt, he believes that it is the figure of the refugee that illustrates the limits of rights rooted in citizenship. By revealing the fiction of assumed bonds between the human and the citizen and between birth and nationality, the refugee, an inherent byproduct of the state, also challenges the order of the state.[100] Since refugees are expected to become citizens or to return to their country of origin, the human, and associated rights, always remains dependent on the state. As Agamben argues, "there is no autonomous space in the political order of the nation-state for something like the pure human in itself".[101] Refugees make it obvious, as noted above, that all humans can be governed by the law and excluded from its protection at the same time. A permanent state of exception applies to their situation, not in the sense that a particular refugee could never escape this state, but in the sense that there is a permanent space that is continuously filled with forms of life that are excluded. As such, refugees are the paradigmatic embodiment of bare life, with minimal or no political freedom, and the camps in which refugees are typically kept symbolize the control of individuals by the sovereign power outside the ordinary legal framework.[102] Agamben claims that the

> refugee should be considered for what it is, namely, nothing less than a limit-concept that at once brings a radical crisis to the principles of the nation-state and clears the way for a renewal of categories that can no longer be delayed.[103]

Importantly, the figure of the refugee exposes not only the biopolitical control that refugees are subjected to but also the inconsistencies of all the legal and political categories associated with the logic of sovereignty, citizenship and human rights, including the idea that the latter are inherent

---

98 For this discussion, see Swiffen, *Law, Ethics and the Biopolitical*, 66–7; Brown, 152.
99 Agamben, "Beyond Human Rights", 90.
100 Agamben, "Beyond Human Rights", 93; see also Agamben, *Homo Sacer*, 131.
101 Agamben, "Beyond Human Rights", 92.
102 Owens, "Beyond 'Bare Life'", 135.
103 Agamben, "Beyond Human Rights", 94.

and inalienable. Therefore, while constituted through its exclusion-inclusion from the law, the figure of the refugee challenges the very existence of state sovereignty: it is "the only category in which one may see today . . . the forms and limits of a coming political community".[104] It is the most emblematic bio-political subject, the one that can be killed with impunity through removal of its subjectivity by placing it outside the law;[105] it is the modern *homo sacer*.

Against the backdrop of Agamben's thorough and critical analysis of the figure of the refugee and the inevitability of the permanent state of exception, and his call for the end of human rights,[106] it is interesting to recall that Arendt was less categorical. Indeed, while Agamben does not consider other possible scenarios,[107] Arendt believed in multiple factors and endings. For instance, totalitarianism is, for her, the crystallization of multiple factors, whereas for Agamben, it is an inherent product of sovereign power.[108] It hence seems important and useful to acknowledge that human rights can and do have different meanings, and that they can evolve and have evolved over time. Emphasizing plurality and the potential of change and new beginnings, as Arendt did, is fundamental to rethink human rights and their subject – a perspective that strongly resonates with other approaches that I explore in more detail in the next chapters.

Questioning Arendt's alleged overemphasis of the political: shortcomings of the figure of the refugee?

Arendt's approach and reasoning have been criticized on several grounds, notably with respect to her view of human rights and the importance attached to being part of a political community, as well as her allegedly strict distinction between the social and political spheres. These critiques, which I discuss in this section, reveal indeed important shortcomings and perhaps even conceptual flaws in Arendt's analysis, and also in subsequent works building on it (such as Agamben's), that would suggest that her theorization of human rights, including her figure of the refugee, cannot grasp and address the complexity of contemporary human rights violations.

104 Agamben, "Beyond Human Rights", 90.
105 Hegarty, 21.
106 Agamben, "Beyond Human Rights", 90.
107 Gündoğdu, 29. Although the scope of this book does not allow engaging with the numerous criticisms of Agamben's work, it is worth mentioning that Agamben has been criticized for his allegedly originalist vision of history and for thinking history in terms of a "decisive and founding event". Swiffen, "Derrida Contra Agamben", 354. Agamben arguably also conceives of sovereign power in a unidirectional manner, erasing the complexity and contingency of the histories of human rights and citizenship. Owens, "Beyond 'Bare Life'", 142; Gündoğdu, 51.
108 Owens, "Beyond 'Bare Life'", 143.

With respect to the argument that Arendt went too far in her conception of the political as distinct from the social and from "the realm of necessity",[109] her stance towards the modern politicization of social issues, such as poverty and housing, have been characterized as negative and "archipolitical".[110] Her attempt to rigidly preserve a clear separation between private life and public/political life has been cast as an attempt "to preserve the political from the contamination of private, social, apolitical life".[111] Arguably, such a conceptual separation allowed her to present the rights of Man as an undue dilemma. According to Jacques Rancière it is a "deceptive trick" to conceive of human rights as belonging exclusively to the social and citizen's rights to the political sphere.[112] Arendt's reasoning, in this perspective, can be understood as either tautological because it grants the rights of Man to those who already have rights as citizens; or it can be understood as void because the rights of Man are the rights of those who have no rights and who have nothing more than the fact of being human, which makes a mockery out of human rights.[113] Said differently, human rights are either equivalent to already existing political rights, making them useless, or they are meaningless because they cannot be enforced, which obviously contrasts with the widespread view that human rights are an important tool in modern politics, even if they are far from perfect.

Rancière also criticizes the way in which subsequent critical thinkers, and in particular Agamben, have utilized Arendt's allegedly exaggerated distinction between what is political and what is social and her emphasis on the political realm. Because of Arendt's categorical separation, Rancière argues, "the political exception is ultimately incorporated in state power, standing in front of bare life – an opposition that the next step forward turns into a complementarity", and politics becomes the same as power.[114] For him, a reliance on Arendt's assumptions in this regard leads Agamben to problematically transpose "an archipolitical statement into a depoliticizing approach" that sets power and repression in a sphere of exceptionality, as exemplified in Agamben's theorization of the *homo sacer*.[115] In contrast, Rancière usefully argues that bare life, and social life more generally, cannot be separated from political life and that politics is a process, not a sphere that would be distinct. In the context of human rights, this means that subjectivization can happen

---

109 Rancière, 298.
110 Rancière, 299.
111 Rancière, 301. For an alternative reading of Arendt's understanding of these two spheres, that is one in which the separation is not as rigid as Rancière suggests, see Benhabib, *The Reluctant Modernism*, xi–xii.
112 Rancière, 298–9.
113 Rancière, 298, 302.
114 Rancière, 302.
115 Rancière, 299.

precisely because of the act of doing something with the rights declared in human rights instruments. Referring to a particular historical event, Rancière points out that if women during the French Revolution could be put to death for their political actions, they had to be considered as political subjects, and not merely as social, apolitical beings who did not have rights. Through their protest and challenge of the idea that only men had rights, women were engaging in what he calls "dissensus", that is a "dispute about the frame within which we see something as given".[116] In other words, they were acting as genuine subjects: "[t]hey acted as subjects that did not have the rights that they had and had the rights that they had not".[117] Rancière therefore rejects what he reads in Arendt as a false dilemma between the social and the political and argues that the concept of Man, presumably presented by Arendt in opposition to the citizen, is not void.

It has also been suggested that the social and the political are distinct in some ways, but that the social is relevant in a political sense, including as a source of rights.[118] For Jean L. Cohen, it is more specifically Arendt's negative assessment of the social in its contemporary form that is problematic and even theoretically flawed.[119] She claims that the plural, flexible and creative elements of modern civil society are missed in Arendt's analysis because of the focus on the political; as a result, the relevance of the social for rights and as a trigger for new types of solidarity and legality is also overlooked.[120] Cohen notes that it is above all civil society actors, and not political actors strictly speaking, that have revived the discourse of human rights towards the end of the 20th century, including the fundamental right to have rights in an Arendtian sense, and have contributed to increasing the impact of human rights.[121] Women's rights organizations, for instance, campaigned for greater equality in the workplace and access to childcare.[122] Convinced of the usefulness of human rights, Cohen strongly disagrees with Arendt's presumed argument that human rights cannot "protect individuals against arbitrary power and lawlessness" and that citizenship necessarily secures the protection of rights.[123] She says that Arendt's general reasoning is flawed in further

---

116 Rancière, 304. 'Consensus' implies for Rancière abandoning politics, resolving conflicts by adjusting interests and preventing possibilities to claim one's rights. Rancière, 306.
117 Rancière, 304.
118 Cohen, 180.
119 Cohen, 165.
120 Cohen, 180.
121 Cohen, 181.
122 It is worth noting that national and regional courts have played an important role in advancing human rights. However, courts can only hear cases that have been brought before them, including by actors like women's rights groups and labor associations, for instance with respect to gender equality at work. See Cohen, n 62 (with reference to Karen Alter's work).
123 Cohen, 164, 171.

ways. For instance, she argues that Arendt mistook historical, external factors that explain why many people lack human rights, such as the collapse of the Austro-Hungarian empire and the rise of nationalism in eastern parts of Europe, for factors inherent to the nation-state and its traditions.[124] Similarly, the problem of the state system, on Cohen's account, does not primarily consist in the relationship between the state and the nation and the negative influence of national identity on the protection of human rights, as Arendt arguably saw it (at least initially), but rather "between unimpeded state sovereignty and constitutionalism", with the former threatening the latter.[125] In this sense, Cohen seems to undermine the importance that Arendt attached to national identity in her analysis, although the notion that one must belong to a group like a nation, as I argue in more detail below, could and still can explain why international human rights are not genuinely accessible to all. Cohen also remarks that citizens lost their rights in the past and nothing in Arendt's argument in favour of the right to have rights suggests that this could not happen again.[126] European Jews, who first lost certain rights and eventually their citizenships in the 1930s and 1940s, are, of course, the archetypical example, but more recent efforts of Western states to denaturalize presumed Islamic terrorists do highlight that expulsion from the political community and denial of the right to have rights remain a possibility. As Arendt would probably have conceded herself, a concept like the right to have rights, while providing the basis for all other rights, can quite obviously not guarantee that this right will be respected in practice.

Other authors agree that giving back a community to refugees would not be a sustainable solution, although they generally understand Arendt's analysis of human rights in a positive light and consider them an important tool. For Benhabib, for instance, trying to reintegrate refugees into a political community – what Arendt, or at least a straightforward reading of her work, proposed – cannot alone prevent the denial of the right to have rights in the future.[127] According to John Lechte and Saul Newman, such attempts would actually reinforce the model of politics based exclusively on the state and the importance of being a citizen.[128] Interestingly, as Christoph Menke, Birgit Kaiser and Kathrin Thiele point out, Arendt never fully explained the idea of a political community of humanity, and the right to have rights conceptually ends up being a right like others, in the sense that it needs mutual agreement to establish it.[129] Moreover, when Arendt claimed that the right

---

124 Cohen, 165–6.
125 Cohen, 171. Cohen notes that Arendt eventually came to a similar conclusion. Cohen, 171–2.
126 Cohen, 171.
127 Benhabib, *The Rights of Others*, 62–3, 134.
128 Lechte & Newman, 529.
129 Menke, Kaiser & Thiele, 750.

to have rights belongs to a new international law, she relied on the same institution – namely the state – and logic that aggravated the problem of statelessness in the first place.[130] It has also been argued that Arendt never fully developed the idea of and offered a convincing source for the right to have right, and that she did not seriously consider international law for such purposes.[131] Instead, according to Cohen, Arendt only underlined the importance of international law under certain specific circumstances, such as for an international penal code and an international court to address crimes against humanity;[132] she missed the fact that international law and national law can work side by side and also that the discourse of international human rights has "symbolic meaning and political effectivity quite different from her own ambivalent assessment".[133] Against the backdrop of such criticism, it can be said that Cohen does not appear to account for Arendt's point that state sovereignty is the foundation of both national and international law. Indeed, Arendt was hesitant *vis-à-vis* international law mainly because it operates on the principle of state sovereignty,[134] which means that states can always invoke their sovereignty to justify inaction towards refugees, with states rarely objecting to the denial of citizenship by another state.[135] Furthermore, international law and its institutions are driven by elites, which is difficult to reconcile with Arendt's vision of participatory politics.[136] Nonetheless, Cohen argues strongly, and persuasively, that human rights discourses have become an essential feature of the global political system that guides and constrains states, which was admittedly not as obvious in Arendt's lifetime. Even oppressive regimes that are often criticized for violating human rights, like China and Saudi Arabia, typically deny such violations and rather claim that they respect human rights.[137] Very much unlike Agamben, as it is worth recalling, Cohen comes to the conclusion that we must find a way to save human rights by reconstructing a universal moral principle.[138]

In light of such critiques, the usefulness of Arendt's thinking about human rights might seem to offer only a limited understanding of contemporary challenges in the field. As a matter of fact, with respect to her figure of the refugee, writers like Rancière and Cohen hardly address this concept. Rancière

---

130 Menke, Kaiser & Thiele, 751.
131 Cohen, 164.
132 Cohen, 177.
133 Cohen, 177.
134 Arendt, *The Origins of Totalitarianism*, 298. For more on this discussion and on major weaknesses of international law according to Arendt, see Cotter, 103–8.
135 Cotter, 99.
136 Williams & Lang, 18.
137 This is illustrated by the reports submitted by all states as part of the Human Rights Council's Universal Periodic Review.
138 Cohen, 183.

only maintains that refugees, like other individuals and groups whose rights are denied, can gain access to rights precisely through a process of dissensus.[139] It is as if refugees are not different from others who are excluded, such as minorities oppressed within a political community, and hence are not a symptomatic group in the Arendtian sense. This is persuasive, since different kinds of marginalized groups can indeed constitute the exception that reveals a flaw within the norm. As discussed, Agamben also makes a case in favour of understanding the exception – exemplified by the refugee – as a good explanation of the general, with the sovereign being able to decide on the difference, and creating a zone of indistinction, between the two.[140] I would nevertheless argue, and I pursue this idea in the next section, that considering the specific position of refugees continues to be particularly insightful, including to grasp other forms of exclusion.

1.3   A creative understanding of Arendt's thinking: human rights, plurality and new beginnings

In spite of certain shortcomings of Arendt's analysis of human rights, it seems useful and possible to remain anchored in Arendt's critical perspective and to build on it in a constructive way to explain contemporary challenges related to human rights and identify possible avenues to improve them, notably by actualizing the figure of the refugee. Arendt's fundamental insights are still relevant, because the profound perplexities of human rights that she highlighted, in particular the problem of statelessness created by the nation-state system, persist. Moreover, it can be argued that there is no universal concept of the "human person", that the legal personhood of migrants – and hence their rights – is often dismissed and that the distinction between citizens and non-citizens proves to be resilient and impacts the actual conditions experienced by migrants.[141] Fundamentally, human rights law continues to leave various categories of migrants with insecure legal standing, because it affirms the principle of territorial sovereignty.[142]

I believe there is great potential in considering Arendt's overall thinking in light of our times, as many events and changes at the international level have taken place since she developed her theory and critique, as well as beyond specific points made in certain texts or contexts. It can be beneficial to read Arendt against Arendt, as Ayten Gündoğdu points out. This means taking into account all her writings and explaining major points with different and

---

139 Rancière, 304.
140 In fact, as Agamben argues, the "exception does not only confirm the rule; the rule as such lives off the exception alone". Agamben, *Homo Sacer*, 16.
141 Gündoğdu, 9–10, 92–3.
142 Gündoğdu, 93. This is an aspect of human rights that is not clearly addressed by some of the authors discussed so far.

sometimes contradictory insights, instead of focusing on the one or two texts usually referred to in the context of human rights. Furthermore, her theory can be appreciated critically by moving back and forth between her writings and today's situations.[143] In this context, Seyla Benhabib usefully recalls that understanding always happens "within a framework that makes sense for us".[144] For instance, human rights have been institutionalized and are now a common language in international politics; they have even become a legitimizing source of the sovereignty of states, since the latter are meant to be the main protectors of individual rights.[145] At the national level, human rights are now manifest in the form of charters, bills of rights and other constitutional guarantees, not only in Western democracies but also in other states that do not necessarily build on a long tradition and logic of human rights.[146] While Arendt's critique of human rights remained, by and large, within the nation-state framework, she had, as Benhabib notes, "more experimental, fluid, and open reflections on how to constitute democratically sovereign communities".[147] These reflections, however, were never fully explored by Arendt, which can be seen as an invitation to pursue them. All this is arguably in line with Arendt's thinking since, as a fervent advocate of critical thinking, she resisted absolutes and final solutions,[148] even her own. On that note, if Arendt has been criticized for offering no or only limited solutions to the problems she identified,[149] it can be argued that finding solutions was not her main objective, which, as it should be emphasized, is not a flaw in itself.

Identifying the perplexities of human rights, as Arendt did, including by illuminating the relationship between human rights and sovereignty, led to a better understanding of the shortcomings of the system and laid the groundwork for conceptual change. In this sense, Arendt did not simply reject human rights, as Agamben, for instance, suggests doing; rather, she usefully distinguished between rights and shed light on the fact that citizen's rights are not the same as human rights. It is also important to keep in mind that Arendt's analysis of the aporias of human rights is related to an understanding of human rights that is independent from both natural law and liberalism; in fact, she questioned the underlying assumptions of these traditions.[150]

---

143 Gündoğdu, 6.
144 Benhabib, *The Reluctant Modernism*, xlviii.
145 Gündoğdu, 8.
146 For instance, the constitutions of Bosnia, Uganda and Guatemala contain numerous references to human rights. As the authors of an empirical study of the constitutions of 189 countries have concluded, "human rights language is now a common feature of national constitutions", see Beck, Drori & Meyer, 497.
147 Benhabib, *The Rights of Others*, 64.
148 Gündoğdu, 32–3.
149 For the argument that Arendt offered political but not conceptual solutions, see Benhabib, *The Rights of Others*, 59.
150 Menke, Kaiser & Thiele, 741.

In sum, I claim it is through a careful reinterpretation – and with an open mind – of some of her key concepts and arguments that Arendt's critique is useful for an analysis of contemporary situations pertaining to human rights, including with respect to refugees and migrants, who represent one of the biggest socio-political challenges to the state-centric system and in the world more generally. It also supports the broader argument with respect to other forms of exclusion created by the human rights system.

A plurality of reiterated claims to reinforce democratic principles

I argue that Arendt's idea of a fundamental right to have rights is still relevant in the current context and can, for instance, be considered as a moral claim of refugees or other stateless persons to citizenship.[151] Benhabib, while departing from Arendt's framework of the nation-state,[152] adapts the right to have rights to highlight the importance of "democratic iterations". Democratic iterations are "complex processes of public argument, deliberation, and learning through which universalist rights claims are contested and contextualized, invoked and revoked, throughout legal and political institutions as well as in the public sphere of liberal democracies".[153] They describe the numerous and multifaceted ways in which the values and norms of the majority are negotiated with cosmopolitan norms, such as human rights. The concept of iteration is drawn from Jacques Derrida, for whom every repetition is a form of variation.[154] There is no "original" or "originary" source of meaning, as "[e]very act of iteration involves making sense of an authoritative original in a new and different context".[155] The various public statements, legal arguments and dialogues in the context of a possible ban of the hijab in the public sphere in France as well as the potential legalization of religious arbitration courts in Canada in the early 2000s are examples of such democratic iterations. For Benhabib, while sovereignty has not become irrelevant, it is through such democratic iterations that established understandings can be disputed and that the right to have rights finds its meaning and is realized. It could hence be argued that the political community that is necessary for the right to have rights to exist in practice can take different forms, both in different places and in different moments in time, which expands on Arendt's notion of a political community. Democratic iterations allow the contestation and re-appropriation of global principles and rights

151 Benhabib, *The Rights of Others*, 56. As noted above, for Arendt, the moral claim that humans have inherent rights does not really have the force of law.
152 Benhabib, *The Rights of Others*, 64–5.
153 Benhabib, *The Rights of Others*, 19.
154 Benhabib, *The Rights of Others*, 179.
155 Benhabib, *The Rights of Others*, 180.

claims as well as the transformation of what counts as authoritative interpretation.[156] In this sense, democratic iterations create fewer exclusions than a static interpretation of sovereignty and related rights. It is through these continuous conversations and interactions, which can be linguistic, legal, cultural, and so on, and which occur in public institutions and civil society, that members of political communities present themselves not only as subjects but also as authors of laws.[157] In addition to altering the meaning and content of rights claims, these processes also affect the self-understandings of the actors involved,[158] as the example of *sans-papiers* will show.

The meaning of rights is also enriched by the plurality of interpretations, which is why Benhabib, through a reasoning reminiscent of Arendt, advocates for the recognition that humans are both distinctive and similar.[159] Differences must be embraced, not only by states but also more broadly in society, and individuals should be thought of "in terms of their identities, particular life histories, beliefs and understandings, needs, desires, feelings, and emotions".[160] In this analysis, migrants thus do not threaten a given political culture, or political liberalism more generally; to the contrary, they contribute to transforming rights "toward a more inclusionary, dynamic, and deliberative democratic project".[161] In fact, it is through the challenge of new groups claiming membership in a political community that both the limits and universality of democratic principles, like rights, are revealed, and that these principles are rearticulated and reinvigorated.[162] This means that contestations and reinterpretations of cultural traditions are a sign of their strength.[163]

Since membership in a community is constantly negotiable and negotiated, with both international and national laws framing these negotiations and, in turn, responding – even if only slowly – to them, the community of actors can eventually include those that are usually excluded, such as refugees and migrants; this does not, however, eliminate exclusion in itself. Creating boundaries and rules concerning membership, which result in exclusions, is inherent to democratic governance according to Benhabib.[164] Political equality cannot be extended to all. Similarly, while noting that state sovereignty is being eroded

156 Benhabib, *The Rights of Others*, 179–80.
157 Benhabib, *The Rights of Others*, 19–20, 113.
158 Benhabib, *The Rights of Others*, 209.
159 Schoolman, xxix.
160 Schoolman, xxix.
161 Benhabib, *The Rights of Others*, 90. As Benhabib also argues, it is only a "static vision of collective-identity formation which makes it plausible . . . to assume that aliens and others may pose a threat to, dilute, or overrun an already attained community of solidarity". Benhabib, *The Rights of Others*, 173.
162 Benhabib, *The Rights of Others*, 197.
163 Benhabib, *The Rights of Others*, 120.
164 Benhabib, *The Rights of Others*, 174.

in several ways, she does not see the end of the state system or the concept of citizenship; as a matter of fact, national borders are still asserted and regulate movements: "Democratic laws require closure precisely because democratic representation must be accountable to a specific people . . . I see no way to cut this Gordian knot linking territoriality, representation, and democratic voice".[165] As for Arendt, in Benhabib's reading, it seems that someone's rights must be coupled with someone else's obligations, and that institutions – "most commonly the state and its apparatus" – are needed to protect these rights.[166] Benhabib also says that new forms of "democratic attachments" at the sub-national and supranational levels are needed, which appears indeed crucial. Nevertheless, in what can be seen as a pragmatic conclusion, she only advocates for porous borders between states as well as for "just membership"[167] (instead of an all-inclusive one), arguing that the existing exclusions can be attenuated by democratic iterations. It is through such iterations that boundaries are adjusted and categories of political membership, such as "citizens" and "others", and their complex relationships, are negotiated and become fluid.[168] However, the problem of the dependency of rights on state sovereignty is clearly not resolved, perhaps because it is irresolvable, and Benhabib, not unlike Arendt, seems to remain closely attached to the reality of current politics and to accept exclusions to an important point.

Notwithstanding the validity of Benhabib's pragmatic concerns, one does wonder why the objective should consist in only mitigating – but not eliminating – exclusions. It might be that it is difficult to imagine a political community without some form of membership and hence also exclusions, but this does not mean that the type and intensity of exclusions that currently exist and that underpin and plague the international human rights system should be accepted. This is why I believe that the underlying political system, and especially the focus on the state and its arguably inherent exclusion of significant parts of humanity that is related to the construction of an idealized subject, needs to be questioned. What may seem empirically impossible within the current paradigm, namely striving for the complete elimination of exclusions, might be conceivable in another paradigm.

Understanding the right to have rights as new beginnings and human rights as practice

The perplexities of human rights identified by Arendt are not necessarily dead ends or unmovable obstacles. In her generous and constructive reading of

---

165 Benhabib, *The Rights of Others*, 6, 219.
166 Benhabib, *The Rights of Others*, 57.
167 Benhabib, *The Rights of Others*, 3.
168 Benhabib, *The Rights of Others*, 21.

Arendt, Gündoğdu conceives of human rights perplexities "as challenging political and ethical dilemmas that can be navigated differently, including in ways that bring to view new understandings of the relationships between rights, citizenship, and humanity".[169] She maintains that these perplexities must be understood as new beginnings, as opportunities to rethink rightlessness. To make this argument, Gündoğdu heavily relies on Arendt's emphasis on natality and the possibilities that new beginnings evoke. For Arendt, action, or inter-action, is a key concept that is closely related to the possibility of new beginnings inherent in birth; newcomers have the capacity of beginning something anew, that is, of acting.[170] It is through human interaction in public spaces that meaningful and concrete freedom, which is not the same as liberty (from oppression or poverty, for example), comes into existence, and that new beginnings are made possible.[171] This is why inter-action, the potential of new beginnings and plurality should be recognized and promoted, and why Arendt feared processes, like in totalitarianism, that would make the plurality, or individuality, of human beings superfluous, and hence humanity eliminable.[172]

Following this insight, the right to have rights can be reinterpreted as a practice of making new rights claims. In fact, it is precisely through the right to have rights that Arendt insisted on critically assessing and rethinking human rights. This right to have rights can be seen as a new beginning itself, since it was not part of the initial rights framework based on citizenship, and it emphasizes the political practice related to human rights.[173] Viewed from this perspective, Arendt's call for a right to have rights is, as Gündoğdu argues, an encouragement "to shift our focus from the question of what grounds human rights to the question of what generates, guarantees, and reinvents them – a shift that demands a close engagement with the *political practices of founding human rights*".[174] The question is not what the external foundation of a new right is, but how it is articulated and given meaning to.[175] In other words, it is possible to think of human rights as being generated through political practice, instead of looking for a moral basis or the normative justification of human rights (something Benhabib, for instance, is still concerned with).[176] For Gündoğdu, Arendt's right to have rights attains universal legitimacy through

169 Gündoğdu, 5.
170 Arendt, *The Human Condition*, 9.
171 Bernstein, 34.
172 Arendt, *The Origins of Totalitarianism*, 457. See also Bernstein, 147; Benhabib, *The Reluctant Modernism*, 67.
173 Gündoğdu, 171.
174 Gündoğdu, 22.
175 Gündoğdu, 181.
176 Gündoğdu, 186. This is also why Gündoğdu maintains, against Rancière, that human rights are not void in Arendt's conception. Rather, it is when they are excluded from the political realm that they lose their democratic potential. Gündoğdu, 81.

the continuous political practice of making new rights claims.[177] The state as a political structure does not become irrelevant, but it is not only within the framework of the state that political action is possible.

It is in this light that rights claims by undocumented migrants, who, for instance, have given themselves assertively the name *sans-papiers* in France and shout "Papers for all!" during demonstrations, and others who are excluded from – but still governed by – the existing framework and initially act without authorization, can be understood. Like the analysis of founding documents of human rights, such as the 1789 *Déclaration*, has shown, rights have always depended on being declared, on being invented; there is no other source of a right than its declaration.[178] As Gündoğdu says, "[h]uman rights owe their origins and continuous reinvention to such inaugural acts [i.e. declarations] that involve the invention and disclosure of a new political and normative world".[179] From that perspective, it is not democratic iterations about existing rights that would allow excluded individuals to gain access to these rights, as in Benhabib's conceptualization; it is about grounding or founding new rights and their potential universality, by public declarations and creative action. In today's context of migration, by declaring rights that are not yet given, such as a right to legal documents and status, *sans-papiers* claim that they are entitled to freedom and equality.[180] *Sans-papiers*, instead of simply accepting their rightlessness, make their speech "audible and intelligible" through creative actions and hence present themselves as political subjects.[181] In a way, Gündoğdu echoes Rancière's argument that subjectivization occurs through practice by pointing out that *sans-papiers* do today what women did during the French Revolution.[182] While it is difficult to establish any clear causal links between these creative actions and concrete changes in the law, it should be noted that gains in terms of formal rights are not the only meaningful achievement; indeed, the recognition of the relevance of new beginnings and rights as a political practice, and the contribution to political debates on their own terms, can enhance the self-understanding and empowerment of those who are largely rightless and improve their situation.

Despite the fact that declaring new rights is of course no guarantee that these rights will be recognized and protected by the political community or that they will attain universal legitimacy, in Gündoğdu's Arendtian approach, the practice of declaring rights, time and again, is an essential precondition.[183]

---

177 Gündoğdu, 23.
178 Gündoğdu, 172.
179 Gündoğdu, 166.
180 Gündoğdu, 172. Gündoğdu also draws on the concept of equaliberty, developed by Etienne Balibar, to argue that human rights are founded on political practices, and not on extra-political sources of authority. Gündoğdu, 23, 183–4.
181 Gündoğdu, 164, 168, 189.
182 Gündoğdu, 187.
183 Gündoğdu, 168.

Such an approach focused on the political practice of declarations has, indeed, great potential since it allows changing existing boundaries of the political community and those that were initially not considered to be entitled to human rights to become political subjects, to claim new rights and to contribute to the development of human rights.[184] In this framework, citizenship loses its privileged status; instead, it is the concept of legal personhood, independent of any nationality, that emerges as foundational for human rights and that allows *personae* to appear in public and assert rights, including new ones.[185] The meaning and significance of human rights, moreover, does not necessarily depend on their formal recognition and enforcement. Said differently, a reinterpretation of Arendt's right to have rights, and a consideration of perplexities as having multiple effects and not necessarily resulting in rightlessness, makes it possible to challenge and reconfigure the existing human rights system. As Gündoğdu argues,

> [t]he divisions that this framework introduces into the "human" of human rights – between citizens and non-citizens, asylum seekers and refugees, legal residents and undocumented migrants, to give a few examples – are by no means settled, and they are now being challenged in various struggles that reinvent the meaning of human rights.[186]

In sum, understanding human rights as a practice might not solve the fundamental problem that Arendt identified with respect to sovereignty, but it is an interesting and constructive approach: it helpfully shifts the focus away from the problem of sovereignty and allows for much-needed alternative understandings of equality, freedom, justice and rights to emerge. At the same time, it should be noted that as with Benhabib's democratic iterations, Gündoğdu's focus on political practices of declaring new rights seems to suggest not only that those who are excluded have agency with respect to rights, but also that the burden to act and to prevent rightlessness lies on them. One can therefore question whether this approach sufficiently takes into account existing power inequalities and genuinely challenges the dominant conception of the subject of human rights.

1.4   Rethinking the human through the figure of the *migrant*

The intensification of migration, combined with certain frequently pursued state policies, has meant that political exclusion resulting from statelessness – or from the lack of protection of the host state in the case of

---

184 Gündoğdu, 185.
185 Gündoğdu, 19.
186 Gündoğdu, 5.

non-citizen migrants who may still have a citizenship of a state that is unable or unwilling to provide effective guarantees – has become more and more common and also accepted.[187] In fact, these exclusions define current global politics, and, as I would argue, the conceptual differences between stateless, refugees and migrants are becoming largely irrelevant in practice. If citizenship and its inherent exclusions were already the foundation of the international order in Arendt's time, the increasingly stringent policing of borders by states, especially in the Global North, has exacerbated the phenomenon of rightlessness resulting from migration. People still embark on the often difficult and dangerous road of migration in spite of these measures, and the conditions experienced by migrants have worsened. Many migrants find themselves in acute situations of vulnerability, frequently facing discrimination and violence.[188] Undocumented migration has been made illegal[189] and even criminal,[190] with state authorities relying on deportation and detention as common strategies of exclusion.[191] The continuous reliance on state sovereignty, which clearly remains an important force behind the (non)respect of human rights, as theorized by Arendt, and the resulting firm defense of borders by state authorities affect individuals from the Global South but also increasingly foreigners from so-called developed countries.[192] Because of the enduring existence of borders, the dichotomy of insiders and outsiders persists, and the latter, as Emma Haddad says, "do not fit into the state-citizen-territory hierarchy, but are forced, instead, into the gaps *between* [and not within] states".[193]

I argue that migrants remain useful to explain contemporary phenomena of rightlessness that are based on an inclusive exclusion, or on a negative relation to law,[194] and even suggest that migration and statelessness could be considered a new approach to human rights and to politics more generally. In this sense, the figure of the *migrant* captures Arendt's core insights and also accounts for some of the limits of her figure of the refugee. It is important to recall, as Arendt already suggested, that the exclusions created by the nation-state and its borders are in no way accidental or incidental; rather, they are continuous and inherent to the international system based on state sovereignty.[195] Therefore, Arendt's figure does not only remain a good starting point to question the idea of the nation and sovereignty and to highlight

187 Hayden, 250.
188 See for instance the reports issued by the United Nations Special Rapporteur on the human rights of migrants.
189 Brown, 153.
190 Gündoğdu, 2–3.
191 Gündoğdu, 207.
192 Gündoğdu, 2–3.
193 Haddad, 7.
194 Dayan, xii.
195 Haddad, 2.

the importance of the right to have rights; the figure can also be expanded to become more comprehensive, and more unsettling. It can be actualized to take into consideration contemporary forms of migration and displacement as well as ensuing political exclusions and forms of rightlessness. Moreover, Arendt's theory can be relied upon in a creative manner, which is consistent with her emphasis on new beginnings leading to new possibilities; in this instance, it is useful to reconfigure legal subjectivity beyond the nation-state framework and the current international human rights system that continues to heavily rely on this framework. This is what the figure of the *migrant* seeks to achieve.

Another reason why the figure of the *migrant* is compatible with what Arendt suggested is that her figure of the refugee can be understood as a changing and socially constructed notion: the identity of the refugee simultaneously included in the law and excluded from its protection is always contingent on the interests of states and their perceptions as to what their priorities should be and who their current enemies are.[196] For instance, it is only between the two world wars that refugees really started to be considered as a problem, and even afterwards, refugees have not always been perceived as a threat; by way of example, during the Cold War, those fleeing communist regimes were supported by and were welcomed in the West.[197]

Drawing on Arendt's ideas and on the theoretical insights achieved by authors who have further developed her thinking on rights and refugees, it is possible to respond to some of the challenges created by contemporary forms of migration. This might address and alleviate the concrete situation of certain migrants, and, more fundamentally, eliminate some of the sources of exclusion lying at the heart of the political system. It is important to bear in mind the negative understanding of statelessness as rightlessness for many individuals in today's world, but also to appreciate its potential as an ideal that allows thinking beyond the current state system and its inherent exclusions. The figure of the *migrant* exposes a fundamental bias of human rights, namely their ontological foundation on an unnecessary connection to the state. In this sense, the figure of the *migrant* goes beyond Arendt's figure of the refugee.

Furthermore, the figure of the *migrant* grasps contemporary forms of rightlessness and exclusions from the international human rights system and from humanity in a broad sense that includes refugees, migrants and also some non-migrants. While it has been suggested that the situation of Arendt's refugees and the one of migrants today are too different to equate,[198] and

196 Haddad, 14, 113. For a discussion on the different definitions of "the refugee" in recent history and related problems, see Haddad, 30–2.
197 Haddad, 113. Contemporary migration is, in fact, characterized by similar dynamics.
198 Schulze Wessel, 55.

although the supremacy of the state is arguably questioned more often and at least some of those who are excluded make their voices heard more actively, I believe that the fundamental exclusion from membership in a political community is very similar for Arendt's refugees and today's migrants. The figure of the *migrant* hence exposes the extent of contemporary rightlessness, comparable to what the figure of the refugee did in Arendt's time. Fundamentally, the concept of the *migrant* recognizes that the traditional difference between refugees and other categories of migrants is no longer tenable. It is often argued that refugees, as defined in the 1951 *Refugee Convention*, are forced to flee and that other migrants choose to leave their home voluntarily,[199] but the distinctions between voluntary and involuntary or forced migration are not as clear-cut as previously assumed. Moreover, individuals can start their journey in one (presumed) category and end up in another.[200] It can also be maintained that the types of situations that the international community recognizes as worthy of being supported are arbitrary and an expression of liberalist thinking. Such categorizations ignore the fact that many are forced to leave their country for lack of a viable alternative. They sustain the idea that some people are more deserving of protection and rights than others[201] and even create "hierarchical divisions within humanity".[202] In fact, all those who find themselves in a foreign state, including so-called economic migrants, asylum seekers (who are often considered guilty of breaking the law until they may be able to prove otherwise[203]) and those who have been "denaturalized" (with the term explicitly conveying the conviction that only citizens are "natural" human beings), share the burden of being in a precarious and dangerous situation.[204] Standing outside the "trinity of state-people-territory",[205] they are without the protection of the law and are hence rightless. It should be noted that in an Arendtian approach, the term "stateless" applies not only to those whose nationality has been legally revoked but also to those who have effectively lost the protection and rights associated with a nationality. Arendt already recognized that both the *de jure* and *de facto* stateless are denied action and speech.[206] In other words, being deprived of one's legal status and/or ability to access and exercise rights is the primary condition of statelessness,[207] and of the *migrant*.

199 Schulze Wessel, 48, 50.
200 Haddad, 165, 170.
201 Gündoğdu, 123–4.
202 Gündoğdu, 124.
203 Gündoğdu, 110–11.
204 Gündoğdu, 3–4.
205 Arendt, *The Origins of Totalitarianism*, 282.
206 Hayden, 255; Gündoğdu, 2.
207 Hayden, 256.

All migrants are relevant as they reveal the importance of citizenship for human rights to be recognized and shed light on how the state-centric paradigm generates exclusions. It can even be argued that the system discriminates between full humans and others, which is an aspect that will be further explored in the next chapters. Reminiscent of Agamben's notion of bare life, it can be argued that migrants are included in the political community through their exclusion: as superfluous stateless, they are *"integrated within the decision-making authority of the state and segregated from the normalized territory of potential host states".*[208] The figure of the *migrant* reflects that while the movements of some people, like international businesspeople and tourists from the Global North, and of goods are less and less limited as a result of global capitalism and free trade agreements, the movements of many others are increasingly restricted. Speaking of a system of global apartheid, Etienne Balibar claims that "[b]orders have thus become essential institutions in the constitution of social conditions on a global scale where the passport and identity card function as a systematic criterion".[209]

It is worth noting that the insistence on migrants should not be seen as denying the condition of rightlessness of many non-migrants. Rightlessness is created in various ways today, and not only via the relation of inclusive exclusion that both refugees and migrants have to sovereignty. As Gündoğdu maintains, there is a growing number of people whose "legal, political, and human standing has been significantly undermined".[210] The experience of rightlessness of nationals who do not benefit from the protection of their state also matters and is, in fact, captured by the figure of the *migrant*. One can think, for example, of political prisoners and people living in extreme poverty or, as it will be discussed below, of the discrimination experienced by persons of colour. In other words, the figure of the *migrant* transcends the conceptual difference between *de jure* and *de facto* statelessness, in the sense that people in both categories cannot effectively access human rights. Migrants, nevertheless, form a large group that, even if it is a heterogeneous one, consistently experiences rightlessness and significant forms of political exclusion on which the system – from state sovereignty to human rights – is built. Migrants hence emerge as one of the most symptomatic contemporary groups that experience rightlessness, which is why the proposed figure is named after them. Finally, while it could be argued that the migrants' rightlessness is not equivalent to a complete loss of rights, as many individuals

---

208 Hayden, 259; see also Haddad, 62. Recent international initiatives like the *Global Compact for Migration*, adopted by states in December 2018 in the form of a legally non-binding instrument, arguably do not alter the fundamental tenets of the framework.

209 Balibar, *We, the People of Europe?*, 113.

210 Gündoğdu, 211.

experienced in the context of totalitarian regimes, it nevertheless describes a particular vulnerable condition.[211]

Importantly, the figure of the *migrant* is conceived neither as a passive victim nor as an active and resilient subject who is responsible for securing its own rights by itself.[212] Considering Arendt's thinking is again insightful in this context. In fact, a fairly cursory reading of Arendt would suggest that she portrayed refugees mostly as rightless and helpless victims, but her emphasis on political action and the potential for change can be understood as attributing a more positive and constructive role to refugees, and to migrants more generally. It is true that in the absence of supranational institutions offering effective protection, losing one's citizenship can imply losing one's rights. However, Arendt's call on Jewish refugees to remain faithful to their identity and values,[213] as mentioned at the beginning of this chapter, suggests that she wanted them to speak and act in the political community, that is to do precisely what they were denied. It also suggests that she would probably support that all those who are denied rights fight for their rights and identities and reject such categories as citizens and non-citizens; she would encourage them to get involved, to be creative and to find their own political solutions. The outsider status that she praised for allowing independent thinking[214] is also the reason why the figure of the *migrant* challenges the system and why actual migrants can engage in avant-gardist political action.[215]

People who are migrating obviously already act politically in various ways. Undocumented migrants, for instance, challenge claims of sovereignty in relation to territory and influence the localization of borders and checkpoints by crossing borders clandestinely and by changing their routes.[216] Indeed, the existence of borders and the shape of border zones actually depend on the actors involved, including – most prominently – those who try to cross borders by defying the authorities. It can even be argued that it is not state authorities but undocumented migrants who determine by their action where borders are drawn: as Julia Schulze Wessel maintains, the undocumented migrant, while certainly being restricted by borders, is a "border actor" who contributes to transforming the border into a border zone, a space characterized by contestation and uncertainty.[217] The previously mentioned case of

---

211 Gündoğdu, 93. The term 'migrant' might evoke a misleading sense of unimpeded movement across borders, but, as Gündoğdu recalls, in this context it invokes a history of banishment and expulsion. Gündoğdu, 4.
212 For critiques of the concept of resilience and notably its affinity with neoliberalism, see e.g. Joseph; Grove.
213 Arendt, "We Refugees", 119.
214 Bernstein, 41.
215 Gündoğdu, 203.
216 Schulze Wessel, 50.
217 Schulze Wessel, 50–3.

the *sans-papiers* is another example of such action. By staging their protests in public spaces and by occupying churches, *sans-papiers* contribute to the important practice of claiming rights and therefore to enhancing public freedom for everyone; as such, their actions "appear as democratic reconquests against the state".[218] In fact, in an Arendtian perspective, these migrants give meaning to the principle of disobedience: through their inclusive exclusion, or exclusion by inclusion, they stand outside the law, but they are still subject to its force and can therefore defy it. In fact, it is precisely by defying the law that they can perhaps "normalize" their condition.[219] This defiance, or disobedience, is crucial for the viability of any political community.[220] It can even be argued, by building both on Benhabib's emphasis on democratic iterations and on Gündoğdu's focus on creative action, that it is this practice of rights – not their abstract deduction – that matters most and that enables the construction of the human.[221]

In sum, as I have argued in this chapter, the figure of the *migrant* exposes the difficult reality and lack of protection of human rights experienced by many migrants, deconstructs the 'human' as a citizen and highlights the fundamental problem that human rights – and every subject – must be connected to a state. The figure of the *migrant* also allows imagining ways of being beyond the current framework and suggests that creative thinking and change are both necessary and possible. This important point will inform and resurface in the discussion in the next chapters. I demonstrate that the 'human' can be reconceptualized on additional grounds and conceived in various ways, as posthumanist theories and theories from the margins usefully suggest, just like law and human rights, which are some of the founding principles of democracy, need to be questioned.

Bibliography

Agamben, Giorgio. *Homo Sacer: Sovereign Power and Bare Life* (Stanford: Stanford University Press, 1998).
———. *State of Exception* (Chicago: University of Chicago Press, 2005).
———. "Beyond Human Rights" (2008) 15 *Social Engineering* 90.
American Declaration of Independence (4 July 1776).
Arendt, Hannah. *The Human Condition* (Chicago: Chicago University Press, 1958).
———. *The Origins of Totalitarianism* (Cleveland: Meridian Books, 1958).
———. "We Refugees" in Marc Robinson, ed, *Altogether Elsewhere* (London: Faber and Faber, 1994) 111.
———. *Elemente und Ursprünge totaler Herrschaft* (München: Piper, 2011).

218 Krause, 343.
219 Arendt, *Elemente und Ursprünge*, 594.
220 This is reminiscent of Rancière's insistence on the importance of contestation and negotiation. Rancière, 302.
221 See also Balibar, "(De)Constructing the Human", 730.

Balibar, Etienne. *We, thePeople of Europe?*, translated by James Swenson (Princeton: NJ: Princeton University Press, 2004).

———. "(De)Constructing the Human as Human Institution: A Reflection on the Coherence of Hannah Arendt's Practical Philosophy" (2007) 74:3 *Social Research* 727.

Beck, Colin J., Gili S. Drori & John W. Meyer. "World Influences on Human Rights Language in Constitutions: A Cross-National Study" (2012) 27:4 *International Sociology* 483.

Benhabib, Seyla. *The Reluctant Modernism of Hannah Arendt* (London: Sage, 1996).

———. *The Rights of Others: Aliens, Residents, and Citizens* (Cambridge: Cambridge University Press, 2004).

Bernstein, Richard. *Hannah Arendt and the Jewish Question* (Cambridge: Polity Press, 1996).

Brown, Chris. "The Only Thinkable Figure? Ethical and Normative Approaches to Refugees in International Relations" in Alexander Betts & Gil Loescher, eds, *Refugees in International Relations* (Oxford: Oxford University Press, 2011) 151.

Cohen, Jean L. "Rights, Citizenship and the Modern Form of the Social: Dilemmas of Arendtian Republicanism" (1996) 3(2) *Constellations* 164.

Convention Relating to the Status of Refugees (adopted on 28 July 1951, entered into force 22 April 1951) 189 UNTS 150.

Cotter, Bridget. "Hannah Arendt and 'the Right to Have Rights'" in Anthony F. Lang, Jr & John Williams, eds, *Hannah Arendt and International Relations: Readings Across the Lines* (New York: Palgrave Macmillan, 2005) 95.

Dayan, Colin. *The Law Is a White Dog: How Legal Rituals Make and Unmake Persons* (Princeton, NJ: Princeton University Press, 2011).

Déclaration des droits de l'homme et du citoyen (1789).

Disch, Lisa J. "More Truth Than Fact: Storytelling as Critical Understanding in the Writings of Hannah Arendt" (1993) 21(4) *Political Theory* 665.

Grove, Kevin. *Resilience* (London: Routledge, 2018).

Gündoğdu, Ayten. *Rightlessness in an Age of Rights: Hannah Arendt and the Contemporary Struggles of Migrants* (Oxford: Oxford University Press, 2015).

Guterres, António. "The World Faces a Pandemic of Human Rights Abuses in the Wake of Covid-19" (22 February 2021) *The Guardian*, <www.theguardian.com/global-development/2021/feb/22/world-faces-pandemic-human-rights-abuses-covid-19-antonio-guterres>.

Haddad, Emma. *The Refugee in International Society: Between Sovereigns* (Cambridge: Cambridge University Press, 2008).

Hayden, Patrick. "From Exclusion to Containment: Arendt, Sovereign, Power, and Statelessness" (2008) 3 *Societies without Borders* 248.

Hegarty, Paul. "Giorgio Agamben (1942-)" in Jon Simons, ed, *Contemporary Critical Theorists* (Edinburgh: Edinburgh University Press, 2010) 14.

Human Rights Watch. "Covid-19 Triggers Wave of Free Speech Abuse" (11 February 2021), <www.hrw.org/news/2021/02/11/covid-19-triggers-wave-free-speech-abuse>.

International Organization for Migration. *World Migration Report 2020*, <https://publications.iom.int/system/files/pdf/wmr_2020.pdf>.

Joseph, Jonathan. "Resilience as Embedded Neoliberalism: A Governmentality Approach" (2013) 1:1 *Resilience: International Policies, Practices and Discourses* 38.

Krause, Monika. "Undocumented Migrants: An Arendtian Perspective" (2008) 7(3) *European Journal of Political Theory* 331.

Lechte, John & Saul Newman. "Agamben, Arendt and Human Rights – Bearing Witness to the Human" (2012) 15:4 *European Journal of Social Theory* 522.

Menke, Christopher, Birgit Kaiser & Kathrin Thiele. "The 'Aporias of Human Rights' and the 'One Human Right': Regarding the Coherence of Hannah Arendt's Argument" (2007) 74:3 *Social Research* 739.

Owens, Patricia. "Beyond 'Bare Life': Refugees and the 'Right to Have Rights'" in Alexander Betts and Gil Loescher, eds, *Refugees in International Relations* (Oxford: Oxford University Press, 2011) 133.

Pavlich, George. *Law and Society Redefined* (Oxford: Oxford University Press, 2010).

Rancière, Jacques. "Who is the Subject of the Rights of Man?" (2004) 103:2 *The South Atlantic Quarterly* 297.

Schoolman, Morton. "Series Editor's Introduction" in Seyla Benhabib, ed, *The Reluctant Modernism of Hannah Arendt* (London: Sage, 1996) xxiii.

Schulze Wessel, Julia. "On Border Subjects: Rethinking the Figure of the Refugee and the Undocumented Migrant" (2016) 23:1 *Constellations* 46.

Swiffen, Amy. "Giorgio Agamben: Thought between Two Revolutions" in Charles Barbour & George Pavlich, eds, *After Sovereignty – On the Question of Political Beginnings* (New York: Routledge, 2010) 166.

———. *Law, Ethics and the Biopolitical* (New York: Routledge, 2010).

———. "Derrida Contra Agamben: Sovereignty, Biopower, History" (2012) 2 *Societies* 345.

Williams, John & Anthony F. Lang, Jr. "Introduction" in Anthony F. Lang, Jr & John Williams, eds, *Hannah Arendt and International Relations: Readings Across the Lines* (New York: Palgrave Macmillan, 2005) 1.

Young-Bruehl, Elisabeth. "Hannah Arendt's Storytelling" (1977) 44:1 *Social Research* 183.

Zouev, Alexandre. "COVID and the Rule of Law: A Dangerous Balancing Act", <www.un.org/en/coronavirus/covid-and-rule-law-dangerous-balancing-act>.

Chapter 2

Human, right? Analysing the subject of human rights through posthumanist approaches

The problems related to the subject of human rights go beyond the citizen-subject discussed in the previous chapter; the 'proper' subject in the humanist tradition that underpins human rights needs to be not only a citizen, as Hannah Arendt usefully pointed out, but also human. Said differently, the only subject that can have rights is a human being. In fact, it must even be human in a particular, idealized way. This is an aspect that Arendt did not engage with, but, as with the citizenship criteria, the idealized human points to fundamental processes of exclusion and inclusion that lie at the heart of the dominant concept of the subject of human rights, which reveals itself as deeply anthropocentric in terms of focus and interests. Relying on posthumanist critiques, which oppose humanist beliefs and refuse to take the human as "an ontological given" or as disembodied and disconnected from nature and animality,[1] hence allows developing a different critique of the concept of the subject of human rights than approaches dealing with the citizen-subject. These approaches are not mutually exclusive, but, as I believe, can usefully inform each other and pinpoint to different yet related reasons why subjectivity, as it is conceptualized in human rights, is not a neutral concept.

In this chapter, I build specifically on the posthumanist critique that discourses centred on conceptions of the 'human', including in the context of human rights, operate with a subject that is defined against and, most importantly, considered superior to the non-human animal.[2] As I argue, this fundamental split and hierarchization in dominant humanist thought between

---

1 Sundberg, 34. Other issues of concerns to some posthumanist writers, such as technological and biological advances that question or threaten the integrity and limits of the human as well as the relations of beings with things, are hence not the focus here.
2 With respect to major challenges that the world faces today, such as threats to the environment and all forms of life on the planet, a dominant idea is that only human beings – thanks to their supposed intellectual superiority – can save the Earth. See Anderson, "Mind Over Matter", 13.

DOI: 10.4324/9781003427957-4

the 'human' and the 'animal'[3] that underlie the conception of subjectivity are responsible for a number of exclusions that manifest themselves even in the context of human rights. It is because of this conception that both non-human animals and, perhaps more surprisingly, many human beings are excluded or kept far away from humanity and precluded from enjoying protections, such as human rights guarantees. These exclusions are made possible by processes of dehumanization and animalization. The human rights project is arguably not simply ancillary to these processes but is entangled with the way in which non-human animals are conceived and treated. As Jacques Derrida argued, "the modern violence against animals . . . is at once contemporary with and indissociable from the discourse of human rights".[4] For instance, and as I will explain, so-called irregular migrants, who do not match the current definition of an ideal subject that stands above the realm of animals because of its alleged greater rationality, and who are subjected to processes of 'othering' through dehumanization and animalization, illustrate this particularly well.[5] For the field of international human rights, which claims to be universal in applicability, these exclusions are paradoxical and highly problematic. As I demonstrate in this chapter, posthumanism presents itself as a useful approach to understand these exclusions, notably because it helps to deconstruct humanist concepts and ideas as well as unveil the false assumption of a necessary and inherent difference between human and nonhuman beings, the resulting alleged superiority of the former, and the related essentialization of groups of beings. Moreover, posthumanist approaches actually allow thinking humanness with openness and fluidity, that is as a constantly shifting mode of being. This, as I will suggest, is captured by a further reformulation of the figure of the *migrant* introduced in the first chapter, namely the figure of the *migrating 'Other'*.

2.1   The flaws of the 'human' according to posthumanist critiques

Posthumanism, which became increasingly influential in Western critical discourses in the 1990s and early 2000s, relies on a number of critical ideas developed in the mid-20th century, often called postmodern or poststructuralist,

---

3 Similar to the 'human', the use of inverted commas around the 'animal' signals the use of a concept.

4 Derrida, *For What Tomorrow*, 74.

5 According to the International Organization for Migration, an irregular migrant is a "person who, owing to unauthorized entry, breach of a condition of entry, or the expiry of his or her visa, lacks legal status in a transit or host country. The definition covers, inter alia, those persons who have entered a transit or host country lawfully but have stayed for a longer period than authorized or subsequently taken up unauthorized employment". International Organization for Migration, *World Migration Report 2015*, 198.

to reveal the limits and contradictions in the dominant understanding of the 'human'.[6] The influence of Derrida, who began to conceive the relationship between the 'human' and the 'animal' in radically new ways, is particularly noteworthy.[7] While posthumanism is not a source of pure consensus, with different definitions existing of what the term refers to,[8] a common objective of all posthumanist theories is to question the anthropocentrism of humanism. These theories try to better understand the relations – and underlying interests and power dynamics – between such categories as human and nature.[9] They problematize the concept of the human and question the ways in which this concept is produced and everything that has been justified for its sake.[10] Posthumanism can hence be seen as disrupting the status quo by radically challenging anthropocentrism and speciesism.[11] As this section demonstrates, posthumanism contests the humanist assumption of humans being fundamentally different from nonhuman animals; condemns the ensuing dominant humanist tendency to think in terms of a hierarchy placing humans above all other beings, as well as the habit of conceiving the 'human' and the 'animal' in terms of binary oppositions that essentialize each group; and even concludes that the 'human', given the lack of genuine specificity, is an empty concept.

Critical posthumanist approaches are particularly useful for the analysis of the subject of human rights: at the same time as exposing inherent problems within humanism and the inadequacy of the human as a concept, they attempt to be aware of the ways in which the 'human' is used precisely by those who critique – and often call for the abandonment of – the concept itself.[12]

It should be noted, before going any further, that humanism refers to a variety of beliefs and methods in the Western world and has hence different meanings. When opposed to scholasticism, for instance, it connotes a certain curriculum and mode of inquiry; when contrasted to postmodern ideas, it has been associated with an essentialist view of the human and belief in its

---

6 Wolfe, *What Is Posthumanism?*, xii. Wolfe highlights the invention of systems theory and Michel Foucault's *The Archaeology of Knowledge* as key developments. Ibid.
7 For a more comprehensive list of philosophers, see Wolfe, *Animal Rites*, xii.
8 Wolfe, *What Is Posthumanism?*, xi. These theories discuss ideas that are irreducible and offer various definitions of the 'human', some of which contradict each other, Castree & Nash, "Editorial", 501. For three modalities of posthumanism, namely as a historical condition, as a set of ontological theses, and as a form of deconstructive reading, see Castree & Nash, "Introduction", 1342. By being highly critical of the concept of the human and everything that is justified in its name, I follow mostly the third modality.
9 Castree & Nash, "Editorial", 503.
10 Sheehan, 8.
11 Wolfe, *What Is Posthumanism?*, xviii–xix.
12 Castree & Nash, "Editorial", 501–2.

individual autonomy.[13] In this latter context, as Carol Quillen has noted, humanism invokes "a variety of assumptions about subjectivity, human agency, and human cultural production that have long grounded canonical constructions of the Western tradition".[14] However, in spite of these different meanings and interpretations, it can be said that there are some underlying and deeply embedded assumptions that are common to most humanist discourses. It is characteristic, above all, to give "special importance to human concerns, values, and dignity" and to emphasize the role of reason.[15] Indeed, a persisting idea among humanist discourses is that reason, especially the human capacity for rationality and scientific reasoning, allowed human beings to progressively move away from the natural realm (and therefore from their animality), thus emancipating themselves from the world they live in.[16] As I demonstrate by relying on posthumanist approaches, this problematic belief in the superiority of human beings, both in terms of intellect and morality, over nonhuman beings and entities has persisted up to today, including in the field of human rights.

The emergence of the 'human' as a problematic concept

The 'human' is a key concept that has long dominated Western philosophical traditions and that has greatly influenced the dominant conception of the world, which is particularly evident in the context of human rights. While human rights texts and discourses do not engage with the concept of the human in any explicit manner, the idea that humans are special – and superior – is arguably built into the very notion of human rights. As article 1 of the *Universal Declaration of Human Rights* stipulates: "All human beings are born free and equal in dignity and rights. They are endowed with reason and conscience".[17] By implication, it can be understood that other beings are not born in dignity, that they are not endowed with reason, and are hence inferior to human beings. Somewhat similarly, the preamble of the *African Charter on Human and Peoples' Rights* notes that "fundamental human rights stem from the attributes of human beings",[18] yet without further elaborating on these "attributes". Here, too, it is assumed that human beings have specific attributes that warrant human rights guarantees.

In the humanist tradition, which has its roots in ancient Greece and was further entrenched by early Christianity, it is the capacity of humans to think, to reason, in other words their intelligence and their capacity to develop and

---

13 Quillen, 1–2. According to Quillen, the term humanism is so loaded that it warrants speaking of a "vexed word". Ibid, 1.
14 Quillen, 2.
15 Law, 263.
16 Murdoch, 1356; Anderson, *Race*, 35–6.
17 *Universal Declaration of Human Rights*, article 1.
18 *African Charter on Human and Peoples' Rights*, preamble.

live according to moral principles,[19] that would not only set humans apart, but also elevate them above animals. In fact, these two traditions can be said to have been erected on the belief in the supposedly unique dignity and worth of human beings.[20] According to Kay Anderson, it is already evident in the writings of Aristotle and Descartes that humanist thought is grounded in a belief in the superiority of human beings over animal life and nature more generally.[21] Then, after centuries during which philosophical thinking was presumably not concerned with the human as an individual, it is as if this individual, its intellect and dignity were rediscovered by Renaissance humanist thinkers.[22] Francesco Petrarca, or Petrarch, who is sometimes considered one of the founding figures of humanism, emphasized in the 14th century that while "man" is an animal, he is a "rational animal" and even "the chief of all animals".[23] According to Petrarch, it is reason alone that "distinguishes [man] from the savagery of the brute, and that it is only by submission to her guidance that he deserves the name of man at all".[24] Towards the end of the 15th century, Giovanni Pico della Mirandola, a prominent Renaissance humanist, further explained why "man is the most fortunate of living things . . . a great miracle and a being worthy of all admiration", which would justify the view that the human stands at the top in the hierarchy of beings.[25] Pico della Mirandola argued that it is the decision of the "Supreme Maker" to set this human "in the middle of the world", as the chosen one that understands and admires god's creation of the world, that explains "the acuteness of [man's] senses, the inquiry of his reason and the light of his intelligence".[26] The human is, in this perspective, "the interpreter of nature", unimpeded by restrictions that apply to all other creatures.[27] This is why Pico della Mirandola conceived the human as the "free and proud shaper of [its] own being", capable of modelling itself according to its own wishes and desires.[28] The alleged superiority of the human that pervades contemporary human rights discourses hence builds on a long tradition in humanist thought.

Posthumanist critiques did not, of course, emerge in a vacuum either and could build on the questioning, from the Enlightenment onwards, of the

19 Sheehan, 7.
20 Anderson, *Race*, 35.
21 Anderson, *Race*, 37–8.
22 For a more nuanced account and critique of this popular understanding of Renaissance humanism, see Martin. While this kind of humanist thought emerged in Europe, it spread to other continents from the 16th century onwards and, as I discuss later, was a fundamental component of and justification for colonialism.
23 Petrarca.
24 Petrarca.
25 Pico della Mirandola, 4–5.
26 Pico della Mirandola, 3, 6–7.
27 Pico della Mirandola, 5, 7.
28 Pico della Mirandola, 7.

superiority of human beings.[29] Modern thinkers such as Karl Marx, Arthur Schopenhauer, Friedrich Nietzsche and T. E. Hulme have all, in one way or another, expressed doubts regarding humanism or certain concepts fundamental to it.[30] More recently, Foucault argued that the 'human' is an accidental invention of the early 19th century and cautioned that "man would be erased" if the arrangements of knowledge that created him in the first place were to disappear.[31] For Foucault, "Renaissance 'humanism' and Classical 'rationalism' were indeed able to allot human beings a privileged position in the order of the world, but they were not able to conceive of man".[32] These critiques suggested something very important, namely that human ways of thinking and being might not necessarily be a given nor admirable, and they facilitated the subsequent development, by posthumanist authors, of more sophisticated arguments to forcefully challenge the distinctiveness and supremacy of the 'human'.

Deconstructing the alleged difference between humans and animals

Posthumanists, as Neil Badmington has noted, criticize humanists above all for their allegedly exaggerated belief in a human nature that sets human beings apart from other animals and for their conviction that human beings also stand at the centre of everything.[33] They contest the idea that the 'human' is a meaningful concept to conceive the world and all relations with other beings and entities and the presumed unique capacity of humans to distinguish between right and wrong. As Simon Glendinning has framed this line of critique,

[m]an is the animal that possesses, in addition to organic traits, say, reason, or spirit, or soul, or mind, or self-consciousness, or language, or is

---

29 It should be noted that modernity and Enlightenment are contested concepts. Comaroff & Comaroff, 2. Moreover, not everything about European modernity and ontology is necessarily negative. The individuality of the subject, for instance, certainly allowed liberating the 'subjected' European subject from very confining social structures. Quijano, 173. Ndlovu-Gatsheni argues that there are bright and dark sides to modernity: "One is seductive and beautiful. The other is fierce, ugly and violent". White people tend to experience the brighter aspects, that is individual liberties, rationality and democracy, while Black people suffered or still suffer from the darker sides, which include the slave trade, material dispossession, and ongoing discrimination. Ndlovu-Gatsheni, 25, 225. Finally, it should be noted that the Enlightenment refers to a period that encompasses several diverse ideas and intellectual movements across Europe, some of which were in contradiction with one another. For more on the diversity and complexity of so-called Enlightenment, see Outram, chapter 1.
30 Sheehan, 2.
31 Foucault, 421–2.
32 Foucault, 347. See also Derrida, "The Ends of Man".
33 Badmington, 1345.

made in God's image or whatever – in any case, traits which are, according to the humanist, a non-natural and uniquely human possession.[34]

A major point of concern for posthumanist writers is hence of definitional nature. Bruce Braun, for instance, maintains that humanism relies on a fundamental anthropological assumption, namely that the human being is radically different from the animal,[35] and on norms and ideals based on this alleged difference. According to this critique, humanism, in the words of Glendinning, "offers an illegitimate delimitation that cannot be other than idealized and distorted – and in both directions, both for 'man' and for 'the animal'".[36] This alleged difference is so central to Western political and philosophical thought that the latter would have no foundation without it.[37] The clear break from the world of animals is seen as necessary for the existence and self-reproduction of the 'human', as Agamben claims:

> It is possible to oppose man to other living things . . . only because something like an animal life has been separated within man, only because his distance and proximity to the animal have been measured and recognized first of all in the closest and most intimate place.[38]

Adopting a posthumanist lens brings to light the fact that humans appear to be in desperate need of this difference and to anxiously hold on to what seems to set them apart from animals. According to Derrida, humanity, through humanism, "is above all careful to guard, and jealous of, what is proper to it"[39] or, as one might add, of what humanity *thinks* is proper to it. Anthropocentrism thus entails more than solely putting the human being on a pedestal; human specificity is defined precisely against whatever beings or entities that are perceived as a threat to humanism and to the very idea of the 'human'.[40]

Unravelling the alleged superiority of human beings

The alleged superiority of human beings within humanism, and implicitly taken up in human rights, remains deeply entrenched in the main contemporary philosophical discourses.[41] It is, in Derrida's terms, seen as "infinite and

---

34 Glendinning, 21. See also Wolfe, *What Is Posthumanism?*, xi.
35 Braun, 1352; Calarco, 6.
36 Glendinning, 22.
37 Braun, 1352.
38 Agamben, *The Open*, 15–16.
39 Derrida, "The Animal That Therefore I Am", 383.
40 Calarco, 53 (referring to Heidegger).
41 For two grand forms of theoretical treatise in regard to the 'animal', see Derrida, "The Animal That Therefore I Am", 382–3. Derrida argues that most philosophers "have taken

par excellence" as well as "*unconditional* and *sacrificial*".[42] The assumption of human exceptionalism sanctions and even requires violence committed by human beings against other beings, as if the capacity to reason would justify human domination. This is even more surprising given that the allegedly defining features of the human have changed over time and actually undergone an interesting evolution. For instance, it was thought, in the 18th century, that the immaterialized soul (or mind) was the supreme, distinctive human characteristic.[43] This was based on Descartes' idea of the mind and body dualism; it also fitted the theological perspective of the time.[44] But already at the beginning of the 19th century, new scientific discoveries, such as in the field of anatomy, challenged the idea of an immaterial soul.[45] With the development of science, the boundaries of the 'human' became more stable and defined.[46] More specifically, anatomical features, most notably the upright position of the human body and the vertical position of the head, were put forward as the main criteria that allowed the development of greater intelligence.[47] This allegedly more advanced physiognomy, together with the belief of the time in the superiority of Europeans, was used as a justification for European colonization of both other human beings and nonhuman beings.[48] As the posthumanist reading of humanist thought can be summed up in this regard, hierarchy among beings and, more specifically, among human beings had a biological basis. The more upright a being, the larger the brain in proportion to sensory organs such as nose and mouth. Since most animals do not stand upright, and since many non-European human beings tend to have more prominent jaws and noses, they were all considered inferior and could hence be colonized. Anderson contends that "it is the very 'knowledge' embedded in colonial stereotypes of non-Europeans that comes to found the far-reaching modern contention that (a uniquely) human mentality is the product of (a uniquely) human anatomy".[49] The idea that some human beings are more human than others on the basis of their assumed distance from nature or their capacity to transcend nature, notably by privileging the presumably higher senses – especially vision – and by suppressing the senses considered lower,[50] persists in Western cultures and

---

no account of the fact that what they call animal could *look at* them and *address* them".
Ibid, 382.
42 Derrida, "The Animal That Therefore I Am", 389–90. Derrida draws here, among others, on biblical and other ancient traditions of sacrificing animals.
43 Anderson, "Mind Over Matter?", 3.
44 Anderson, "Mind Over Matter?", 5.
45 Anderson, "Mind Over Matter?", 7.
46 Agamben, *The Open*, 24.
47 Anderson, "Mind Over Matter?", 6–8.
48 On the animalization of the colonized, see Hudson, 1664–5.
49 Anderson, "Mind Over Matter?", 10.
50 This will be explored in more detail in Chapter 5.

continues to influence the concept of the 'human' and the implementation of human rights, as I explore below.

Resisting binary oppositions and resulting essentializations

Drawing on posthumanist critics also helps to reveal that the creation of binaries and associated processes of essentialization within humanism are unhelpful, especially because they create a much-needed 'Other' against which the 'human' can be defined. Indeed, most humanist discourses rely on an array of binary oppositions, some of which are obvious while others are more implicit: human/inhuman, culture/nature, self/other and subject/object.[51] A related binary in dominant humanist thought sets human reason apart from the instinct associated with animality. Implied in such a way of thinking – as criticized by posthumanism – is the idea that humans are seen as the sum of a specific set of criteria *vis-à-vis* another set of criteria constituting animals. As with all binaries, the opposing terms in the relation are envisaged as fundamentally different from one another, and each term is rendered equally fundamentally homogenous (which does not preclude processes of dehumanization and animalization, as will be discussed). Each term is fixed and conveys an impression of stability, as if evolution could be swept out of the equation and the subjects enclosed by the binary terms never changed. However, taking a historical perspective, one can understand that the 'human' is not a static entity. Humanness is not a fixed pole that is part of a dichotomy, but should rather be understood, in the words of Anderson, as a "shifting mode of being".[52] The flattening of differences – it is common to speak of *the* human and *the* animal, for instance – also hides the fact that there is great variety within these categories and especially, though often ignored, among nonhuman animals. Derrida argued that the essentialization of animals is widespread, even in the Western philosophical tradition[53] (which is, of course, itself deeply anthropocentric[54]), whereas there is a profound heterogeneity in the animal realm.[55] He has challenged most famously the homogeneity presumed in 'the animal' which is used to create an 'Other', and

---

51 Badmington, 1345.

52 Anderson, *Race*, 2.

53 Derrida writes that "philosophers have always judged and *all* philosophers have judged [the limit between man and the animal] to be single and invisible, considering that on the other side of that limit there is an immense group, a single and fundamentally homogenous set . . . the set of the Animal in general, the animal spoken of in the general singular". Derrida, "The Animal That Therefore I Am", 408–9. See also Calarco, 63.

54 Calarco, 8.

55 Derrida, "The Animal That Therefore I Am", 399. Interestingly, in spite of this diversity, and as Glendinning points out, humans cannot simply be included in the group of animals. Glendinning, 23.

then deployed to define the 'human' and create exclusions. He has argued that speaking of 'the animal' in the singular form to designate very different organisms such as a bee, a giraffe, a fish, a microbe and so on, is not only a conceptual simplification, but most importantly a very violent act against animals; and that it is this act of violence that permits the existence of slaughterhouses and the use of animals in the industrial domain.[56] To denounce the common trend of lumping all animal species together to create a homogenous 'Other',[57] Derrida created a neologism, namely *l'animot*, which is the result of blending the French terms for animal (*animal*) and word (*mot*), hence emphasizing the role of language: "*Ecce animot*. Neither a species nor a gender nor an individual, it is an irreducible living multiplicity of mortals, . . . a sort of monstrous hybrid".[58] With *animot*, Derrida stressed that we must start to think of living creatures in the plural form. Moreover, symbolically bringing the *mot*, in other words language, back to animals, does not mean simply "giving speech back to animals"; rather, Derrida insisted that – even if most humans have thought of animals as being deprived of language – the absence of the word be considered as something other or something more than mere privation.[59] Although scientific studies have shown that at least some animals have a language,[60] which can be quite sophisticated, language has often been taken to be reserved for human animals, either as a particular supplement to distinguish them from other animals, or as a marker to define them. In a way, this idea even transpires in prominent human rights instruments. The *Universal Declaration of Human Rights* takes up this idea from the outset, in the second paragraph of its preamble, by proclaiming to aspire to "a world in which human beings shall enjoy freedom of speech".[61]

This critique hence reveals the false homogeneity, plenitude and coherence that result from the creation of binaries and tendencies to essentialize, which means that alterity within categories tends to be ignored, and humans as well as animals are often reduced to figures; as such, both the 'human' and

56 "Jacques Derrida and the Question of 'the Animal'". See also Derrida, "The Animal That Therefore I Am", 416.
57 For more on this, see Braun, 1353.
58 Derrida, "The Animal That Therefore I Am", 409.
59 Derrida, "The Animal That Therefore I Am", 415–16. Calarco has argued that, according to the Western philosophical tradition, it is by acquiring language that humans can break away from their animal instinct. Calarco, 83. The author relies on Agamben to point out that humans are born without language and that they have "to receive it from outside themselves". Calarco, 85. For a more detailed discussion on language as a 'human marker', see Agamben, *The Open*, 34–7. See also Wolfe, *Animal Rites*, chapter 2.
60 For a study that described the language of prairie dogs already in 1991, see C. N. Slobodchikoff et al, "Semantic Information". For a more recent study, see Slobodchikoff et al, "Prairie Dog Alarm".
61 *Universal Declaration of Human Rights*, preamble. Moreover, article 19 of the *Declaration* contains the right to freedom of opinion and expression.

the 'animal' carry the responsibility of representing all human beings and all animals.[62] In fact, it can be argued that it is through the *figure* of the animal that humanism has created the *figure* of the human.[63] In other words, an undifferentiated 'Other' was produced through a simplified and limited understanding of the animal, against which the human being can be compared, measured, and defined. The human being, in turn, becomes the norm, in the face of which everything else becomes inhuman.[64]

The 'human': an empty concept

Against the common humanist belief in the superiority and specificity of the human being, it can be maintained that there is, in reality, no specific characteristic or distinctive mark to define human beings and to separate them from animals. Having the capacity to reason, to speak and to make tools have, among others, been put forward, but each of them fails to establish the difference.[65] Either some nonhuman animals show the supposedly unique human characteristic, or some humans fail the test. For instance, certain animals, like apes and crows, also make and use tools, whereas some humans, such as infants or persons having certain disabilities, are still considered human without being able to perform these tasks.[66] Although the ability to suffer has been considered a more appropriate criterion to separate beings, as already suggested by Jeremy Bentham,[67] scientists have shown that human beings are not the only animals that demonstrate complex emotions and feeling: a form of grief, for instance, is clearly felt by different species, such as whales.[68] Derrida also claimed that listing unique human properties will always involve a configuration, which means that there is no single characteristic that can be isolated to define human beings. Rather, a "nonfinite number of other concepts, beginning with the concept of a concept" can be added to the list.[69]

If there is no specific human marker, and since the 'human' is defined by means of exclusion, negation or opposition to the 'animal',[70] it can be concluded, based on posthumanist critiques, that the concept of the human remains abstract, and human uniqueness a fantasy. Some posthumanist authors even suggest that the centre of the 'human' is always empty or, as Badmington

---

62 Badmington, 1348.
63 See the discussion in Braun, who draws on Badmington, Derrida and Agamben. Braun, 1352.
64 Braun, 1352.
65 See for instance Wolfe, *Animal Rights*, 40; Braun, 1353 (explaining Derrida's point).
66 Singer, 5.
67 Bentham, 310, n 1.
68 For a discussion of a grieving female orca who carried her dead baby for 17 days and other examples, see King.
69 Derrida, "The Animal That Therefore I Am", 373–4.
70 Anderson, *Race*, 11.

says, that it is "devastatingly absent".[71] Agamben also explains the 'human' in terms of indeterminacy and emptiness through what he calls the "anthropological machine".[72] For him, humanity "is neither a clearly defined species nor a substance; it is, rather, a machine or device for producing the recognition of the human".[73] This machine refers to the humanist mechanisms that allow differentiating humans from animals. Agamben distinguishes between two ways the anthropological machine works, both of which involve inclusion and exclusion. The modern process consists in an isolation of the nonhuman within the human, or an animalization of the human; the objective, here, is to identify and exclude animality from human life. The other, premodern process works through an inclusion within humanity of the excluded animal; through this variation of the machine, the animal is humanized. During the transatlantic slave trade, for example, slaves were considered to be animals in human form. Both processes put forward by the anthropological machine take the 'human' for granted, and, as a result, produce an empty space.[74] To fill this void, humanism must rely on conceptions that stem from religion, science, or politics; in turn, the very same conceptions are justified and given meaning by humanism.[75] As posthumanist writers point out, humanism can hence be seen as its own dogma that is constructed and sustained through a number of anthropological prejudices,[76] which can explain the construction of an idealized subject in human rights and the resulting inaccessibility of these rights for many individuals and groups.

2.2   The paradoxical exclusion of humans from human rights

Because humanism and its problematic anthropological assumptions are at the core of the concept of human rights, both international and national human rights systems are consequently prone to the same criticisms. Indeed, the desire to distinguish humans from animals is deeply entrenched here, too. It can even be said, as W.J.T. Mitchell does, that the rights human beings recognize for themselves in the documents that established and consolidated the dominant liberal rights paradigm, such as the 1789 *Déclaration des droits de l'homme et du citoyen* and the 1948 *Universal Declaration of Human Rights*, are grounded in the supposed superiority of the human and the absence of rights of animals.[77] Moreover, as a posthumanist lens also helps understand,

---

71 Badmington, 1348.
72 The discussion here relies heavily on Agamben, *The Open*, 37 and Calarco, 92–4.
73 Agamben, *The Open*, 26.
74 Agamben, *The Open*, 37.
75 Foucault in Rabinow, 44.
76 Wolfe, *What Is Posthumanism?*, xiv.
77 W.J.T. Mitchell, ix, xiii.

and as I will now discuss, it has always been possible to deny certain human beings access to human rights through processes of dehumanization, and notably through animalization. Certain individuals and groups of humans have been animalized precisely because of the assumed superiority of humans over animals and the attribution of this alleged inferiority of certain animals, and characteristics like brutality, to these individuals and groups.[78] This assumed superiority is left implicit, perhaps precisely because it is taken for granted; yet it has important consequences that need to be exposed.

While the human being is the only genuine subject of humanism, and therefore also of human rights, the various constructions of the human as a concept have discriminated against both nonhuman beings and some, or rather many, human beings. As Matthew Calarco claims, it is

> always one version or another of *the human* that falsely occupies the space of the universal and that functions to exclude what is considered nonhuman (which, of course, includes the immense majority of human beings themselves, along with all else deemed to be nonhuman) from ethical and political consideration.[79]

As noted by Noel Castree and Catherine Nash, there is a long history in dominant humanist thought of using differences to recognize the humanness of certain humans and to deny it in the case of others, who are considered less worthy.[80] Those who are to be afforded rights by the human rights system need to correspond to an "abstract and idealised human subject"[81] on which this system relies and which is typically associated with a white, male citizen. At the same time, given the large proportion of humans who are animalized, in other words considered and treated like animal 'Others', through the anthropological machine, it has been argued that locating the 'human' is becoming increasingly difficult.[82]

Migrants, once again, exemplify the ways in which humans can be excluded from humanity and denied the protection of presumably inalienable rights. Implicitly or explicitly, migrants all over the world experience processes of dehumanization and animalization. With an estimated 272 million international migrants worldwide,[83] many states are considering new practices to

---

78 Roberts, x.
79 Calarco, 10. See also Glendinning, 21.
80 Castree & Nash, "Editorial", 501. As Dayan has pointed out, while key writers like John Locke actually questioned the idea of a fixed boundary of the human species, even Locke's arguments were subsequently misused to "embrace the natural human hierarchy that he so fundamentally questioned". Dayan, 124.
81 Vaughan-Williams, 2.
82 Hudson, 1664.
83 These are the estimations of the United Nations in 2019. See United Nations, "Global Issues: Migration".

face what is often seen as a major challenge, or even 'threat' to their national security. For instance, European states increasingly rely on detention centres situated in Libya and Morocco as well as in Greece, Italy and other southern European states to deal with migrants and their refugee claims. Many migrants that are or have been held in detention centres report that their encounter with border security forces have been marked by violent practices that question their humanness.[84] To describe this encounter, migrants use language and metaphors that compare their treatment to the one of animals and to processes of animalization, for instance: "even if they [the authorities] treated us according to the EU law for the correct treatment of animals, it would be better than what they do now!", or "we had to eat on the floor like animals".[85] The terrible conditions of detention have hence been described and denounced as places of dehumanization.[86]

The discourse of being treated like animals – or, given that the treatment of animals is regulated in many countries, not even being treated like animals according to such rules – is more than just a metaphor used as a linguistic tool by migrants or human rights organizations; it is a response to processes of dehumanization and animalization used by political authorities to discriminate and exclude. Indeed, these processes can be understood as a strategy to control borders, as in the case of the southern borders of the European Union and the United States. Nick Vaughan-Williams, relying on Derrida's argument that it is precisely at the border between humans and animals that the sovereign power works, claims that

> the material conditions of certain detention spaces and their animalising effects can be read as a symptom of the zoopower that seeks to (re)produce sovereign lines of distinction between the "proper" life of the "regular" citizen-subject whose humanity is assured and the "improper" life of the "irregular" migrant whose belonging to humanity is habitually called into question: the former is made possible by and given meaning in contradistinction to the latter.[87]

Put even more provocatively, the discourse of animality serves to discriminate between what is legal and what is illegal, to mark what/who is included and what/who is excluded from humanity. The conditions of detention in overcrowded, zoo-like spaces, where humans are locked up and often treated like animals in industrial farms, without access to essential resources and

---

84 Vaughan-Williams, 5. As Wolfe notes, "all manner of brutalizations carried out by cultural prescription can serve to animalize humans". Wolfe, *Animal Rites*, 101.
85 Pro Asyl, *Walls of Shame*, 59, 43.
86 Vaughan-Williams, 2, 4.
87 Vaughan-Williams, 8.

services, such as food, water, sanitation and medical care,[88] show that the question does not revolve around an acceptable or practical implementation of human rights; rather, the main question is which forms of life are worthy or, in Arendtian terms, who has the right to have rights. All relevant frameworks – whether they stem from theology, philosophy, politics, ethics or jurisprudence – are contingent on, or, as Agamben says, "suspended in the difference between man and animal".[89]

Building on a posthumanist critique that is alert to such forms of exclusion, it can hence be argued that the protection of migrants' rights – and the larger political-ethical project based on human rights – will remain ineffective as long as the impact of the common rejection of animality and related processes of animalization are not recognized. It is, in particular, the construction of the human against an animal 'Other' that has facilitated violence against both nonhuman animals and many humans on the basis of their alleged animality. Since some, or rather many, human beings are inherently discriminated against because of the engrained biases of humanism, W.J.T. Mitchell has argued persuasively that "the claim to humanity and human rights will never succeed until it has reckoned with the irreducible plurality and otherness of nonhuman or posthuman life forms, including those that (like ourselves) wear a human face".[90] The justification that some humans enjoy a privileged place among other humans and other beings is indeed untenable,[91] even more so if such a privilege implies the exclusion of these 'Others'.

2.3 Decentring the subject: posthumanist calls for radical openness

So far, I have focused on posthumanist critiques highlighting that dominant humanist thought has always needed an 'Other', more precisely an animalized 'Other', to define its subject and has always remained indebted to what has been persistently ignored or rejected. As Calarco has noted, "the notion of the subject . . . is founded on the forgetting of an alterity that both founds and continually disrupts subjects".[92] This anthropocentric speciesism sacrifices what is considered animalistic and allows discourses that enable various

---

88 As noted, for instance, by Human Rights Watch with respect to the Moria camp on Lesbos, Greece, in 2019. Human Rights Watch, "Greece: Camp Conditions Endanger Women, Girls".

89 Agamben, *The Open*, 22. Derrida similarly argues that "the question of the living and of the living animal . . . will always have been the most important and decisive question". Derrida, "The Animal That Therefore I Am", 402.

90 W.J.T. Mitchell, xii.

91 Anderson, "Mind Over Matter", 4.

92 Calarco, 11. See also Glendinning, 26.

forms of domination, even within the same species and based on such factors as class, gender or ethnicity.[93] Posthumanist writers, such as Sarah Whatmore, hence suggest that the thinking human subject must be dislodged and subjectivity recognized not along neatly defined boundaries but in a less exclusive manner, and in other beings.[94] This is, I believe, an important point that is of particular relevance to the analysis of the subject of human rights.

A central aspect of subjectivity that has been taken for granted in modern Western thought concerns human modes of experiencing the world. This is especially problematic since the Enlightenment's attempt to desubstantialize and purify the subject from any links to nature, animality and body as well as context.[95] A major dogma associated with dominant humanist thought, as emphasized by Cary Wolfe, is that to be human, everything related not only to animal origins, but also to the biological and to materiality had to be suppressed.[96] This alleged cognitive privilege must be dismissed: as I explore in more detail in the next chapters, perception does not only occur through the eyes and thinking not only in the mind but through the body more broadly: senses, feelings and emotions all matter.

Against the backdrop of the ubiquitous anthropocentrism and vision-centredness in dominant Western modern thought, with vision having become inseparable from knowledge and contrasted with the presumably lower senses of touch, smell and taste, it can be argued that the 'human' and its supposedly supreme rational consciousness as well as its taken-for-granted modes of perception ought to be decentred. Moreover, the fuller sensorium of other beings and, more generally, their ways of conceiving the world and bodily practices should be turned to.[97] This sensorium could arguably be retrieved since, in an evolutionary sense, it is inborn and part of humans (who are, after all, animals themselves from a biological point of view).[98] This also means that the 'human' should not be used, implicitly or explicitly, as the defining reference point for other kinds of being and ways of experiencing the world.[99]

Influenced by posthumanist approaches that offer useful critical perspectives to analyse and deconstruct the 'human', it is possible to reconceive relationships between beings and with things with an openness that humanism has never had. It is an openness not only towards others – whatever or

---

93 Wolfe, *Animal Rites*, 7–8.
94 Whatmore, *Hybrid Geographies*, 36; Murdoch, 1356–7.
95 Wolfe, *Animal Rites*, 109.
96 Wolfe, *What Is Posthumanism?*, xv.
97 Anderson, "Mind Over Matter?", 4.
98 Wolfe, *Animal Rites*, 3.
99 Wolfe, *Animal Rites*, 4; Wolfe, *What Is Posthumanism?*, xxv; Anderson, "Mind Over Matter", 14.

whoever these others may be – but also to the uncertain and unfixed.[100] I also believe that what is needed is not another attempt to include what never fits in or is traditionally excluded, from animals to migrants, but a realization that the currently dominant concepts and modes of thinking simply do not allow such 'fitting in'.[101] As Glendinning has argued, we need "an openness to what cannot be appropriated, access to what cannot be assimilated".[102] This would, I think, allow recognizing each living being for its own wonder and uniqueness, that is precisely because of its difference, not for what it is worth in the human *Weltanschauung*. Such an approach therefore goes beyond the idea that the 'human' or subjectivity can simply be extended.[103] This is quite different from animal rights philosophy, for instance, which seeks to establish that animals are in many ways the same as human beings. Since it is profoundly anthropocentric, as Calarco, among others, has argued, this reasoning – and associated rights claims – could only ever apply to a few animals, namely those that resemble human beings.[104] Wolfe therefore suggests that animal rights philosophy risks reinforcing the same humanism that created a hierarchy between humans and animals in the first place.[105] In other words, it should not be assumed that human concepts can apply to other beings. This means that in the context of international human rights, the inherent limitations of the dominant concept of subjectivity and of human rights cannot be resolved by extending the application of certain rights to animals and other entities. Rather, humans themselves might have to change, transcend the logic of superiority, and accept ongoing transformations that they cannot control. This includes a different relation to animals and to humans' own animality.[106] In that sense, a fundamental change in the nature of thought, which implies resisting hegemonic discourses and rethinking the relationships between beings and with things in nonanthropocentric terms, would be required. As Agamben explains,

> [w]hen the difference [between the 'human' and the 'animal'] vanishes and the two terms collapse upon each other . . . the difference between being and the nothing, licit and illicit, divine and demonic also fades away, and in its place something appears for which we seem to lack even a name.[107]

Indeed, it is quite possible that contemporary dominant discourses are not yet adequate to grasp and describe the richness of human beings that are often

100 Calarco, 4; Glendinning, 22.
101 Glendinning, 23.
102 Glendinning, 24.
103 Wolfe, *What Is Posthumanism?*, xvi.
104 Calarco, 8. See also Glendinning, 22.
105 Wolfe, *Animal Rites*, 192.
106 Hudson, 1675.
107 Agamben, *The Open*, 22.

excluded, such as refugees and migrants, as well as the variety of non-human animals and their perspectives. This helps understand why the current human rights system and its discourses are of very little usefulness to many migrants who, under this system, are often excluded and dehumanized, not only as non-citizens but also on the basis of their alleged proximity to animals, which, as explained above, serves as an implicit justification for their detention in zoo-like spaces.[108] Rather than forcing beings to use already existing modes of being, perception and expression that contribute to their exclusion, we must be open to new ones, as Calarco has argued: we "need new languages, new artworks, new histories, even new sciences and philosophies".[109]

Considering the anthropocentrism of the 'human' as well as posthumanism's call for greater openness in the context of subjectivity, one might argue that being concerned with the exclusion and the dehumanization of some human beings is itself an anthropocentric endeavour, which would be flawed according to some posthumanists. However, it is worth emphasizing that posthumanism is not necessarily anti-human,[110] and the 'post' of posthumanism does not automatically lead to the end of the 'human'.[111] Wolfe has argued that "the point is not to reject humanism tout court – indeed, there are many values and aspirations to admire in humanism – but rather to show how those aspirations are undercut by the philosophical and ethical frameworks used to conceptualize them".[112] Instead of simply dismissing the 'human', this kind of humanized posthumanism, as suggested by writers like Jonathan Murdoch and Cary Wolfe, helpfully seeks to make sense of the world's complex "entangled ecologies"[113] by deconstructing dominant concepts relating to humans, animals, justice, rights and nature and, in particular, by shedding light on the fiction of a rational and autonomous human subject that has little connection to nature and its body.[114]

While posthumanist approaches can hence be useful to deconstruct fundamental concepts like the 'human' and also to imagine new modes of being, it should also be said that they have important biases because of their

108 Similar arguments have been made with respect to the "inhumane" treatment of prisoners. See Dayan, 184.
109 Calarco, 6. Although the author makes this claim in the specific context of the animal, it can be applied more broadly.
110 Wolfe, *What Is Posthumanism?*, xv.
111 Badmington, 1349. Since the 'human' never was and should rather be considered a work in progress, the term posthumanism is somewhat confusing and perhaps even contradictory. This is why Whatmore proposes the term 'more-than-human' instead of posthuman, since "it is what exceeds rather than what comes after the human . . . that is the more promising and pressing project". Whatmore, 1361.
112 Wolfe, *What Is Posthumanism?*, xvi. It should also be highlighted that humanism is not an entirely uncritical approach. For more on the humanist contributions to be saved, see Wolfe, *Animal Rites*, chapter 1.
113 Murdoch, 1359.
114 Murdoch, 1359; Wolfe, *What Is Posthumanism?*, xv.

philosophical foundations that should not be ignored in a discussion on the subject of human rights. Posthumanism actually has a tendency to essentialize and to make universalizing claims, which is problematic.[115] Moreover, as Castree and Nash note, it is important to be aware of the tendency of some posthumanist authors to presuppose the 'human' as a stable category.[116] Anderson usefully demonstrates that unlike what some posthumanist writers suggest, humanism has never been entirely fixed and has consisted of different and evolving strands.[117] With respect to critiquing the subject of human rights, the insights that posthumanist approaches have their own limits and that humanism has not always relied on a clear separation between mind and body mean that it might be possible to reconceptualize the fundamentally humanist notion of the 'human' within humanism itself (although this reconceptualization could still be informed by posthumanist critiques). However, as it should be noted, posthumanism has a tendency not only to essentialize and to generalize but also – and this emerges as an important shortcoming, including for the discussion of the subject of human rights – to ignore and even

115 Many posthumanist texts explicitly reject common binaries, but they are themselves founded on the dualist notion of humanism/posthumanism: quite obviously, 'the posthuman' only makes sense when considered in relation to the 'human', and humanism and posthumanism are necessarily and inherently entangled W.J.T. Mitchell, xiv. On the contingency of humanness and the ways in which 'the inhuman' partly constitutes the 'human', see the discussion in Sheehan, 8–10; see also Anderson, "Mind Over Matter", 4. As Murdoch points out, posthumanist critics "have paid too little attention to critical and emancipatory practices that occur *inside* humanism". Murdoch, 1357. In this sense, it is important to recognize the inevitability of the 'human' and to be aware of essentializing tendencies, as critical posthumanist approaches are.
116 Castree & Nash, "Editorial", 501–2.
117 For example, not all humanist approaches actually adhered to the split between mind and body and resorted to immateriality to justify the alleged human exceptionalism. And while some critical scholars relying on posthumanism seek to decentre the human subject by recuperating its materiality, thus challenging one of the West's central dualisms, which also underpins the concept of human rights and its subject, and favouring coexistence of different beings and things, it is, as Anderson notes, precisely by appealing to the materiality of the body that 19th-century humanism was able to perpetuate the idea of human exceptionalism and superior intelligence: the claimed superiority of human beings was no longer grounded in the metaphysics of the mind or the immateriality of the soul, but was directly related to the human body. Consequently, Anderson puts forward the interesting argument that the posthumanist understanding of humanism built on immaterialism risks tracing human exceptionalism "to the uncritical premise that humans are ontologically distinct". Anderson, "Mind over Matter?", 4–5, 10. This very materiality of humanism needs to be understood in order to reveal and undo the idea of human exceptionalism, which is why I believe it is important to continue to engage with and tackle humanism, instead of simply dismissing it, including in the context of a critique of the subject of human rights. Similarly, Zakiyyah Iman Jackson, writing from a Black studies perspective that focuses on the dimension of race and the Black body – which will be explored in more detail in the next section – claims that 'post' movements continue to be fundamentally humanist in their philosophy and approach. Z. I. Jackson, "Animal", 682.

to silence important issues and beings because of its Eurocentrism. Indeed, posthumanist theories rely heavily on Western ideas, and in particular on postmodern and poststructuralist thought. Moreover, in posthumanist schol-arship, as it is often the case in Western scholarship more generally, the loca-tion of enunciation is rarely mentioned: there is really no established practice of situating oneself in regard to space and in terms of one's background. As Juanita Sundberg argues, ignoring the fact that posthumanism has emerged from a particular context – and that this context is Euro-American – implies that Western theory is presumed and implicitly presented as universal, and as the only relevant body of knowledge and epistemology.[118] Presuming the universality of Western, Eurocentric theory means that certain concepts, like agency and rights, are unduly privileged, as are certain "human-nonhuman assemblages".[119]

Although it is problematic that some of the concepts and beliefs that post-humanism presumes to be universal are clearly products of Western moder-nity, I believe that many posthumanist insights nevertheless remain useful, including to deconstruct the ideal(ized) subject of human rights. They help understand, in particular, that the 'human' of human rights has been con-structed in opposition to an animalized 'Other' and is hence the source of significant exclusions.

2.4   Further reconsidering subjectivity through the *migrating 'Other'*

Understood through the posthumanist approaches that I have discussed, hu-manness itself can be thought of with openness and fluidity, as a mode of being that is constantly shifting and without an essence, which, as I submit, is captured by a further reformulation of the figure of the *migrant* introduced in the first chapter, namely the figure of the *migrating 'Other'*.

The *migrating 'Other'* allows imagining subjectivity as open-ended, without closure, and the subject as "on the move . . . as constantly home and away, as migrant or wanderer, as nomad".[120] The grammatical form *migrat-ing* expresses the oftentimes changing condition or fluidity and inse-curity experienced by migrants and many, if not all, other beings. In contrast to terms like the 'migrant', the 'stateless' or even the 'human', which convey the idea of a static condition, *migrating* reflects the fact that migration – and being more generally – is a process, oftentimes without clear starting and end

---

118 Sundberg, 36.
119 Sundberg, 34 (citing Watson & Huntington). The divide between nature and culture, for instance, is so fundamental to Eurocentric thought and posthumanist critique that it is referred to as if it was universal; this, in the end, contributes to perpetuating the very same idea of universality. Sundberg, 35.
120 Glendinning, 25.

points. Indeed, some individuals may be migrating for years or even the rest of their lives. It also points to the importance of recognizing the plurality and fluidity of ontologies, and the opportunities created by such an emphasis on process, which I discuss in more detail in the next chapter.

The *migrating 'Other'* also captures additional elements of contemporary forms of rightlessness and exclusion, notably thanks to the addition of the term 'other'. Indeed, there are many 'others' who are excluded, whether human or non-human; the human being is one among – and certainly not above – a multitude of beings. It is also important to understand that challenges, including environmental and social ones, are never just the problems of human beings.[121] Human beings alone cannot find solutions to all current and future challenges, and there are no simple stories that could be told only by human perspectives.[122] This means that any project that operates with an exclusively anthropocentric perspective and that conceives human beings as the only possible subjects, such as in the current human rights system, is not justifiable. It will remain inherently limited and ineffective unless it fully considers and embraces other modes of being and perceiving the world, including by a boundless subject, as expressed by the figure of the *migrating 'Other'*.

While the use of the term 'other' may appear paradoxical if the objective of the figure is to pursue a more inclusive analysis and transcend boundaries and borders, I believe that the processes through which migrants and many other beings are alienated and excluded must be denounced strongly and should be echoed in the name of the figure. The *migrating 'Other'* is, in this sense, not an 'Other' or a threat against which one should define oneself in sustaining the idea of a nation or of an essentialized humanity;[123] the perceived strong dichotomy between presumably heterogeneous group, like nationals or humans, and 'Others' is, in any event, a fiction, as the categories are actually less stable than they are often thought of.[124] Rather, as a limit-concept exposing the system's biases,[125] the figure of the *migrating 'Other'* is meant to reflect the current reality that must be changed. This is why the *migrating 'Other'*, even if migration itself will continue to exist, should only be of temporary relevance as a concept.

Finally, it is worth noting that this figure, as the approaches that I have discussed so far, are compatible with other approaches. They can even be enriched by other critical theories and the idea of a plurality of ontologies, as I discuss in the next chapter.

---

121 Hudson, 1675.
122 Badmington, 1349. As Badmington also argues, "histories and geographies are made by more than human subjects". Ibid, 1345.
123 Haddad, 54.
124 Benhabib, *The Rights of Others*, 210.
125 Krause, 337; Lechte & Newman, 532.

Bibliography

African Charter on Human and Peoples' Rights (adopted on 27 June 1981, entered into force 21 October 1986) 1520 UNTS 217.

Agamben, Giorgio. *The Open: Man and Animal* (Stanford: Stanford University Press, 2004).

Anderson, Kay. *Race and the Crisis of Humanism* (London: Routledge, 2007).

———. "Mind over Matter? On Decentring the Human in Human Geography" (2014) 21:1 *Cultural Geographies* 3.

Badmington, Neil. "Mapping Posthumanism" (2006) 7:4 *Social & Cultural Geography* 1344.

Benhabib, Seyla. *The Rights of Others: Aliens, Residents, and Citizens* (Cambridge: Cambridge University Press, 2004).

Bentham, Jeremy. *Introduction to the Principles of Morals and Legislation* (Oxford: Clarendon Press, 1879).

Braun, Bruce. "Modalities of Posthumanism" (2006) 7:4 *Social & Cultural Geography* 1352.

Calarco, Matthew. *Zoographies: The Question of the Animal from Heidegger to Derrida* (New York: Columbia University Press, 2008).

Castree, Noel & Catherine Nash. "Introduction: Posthumanism in Question" (2004) 36:8 *Environment and Planning A* 1341.

———. "Editorial: Posthuman Geographies" (2006) 7:4 *Social & Cultural Geography* 501.

Comaroff, Jean & John L. Comaroff. *Theories from the South: Or, How Euro-America Is Evolving toward Africa* (Boulder, CO: Paradigm Publishers, 2012).

Dayan, Colin. *The Law Is a White Dog: How Legal Rituals Make and Unmake Persons* (Princeton, NJ: Princeton University Press, 2011).

Derrida, Jacques. "The Ends of Man" (1969) 30:1 *Philosophy and Phenomenological Research* 31.

———. "The Animal That Therefore I Am (More to Follow)" (2002) 28:2 *Critical Inquiry* 369.

Derrida, Jacques & Elisabeth Roudinesco. *For What Tomorrow . . .: A Dialogue*, translated by Jeff Fort (Stanford: Stanford University Press, 2004).

Farbota, Kim. "Black Crime Rates: What Happens When Numbers Aren't Neutral" (9 February 2015) *Huffington Post*, <www.huffingtonpost.com/kim-farbota/black-crime-rates-your-st_b_8078586.html>.

Fischer-Lescano, Andreas & Tillmann Löhr. *Legal Opinion: Border Controls at Sea: Requirements under International Human Rights and Refugee Law* (European Center for Constitutional and Human Rights, 2007).

Foucault, Michel. *The Order of Things: An Archaeology of the Human Sciences* (London: Routledge, 1970).

Glendinning, Simon. "From Animal Life to City Life" (2000) 5:3 *Angelaki: Journal of the Theoretical Humanities* 19.

Haddad, Emma. *The Refugee in International Society: Between Sovereigns* (Cambridge: Cambridge University Press, 2008).

Hudson, Laura. "A Species of Thought: Bare Life and Animal Being" (2011) 43:5 *Antipode* 1659.

Human Rights Watch. "Greece: Camp Conditions Endanger Women, Girls" (4 December 2019), <www.hrw.org/news/2019/12/04/greece-camp-conditions-endanger-women-girls>.

International Organization for Migration. *World Migration Report 2015 – Migrants and Cities: New Partnerships to Manage Mobility*, <http://publications.iom.int/system/files/wmr2015_en.pdf>.

Jackson, Zakiyyah Iman. "Animal: New Directions in the Theorization of Race and Posthumanism" (2013) 39:3 *Feminist Studies* 669.

King, Barbara J. "The Orca's Sorrow" (2019) 320:3 *Scientific American* 30.

Krause, Monika. "Undocumented Migrants: An Arendtian Perspective" (2008) 7:3 *European Journal of Political Theory* 331.

Law, Stephen. "Humanism" in Stephen Bullivant & Michael Ruse, eds, *The Oxford Handbook of Atheism* (Oxford: Oxford University Press, 2013) 263.

Lechte, John & Saul Newman. "Agamben, Arendt and Human Rights – Bearing Witness to the Human" (2012) 15:4 *European Journal of Social Theory* 522.

Martin, John Jeffries. "The Myth of Renaissance Individualism" in Guido Ruggiero, ed, *A Companion to the Worlds of the Renaissance* (Malden, MA: Blackwell, 2007) 208.

Mitchell, W.J.T. "Foreword: The Rights of Things" in Cary Wolfe, ed, *Animal Rites – American Culture, the Discourse of Species, and Posthumanist Theory* (Chicago: University of Chicago Press, 2003) ix.

Murdoch, Jonathan. "Humanising Posthumanism" (2006) 7:4 *Social & Cultural Geography* 1356.

Ndlovu-Gatsheni, Sabelo J. *Empire, Global Coloniality and African Subjectivity* (New York: Berghahn Books, 2013).

Outram, Dorinda. *The Enlightenment* (Cambridge: Cambridge University Press, 2011).

Petrarca, Francesco. *Petrarch's Secret or the Soul's Conflict with Passion: Three Dialogues between Himself and S. Augustine*, translated by William H. Draper (London: Chatto & Windus, 1911).

Pro Asyl. *Walls of Shame: Accounts from the Inside: The Detention Centers of Evros* (2012), <www.proasyl.de/fileadmin/fm-dam/q_PUBLIKATIONEN/2012/Evros-Bericht_12_04_10_BHP.pdf>.

Quijano, Aníbal. "Coloniality and Modernity/Rationality" (2007) 21:2–3 *Cultural Studies* 168.

Quillen, Carol Everhart. *Rereading the Renaissance: Petrarch, Augustine, and the Language of Humanism* (Ann Arbor: University of Michigan Press, 1998).

Rabinow, Paul, ed. *The Foucault Reader* (New York: Pantheon, 1984).

Roberts, Mark S. *The Mark of the Beast: Animality and Human Oppression* (West Lafayette, IN: Purdue University Press, 2008).

Sheehan, Paul. "Introduction – Contingencies of Humanness" in Paul Sheehan, ed, *Becoming Human: New Perspectives on the Inhuman Condition* (Westport, CT: Praeger, 2003) 1.

Singer, Peter. "Prologue: Ethics and the New Animal Liberation Movement" in Peter Singer, ed, *In Defense of Animals* (New York: Blackwell, 1985) 1.

Slobodchikoff, C. N. et al. "Semantic Information Distinguishing Individual Predators in the Alarm Calls of Gunnison's Prairie Dogs" (1991) 42 *Animal Behavior* 713.

———. "Prairie Dog Alarm Calls Encode Labels about Predator Colors" (2009) 12:3 *Animal Cognition* 435.

Sundberg, Juanita. "Decolonizing Posthumanist Geographies" (2014) 21:1 *Cultural Geographies* 33.

United Nations. "Global Issues: Migration", <www.un.org/en/global-issues/migration>.

Vaughan-Williams, Nick. "We are *Not* Animals! Humanitarian Border Security and Zoopolitical Spaces in EUrope" (2015) 45 *Political Geography* 1.

Whatmore, Sarah. *Hybrid Geographies* (London: Sage, 2002).

Wolfe, Cary. *Animal Rites – American Culture, the Discourse of Species, and Posthumanist Theory* (Chicago: University of Chicago Press, 2003).

———. *What is Posthumanism?* (Minneapolis: University of Minnesota Press, 2010).

Chapter 3

Contesting the dominant ontology and epistemology through critical theories from the margins

Critical theories that do not have their origins in Eurocentric traditions are useful to understand the ongoing debates concerning the concept of the human that underpins international human rights law. I draw, in particular, on decoloniality, Black[1] and Indigenous approaches, which reveal and oppose Western domination over various aspects of life, such as with respect to citizenship and migration policies, and help critique the dominant concept of the subject and its focus on the white individual. As discussed above, although every human being is supposed to have human rights, it is citizenship and immigration status that often determine if these rights can actually be accessed, with many relevant laws and policies being highly discriminatory, typically along the line of skin colour and ethnicity. Highlighting this relationship between human rights, citizenship and racial discrimination, Tendayi Achiume, the UN Special Rapporteur on contemporary forms of racism, racial discrimination, xenophobia and related intolerance, has noted that "[s]tates have long used access to citizenship and immigration status as a discriminatory tool to curtail the rights and benefits of marginalized groups".[2]

The critical theories I discuss in this chapter are different from each other in their respective focus and conclusions; yet they all critique the dominant approach, including the construction of the modern subject in opposition to an 'Other'. In this sense, and without wanting to reinforce an inflated binary opposition between the centre and the margins, since both terms are constructions and more closely related to and dependent on each other than what is often assumed, I believe that non-dominant approaches offer powerful insights by critically assessing what is at the centre, or dominant, or assumed to be dominant. They highlight, in particular, that human rights are highly dependent on the Eurocentric construction of the 'human' and

---

1 Following the practice of some authors, the words Black and Blackness are capitalized to assert their importance as ontological positions.
2 *Report of the Special Rapporteur on Contemporary Forms of Racism, Racial Discrimination, Xenophobia and Related Intolerance*, A/HRC/38/52, para 11.

DOI: 10.4324/9781003427957-5

humanist values, and that non-white bodies reveal inherent shortcomings and failures of the system.

Although some of these dynamics of domination have also been pointed out by posthumanist scholars, as noted in the preceding chapter, the theories from the margins I rely on here arguably make more profound critiques about Western modernity[3] and the dominant subject than theories like posthumanism could offer, including at the level of knowledge and knowledge production. Indeed, and in addition to the points of criticism previously discussed, posthumanism, when considered from these margins, seems to presume that the world can only be understood through Eurocentric concepts and categories, and that only the West can elicit genuine critiques, including *vis-à-vis* dominant Western thought. This leads to the silencing of other epistemologies and ontologies, such as those that could potentially disrupt the West's supremacy. Indigenous and Black approaches, and epistemes more generally, are largely excluded.[4] Race and Blackness are also rarely addressed by posthumanism. As Zakiyyah Iman Jackson says, "far too often, gestures toward the 'post' or the 'beyond' effectively ignore praxes of humanity and critiques produced by black people, particularly those praxes which are irreverent to the normative production of 'the human'".[5] Race, she argues, is an issue that posthumanism is trying to escape and even dissimulate; because of the usually presumed absence of any other persuasive critical theories, Eurocentric theory is considered the only one that is able to judge the "political significance and vitality of nonhumans".[6] These tendencies of silencing and excluding contribute to perpetuating Eurocentric and colonial ideas of dualisms, such as between educated, rational subjects and naive 'Others',[7] with knowledge production being the privilege of the former.

I argue in this chapter that, when used together in a constructive manner, theories from the margins allow developing a powerful critique of the currently dominant conception of the human that is at the basis of the international human rights system. Instead of considering specific historical processes

---

3 For an insightful critique of Western modernity, see Mignolo, *The Darker Side of Western Modernity.*

4 In those few cases when posthumanist scholarship does refer to Indigeneity, it tends to do so without properly naming sources, and without sincerely engaging with Indigenous worldviews. Of note, Indigeneity, which is "the socio-spatial processes and practices by whereby Indigenous people and places are determined as distinct (ontologically, epistemologically, culturally, in sovereignty, etc.) to dominant universals", has recently become an important analytical concept. Radcliffe, "Geography and Indigeneity I", 221. Indigeneity allows to consider how Indigenous peoples' identities are constructed, and to show that "indigenous embodiment and subjectivities continue to be produced in the interstices of the colonial present". Radcliffe, "Geography and Indigeneity II", 437–8.

5 Z. I. Jackson, "Outer Worlds", 215–16.

6 Sundberg, 38.

7 Sundberg, 37.

or forms of suffering and discrimination separately, as many approaches and authors tend to do,[8] I believe that it is important and even necessary to both highlight common concerns and bring together specific arguments in order to gain a better understanding of the creation of complex dominant concepts and to deconstruct them.[9] In fact, theories from the margins were not developed in isolation: for instance, while decolonial studies emerged in Latin America and Black studies in North America, they have some common intellectual origins and have influenced each other.[10] Importantly, as it should be noted, the margins – or the South – are not limited to the geographical localization but are "a metaphor for the systematic suffering inflicted upon large bodies of population by Western-centric colonialism, capitalism, and patriarchy"; they are found both outside and inside Europe, North America and other industrialized societies.[11]

The subjection of non-white people has insidiously continued in daily life, even if the situation of historically oppressed groups has certainly changed over time.[12] It is true that slavery was formally abolished in the 19th century and that the civil rights movement brought about important improvements in the mid-20th century. Moreover, movements like Idle No More and Black Lives Matter and institutions like the Canadian Truth and Reconciliation Commission on the Indian residential school system continue to occupy an important place in contemporary political discourses. Yet inequality based on historical oppression, and also unequal access to human rights, remains a reality. The killings of unarmed 17-year-old Trayvon Martin in 2012 by a white self-appointed surveillance patrol, who was acquitted on the basis of self-defence, and of unarmed George Floyd, who was suffocated by white police officers in 2020, are only two (sadly) famous cases of the profound vulnerability and ongoing fungibility of Black people in the United States of America, and routine violation of their rights, in this case the right to life.[13] The killing of 17-year-old Nahel Merzouk, a French citizen of north African descent, who was also unarmed, by a police officer in France in 2023 illustrates that non-white people are not protected from similar threats in Europe.[14] Black agency, in fact, rarely has a positive connotation; it is rather

8 There are, of course, exceptions. Rinaldo Walcott, for instance, makes a powerful argument that brings together Black studies and a critique of the capitalist neoliberal system in the Indigenous context in Canada.

9 This is why this chapter does not discuss each approach in isolation but builds on both specific and shared insights to pursue the analysis.

10 See e.g. Mignolo, "Introduction – Coloniality of Power and De-Colonial Thinking", 164.

11 Santos, "Epilogue", 175–6.

12 Sithole, 24–5.

13 See Marshall for an explanation of the political dimensions of fungibility in the case of Trayvon Martin.

14 The Observer France.

associated with criminality to justify contemporary anti-Black laws and practices.[15]

In white settler societies, such as the United States and Canada, not only are non-white people more likely than white people to be arrested when suspected of a crime, to be convicted for the same crime, and to receive higher sentences;[16] they also face significant wealth inequalities and discrimination in housing, health and employment.[17] According to the United Nations, Indigenous people around the world are almost three times more likely than non-Indigenous people to live in extreme poverty.[18] To cite a few specific instances of violations of the right to health and the right to life of Indigenous peoples in Canada, several Indigenous communities do not have access to safe drinking water, and the suicide rate is significantly higher, namely up to nine times in the case of Inuit, than for non-Indigenous people.[19] These human rights violations have their roots in historical and ongoing forms of colonialism. As the National Inquiry into Missing and Murdered Indigenous Women and Girls, which submitted its final report in 2019, found, the higher rates of violence against Indigenous women and girls are a result of the "significant, persistent, and deliberate pattern of systemic racial and gendered human rights and Indigenous rights violations and abuses – perpetuated historically and maintained today by the Canadian state, designed to displace Indigenous Peoples from their land, social structures, and governance and to eradicate their existence as Nations, communities, families, and individuals".[20] It is intriguing and troubling that the names of Indigenous individuals who died as a result of police misconduct, such as Neil Stonechild, Lawrence Wegner and Rodney Naistus,[21] are rarely mentioned and remembered by Canadians, like the hundreds of missing and murdered Indigenous women and girls. This suggests an acute vulnerability and disposability of Indigenous people. To give another recent example of unequal protection of rights, Indigenous people, as highlighted by the UN Special Rapporteur on the Rights of Indigenous Peoples, are more likely to contract and to die of COVID-19.[22]

---

15 Marshall.
16 See United States Sentencing Commission. See also Farbota.
17 See e.g. Pager & Shepherd. For a thorough discussion of the relationship between racial discrimination and the poor health and well-being of Indigenous peoples in New Zealand, see Reid, Cormack & Paine.
18 UN Office of the High Commissioner for Human Rights, "About Indigenous Peoples and Human Rights".
19 On the lack of access to safe drinking water of Indigenous people in Canada and the failure of the state to meet its human rights obligations, see the report of the Office of the Auditor General of Canada; on the suicide rate among Indigenous peoples, see Statistics Canada.
20 National Inquiry into Missing and Murdered Indigenous Women and Girls, 60.
21 El-Hadi.
22 UN Office of the High Commissioner for Human Rights, "Indigenous Peoples have been disproportionately affected by COVID-19".

These cases and statistics reveal that the human rights – in terms of both civil and political rights and social, economic and cultural rights – of marginalized people are not protected and promoted to the same extent as the rights of those who belong to the dominant society. As Jaime Amparo Alves argues by referring to Brazil, the main gesture of the state towards people of colour, in particular those living in poverty, is punitive because they are not considered full citizens, or humans: "democracy itself entails a dialectical antagonism between endangered White civil society and a dangerous racial other".[23] As for Europe, there are many manifestations of the almost limitless anti-Black feeling,[24] as exemplified by the stringent border policies targeting in particular African migrants. In the terms of Sabine Broeck:

> practices range on a continuum from pejorative media, through ritualistic forms of Black debasement in advertisement, through aggressive exorcisms and ridicule in popular customs such as the Netherland's *Zwarte Piet*, or the return of the *Sarotti Mohr* in German chocolate consumer culture, through what amounts to an overall denial of anti-racist change in institutions of higher education, to massive and indeed murderous forms of violence within and outside of the state apparatus, to criminal fascist attacks on Black people and to the anonymous death of migrants from the African continent in the Mediterranean, watched over by the FRONTEX regime.[25]

A key insight from theories from the margins is that the Western domination, founded on an alleged superiority, and resulting colonialism have never been completely erased and that the aftermaths of colonialism can still be felt. Political colonialism might have been abolished and colonial administrations disappeared, but the colonial domination and exploitation of non-Westerners nonetheless persist today, on the grounds of their assumed inferiority, with various intensities.[26] As Boaventura de Sousa Santos, who has challenged dominant epistemologies, especially with respect to law, writes, there is "an entrenched colonialist prejudice that has outlived historical colonialism for many decades".[27] As a result, the Western point of view, its ideas and claimed universals still reign, including the separation of humans from nature and of

---

23 Amparo Alves, 152.
24 Sexton, 47. Some authors claim that anti-Black sentiments have not spared European and North American academia, where few scholars study race and racism, with long-lasting consequences for the production of knowledge. See Broeck, 113–14 and Gilroy, "Multiculture", 98.
25 Broeck, 110.
26 Quijano, 169. For an analysis of the ongoing effects of colonial ideas about ethnicity in defining Indigenous peoples, see Napoleon, "Extinction by Number".
27 Santos, "Epilogue", 173.

the mind from the body, and the resulting construction of an ideal subject that underlies human rights.

Theories from the margins challenge this idea of one valid point of view. They argue that so-called universal ideas are fallacious and that Western knowledge is historically determined and only one among other forms of knowledge. Moreover, they put forward the argument that coloniality is actually constitutive of modernity; without the former, the discourse and practice of modernity would not exist, which is why modernity has an interest in perpetuating coloniality.[28] A related crucial point is that the modern subject could only constitute itself in opposition to the non-European body, and that this had important consequences for the way in which the 'human' was and still is conceived in the context of human rights.[29] As the critical visual discourse analysis in the next chapter will further reveal, these dynamics and resulting exclusions are entrenched through the vision-centredness of Western modernity that also characterizes international human rights. The act of looking is never neutral but constructs the one who is looked at – or represented – in certain ways. To take a telling example, in the case of Black bodies, and more generally of non-white migrants nowadays, this act of looking continues to be violent, to create exclusions and to deny them subjectivity and, as a result, the protection of human rights.

Another reason why these theories from the margins are important for the present analysis of the subject of human rights is that they conceive the human not into a *fait accompli* but as an interrogating model, subject to change and critique,[30] like the figure of the *migrating 'Other'* proposed in the previous chapter. In fact, to embody the commitment to the plurality of knowledges and beings as well as the possibility of change, I will propose the plural form *migrating 'Others'* as a final variation of the figure developed in the previous chapters.

Indeed, theories from the margins can be a useful resource to analyse and deconstruct the modern Western conception of the human and of humanity embedded in human rights discourses, for instance because of Black studies scholars' particular vigilance of hierarchizations of different groups of humans.[31] I would like to emphasize that in spite of the claim of certain authors working on Blackness that Black people occupy a particular position in the relationship between dominant and dominated subjects, as will be further discussed below, different theories from the margins put the finger on different dynamics of and explanations for oppression, and that exclusions

28 Maldonado-Torres, 244.
29 Similarly, following Spivak (see e.g. Spivak, *A Critique of Postcolonial Reason*, 116–17), it can be argued that dominant humanist discourses are based on the exclusion of marginal figures.
30 Weheliye, 8, 19.
31 Weheliye, 3.

can take different forms. My purpose is therefore not to establish or follow a particular hierarchy of oppression, but to build on the respective insights from the different theories. This, as I believe, helps to deconstruct dominant concepts such as the 'human' of human rights, and hence to adopt a critical perspective on the international human rights system, and has the potential to lead to greater justice, including epistemic justice.[32]

There are, of course, authors from the Global North who also believe that the dominant conception of the human is problematic and discriminatory *vis-à-vis* certain groups, but implicitly or explicitly, they do not sufficiently address the extent to which racialization lies at the core of the 'human' and its body.[33] For instance, Judith Butler has claimed that one of the core issues of human rights law

> is not just that some humans are treated as humans, and others are de- humanized; it is rather that dehumanization becomes the condition for the production of the human to the extent that a "Western" civilization defines itself over and against a population understood as, by definition, illegitimate, if not dubiously human.[34]

While it is useful to appreciate that the 'human' is now constructed against a diverse 'Other', in the sense that there are many disadvantaged and op- pressed groups, one problem with most Western critical theories, including postmodernism and poststructuralism, and the concepts that they have devel- oped, such as biopolitics and bare life, is that they often fail to recognize their own specific white-European historical, philosophical and political founda- tions and therefore perpetuate a coloniality of power and knowledge. As Ramón Grosfoguel writes, authors who rely on a Western epistemology and only follow Eurocentric authors such as Foucault and Gramsci "constrained and limited the radicality of their critique".[35] Alexander G. Weheliye has forcefully argued that "[b]are life and biopolitics discourse not only mis- construes how profoundly race and racism shape the modern idea of the human, it also overlooks or perfunctorily writes off theorizations of race, subjection, and humanity found in black and ethnic studies".[36] Other theo- ries that focus on the construction of the human as a citizen or in opposition to non-human animals, while offering crucial insights, arguably do not meet the challenge posed by racism either, because they do not (or not seriously)

---

32 On the importance of epistemic justice, see Santos, *Epistemologies of the South*, 42.
33 Weheliye, 4. There are, of course, exceptions. Broeck, for instance, offers interesting ar- guments on the legacies of white abjectorship and the "enslave-ability" of Black people. Broeck, 109.
34 Butler, *Precarious Life*, 91.
35 Grosfoguel, 211–12.
36 Weheliye, 4.

take into consideration the central factor of race and colonialism and largely ignore minority discourses and ways of being[37] as well as some of the fundamental reasons why many individuals and groups cannot effectively access human rights.

3.1   Revealing ongoing forms of coloniality

The impacts of colonialism persist, including with respect to the definition of the human and related exclusions, which reveals, as I argue by building on decoloniality theory, that a form of coloniality is also at work in international human rights.[38] Colonialism persists today in the form of coloniality, which captures phenomena well beyond the limits or direct results of colonialism and colonial administration, namely more subtle and enduring effects on social life. Decoloniality theory was developed mainly in Latin America in the 1920s, among others by the Peruvian José Carlos Mariátegui, and spread in the 1970s, but its inspiration can be traced back to thinkers and approaches from various colonies and ex-colonies, such as Mahatma Gandhi in India, Aimé Césaire and Frantz Fanon in the French Caribbean and Indigenous activists in settler countries like Canada and Australia.[39] These authors emphasize that colonial powers imposed their own ways of producing knowledge and meaning and also mystified these ways and made them attractive, with the purpose of co-opting the perspectives of those colonized. Aníbal Quijano argues that colonialism should be understood as comprising the repression, from the 15th and 16th centuries onwards, of knowledge, beliefs and symbols considered not useful or detrimental to the colonial powers, and also ways of knowing and modes of producing knowledge, perspectives, images, signification and so on.[40] Coloniality, in the words of Nelson Maldonado-Torres, "refers to long-standing patterns of power that emerged as a result of colonialism, but that define culture, labor, subjective relations, and knowledge production".[41] It can even be argued that coloniality continues to represent the main contemporary form of domination and exploitation of non-European people: "as modern subjects we breathe coloniality all the

---

37 Weheliye, 9–10.
38 The ongoing forms of coloniality have also been pointed out by Indigenous authors. See for instance Simpson.
39 Mignolo, "Introduction – Coloniality of Power and De-Colonial Thinking", 163–4. Both post-colonialism and decoloniality have contributed to questioning and contesting colonialism, but there is a notable difference between the two approaches: while post-colonialism is "an attempt to bring multiplicity and difference within the modern", decoloniality is "a more radical effort to challenge discourses of modernity and refuse them". M. Jackson, xiii–xiv.
40 Quijano, 169.
41 Maldonado-Torres, 243.

time and everyday".[42] All aspects of life, including how one feels and sees one-self, are imbued with these well-entrenched power dynamics. With respect to Indigenous peoples in settler countries, as Val Napoleon writes, colonial imperialism continues to shape even concepts, such as self-determination, that are used by Indigenous peoples because of their supposedly emancipatory potential: "colonial imperialism has been able to successfully refashion its outward appearance so as to seem non-imperial, and to pervade indigenous political projects".[43]

Coloniality exists at different, if interrelated, levels, namely at the levels of power, knowledge and being, as Grosfoguel has usefully pointed out, and, as I would argue, this is also true in regard to human rights: coloniality – of power, knowledge and being – is at work in the international human rights system, perpetuating the domination of Western thought and ideas in relation to rights and subjectivity. The coloniality of *power* is reflected in various entangled hierarchies that structure virtually all relations on a global scale. It is through a number of interrelated processes touching on political, socio-economic and religious spheres that these hierarchies were created. One can cite the imposition of the Western-rooted capitalist system and a global division of labour; the emphasis on the modern state system and associated military organizations; and the privileging of Europeans and Christians over non-Europeans and non-Christians, as well as of men over women and of heterosexuals over homosexuals.[44] It should be noted that while some of these hierarchies are not specific to Western societies, they have all been prominent sources of discrimination in the West. Because the international human rights system has its origins in Western thought and philosophy, many of these hierarchies are also, and almost naturally, perpetuated here. The fact that it is modern states, a construction of the West – and not other political entities – that are the primary duty bearers and occupy hence a highly privileged status with respect to the promotion, protection and implementation of human rights, is a stark illustration of this bias. Moreover, it took a long time for women's rights to be recognized as human rights, which had been strongly associated with men; the recognition of discrimination based on sexual orientation as a human rights violation is an even more recent phenomenon.[45] Furthermore, the imposition of a legal system based

---

42 Maldonado-Torres, 243. See also Quijano, 170; Grosfoguel, 220. Grosfoguel also refers to the role of international institutions like the International Monetary Fund and the World Bank.

43 Napoleon, "Aboriginal Self Determination", 33.

44 Grosfoguel, 216–17. Further hierarchies could be added, including the domination of 'abled' over 'disabled' bodies. For instance, for a critique, based on a critical disability studies approach, that Western modernity produced a 'normative sensory subject' that is able to see, see Davis.

45 See for instance Bunch; McGoldrick.

on Western ideas of justice, agency and claimable rights is a significant example of the coloniality of power. The concept of self-determination, which
was developed by the colonial power and has always been understood in
such terms, is another good example. Napoleon contends that it is always
only in the terms of this understanding of self-determination that Indigenous
peoples are potentially considered as legitimate actors.[46] Napoleon also notes
that in Canada, "colonialism was imposed in gendered forms with aboriginal
women bearing the primary consequences".[47] She argues that both the band
council structure and the *Indian Act*, which were imposed on Indigenous
peoples by the Canadian state, are based not only on Western models of
leadership and democratic representation but also on discrimination against
Indigenous women.[48]

The privileging of Western thought and cosmology, as part of the coloniality of power, led to a coloniality of *knowledge*. In dominant discourses, such
as in international human rights, the *real* knowing and thinking subject is in
the West, imagined as European or of European descent, while the rest of the
world is condemned to the realm of nature, and is made absent.[49] According
to Jean Comaroff and John L. Comaroff, non-Western worlds were and are
still considered by dominant actors to be incapable of producing knowledge
themselves and are regarded as mere "reservoirs of raw fact".[50] Depicted
by the colonizers as deprived of reason, colonized peoples were and still are
hence ontologically excluded: "Beneath the 'I think' we can read 'others do
not think', and behind the 'I am' it is possible to locate the philosophical
justification for the idea that 'others are not' or do not have being".[51] The
increasing focus, from the Enlightenment onward, on the individual was, of
course, instrumental for the emergence of the concept of human rights, as
was the idea that the modern subject had to own property to be a genuine
subject, which explains the importance attached to the right to property in
human rights, as I explore in more detail below. These problematic dynamics,
which also mean that it is typically white Westerners who speak on behalf
of people in the Global South whose voices are not heard, have arguably
plagued the international human rights system from its beginning.[52] In fact,
it is only the European subject that can enter into communication with the
rest of the world to share knowledge; colonized people are prevented from

46 Napoleon, "Individual Self and Collective Selves", 33–4.
47 Napoleon, "Individual Self and Collective Selves", 38.
48 Napoleon, "Individual Self and Collective Selves", 36–7. For an historical account of legal
    actions taken by the Canadian state against Indigenous women, see Napoleon, "Extinction
    by Number", 115–24.
49 Quijano, 173.
50 Comaroff & Comaroff, 1.
51 Maldonado-Torres, 252.
52 See for instance Kennedy, "Spring Break".

contributing – or of contributing on their own terms – to exchanges of knowledge with the colonizers as well as with others that are also colonized.[53] The possibility of having and giving, for instance, which signifies one's self and is the basis of communication with others and of a common world, is denied from the colonized;[54] that this is problematic is particularly obvious in the case of many Indigenous peoples, for whom gift-giving is fundamental to transmit knowledge and traditions and to build relationships with everyone and everything.[55]

The coloniality of both power and knowledge affects the understanding of being and the creation of identities, which is captured in the concept of the coloniality of *being* and can explain, as I maintain, why international human rights are still effective only for some beings but not for others. Maldonado-Torres claims that modernity introduced a colonial difference between the person of the conqueror and the conquered, and that people of colour were dehumanized and rendered invisible through the idea of race.[56] Race is, for several authors from the margins, the main organizing principle of this coloniality of power and being, which structures and affects all the other hierarchies.[57] In this logic, it is race, that is the idea of the "nonhomogeneity of the human species",[58] that became the key criterion for the creation of new social and geocultural identities[59] and that created a stark distinction between presumably superior and inferior people. Scholars working on Blackness, such as Tendayi Sithole and Rinaldo Walcott, explain how the humanness of Black people, because they lack whiteness, is never taken for granted; they must constantly justify themselves, and they often suffer from a complex of inferiority.[60] In this perspective, colonizers not only saw

53 Quijano, 171–4.
54 Maldonado-Torres, 258.
55 For a discussion on the importance of gift-giving for most Indigenous cultures, see Kuokkanen. As a site of knowledge production of the dominant society, the current university system arguably contributes to this coloniality of knowledge and to epistemic violence. Hunt, 29; see also M. Jackson, 3. When Indigenous people, for instance, try to speak by relying on their own epistemological frameworks in an academic setting, they are not, or rarely, heard; they are confronted with what Rauna Kuokkanen calls academia's "epistemic ignorance". Kuokkanen, 60–3. Mignolo also specifies that academic disciplines such as the humanities are sites of coloniality and that it is largely dominant actors that speak on behalf of the marginalized. Mignolo, "Further Thoughts on Decoloniality", 34. In settler societies like Canada and Australia, these dynamics are part of a larger, ongoing and far-reaching strategy of colonization that transformed Indigenous societies and their environment, including at the conceptual level. Hunt, 29. On the reproduction of racial privilege in academia in Europe, see Araújo & Maeso.
56 Maldonado-Torres, 245, 276–7.
57 See e.g. Quijano, 171; Grosfoguel, 217.
58 Wynter, "1492", 34.
59 Quijano, 171.
60 Sithole, 31–6; Walcott, 93.

inferiority in everyone else; they attempted, often with success, to make everyone feel inferior to them. Césaire describes this as an almost innate feeling, with millions having been taught "la peur, le complexe d'infériorité, le tremblement, l'agenouillement, le désespoir, le larbinisme",[61] which, Fanon argues, further entrenches the relation of 'Other' and, as a result, instils a desire to escape their Black identity or to obliterate their self.[62] A mental process seems to occur that consists in removing from their consciousness everything that is Black about themselves. The goal of their actions and decisions is oriented towards white people, because it is only through the latter that they can be valued.[63] Fanon argues Black people experience constantly fighting their own image.[64] Sylvia Wynter speaks of how she had to face her own prejudices, which characterizes all her work:

> How do you deal with the stereotyped view of yourself that you yourself have been socialized to accept? . . . It is that given the conception of what it is to be human, to be an imperial English man or woman, you had to be seen by them as the negation of what they were. So *you*, too, had to *circumcise* yourself of yourself, in order to be fully human.[65]

Similarly, Fanon describes that many Black people have the impression – induced and sustained by white people – that they do not even exist for themselves: "Sentiment d'infériorité? Non, sentiment d'inexistence".[66] What Fanon means is how Black people must adapt to and adopt white standards; they must "act White".[67] By way of example, Black people had and often still have no choice but to embrace the language of the colonizers: "le Noir Antillais sera d'autant plus blanc, c'est-à-dire se rapprochera d'autant plus du véritable homme, qu'il aura fait sienne la langue française".[68] In other words, Black individuals, as described by Fanon, often experience that they have no value in or for themselves, and that they depend entirely on the existence of those who are constructed as full subjects, namely white persons. In fact, following a strategy of coloniality of being, the colonized were made not only inferior but also dispensable: in order for the white Euro-American ontologies to be preserved, the humanness of certain beings, in particular

---

61 Césaire, *Discours sur le colonialisme*, 24.
62 Fanon, *Peau noire, masques blancs*, 48.
63 Fanon, *Peau noire, masques blancs*, 124.
64 Fanon, *Peau noire, masques blancs*, 156.
65 Wynter, "The Re-Enchantment of Humanism", 131–2.
66 Fanon, *Peau noire, masques blancs*, 112.
67 Sithole, 26.
68 Fanon, *Peau noire, masques blancs*, 14. This requirement to speak the language and follow the logic of the colonizer is, of course, not limited to Black people but also applies to other colonized and marginalized people.

Indigenous and Black human beings, was and continues to be denied, with these beings having been turned into objects of knowledge.[69] Similar dynamics have shaped the colonization of Indigenous peoples, who often had to adopt ideas and concepts of the colonizers, as in the case of the above-mentioned example of self-determination, and even when trying to resist colonization.[70] Again, coloniality runs deep, with the mind, imaginations and identities all being colonized.[71]

While Western modernity and its concepts of subjectivity and rights put forth the idea that the Western individual produces knowledge by himself,[72] from a decolonial perspective, the individual needs other subjects to exist and forms itself precisely in relation with them: "Every individual discourse, or reflection, remits to a structure of intersubjectivity. The former is constituted in and vis a vis the latter".[73] In many Indigenous cosmologies, individuals are necessarily connected to each other.[74] This is not, however, how human rights are usually framed: with a strong focus and explicit wording, human rights are first and foremost thought and expressed as rights that individuals hold by themselves, and not in relation with others or as part of a community. Almost all the rights listed in the *International Covenant on Civil and Political Rights*, one of the key treaties of the international human rights system, are primarily individual rights; only very few, like the right to self-determination and certain rights of ethnic, religious and linguistic minorities, have a collective dimension, although this does not mean that groups or peoples can claim these rights as collective entities.[75] Some Indigenous peoples are therefore reluctant to use human rights because of their dominant liberal-individualistic focus, and would rather frame their claims as collective rights or highlight, as Napoleon does, that individual and collective claims are interdependent.[76]

Coloniality continues to impact global relations and the way in which the 'human' is conceived, thus sustaining and creating further exclusions, including in human rights. Global capitalism and (neo)liberalism, which are arguably the main forms of coloniality today, still foster differences, structure relations and configure subjectivities in a colonial logic and, importantly, determines whether a subject is considered a full human being and can effectively

69 Quijano, 172–4; Maldonado-Torres, 245, 247, 259.
70 Napoleon, "Individual Self and Collective Selves", 33–4.
71 Maldonado-Torres, 242.
72 The use of the masculine pronoun is intentional and reflects the fact that the Western modern subject was for a long time constructed by and as (white) men.
73 Quijano, 173.
74 I return to this point as part of my analysis of some works of Indigenous artists in the next chapter.
75 *International Covenant on Civil and Political Rights*, articles 1 and 27. For the distinction between individual rights, group rights and collective rights, see Sanders.
76 Napoleon, "Aboriginal Self Determination". See also Holder & Corntassel, 128; Anaya, 42–5, 77–80.

access human rights. Global capitalism is often deployed through the logic of development, which is sometimes even cast as a "right to development". The *Vienna Declaration and Programme of Action*, which was adopted by consensus at the 1993 World Conference on Human Rights, indeed affirms that the right to development is "a universal and inalienable right and an integral part of fundamental human rights".[77] This right is also enshrined in the *African Charter on Human and Peoples' Rights*.[78] Another example is that of the *United Nations Millenium Development Goals*: adopted by all states and driving the work of international development institutions from 2000 to 2015, these goals have been explicitly linked to international human rights, including the right to development.[79] It is useful to recall Arturo Escobar's argument that development is a "historically produced discourse" and regime of representation that entrenches an imbalance of power and represents the latest source of cultural, social and economic domination by the West.[80] Discourse, as it is worth recalling, is here understood as a "process through which social reality comes into being"; what can be said or imagined is limited by the space created by the discourse.[81] In the case of development, it is only the modern Western knowledge system that has been relied upon, and although some of the structures and strategies of development discourses have changed over time, the underlying relations between the elements that make up the discourse have not changed.[82] Through the discourse of development, different forms of power – related to race and nationality, among others – were introduced and perpetuated, and it is through development that the idea of the "Third World" as underdeveloped, poor, overpopulated and in need of Western knowledge and governance was produced from the 1950s onwards.[83] Like other concepts that have emerged in the West, such as citizenship and statehood, development could never be genuinely questioned, and it remains difficult to imagine social reality in any other way than through this prism. Indeed, the doctrine of development is still prevalent even though it failed to deliver most of its promises and actually led to underdevelopment, further exploitation and oppression on a large scale.[84] But, from a decolonial perspective, the idea of development is problematic in any event,

---

77 *Vienna Declaration and Programme of Action*, para 10. For an early account and critique of the right to development, see Alston. For an historical overview, including opposition to the right to development, see Marks.
78 *African Charter on Human and Peoples' Rights*, article 22.
79 UN Office of the High Commissioner for Human Rights, "Millennium Development Goals".
80 Escobar, *Encountering Development*, vii, 5–6, 10. It should be noted that Escobar focuses on development, but he says the same is also happening with other globalization discourses. Ibid, xxxii.
81 Escobar, *Encountering Development*, 39.
82 Escobar, *Encountering Development*, 13, 42.
83 Escobar, *Encountering Development*, 9, 12, 43.
84 Escobar, *Encountering Development*, 4.

whether the project succeeds or fails to bring about economic improvement, because it is an ideological export. It is always an act of cultural imperialism that seeks to impose Western standards and that has important political, economic and cultural consequences.

It is hence important to reveal not only specific periods or the most obvious facets of colonialism as it is usually conceived, but also ongoing forms of exploitation that are enabled notably through the logic of development in the Global South, and of global capitalism and (neo)liberalism more generally speaking. Walcott usefully highlights that ongoing forms of colonialism also exist in the Global North and were able to maintain themselves over time through capitalism: rooted in the enslavement and commodification of Black bodies, the neo-colonial project continues not only to exploit non-white bodies but also to conceive them, including Indigenous peoples and other marginalized human beings, as out of place and disposable and to deny them full membership in humanity on the basis of their 'race' and economic worth.[85] These factors are part of the reasons why Black and Indigenous persons still have greater difficulty to have their human rights respected, from the right to life to the right to vote and the right to health.

3.2   The fallacy of one universal point of view

A key insight from theorists from the margins is that they challenge the well-entrenched belief that only European thought, that is the philosophy, science, religious tradition and idea of progress developed by Europeans and people of European descent – yet presented as objective truth – could govern and solve the problems of the entire world. In addition to colonialism and evangelization, foreign aid, development programs and neo-colonial economic practices, the human rights project is also part of this logic.[86] Theories from the margins usefully highlight that most ideas and concepts that have their origins in the West are biased and founded on violence and exclusions. As I would argue, the claim to universality of international human rights is particularly problematic, and notably the existence of one neutral and objective point of view that could express a universal truth. If everyone in the world, without any discrimination, is supposed to be able to benefit from human rights guarantees, then the human rights system should be based not only (or mainly) on its European origins but on a variety of beliefs and perspectives.

Indeed, one of the central problems of the human rights system consists in Western modernity's implicit pretention of an ideal subject that is disconnected from the non-human world and the community, which also led to the

85 Walcott, 101.
86 Santos, "Epilogue", 173.

conceptualization of Western knowledge as superior to all other knowledges and people.[87] The allegedly rational, disembodied and objective Western subject was and is expected to exist independently of its epistemic location and background, be it ethnicity or gender, among others, and human rights are supposed to apply and to be enjoyed by everyone, as if one's identity and worldview did not matter, and as if human rights were not based on specific humanist ideas and values. As Ramón Grosfoguel points out, what is presented as "truthful universal knowledge" hides the identity of the speaker and "the geo-political and body-political epistemic location in the structures of colonial power/knowledge".[88] Modern ontology, in other words, presumes a singular universe, and knowledge in the Western world is still, to a very large extent, produced from this "point zero".[89] This enables and is further entrenched by global capitalism, neo-colonial discourses and, as I argue, also human rights discourses, that elevate humans over non-humans and some humans over others, the individual over the community, and reason and science over other forms of knowledge.[90]

It is important to understand any claim to universality, as the one that human rights make, as situated claims. There is not one "real world",[91] as Walter Mignolo writes, and knowledges (in the plural form) are arguably always situated, which means they are tied to the specific location within the power structures and hierarchies from which they emerge.[92] With respect to the supposedly disembodied and dis-located subject or 'human', Mignolo argues that "the 'aboutness' of what we think, write, talk and argue does not have an existence independent of the 'who' – the agency of enunciation, and of the 'universes of meaning' in which our thinking, talking, writing, arguing is framed".[93] This "aboutness" is even created at the same time as the subject constitutes itself as such.[94] Said differently, knowledge cannot be produced in isolation: it is relative and contextual, and identity and being are always constituted through the connections between one's own self and others.[95] In that sense, and as already discussed in the previous chapter, the 'human' of human rights is not a universal concept but is historically determined; the claims associated with what it means to be human reflected in human

---

87 Grosfoguel, 213–14; Escobar, *Encountering Development*, xxii.
88 Grosfoguel, 213.
89 Grosfoguel, 215.
90 Escobar, *Encountering Development*, xxvii.
91 Mignolo, "Further Thoughts on Decoloniality", 46.
92 Grosfoguel, 213. As Grosfoguel highlights, feminists such as Patricia Hill Collins and Donna Haraway also made this point several decades ago. Ibid. That knowledge and arguments are always situated and "to be understood in terms of historical context" has also been recognized by philosopher Alasdair MacIntyre. MacIntyre, 9.
93 Mignolo, "Further Thoughts on Decoloniality", 22.
94 Mignolo, "Further Thoughts on Decoloniality", 24.
95 Blaser, "Life Projects", 29–31, 40.

rights discourses are always located in a "euro(andro)(anthropo)centric" way.[96] One of the main problems is, of course, that non-dominant or, in a Gramscian sense, non-hegemonic subjects cannot contribute to these discourses; the "subaltern", as Gayatri Chakravorty Spivak has argued from a feminist post-colonial perspective, cannot speak in the sense of expressing herself – because she is not heard – and cannot exercise her subjectivity.[97]

While contemporary discourses of human rights are often presented as emancipatory, they are hence not based on neutral "normative universal categories";[98] rather, as I wish to highlight, they reflect situated histories and arguably perpetuate, explicitly or implicitly, violence and exclusions, because of their rootedness in values and concepts developed by humanism and the Enlightenment. Ironically, the humanist subject is still often considered a universal standard, as something to look up to, even in the Global South.[99] As Broeck has argued, "the Enlightenment, with its impetus for individual self-ownership, self-responsibility, subjective and objective rights to freedom, and productive self-realization, learned to operate within a system of a large-scale racist parasitism".[100] In fact, the existence of biased concepts based in European thought led thinkers from the colonies like Césaire to criticize humanism as "sordidly racist" and label it "pseudo-humanism".[101]

These criticisms hence help understand why Western concepts of human rights are not always useful remedies and may not do justice to a range of worldviews. The idea that agency as conceived in human rights discourses, for instance, can or should be granted to everyone and everything is problematic: among others, the prevalent focus on agency in its current form hides and diminishes the importance of relationality and the rich processes that some Indigenous authors call "co-constitution" and "co-becoming".[102] Other problems are assumptions about the right to property and ownership of land and the way that these ideas were imposed, notably on Indigenous peoples, through colonialism and capitalism.[103] According to some authors, it is also through the continuity of the capitalist system and ensuing forms of exploitation that emerged with the enslavement of Africans that the aftermaths of slavery are still felt by Black people as descendants of slaves.[104]

96 Z. I. Jackson, "Outer Worlds", 217.
97 Spivak, "Subaltern Talk", 292.
98 Amparo Alves, 152.
99 Spivak, "Criticism, Feminism, and the Institution", 7. This also explains Spivak's critique of other Western political concepts, such as nationhood and citizenship, and their ahistorical transplantation into other contexts. Morton, 214.
100 Broeck, 119 (references omitted).
101 Césaire, *Discours sur le colonialisme*, 14 (my translation).
102 Bawaka Country, "Co-Becoming Bawaka", 464.
103 For a discussion on land rights in relation to Indigenous peoples in Canadian case law, see Niezen.
104 See e.g. Walcott, 98–9.

Fundamentally, Western notions of self-determination, state- and nation-hood as well as citizenship, where membership is conceived exclusively and in the form of hard boundaries, contrast with Indigenous approaches. As Napoleon has argued, "pre-contact aboriginal societies practiced forms of nationhood that were deliberately inclusive in order to build strong nations with extensive international ties".[105] With respect to notions of freedom and empowerment assumed in human rights discourses, they are informed by ideas of domination and the (presumed) absence of domination, and legal subjectivity has been made dependent on ownership, with the ownership of slaves being a crude example.[106]

In addition to emphasizing situatedness and relationality, several theories from the margins maintain that the Western reliance on dualisms, which, as I argue, is also prevalent in human rights, is highly problematic. As with all binary relations, the opposing terms are envisaged as fundamentally different from one another, and each term is rendered equally fundamentally homogenous: a particular conduct will always be characterized as either legal or illegal, as respecting human rights or as violating them. The common flattening of differences – which, as it is worth recalling, some posthumanist writers also highlight – hides the fact that there is great variety within supposedly binary categories. Each term is constructed as fixed and associated with stability, as if diversity could be swept out of the equation and the subjects enclosed by the binary terms could never change. Although thinking in terms of such binaries has become pervasive not only in Western societies, other perspectives may traditionally not operate with them, or may rely on them only to some extent. In many Indigenous perspectives, for instance, there is no universal/particular, individual/collective or global/local dualism; for some Indigenous peoples, as Mario Blaser has noted, such a binary way of seeing the world actually always involves an issue of domination or control by one element over the other: by the self over the 'Other', by the knower over the known, by the colonizer over the colonized, and so on.[107] This heavy reliance on binaries and its sometimes violent consequences for non-dominant subjects, who do not fit into the predetermined categories established by a framework like human rights, explains why it can be difficult for many individuals and groups, such as migrants and Indigenous peoples, to successfully claim their rights. The Convention on the Elimination of All Discrimination against Women is a good example and makes it particularly obvious that international human rights law operates with such binary understandings, in

---

105 Napoleon, "Aboriginal Self-Determination", 38. On Indigenous nationhood, see also Napoleon, "Extinction by Number"; Simpson; for an analysis of the concept of Aboriginal citizenship in Canada, see Borrows, "Uncertain Citizens".
106 Weheliye, 4, 11.
107 Blaser, "Life Projects", 39. Williams highlights that the Western penchant for dualist thinking has its roots in ancient Greece. Williams, 6.

this context with respect to sex and gender. In this landmark 1979 treaty that continues to be the main point of reference for women's rights,[108] subjects can only be female or male: article I explains that discrimination against women is to be assessed "on a basis of equality of men and women".[109] Feminist and queer authors have usefully critiqued this particular bias within international law. Gabrielle Simm, for instance, has highlighted the colonial influences at play here, and that gender identity and sexuality may not be categorized in non-Western contexts in the same way as in dominant human rights discourses.[110] Similarly, Dianne Otto criticizes international human rights law for assuming an "interdependence of the male/female gender binary" that "empowers and privileges corresponding male subjectivities which are constituted as fully human, which includes the expectation that they provide protection for women".[111]

Finally, the theories from the margins I engage with argue that the fallacy of one point of view is well entrenched: even critical discourses within the currently dominant epistemological framework are based on strategies of alterization. As Escobar writes, "most accounts of identity in liberation discourses in philosophy and other fields have relied on postulating a foundational alterity and a transcendental subject that would constitute a radical alternative in relation to an equally homogenized modern/European/North American Other".[112] Yet identities are always heterogeneous and partial, and ontologies multiple and shifting, which is hardly acknowledged in international human rights. For many non-Western ontologies, the world can only be conceived as a pluriverse, not as a universe, as it is suggested by the title of the foundational document of modern international human rights law, the *Universal Declaration of Human Rights*. A commitment to a pluriverse implies recognizing that different perspectives exist in and about the world and, more profoundly, that there are multiple realities and different worlds that are "animated in different ways".[113]

3.3   White human rights? A dominant paradigm based on racial exclusions

It can be argued that the subject of human rights is defined, even if implicitly, by European understandings of race constructed largely by white people and

---

108 Simm, 375.
109 *Convention on the Elimination of All Forms of Discrimination against Women.*
110 Simm, 376.
111 Otto, 197.
112 Escobar, "Worlds and Knowledges Otherwise", 200.
113 Blaser, "Ontology and Indigeneity", 51.

against white standards.[114] According to Black studies scholarship, it is race, and Black slavery more specifically, that allowed the European white man to rise as the sole genuine subject that is free and has rights, thus monopolizing the claim to define humanness.[115] Similar arguments have been made by Indigenous author Robert A. Williams with respect to the construction of 'savages' in the history of the West, which were eventually personified by Indigenous peoples, hence allowing Europeans to affirm themselves as 'civilized'.[116] These dynamics can be directly related to the current international law framework: as the UN Special Rapporteur on contemporary forms of racism has maintained, international law did not only "allocate human rights on a racial basis", but it also played an active role in "consolidating and furthering global structures of racial domination and discrimination".[117] In this view, human rights have been developed on the basis of race and have contributed to entrenching exclusions.

Although Western understandings of the 'human' and discourses of human rights have evolved through time, they have arguably always been and are still founded on exclusions and led to and justified various forms of violence and domination. The worldview centred on the individual,[118] which underpins human rights, as demonstrated above, is not open to everyone. If exclusions may be grounded in sex, gender, class and other categorizations, race is the key criterion identified by several theories from the margins. Following Weheliye's definition, race and racial identities are understood here as

> ongoing sets of political relations that require, through constant perpetuation via institutions, discourses, practices, desires, infrastructures, languages, technologies, sciences, economies, dreams, and cultural artifacts, the barring of nonwhite subjects from the category of the human as it is performed in the modern west.[119]

From this perspective, race refers to socio-political processes that differentiate, hierarchize and hence separate humanity into exclusionary categories,

---

114 Sithole, 34. This also resonates with Indigenous critiques of international law. See for instance Anaya, 48, 52.
115 Z. I. Jackson, "Outer Worlds", 216–17.
116 Williams, 1, 8.
117 *Report of the Special Rapporteur on Contemporary Forms of Racism, Racial Discrimination, Xenophobia and Related Intolerance*, A/74/321, para 18.
118 It has been argued that nowadays, the Western world understands the 'human' in a primarily economic way: that is, to be recognized as a human being in "our breadwinner-democracy", one must be a member of the middle-class or the bourgeoisie. Wynter, "The Re-Enchantment of Humanism", 157.
119 Weheliye, 3–4.

such as full humans and nonhumans.[120] While racism is most often conceived in terms of skin colour, it is important to remember that the marker of difference can also be language, religion, or culture more generally.[121]

Race seems a particularly useful modality to analyse historical and ongoing political violence and dehumanization, and this lens also helps reveal important but underappreciated biases inherent to international human rights. Racial violence and discrimination can be seen as infusing all levels and spheres of life: thinking, acting and even ways of being.[122] For Weheliye, all aspects of the 'human' are racialized.[123] As it has been argued in the context of the United States, racism is not confined to the level of ideology but has been instrumental for the construction of the political economy and the definition of social classes.[124] Hierarchies based on race are integral to contemporary social and political relations[125] and may account for the suspension of legal protection. As Paul Gilroy writes:

> The old notions of racial and absolute ethnic difference that characterized nineteenth-century empires appear to be quietly active within the calculus that currently assigns differential value to lives lost according to their locations and supposed origins and considers that some abject human bodies are more easily and appropriately tortured, humiliated, imprisoned, shackled, starved, and destroyed than others.[126]

Fundamentally, race and racism are essential to white matters,[127] because they facilitated the creation and perpetuation of relations of domination and exploitation. Through imagined, enhanced and misinterpreted differences, racism has permitted the white body to conceive non-white people as inhuman, and to justify control over these people.[128] It is arguably the reformulation of human exceptionalism in colonial times that called upon the concept of race to justify a difference between what was seen as human and nonhuman and, at the same time, created a hierarchy between human beings. Wanting to move away from Descartes' split between mind and body, colonial stereotypical thinking forged the idea that human uprightness and

---

120 Santos and Sena Martins speak of "forms of sub-humanity". Santos & Sena Martins, 6–7. A middle category of 'not-quite-humans' or 'half-humans' is sometimes added; Indigenous peoples, for instance, as Wilderson says, are socially half-dead or half-alive. Wilderson, 23.
121 Reid, Cormack & Paine, 120.
122 Wilderson, 2.
123 Weheliye, 8.
124 Marable, 31.
125 Gilroy, *Against Race*, 1.
126 Gilroy, "Multiculture", 102.
127 Sithole, 26. See also Reid, Cormack & Paine, 120.
128 Mbembé, 17.

related cranial development explained human exceptionalism,[129] with the human cognitive abilities being a product of physical, and hence material, features. In particular, the size and shape of the head, and by implication of the brain, were used to assess these abilities.[130] The belief was that the more a being stood upright, the more its facial profile was vertical and the larger was its brain in relation to the sensory organs associated with smell and taste, two senses that were said to belong to the realm of animals. As a consequence, a new hierarchy was created based on biological features, with some human groups, namely white people, seen as superior to people of colour. Alleged racial differences between the Western subject and its 'Other' even led to what has been called modernity's "structure of terror".[131] In fact, the colonial project of Europe required and further entrenched the degradation and dehumanization of non-European 'Others', which allowed modernity to emerge, along with its very narrow conception of the thinking, rational, enlightened 'human'.[132] As Wynter has argued, Renaissance humanism radically split the human species in two: the West was able to "re-invent its *true Christian self* as that of Man only because, at the same time, Western discourses were also inventing the *untrue Other* of the Christian self, as that of Man's human Others".[133] In this sense, race does not refer to objective facts distinguishing different groups but is an object of knowledge that determines, through hierarchical power structures, who is considered a full human being.[134]

Following this reasoning, it can be argued that some human beings could dominate 'Others' who were considered inferior mainly because of their assumed lack of rationality: in the European hierarchy of human beings, white people were considered the most mentally developed and rational beings and hence superior to people of colour, with Black people being at the very bottom, below all other non-white people.[135] Individuals and groups of African descent were represented as non-evolved and even as the inferior 'Others' against whom Europeans could define themselves.[136] In this perspective, Black people are the ultimate 'Other' and constitute the prototype of abjection.[137] And while it does not seem helpful to engage in a discussion of a

129 Anderson, "Mind over Matter?", 7–8.
130 Anderson, "Mind over Matter?", 8.
131 Amparo Alves, 153 (referring to Spillers). It is important to be aware of the fact that invoking an 'Other' implies, to some extent, following the logic of Eurocentric thought (Walcott, 95); yet it seems at least equally important to reveal the dynamics of 'othering'.
132 David Scott in Wynter, "The Re-Enchantment of Humanism", 120.
133 Wynter, "The Re-Enchantment of Humanism", 175–6. Wynter uses 'Man' with a capital letter as a synonym of the 'human' conceived by Western modernity.
134 Weheliye, 19.
135 Wynter, "1492", 39.
136 Wynter, "1492", 37.
137 Walcott, 100–1.

potential hierarchy of oppression, the argument that the creation of the Black 'Other' paved the way for the creation of other 'Others' seems convincing. Indeed, in the contemporary context, including in human rights, the continuous exclusion of Black people should be seen as a significant – but not the only – iteration of the prevalent phenomenon of 'othering' that affects many other beings, including non-citizens and non-human beings, as previously discussed. Similarly, Indigenous people were seen as 'savages' who, at best, needed to be taught how to behave in a civilized manner or, at worst, could be erased.[138] Wynter actually argues that it was the idea of race, the "ultimate mode of otherness", that enabled the creation of other forms of 'Otherness'.[139] Race thus became the symbolic construct and the basis of the modern order,[140] which arguably explains both historical and contemporary forms of exclusion, including in international human rights.

Black studies scholars argue the West invented Blackness as a racial category to be able to conceive separately white enlightened humans as free, rights-bearing subjects, with white humans defined against (Black) slaves; in this colonial ordering, as Walcott maintains, the Black body became a commodity that could be – and still is – excluded from humanity.[141] These critiques have their roots in the intellectual traditions of African Americans, such as Frederick Douglass and Ida B. Wells, who fought for the abolition of slavery and civil rights. Yet even if Blackness was first developed in the wake of the European exploration of the African continent and the enslavement of African populations, the concept remains relevant, both because Blackness continues to signify exclusion and as an analytical tool that helps understand these exclusions. Indeed, the coloniality of being and its particular impact on Black people are pervasive and persist today.[142] While there may be numerous differences in being a Black person, including whether one lives, for instance, in the United States, the Caribbean, Europe or Africa,[143] some scholars argue that Blackness has also come to represent a community for people from Africa or African descent that is united by particular structural vulnerabilities.[144] For these scholars, the common experience for contemporary Black

---

138 Douzinas, "The Paradoxes of Human Rights", 53.
139 Wynter, "1492", 42.
140 Wynter, "1492", 34.
141 Walcott, 94–5.
142 Walcott, 94.
143 Moreover, it is interesting that the very notion of Blackness to refer to 'Otherness' has changed over time: for instance, while people from the former British colonies in Africa, Asia and the Caribbean were collectively called Blacks by the colonizers, the discourse is now more nuanced and communities are referred to as Hindu, Sikh, Muslim, etc. See Nimako, 60–1.
144 See Marshall. A major objective of Black studies has been to break with well-entrenched misconceptions regarding the alleged inferiority of Black people and to restore African social and intellectual heritage. Bobo, Hudley & Michel, 1.

people is hence not necessarily their skin colour; as Césaire already said, it is rather the fact that they constitute groups that were affected by some of the worst forms of violence in human history and that they continue to suffer from oppression:

> la Négritude . . . fait référence à quelque chose de plus profond, très exactement à une somme d'expériences vécues qui ont fini par définir et caractériser une des formes de l'humaine destinée telle que l'histoire l'a faite: c'est une des formes historiques de la condition faite à l'homme.[145]

Anti-Blackness is widespread and institutionalized, and Black people are often still considered less human in various and pernicious ways, which obviously also affects the enjoyment of their human rights. Black studies scholars denounce this anti-Black reality that is so deeply embedded in countless contemporary normativities that it is often overlooked. They argue that Blackness, because of its ongoing relevance for widespread exclusions, discrimination and human rights violations, must be analysed in the context of the history of the West, not as a phenomenon that is local or ethnographic. With respect to international human rights, the UN Special Rapporteur on contemporary forms of racism laments that "human rights analysis . . . is often ahistorical and colour-blind", meaning that the human rights framework treats all subjects of human rights in the same way and ignores the specific history and context of violence and human rights violations.[146] This is why she argues that the dominant approach does not genuinely challenge racial discrimination and the structures that enable exclusions on that basis.[147]

I believe that both the theoretical underpinnings and methodologies of Black studies can explain various forms of domination, exploitation and political violence and thus have the potential of being applied broadly, that is beyond human rights violations experienced by Black people, including to understand some of the fundamental reasons and dynamics behind the numerous and well-entrenched paradoxical exclusions in the field of human rights.[148] Most scholars working on Blackness do not deny the fact that many groups and individuals – that is not only Black people – are oppressed or face discrimination. Fanon, for instance, already emphasized that exploitation can take different forms but – in an evidently humanist perspective that

---

145 Césaire, Discours sur la Négritude, 80–1.
146 Report of the Special Rapporteur on Contemporary Forms of Racism, Racial Discrimination, Xenophobia and Related Intolerance: Global Extractivism and Racial Equality, A/HRC/41/54, para 14.
147 Report of the Special Rapporteur on Contemporary Forms of Racism, Racial Discrimination, Xenophobia and Related Intolerance: Global Extractivism and Racial Equality, A/HRC/41/54, para 14.
148 Weheliye, 3–4.

seems to ignore the exploitation of non-human beings – that it always targets a human being: "Toutes les formes d'exploitation se ressemblent . . . Toutes les formes d'exploitation sont identiques, car elles s'appliquent toutes à un même 'objet': l'homme".[149] As explained previously, contemporary forms of oppression often come in a modern attire of coloniality, which prevails, in particular, through neoliberal ideas related to individualism, ownership, identity and belonging, and whose impact is felt in the political, cultural and economic spheres. This has a tremendous impact on all groups, including, as in the North American context, Black, Indigenous and white people, and has contributed to creating a climate of competition between disadvantaged groups.[150] Some scholars working on Blackness nonetheless insist that the extent and the particular violence of Black slavery set it apart from other forms of exploitation.[151] And it is this historical discrimination of Black people that allowed the emergence of the free white human that continues to underpin human rights.

If Black slavery can be said to constitute, as forced labour, the basis of today's neoliberal economy for it allowed cheap and renewable labour for the formation and then the expansion of capitalism,[152] I argue it had another *raison d'être*: Black slaves were used – similarly to Indigenous people[153] – as a category of inferior beings against which white Europeans could erect themselves as pure and powerful subjects that hold rights. Put differently, slavery is the ontological basis of white societies, on which the modern human arose. Black studies scholars such as Walcott and Broeck claim that the self-empowerment of European men, and later of European women, was

---

149 Fanon, *Peau noire, masques blancs*, 71.

150 Walcott, 98. Walcott argues that these dominant notions have led to the creation of "relationships to capital that force, but also allow white and non-white groups to act within the historical legacies of colonial racial ordering". Ibid, 98–9.

151 For an analysis of the distinct character of slavery in opposition to other forms of exploitation and oppression as well as a historical overview of the phenomenon, see Patterson. The nature, scale and longevity of the Atlantic slave trade and plantation system in the United States and the Caribbean have impacted Black people to such an extent that they – and with them the concept of the human – have not fully recovered, even though the slave trade ended well more than a century ago. It may be useful to recall that an estimated 12.5 million Africans were forcibly transported to the Americas between the 16th and the 19th centuries. For detailed information and data, see the Trans-Atlantic Slave Trade Database. Importantly, according to Walcott, highlighting this specificity does not necessarily imply claiming that Black human beings are in a worse situation than Indigenous people, for instance; it rather points to the fact that "the Black body is the template of how the abjection by which the Human was produced . . . [and how] all non-white bodies are mastered into a project of disposability". Walcott, 100–1. Of note, some authors use the term "Human" with a capital letter to refer to the Western understanding of the 'human' and the fact that this understanding is imposed on others.

152 Walcott, 101–2.

153 Williams, 8–9.

enabled through transatlantic enslavism.[154] It seems that an 'Other' was needed to bring to an end to a social structure that legally kept the vast majority of the population in an everlasting position of subordination *vis-à-vis* the few who possessed the land. According to Fanon, in European culture the *nègre* had the function of incarnating the negative side of the human being, of representing bad or 'dark' feelings, thoughts and habits. Eurocentric culture projects on the Black body everything that the European tries to avoid being;[155] it symbolizes evil, misery, sins and war, which makes it the 'dark side' of the human soul: "[l]e péché est nègre comme la vertu est blanche".[156] The European subject therefore transformed this 'Other' into the incarnation of his own abject part.[157] Moreover, to become genuinely free in the context of the emergence of the new global economic system, one also had to possess this abject 'Other'. As Cheryl I. Harris has argued, "'Black racial identity marked who was subject to enslavement; 'white' racial identity marked who was 'free' or, at a minimum, not a slave".[158] This can be seen as another important reason why the European subject enslaved African populations and made them his property, and why freedom and slavery are inherently connected.

It is precisely the Black body's fungibility that secured and enhanced the superiority of the European man: turned into a commodity, the Black body is easily replaceable and, according to Saidita V. Hartman, acts as "an abstract and empty vessel vulnerable to the projection of others' feelings, ideas, desires, and values" and "as a sign of power and domination".[159] At the symbolic level, the slave ship and the plantation represent the free, unlimited and empowering form of violence through which white subjectivity was constructed and affirmed: as Broeck argues,

[t]he free citizen of Europe gained this very freedom, this "mastery" of his (and eventually her) destiny by the creation of a mental, physical, political, and social border around the free human, which was marked and maintained by the existence of the Black/"slave", by the free human subject's "n–."[160]

154 Broeck, 117; see also Walcott, 93–4.
155 Spillers, 155.
156 Fanon, *Peau noire, masques blancs*, 112. It is worth mentioning that the Black/white binary is, of course, a fairly recent invention in the West that is not necessarily shared by other traditions. See Pastoureau. For a discussion on Blackness as a supposed absence of colour and its meaning for Black life, see Moten.
157 Broeck, 118.
158 Harris, 1718.
159 Hartman, 21. Through the Black female body, the slave is also easy to reproduce. Sexton, 33. For a more detailed account of sexual violence against Black female slaves, see Hartman, 82–6.
160 Broeck, 119–20.

The structural violence exerted specifically against Black people since the beginning of modernity – compared to almost everyone in Europe in the Middle Ages – and which became a definitional marker of the Black being, was arguably a prerequisite for the emergence of modern discourses of emancipation, such as Marxism and feminism and, as I would add, of human rights.[161] Broeck has even argued that modernity divided the world in two categories: human beings on one side, and Black slaves on the other.[162] In the words of Sithole, "the human *qua* human is the ontological domain of Whiteness"[163] that stands in opposition to Blackness. Taken together, these ideas suggest that Black slavery, and Blackness more generally, allowed the European man to declare himself free and, perhaps more importantly, was hence instrumental in defining humanness as the term is still understood in the modern Western world.[164]

Because Black people were slaves owned by white people, they had no way of acceding to free subjectivity as conceived by Europeans,[165] and I would suggest this argument put forward by Broeck can be applied to the question of being a subject of human rights. As a result of this historical development, the existence of Black beings as human beings continues to be questioned in the context of human rights.[166] They are conceived as if they belonged nowhere, which makes them vulnerable to various forms of colonial violence and discrimination and related violations of their human rights. As noted above, the paradigmatic Black body is situated by some scholars at the ontological fringes of humanity,[167] as constantly being "out-of-place", because of white domination.[168]

Because their humanness is routinely denied, Black people – and arguably other non-white people too – do not exist in the way that the dominant subject of human rights does,[169] and since they do not exist, they can rarely enjoy their rights or make successful claims. This is particularly clear in the context of migration from the Global South to Western countries. If the right to claim asylum and the principle of *non-refoulement*, for instance, exist in theory,[170]

---

161 Wilderson, 20.

162 Broeck, 118.

163 Sithole, 30. Humanness is not necessarily limited to white people from Europe or European descent; Wilderson includes, for instance, Asians and Arabs into the "race of Humanism". Wilderson, 20.

164 Walcott, 93.

165 Broeck, 119.

166 Walcott, 93.

167 Sithole, 35.

168 Walcott, 97.

169 Sithole, 27. For the same reasons, the integration of Indigenous peoples into the capitalist economy or political life – as a form of justice for past prejudices – cannot bring genuine recognition of the Indigenous being.

170 For a useful analysis, see Fischer-Lescano & Löhr.

the barriers that have been erected in particular by Western states and re-lated pushback operations, arbitrary detention and ill-treatment to prevent migrants from the Global South to even enter their territory, show that these rights are often meaningless in practice.[171] The conditions in refugee camps in northern Africa and Europe discussed in the second chapter are another stark illustration of the fact that many humans are not considered full sub-jects of human rights. While these conditions have, of course, been criticized by human rights organizations and, in the case of camps on European soil, found to violate the European Convention on Human Rights,[172] the actual experience of those detained proves that the very idea of human rights often remains almost entirely abstract in this context. The success of certain ap-plications, as for instance to the European Court of Human Rights with re-spect to the prohibition of inhuman and degrading treatment under article 3 of the European Convention on Human Rights, confirms that these rights violations do occur, but such successful cases are rare and, as I would argue, should not hide the persisting systematic violation of non-Western migrants' human rights and inaccessibility of human rights to these migrants.

It is hardly surprising that anti-Blackness, and anti-'Otherness' more generally, still exists in endless forms today, and that effective remedies are difficult to imagine. Human rights, as discussed, are rooted in so-called hu-manist and universal values and ideas that are supposed to provide justice but that embrace the same racist biases as the dominant conception of the human itself. It is, in particular, the insight that Black slavery facilitated the emergence of the free, rights-bearing European subject that reveals one of the profound conceptual shortcomings that the contemporary human rights system continues to bear. According to this interpretation, the modern state and political community are based on 'othering', and continue to conceive Black people and arguably many 'Others', as discussed, as "outlawed, ab-ject, and non-human",[173] for whom human rights remain empty and justice a fantasy.[174] It is, as I argue, this well-entrenched idea of a certain human that continues to underlie human rights – and determines who is a full or genu-ine subject who can benefit from human rights – that explains not only the routine violation of their rights but also why attempts made within the domi-nant paradigm of humanism and human rights to redress this situation have largely failed. This suggests that trying to meet Black people's ontological

171 Pro Asyl, *pushed back*. While particularly striking in the context of Western countries, dis-crimination and severe human rights violations of migrants also take place in non-Western countries. See, for instance, Human Rights Watch, "Saudi Arabia".
172 For an overview of judicial decisions, see European Court of Human Rights. For a report on detention conditions in Greece, see Pro Asyl, *Walls of Shame*.
173 Amparo Alves, 145, 147.
174 Amparo Alves, 147.

demands, or "ontological sovereignty",[175] would require a different strategy. Indeed, even if slavery may have been abolished, the humanness of Black people – and of other 'Others' – has arguably never been fully recognized. To the contrary, the system has continued to be based on and operate with the unavowed continuation of white superiority and domination.[176]

3.4 Embracing the plurality of knowledge and being: the figure of *migrating 'Others'*

In light of the critique of Western thought and ways of living as being based on and having entrenched various forms of domination and exclusion, the unsustainability of the Western model seems undeniable, which is why theories from the margins call for change. Taking up the insights suggested by these theories requires, as a start, a perpetual decolonization of knowledge[177] and shifting "the locus of enunciation" from the white man to other perspectives in order to enable a more complex and representative understanding of the world, or rather worlds, and to achieve greater justice.[178] Crucially, considering that the idea of a linear history, or of moving progressively from old to new, is part of the unhelpful legacy of Western modernity, what theories from the margins demand is not an entirely new paradigm, but *another* one that builds on existing alternative worldviews.[179]

The possibility of change

The theories from the margins that I have discussed do not suggest making cosmetic modifications to a necessarily simplifying universal, grand theory about the world; they all call for fundamental changes. They demand new socio-economic and institutional arrangements, progress in terms of nonmaterial human fulfillment, interconnectedness, dematerialized production, and emphasis on values such as solidarity and community.[180] These changes also affect human rights and how they are imagined and implemented. An example consists in the inclusion of the rights of nature, such as Pachamama as

---

175 Wynter, "The Re-Enchantment of Humanism", 136. In this perspective, the very idea of human rights hinges on Black social death, which means that changing the system from within could never satisfy the ontological demands of Black people. While most so-called Afro-pessimist scholars do not specifically address the idea of human rights, it should be noted that critical race theory, or "blackcrit theory", has analysed the role of race and racial dimensions of the structure and operation of the international human rights system. For an overview, see Lewis.

176 Sexton, 35.

177 Mignolo, "Further Thoughts on Decoloniality", 26.

178 Grosfoguel, 216.

179 Escobar, "Worlds and Knowledges Otherwise", 180.

180 Escobar, *Encountering Development*, xxii.

an earth-being that has rights, in some Latin American constitutions, which hence perceive nature as an inevitable subject and disrupt dominant ontologies and conceptions of what is political.[181] The belief shared by theories from the margins in the possibility and necessity of change stands in contrast to the currently dominant paradigm, which arguably cannot envisage any genuine alternative. Theories from the margins, as noted by Escobar for instance, suggest other epistemologies to imagine "*an altogether different world*"[182] that is not grounded on the major narratives of Western modernity, such as liberalism and Marxism.[183] They argue persuasively that there is a crucial need to go beyond Western critiques of the modern paradigm, since these critiques are always and inherently limited. As for humanism and associated discourses, they need to take their own historical and contemporary racial biases more seriously.[184]

Such a radical change of paradigm would, of course, have important consequences for the human rights system, since it would require a significant reconceptualization or even abandoning the idea of human rights altogether. As I have argued, human rights are naturally highly dependent on the 'human' – an exclusionary figure – and humanist values; non-white bodies, in particular, reveal the inherent shortcomings and failures of the current system. An intrinsically biased system, which has been constructed on fallacious universals and in deeply problematic opposition to an 'Other', cannot simply include this 'Other', and therefore seems hardly salvageable. In this perspective, rejecting the pervasive logic of belonging and the deceptive discourses of rights and freedoms could contribute to generating new social relationships and ways of being human beyond the (post)modern paradigm.[185] Yet the existence and knowledge of non-white bodies also stress the numerous possibilities of a reinvented concept of the human. Césaire actually argued that the West has never lived a true humanism,[186] meaning one in which all

---

181 Blaser, "Ontology and Indigeneity", 51; Escobar, *Encountering Development*, xxviii.
182 Escobar, *Encountering Development*, xx.
183 Escobar, "Worlds and Knowledges Otherwise", 180.
184 Walcott, 7. Even posthumanist approaches are, in fact, conservative in regard to their engagement with other ontologies, since membership is extended solely to what the West can understand. See Blaser, "Ontology and Indigeneity", 50–1. As an example, the posthumanist approaches discussed above focus on those more-than-human entities that make sense to Western, liberal and secular thought and fit into ontological categories that are considered legitimate. Gods and other spiritual creatures, for instance, are not seriously considered. But for many other ontologies, such as many Indigenous ones, these entities are central. By way of example, "Country" is such an inescapable subject and indisputably part of the web of relationships for Aboriginals in Northern Australia that it even deserves to be the lead author of a series of academic articles on Indigenous ontologies. See Bawaka Country. For a detailed account of the importance of creation stories, see McGregor, 74–7.
185 Walcott, 103.
186 Césaire, *Discours sur le colonialisme*, 68.

human beings could live without oppression, and that it would be somewhat premature to abandon humanism and its concepts and values. Understanding the full meaning and repertoire of the human and subjectivity have
even been highlighted as a core task for human rights law, which should be
open to the idea of a heterogeneity of values, precisely to allow developing
a more expansive conception of the human,[187] or, in a less anthropocentric
approach, of being more generally. In this perspective, Fanon's call for a radically new humanism[188] could be taken up in order to imagine a less white – in
fact, non-racial – and hence more inclusive version of humanism and human
rights.

Inspired by theories from the margins, I suggest that to reinvent, or rather
re-configure, its subject, the system of human rights – or any alternative system that may or may not hold similar claims to universality – can turn to a
rich and already available repertoire of ways of being and knowing.[189] It is
possible to build on alternative approaches that have been oppressed in the
modern world and that offer other ways of being, thinking, knowing and, as
I will discuss in more detail in the next chapters, of sensing. Different peoples
and philosophies have, indeed, been developing their own ways for a long
time. In Mark Jackson's words, "[w]e need to recognize that other people,
other philosophies, other worlds, and other ideas have been making similar
claims on wider ecological relations for hundreds, sometimes tens of thousands, of years, and crucially, in critical ways".[190] The long history of violence, including at the ontological and epistemic levels and against non-white
people in particular, has had dramatic consequences that are still felt today,
but it has not annihilated these people.[191] Indigenous cosmologies, for instance, have been brutally disrupted but not destroyed. Certain Indigenous
ceremonies were outlawed in settler states, with the objective of stripping
Indigenous peoples of their distinct identity and membership by destroying
their ways of living. Yet, they were still practised in secret: in Canada, for
instance, Indigenous peoples managed to sustain the tradition of potlatches,
which are festive events – and integral to governing – that strengthen social
cohesion through the exchange of gifts and distribution of wealth, although
they were criminalized through the *Indian Act* from the 1880s to 1951.[192]
Despite very oppressive state practices, Indigenous cultures still exist, and
their traditions and ways of living could be – and have been – maintained and

---

187 Butler, *Precarious Life*, 91.
188 Fanon, *Les damnés de la terre*, 301–5.
189 Weheliye, 12.
190 Jackson, M., xii.
191 See for instance Napoleon, "Individual Self and Collective Selves", 37.
192 On the relevant changes in the Canadian *Indian Act*, see Treaties and Historical Research
    Centre. See also University of British Columbia.

revived.[193] Similarly, Blackness has never been entirely passive: Black people have always resisted oppression in numerous, if oftentimes small, ways.[194] Even in times of slavery, as Weheliye argues, there were "minuscule movements, glimmers of hope, scraps of food, the interrupted dreams of freedom found in those spaces deemed devoid of full human life".[195] Black slaves always found some way of contesting desocialization, for instance through a particular cherishing of kin relations that were, under slave law, considered illegitimate.[196] They also managed to retain, to a certain extent, their own perspectives *vis-à-vis* time and their selves, and to express their humanness in various ways, such as through music and bodies that were legally owned by white "masters".[197] In other words, different conceptions of the human than the dominant Eurocentric one have survived the structural violence of Black slavery and colonialism; the insistence of Black and colonized people to defend their own humanness has, in fact, always influenced the dominant conception of the human.[198] The so-called socially dead are not entirely dead, and considering them alive enables a panoply of possibilities, which would also bring us closer to imagining the 'human' in all its ontological complexity,[199] and to transcend the idea of an exclusive subject of human rights.

Regarding (neo)liberal discourses of individual rights, agency and development, a range of alternative theories and understandings regarding ecology, culture and spirituality also already exists. The above-mentioned enshrinement of the rights of nature in some constitutions represents an important shift from an individual-anthropological to a relational and even biocentric perspective,[200] in which nature is considered a subject and the self is understood as interconnected with the environment. The concept of *sumac kawsay* in Quechua (or *buen vivir* in Spanish) is perhaps an even more important departure from the dominant individualistic and development-oriented paradigm, which arguably also breaks with prominent phenomenological accounts, such as those put forward by Césaire and Fanon, that – while important and groundbreaking at the time – overly depend on a notion of the human and human experience and are hence exclusionary. *Sumac kawsay/ buen vivir* is rooted in non-linear cosmovisions of Indigenous peoples that

193 Mignolo, "Further Thoughts on Decoloniality", 43. See also Borrows, "Indigenous Constitutionalism", 17.
194 As Césaire already noted in *Discours sur la Négritude*, 84.
195 Weheliye, 12.
196 Patterson, 337.
197 Mbembé, 22. To name just a few well-known examples, jazz and Black literature emerged as ways of contesting white supremacy and contributed in a positive manner to humanity in a general sense. Walcott, 104.
198 Walcott, 94.
199 Weheliye, 32.
200 Escobar, *Encountering Development*, xxvi.

elevate ecological criteria, dignity and social justice over economic development.[201] The focus on the present moment and not the future, yet without compromising the well-being of future generations, which is another feature of many Indigenous cosmovisions, also radically breaks with the Western notion of development.[202] *Buen vivir* is an opportunity to envisage and construct collectively new forms of being and knowing.

Decolonizing knowledge

I contend that theories from the margins are highly relevant because they question dominant discourses and categories of knowledges, languages, actors and institutions,[203] and because they propose to engage in meaningful dialogue.[204] They usefully point out that there are various coexisting geopolitical struggles and ontological conflicts, and that the West – even critical, sensitized and well-intentioned scholars, as within posthumanism – cannot speak for others. The Western imaginary of Indigeneity, for instance, cannot replace Indigenous ontologies, because Indigenous ontologies and Western conceptions of Indigeneity and of Indigenous ontologies are different things.[205] By way of example, Western scholars and policy-makers tend to focus on land and territory, and to conceive of the relationship of humans with land and territory in terms of rights and ownership; other ways to imagine this relationship and other fundamental social aspects, such as family relationships and the ways in which children are raised, are usually left aside. Sarah de Leeuw asks pointedly: "Why does so much research about Indigeneity and ontology . . . remain fundamentally tied to ecology, ecosystems, land, or macro-scale geographies and not attuned to Indigenous children's bodies and homes?"[206] In fact, even the meaning of the term ontology is contested by some Indigenous scholars. For these scholars, to speak of Indigenous ontologies is the equivalent of playing the colonial game; as Emilie Cameron, Sarah de Leeuw and Caroline Desbiens note, "they are wary of how Indigenous knowledges, beliefs, and practices are represented and mobilized within colonial structures of knowledge production".[207] Therefore, it would be important to work simultaneously towards the disavowal of the hegemonic

---

201 Escobar, *Encountering Development*, xxvi.
202 Blaser, "Life Projects", 38.
203 Mignolo, "Further Thoughts on Decoloniality", 39.
204 Maldonado-Torres, 261.
205 Hunt, 28.
206 de Leeuw, 60.
207 Cameron, de Leeuw & Desbiens, 19. As Sundberg maintains, even "geographical engagements with posthumanism tend to reproduce colonial ways of knowing and being by enacting universalizing claims and, consequently, further subordinating other ontologies". Sundberg, 34.

discourse and ontology and, in Mignolo's words, towards "inscribing an ontology that corresponds with the experience of the victims of patriarchal masculinity and racism – building and rebuilding worlds not based on economic success and heroic leadership, but on communal and decolonial love".[208] Listening and engaging in genuine dialogue hence also means that different ways of being and knowing must be recognized on their own terms.

It is worth noting that some of the conceptual ways in which colonialism was resisted were also limiting, which is why they, too, might need to undergo a process of decolonization. Maybe as a result of the coloniality of knowledge, most liberation movements in Africa first followed a revolutionary logic imposed by modernity, instead of looking for real alternatives to the Eurocentric model.[209] It has been argued that negritude, for instance, was not a re-imagination of Africans by Africans outside the Eurocentric perspective; among others, it reproduced the same dichotomy based on 'race' that had been imposed by colonialism.[210] This can easily be explained by the omnipresence of colonialism and hegemonic discourses: colonized peoples were victims of various and complex technologies of subjectivation, including the strategic re-invention of African concepts and values to facilitate colonial governance and more recent discourses of human rights and democracy. As a result, they integrated parts of the imperialist and colonialist logic, as if they saw themselves as lacking something and as having to catch up.[211] As Sabelo Ndlovu-Gatsheni writes,

> [t]he attempts by Africans to construct, name, and represent themselves have remained hostage to invented colonial discourses, Western racial templates that were developed during the age of colonial encounters, and African counter-discourses that were finding it difficult to free their liberatory episteme from the immanent logic of colonial racism.[212]

It has therefore been suggested that, in order to realize their full potential, all those who are not considered full subjects in the dominant modern paradigm ought to detach themselves (and their own conception of themselves) from Eurocentric thinking and actively reject concepts like freedom, justice, equality and even human rights that only speak to "White liberal sensitivities" and contribute to exclusion and oppression.[213] In this perspective,

208 Mignolo, "Further Thoughts on Decoloniality", 38.
209 Ndlovu-Gatsheni, 27.
210 Ndlovu-Gatsheni, 39.
211 Ndlovu-Gatsheni, 106–7, 227. Fanon most famously theorized these dynamics and their implications for the construction of one's identity and subjectivity in his *Peau noire, masques blancs*.
212 Ndlovu-Gatsheni, 104.
213 Sithole, 25.

instead of participating in politics of resistance or affirmation – which are illusionary – those who are excluded or marginalized should engage in politics of antagonism and put forward their own ontology to be recognized as full human beings.[214] They must have their own register,[215] their own episteme. While this approach may appear rather prescriptive, it is certainly important to recognize that there are alternatives to the imposed negative representation of non-white people as always lacking intelligence, development and democracy.

Decoloniality means, indeed, that marginalized perspectives are rendered visible and audible in their own terms, and in a way that forces dominant approaches to engage with them, to be open to different interpretations and to appreciate that identities are complex and evolve.[216] It can even be argued that to move beyond conceptions of the human that are based on citizenship and that are built in opposition to the non-human animal and also exclude many humans, humanity can only be viewed through a radically altered lens. Zakiyyah Iman Jackson maintains that "an anamorphic view *of* humanity, a queering of perspective and stance that mutates the racialized terms of Man's praxis of humanism" is needed.[217] As discussed above, posthumanism, for instance, usefully decentres the human, but it needs to integrate insights from the Global South to highlight the dramatic implications of race and gender.[218] This shows, once again, that liberal humanist concepts cannot easily be expanded to include further subjects; in this case, it is the concept of the human that must undergo significant change or that must be displaced and replaced by another concept.

It is quite possible that other paradigms that could replace the currently dominant one can only come from the margins; real radicality can arguably only come from those that have been oppressed. In Mark Jackson's words, it is

> at the boundaries, in the "between spaces", in negotiating the questions difference makes to decentring ideas of the human, and to re-defining stories of humanness, that there are significant discursive overlaps and potentials for concepts to be created, [and] bridges built.[219]

Several authors working with and further developing the theories from the margins hence ask how the world would be if the margins were to become the locus of enunciation.

---

214 Sithole, 38. See also Amparo Alves, 154.
215 Sithole, 26.
216 Ndlovu-Gatsheni, 129. See also Escobar, *Encountering Development*, xxx.
217 Z. I. Jackson, "Outer Worlds", 217.
218 Z. I. Jackson, "Animal", 673. As Jackson notes, posthumanism is beginning to open itself to critiques focused on "race, gender, sexuality and dis/ability". Ibid, 674.
219 M. Jackson, 9.

Shifting the locus of enunciation and valuing plurality

Theories from the margins propose to dislodge the dominant and hegemonic forms of knowledge and practices that stem from what is still perceived as the centre,[220] which has obvious consequences for the dominant subject in Western legal thought. Interestingly, this has already been taken up by some theorists from the Global North who are aware of and question the dominant Western epistemology. As Santos, for instance, has argued, it is imperative to go South and to learn from the South.[221] Comaroff and Comaroff similarly point out that historical processes have always involved both the core and the peripheries; it is the populations in the Global South that have been the first and most affected by decisions made by the West; and there are already relevant theories in the Global South, including with respect to what the North is experiencing.[222] Those who have been silenced should finally be considered as producing knowledge.[223] To cite Mark Jackson again, "[o]ther ways of life, other languages, other forms of social interaction, prove extremely insightful and resilient, perhaps because they frame human exceptional capacities and ecological relationships in profoundly different ways".[224] Such a decolonial perspective is an invitation – or suggests a responsibility for dominant actors – to think of modernity from a variety of epistemic positions and experiences, particularly of those who suffered and still suffer from coloniality, to consider the mechanisms that have allowed such suffering and erasing, and to start a dialogue between different beings.[225]

Indeed, life can be embraced in all its forms and can be considered holistically. Instead of creating artificial distinctions and categories, the ontological, the cultural, the political, the social, the ecological and the spiritual can be understood as inherently related and inseparable dimensions of life.[226] Indigeneity, for instance, is much more than a theoretical concept and is not fixed in ways that would make sense in a Western epistemological or ontological frame; it is also lived and practiced.[227] For many Indigenous peoples,

220 Mignolo, "Introduction – Coloniality of Power and De-Colonial Thinking", 160.
221 Santos, *Epistemologies of the South*.
222 Comaroff & Comaroff, chapter 1. On the influence of Indigenous peoples on Western thought, and more specifically in the context of anthropology, see Wilner.
223 Maldonado-Torres, 261–2.
224 M. Jackson, 9. Some authors have already tried to make this shift towards the South: the Comaroffs and Ndlovu-Gatsheni, for instance, make Africa the locus of enunciation and show that the continent has always been a striving epistemic site. Comaroff & Comaroff; Ndlovu-Gatsheni. Various movements in the Global South could, in fact, be considered through this lens. For a concrete example of shifting the locus by considering Rastafari as a "culture of decolonization", see McPherson, 355.
225 For an early example of considering human rights from the perspective of those who have been historically oppressed, see Baxi, "From Human Rights to the Right to Be Human".
226 Escobar, *Encountering Development*, xxi.
227 Hunt, 29.

intellectual life and everyday life are entangled, and knowledge production happens at different levels. Theory cannot be separated from life: life includes theory, and theory also concerns life. As in other worldviews, 'facts' and events, thoughts and feelings are all relevant. This is exemplified by the human and more-than-human collective that calls itself Bawaka Country, and for which ontology and research are relational, and everything is knowledgeable and interconnected. Human beings and their environment – the land, broadly speaking – mutually influence each other. Significantly, the land not only refers to territory that could be possessed or inhabited in a Western sense; it encompasses "all the beings (human and nonhuman, corporeal and non-corporeal), processes, affects, songs, dreams and relationships".[228] Contrary to the dominant Western humanist perspective, humans are a part but not the centre of the universe, or cosmos: "Humans are part of Country along with the mullet, the tides, the moon, the songs and the stories, along with the spirits, the plants and animals, the feelings and dreams".[229] Recognizing that everything is constituted as part of a web of relationships and that everything is always changing and in the process of "becoming together",[230] means attending, listening, feeling and so on in order to understand oneself, to care and to interact.[231]

The ontological violence inflicted by Eurocentric epistemologies, which has long affected and still affects all aspects of life, needs to be exposed and opposed both in scholarship and everyday life. And while it is difficult to pinpoint with precision everything that counts as part of a process of decolonization, this process must start by focusing on what decolonization implies for oneself.[232] In the context of human rights, this implies that all actors involved, including human rights experts, practitioners and advocates, ought to be aware of who they are, how they think and what they do. In Mignolo's words, as it is worth recalling, decolonial thinking is simultaneously "a way of being, thinking, doing, and becoming in the world".[233] Sundberg, who writes from a Western point of view but has usefully articulated these ideas, argues that one has to recognize one's locus of enunciation – as Arendt already recognized and put in practice by integrating her own story and experiences into her analysis of refugees and human rights – and eventually take responsibility for one's own biases and assumptions, including at the ontological and epistemological levels.[234] Furthermore, in a holistic approach, it

---

228 Bawaka Country, "Working with and Learning from Country", 270–1.
229 Bawaka Country, "Working with and Learning from Country", 273.
230 Bawaka Country, "Working with and Learning from Country", 275. As Blaser notes, Indigenousness is also always in the making. Blaser, "'Way of Life' or 'Who Decides'", 54.
231 Bawaka Country, "Working with and Learning from Country", 275.
232 Mignolo, "Further Thoughts on Decoloniality", 35–8.
233 Mignolo, "Further Thoughts on Decoloniality", 33.
234 Sundberg, 34–5.

is by doing that one knows, and this active knowing brings about responsibilities; it brings about an ethics of care[235] or, in other words, solidarity, responsiveness, respect and trust, and responsibility to each other to ensure this co-becoming.[236]

The recognition that coexistence with others, whether they are human or non-human animals and entities, is a reality that requires collaborative and active dialogue in various forms hence emerges as a key point. Conceiving beings in relation with one another would reveal and contribute to addressing various dynamics of domination.[237] Acknowledging the importance of diversity and difference would indeed contribute to decolonizing subjectivity and to the liberation of suppressed or silenced modes of knowledge production.[238] This would arguably be beneficial for all beings and could also contribute to re-humanizing the colonizer.[239] Importantly, building bridges and engaging in dialogue does not imply rendering equal; difference always remains valuable.[240] As discussed above, the idea of a plurality of human voices and its significance were already recognized by Arendt (although, when assessed through a contemporary lens, in a less radical manner than what some theories from the margins suggest), and posthumanist writers have highlighted the plurality of life forms more generally. Moreover, for theories from the margins, each worldview is and, in fact, can remain unique: "The beauty and the promise of life projects is that they trace a possible path towards the idea of unity in diversity".[241] There is a "heterogeneity of heterogeneous assemblages", where each assemblage, or world, constitutes itself in relation to other worlds.[242] This heterogeneity calls for political openness and sensitivity, for a recognition of and genuine commitment to the plurality of knowledges and beings, to the pluriverse.

I would argue that to embody this commitment to the plurality of knowledges and beings as well as the possibility of change and the decolonization of knowledge, the figure of the *migrating 'Other'* suggested above needs further refinement. Since the key aspect of plurality should also be captured in the name of the figure, I propose, as a further variation, the plural form *migrating 'Others'*. With this figure, I seek to capture the great diversity of being in and experiencing the world, beyond a specific mode or model that dominates, silences and ultimately suppresses others. Reconceptualizing the

235 Bawaka Country, "Co-Becoming Bawaka", 467.
236 Bawaka Country, "Working with and Learning from Country", 278; Sundberg, 41.
237 Weheliye, 13.
238 Quijano, 177.
239 On the dehumanizing effect of colonization on the colonizer, see Césaire, *Discours sur le colonialisme*, 18. See also Fanon, *Peau noire, masques blancs*, 48.
240 M. Jackson, 5.
241 Blaser, "Life Projects", 35.
242 Blaser, "Ontology and Indigeneity", 51, 55.

currently dominant subject of international human rights along the lines of this figure, which is inspired by the combined insights of the theories from the margins that I have discussed, namely decoloniality, Black and Indigenous approaches, could arguably contribute to ending epistemic violence and to creating a more just world, or rather worlds, where rights are not the privilege of a few.

Bibliography

African Charter on Human and Peoples' Rights (adopted on 27 June 1981, entered into force 21 October 1986) 1520 UNTS 217.

Alston, Philip. "Making Space for a New Human Rights: The Case of the Right to Development" (1988) 1 *Harvard Human Rights Yearbook* 3.

Amparo Alves, Jaime. "Neither Humans nor Rights: Some Notes on the Double Negation of Black Life in Brazil" (2014) 45:2 *Journal of Black Studies* 143.

Anaya, James. *Indigenous Peoples in International Law* (Oxford: Oxford University Press, 2004).

Anderson, Kay. "Mind over Matter? On Decentring the Human in Human Geography" (2014) 21:1 *Cultural Geographies* 3.

Araújo, Marta & Silvia R. Maeso. "The Power of Racism in Academia: Knowledge Production and Political Disputes" in Boaventura de Sousa Santos & Bruno Sena Martins, eds, *The Pluriverse of Human Rights: The Diversity of Struggles for Dignity* (New York: Routledge, 2021) 186.

Bawaka Country. "Working with and Learning from Country: Decentring Human Authority" (2015) 22:2 *Cultural Geography* 269.

———. "Co-Becoming Bawaka: Towards a Relational Understanding of Place/Space" (2016) 40:4 *Progress in Human Geography* 455.

Baxi, Upendra. "From Human Rights to the Right to Be Human: Some Heresies" (1986) 13:3/4 *India International Centre Quarterly* 185.

Blaser, Mario. "Life Projects: Indigenous Peoples' Agency and Development" in Mario Blaser, Harvey A. Feit & Glenn McRea, eds, *In the Way of Development: Indigenous Peoples, Life Projects, and Globalization* (New York: Zed Books, 2004) 26.

———. "'Way of Life' or 'Who Decides': Development, Paraguayan Indigenism and the Yshiro People's Life Projects" in Mario Blaser, Harvey A. Feit & Glenn McRea, eds, *In the Way of Development: Indigenous Peoples, Life Projects, and Globalization* (New York: Zed Books, 2004) 52.

———. "Ontology and Indigeneity: On the Political Ontology of Heterogeneous Assemblages" (2014) 21:1 *Cultural Geographies* 49.

Bobo, Jacqueline, Cynthia Hudley & Claudine Michel. "Introduction" in Jacqueline Bobo, Cynthia Hudley & Claudine Michel, eds, *The Black Studies Reader* (New York: Routledge, 2004).

Borrows, John. "Uncertain Citizens: Aboriginal Peoples and the Supreme Court" (2001) 80 *Canadian Bar Review* 15.

———. "Indigenous Constitutionalism: Pre-Existing Legal Genealogies in Canada" in Peter Oliver, Patrick Macklem & Nathalie Des Rosiers, eds, *The Oxford Handbook of the Canadian Constitution* (Oxford: Oxford University Press, 2017).

Broeck, Sabine. "Legacies of Enslavism and White Abjectorship" in Sabine Broeck & Carsten Junker, eds, *Postcoloniality – Decoloniality – Black Critique – Joints and Fissures* (Frankfurt: Campus Verlag, 2014) 109.

Bunch, Charlotte. "Women's Rights as Human Rights: Toward a Re-Vision of Human Rights" (1990) 12 *Human Rights Quarterly* 486.

Butler, Judith. *Precarious Life* (London: Verso, 2004).

Cameron, Emilie, Sarah de Leeuw & Caroline Desbiens. "Indigeneity and Ontology" (2014) 21:1 *Cultural Geographies* 19.

Césaire, Aimé. *Discours sur le colonialisme* (Paris: Présence africaine, 1955).

———. Discours sur la Négritude in Aimé Césaire, ed, *Discours sur le colonialisme, Suivi de Discours sur la Négritude* (Paris: Présence africaine, 2000).

Comaroff, Jean & John L. Comaroff. *Theories from the South: Or, How Euro-America Is Evolving toward Africa* (Boulder, CO: Paradigm Publishers, 2012).

Convention on the Elimination of All Forms of Discrimination against Women (adopted on 18 December 1979, entered into force 3 September 1981) 1249 UNTS 13.

Davis, Elizabeth. "Structures of Seeing: Blindness, Race, and Gender in Visual Culture" (2019) 14:1 *The Senses and Society* 63.

de Leeuw, Sarah. "State of Care: The Ontologies of Child Welfare in British Columbia" (2014) 21:1 *Cultural Geographies* 59.

Douzinas, Costas. "The Paradoxes of Human Rights" (2013) 20:1 *Constellations* 51.

El-Hadi, Nehal. "Harlem on the Prairies: How Blackness Is Harmfully Used as Shorthand" (15 April 2021) *CBC News*, <www.cbc.ca/news/canada/saskatchewan/black-on-the-prairies-harlem-1.5986189>.

Escobar, Arturo. "Worlds and Knowledges Otherwise – The Latin American Modernity/Coloniality Research Program" (2007) 21:2–3 *Cultural Studies* 179.

———. *Encountering Development: The Making and Unmaking of the Third World* (Princeton, NJ: Princeton University Press, 2012).

European Court of Human Rights. "Factsheet – Migrants in Detention" (March 2021), <www.echr.coe.int/Documents/FS_Migrants_detention_ENG.pdf>.

Fanon, Frantz. *Peau noire, masques blancs* (Paris: Les Éditions du Seuil, 1952).

———. *Les damnés de la terre* (Paris: La Découverte, 2002).

Gilroy, Paul. *Against Race: Imagining Political Culture beyond the Color Line* (Cambridge, MA: Harvard University Press, 2000).

———. "Multiculture and the Negative Dialectics of Conviviality" in Rebecka Rutledge Fisher & Jay Garcia, eds, *Retrieving the Human: Reading Paul Gilroy* (Albany, NY: SUNY Press, 2014).

Grosfoguel, Ramón. "The Epistemic Decolonial Turn – Beyond Political-Economy Paradigms" (2007) 21:2–3 *Cultural Studies* 211.

Harris, Cheryl I. "Whiteness as Property" (1993) 106:8 *Harvard Law Review* 1707.

Hartman, Saidita V. *Scenes of Subjection – Terror, Slavery, and Self-making in Nineteenth-Century America* (New York: Oxford University Press, 1997).

Holder, Cindy L. & Jeff J. Corntassel. "Indigenous Peoples and Multicultural Citizenship: Bridging Collective and Individual Rights" (2002) 24:1 *Human Rights Quarterly* 126.

Human Rights Watch. "Saudi Arabia: Mass Killings of Migrants at Yemen Border" (21 August 2023), <www.hrw.org/news/2023/08/21/saudi-arabia-mass-killings-migrants-yemen-border>.

Hunt, Sarah. "Ontologies of Indigeneity: The Politics of Embodying a Concept" (2014) 21:1 *Cultural Geographies* 27.

International Covenant on Civil and Political Rights (adopted on 16 December 1966, entered into force 23 March 1976) 999 UNTS 171.

Jackson, Mark, ed. *Postcolonialism, Posthumanism and Political Ontology* (London: Routledge, 2017).

Jackson, Zakiyyah Iman. "Animal: New Directions in the Theorization of Race and Posthumanism" (2013) 39:3 *Feminist Studies* 669.

———. "Outer Worlds: The Persistence of Race in Movement 'Beyond the Human'" (2015) 21:2–3 *Gay and Lesbian Quarterly* 215.

Kennedy, David. "Spring Break" (1984) 63 *Texas Law Review* 1377.

Kuokkanen, Rauna. "What Is Hospitality in the Academy? Epistemic Ignorance and the (Im)Possible Gift" (2008) 30:1 *Review of Education, Pedagogy, and Cultural Studies* 60.

Lewis, Hope. "Reflections on 'BlackCrit' Theory: Human Rights" (2000) 45 *Villanova Law Review* 1975.

MacIntyre, Alasdair. *Whose Justice? Which Rationality?* (Notre Dame, IN: University of Notre Dame Press, 2020).

Maldonado-Torres, Nelson. "On the Coloniality of Being – Contributions to the Development of a Concept" (2007) 21:2–3 *Cultural Studies* 240.

Marable, Manning. "Black Studies and the Racial Mountain" (2000) 2:3 *Souls: Critical Journal of Black Politics & Culture* 17.

Marks, Stephen. "The Human Right to Development: Between Rhetoric and Reality" (2004) 17 *Harvard Human Rights Journal* 137.

Marshall, Stephen H. "The Political Life of Fungibility" (2012) 15:3 *Theory and Event* (no page).

Mbembé, Achille. "Necropolitics" (2003) 15:1 *Public Culture* 11.

McGoldrick, Dominic. "The Development and Status of Sexual Orientation Discrimination under International Human Rights Law" (2016) 16:4 *Human Rights Law Review* 613.

McGregor, Deborah. "Traditional Ecological Knowledge and Sustainable Development: Towards Coexistence" in Mario Blaser, Harvey A. Feit & Glenn McRea, eds, *In the Way of Development: Indigenous Peoples, Life Projects, and Globalization* (New York: Zed Books, 2004) 72.

McPherson, Annika. "Rastafari and/as Decoloniality" in Sabine Broeck & Carsten Junker, eds, *Postcoloniality – Decoloniality – Black Critique – Joints and Fissures* (Frankfurt: Campus Verlag, 2014) 353.

Mignolo, Walter D. "Introduction – Coloniality of Power and De-Colonial Thinking" (2007) 21:2–3 *Cultural Studies* 155.

———. *The Darker Side of Western Modernity: Global Futures, Decolonial Options* (Durham: Duke University Press, 2011).

———. "Further Thought on (De)Coloniality" in Sabine Broeck & Carsten Junker, eds, *Postcoloniality – Decoloniality – Black Critique – Joints and Fissures* (Frankfurt: Campus Verlag, 2014) 21.

Morton, Stephen. "Gayatri Chakravorty Spivak (1942-)" in Jon Simons, ed, *Contemporary Critical Theorists* (Edinburgh: Edinburgh University Press, 2010) 210.

Moten, Fred. "The Case of Blackness" (2009) 50:2 *Criticism* 177.

Napoleon, Val. "Extinction by Number: Colonialism Made Easy" (2001) 16:1 *Canadian Journal of Law and Society* 113.

———. "Aboriginal Self-Determination: Individual Self and Collective Selves" (2005) 29:2 *Atlantis* 31.

———. "Thinking about Indigenous Legal Orders" in René Provost & Colleen Sheppard, eds, *Dialogues on Human Rights and Legal Pluralism* (Dordrecht: Springer, 2013) 229.

National Inquiry into Missing and Murdered Indigenous Women and Girls. "Executive Summary of the Final Report" (2019), <www.mmiwg-ffada.ca/wp-content/uploads/2019/06/Executive_Summary.pdf>.

Ndlovu-Gatsheni, Sabelo J. *Empire, Global Coloniality and African Subjectivity* (New York: Berghahn Books, 2013).

Niezen, Ronald. "Culture and the Judiciary: The Meaning of the Culture Concept as a Source of Aboriginal Rights in Canada" (2003) 18:2 *Canadian Journal of Law and Society* 1.

Nimako, Kwame. "Location and Social Thought in the Black: A Testimony to Africana Intellectual Tradition" in S. Broeck & C. Junker, eds, *Postcoloniality – Decoloniality – Black Critique* (Frankfurt: Campus Verlag, 2014) 53.

The Observer France. "The Observer View on the Riots in France: A Grim Tale of the Growing Gulf between Haves and Have-Nots" (2 July 2023), <www.theguardian.com/commentisfree/2023/jul/02/observer-view-riots-france-nahel-merzouk>.

Office of the Auditor General of Canada. "Access to Safe Drinking Water in First Nations Communities – Indigenous Services Canada" (2021), <https://opencanada.blob.core.windows.net/opengovprod/resources/7445c056-703f-4dee-85a0-886102794011/parl_oag_202102_03_e.pdf?sr=b&sp=r&sig=VgNsS5jGt9UlRw7CzKntUUT8z5%2B/qkFwaOM/HlspiAE%3D&sv=2015-07-08&se=2021-10-04T21%3A02%3A24Z>.

Otto, Dianne. "International Human Rights Law: Towards Rethinking Sex/Gender Dualism" in Vanessa E. Munro & Margaret Davies, eds, *The Ashgate Research Companion to Feminist Legal Theory* (New York: Routledge, 2013) 197.

Pager, Devah & Hana Shepherd. "The Sociology of Discrimination: Racial Discrimination in Employment, Housing, Credit, and Consumer Markets" (2008) 34 *Annual Review of Sociology* 181.

Pastoureau, Michel. *Noir: histoire d'une couleur* (Paris: Seuil, 2008).

Patterson, Orlando. *Slavery and Social Death: A Comparative Study* (Cambridge: Harvard University Press, 2000).

Pico della Mirandola, Giovanni. *Oration on the Dignity of Man*, translated by A. Robert Caponigri (Chicago: Henry Regnery, 1956).

Pro Asyl. *Walls of Shame: Accounts from the Inside: The Detention Centers of Evros* (2012), <www.proasyl.de/fileadmin/fm-dam/q_PUBLIKATIONEN/2012/Evros-Bericht_12_04_10_BHP.pdf>.

———. *Pushed back: systematic human rights violations against refugees in the aegean sea and the greek-turkish land border* (2013), <www.proasyl.de/wp-content/uploads/2015/12/PRO_ASYL_Report_Pushed_Back_english_November_2013.pdf>.

Quijano, Aníbal. "Coloniality and Modernity/Rationality" (2007) 21:2–3 *Cultural Studies* 168.

Radcliffe, Sarah A. "Geography and Indigeneity I: Indigeneity, Coloniality and Knowledge" (2017) 41:2 *Progress in Human Geography* 220.

———. "Geography and Indigeneity II: Critical Geographies of Indigenous Bodily Politics" (2017) 42:3 *Progress in Human Geography* 436.

Reid, Papaarangi, Donna Cormack & Sarah-Jane Paine. "Colonial Histories, Racism and Health – The Experience of Māori and Indigenous People" (2018) 28 *European Journal of Public Health (Supplement 1)* 3.

Report of the Special Rapporteur on Contemporary Forms of Racism, Racial Discrimination, Xenophobia and Related Intolerance, UN Doc A/HRC/38/52 (25 April 2018).

Report of the Special Rapporteur on Contemporary Forms of Racism, Racial Discrimination, Xenophobia and Related Intolerance: Global Extractivism and Racial Equality, UN Doc A/HRC/41/54 (14 May 2019).

Report of the Special Rapporteur on Contemporary Forms of Racism, Racial Discrimination, Xenophobia and Related Intolerance, UN Doc A/74/321 (21 August 2019).

Sanders, Douglas. "Collective Rights" (1991) 13 *Human Rights Quarterly* 368.

Santos, Boaventura de Sousa. *Epistemologies of the South – Justice against Epistemicide* (Boulder, CO: Paradigm Publishers, 2014).

———. "Epilogue: A New Vision of Europe: Learning from the South" in G. Bhambra & J. Narayan, eds, *European Cosmopolitanism: Colonial Histories and Postcolonial Societies* (New York: Routledge, 2017) 172.

Santos, Boaventura de Sousa & Bruno Sena Martins. "Introduction" in Boaventura de Sousa Santos & Bruno Sena Martins, eds, *The Pluriverse of Human Rights: The Diversity of Struggles for Dignity* (New York: Routledge, 2021) 1.

———, eds. *The Pluriverse of Human Rights: The Diversity of Struggles for Dignity* (New York: Routledge, 2021).

Sexton, Jared. "People-of Color-Blindness: Notes on the Afterlife of Slavery" (2010) 28:2 *Social Text* 31.

Simm, Gabrielle. "Queering CEDAW? Sexual Orientation, Gender Identity and Expression and Sex Characteristics (SOGIESC) in International Human Rights Law" (2020) 29:3 *Griffith Law Review* 374.

Simpson, Audra. "Paths Toward a Mohawk Nation: Narratives of Citizenship and Nationhood in Kahnawake" in Duncan Ivison, Paul Patton & Will Sanders, eds, *Political Theory and the Rights of Indigenous Peoples* (Cambridge: Cambridge University Press, 2000) 113.

Sithole, Tendayi. "The Concept of the Black Subject in Fanon" (2016) 47:1 *Journal of Black Studies* 24.

Spillers, Hortence. *Black, White, and in Colour: Essays on American Literature and Culture* (Chicago: Chicago University Press, 2003).

Spivak, Gayatri Chakravorty. "Criticism, Feminism, and the Institution" in Sarah Harasym, ed, *Gayatri Chakravorty Spivak: The Post-Colonial Critic* (New York: Routledge, 1990) 1.

———. "Subaltern Talk: Interview with the Editors" in Donna Landry & Gerald MacLean, eds, *The Spivak Reader: Selected Works of Gayatri Chakravorty Spivak* (New York: Routledge, 1996) 287.

———. *A Critique of Postcolonial Reason: Toward a History of the Vanishing Present* (Cambridge, MA: Harvard University Press, 1999).

Statistics Canada. "Suicide among First Nations People, Métis and Inuit" (2011–2016), <www150.statcan.gc.ca/n1/pub/99–011-x/99–011-x2019001-eng.htm>.

Sundberg, Juanita. "Decolonizing Posthumanist Geographies" (2014) 21:1 *Cultural Geographies* 33.

Trans-Atlantic Slave Trade Database (hosted by Emory University), <www.slavevoyages.org>.

Treaties and Historical Research Centre, P.R.E. Group, Indian and Northern Affairs. "Historical Development of the Indian Act" (1978).

United States Sentencing Commission. *Booker Report 2012*, <www.ussc.gov/sites/default/files/pdf/news/congressional-testimony-and-reports/booker-reports/2012-booker/Part_A.pdf#page=55>.

University of British Columbia. "First Nations & Indigenous Studies", <http://indigenousfoundations.arts.ubc.ca/the_indian_act/#potlatch>.

UN Office of the High Commissioner for Human Rights. "Indigenous Peoples Have Been Disproportionately Affected by COVID-19 – Senior United Nations Official Tells Human Rights Council" (28 September 2021), <www.ohchr.org/EN/NewsEvents/Pages/DisplayNews.aspx?NewsID=27556&LangID=E>.

———. "About Indigenous Peoples and Human Rights", <www.ohchr.org/EN/Issues/IPeoples/Pages/AboutIndigenousPeoples.aspx>.

———. "Millennium Development Goals and Human Rights Standards", <www.ohchr.org/EN/Issues/SDGS/Pages/MDGsStandards.aspx>.

Vienna Declaration and Programme of Action (adopted on 12 July 1993), UNGA Res 48/121 (20 December 1993).

Walcott, Rinaldo. "The Problem of the Human: Black Ontologies and 'the Coloniality of Our Being'" in Sabine Broeck & Carsten Junker, eds, *Postcoloniality – Decoloniality – Black Critique – Joints and Fissures* (Frankfurt: Campus Verlag, 2014) 93.

Weheliye, Alexander G. *Habeas Viscus: Racializing Assemblages, Biopolitics, and Black Feminist Theories of the Human* (Durham: Duke University Press, 2014).

Wilderson III, Frank B. *Red, White & Black – Cinema and the Structure of U.S. Antagonisms* (Durham: Duke University Press, 2010).

Williams, Robert A. *Savage Anxieties: The Invention of Western Civilization* (New York: Palgrave Macmillan, 2012).

Wilner, Isaiah Lorado. "A Global Potlatch: Identifying the Indigenous Influence on Western Thought" (2013) 37:2 *American Indian Culture and Research Journal* 87.

Wynter, Sylvia. "1492: A New Worldview" in V Hyatt & R Nettleford, eds, *Race, Discourse, and the Origin of the Americas* (Washington, DC: Smithsonian Institution Press, 1995) 5.

———. "The Re-Enchantment of Humanism: An Interview with Sylvia Wynter" (2000) 8 *Small Axe* 119.

Concluding reflections on the 'human' of human rights

Rethinking the 'human' of human rights – including the reasoning for the existence of such a concept – in a creative manner, as inspired by the different approaches discussed in this Part, would require the human rights system to go far beyond the common logic of exceptions and inclusions that are always assessed against a norm presented as universal.[1] Indeed, in a state system that is increasingly under pressure because of its inherent shortcomings, including with respect to human rights, new forms of legal and political subjectivity seem to be needed.[2]

In line with what has been highlighted and expressed – in certainly different but not incompatible ways – by an Arendtian perspective, by posthumanist approaches and perhaps even more forcefully by several theories from the margins, ontological openness could be the basis of a new form of political community.[3] The figure of *migrating 'Others'* that I have suggested embodies an openness to what is in flux, unknown and undefined and embraces the plurality of beings. Arendt did not believe in firm or fixed foundations upon which our thinking could be based but valued unpredictability and uncertainty; in this Part, this has been interpreted as the possibility for the 'human' to forsake traditionally defining characteristics, including the citizenship criterion.[4] Since statelessness "is an authentic mode of being human",[5] one can be a subject and human without the state. Importantly, because it should eventually be possible to conceive the human without a negative link to the state, the figure of *migrating 'Others'* and the condition of statelessness might turn out to be only intermediate concepts. The human might not have to be defined, neither in relation to the state nor against 'Others', whether non-human or human, as it is not a concept to be realized or

---

1 Weheliye, 11.
2 For a similar argument, see Benhabib, *The Rights of Others*, 179.
3 Lechte & Newman, 529.
4 Williams & Lang, 6.
5 Lechte & Newman, 530.

DOI: 10.4324/9781003427957-6

an ideal to attain. Openness and indeterminacy are perhaps even the greatest strengths of the 'human'; they also ground human rights without confining them, and they allow much-needed creativity.[6]

Following the insights from the posthumanist approaches and the theories from the margins that I discussed, the field of human rights should engage critically with its humanist biases and its colonial and racist past,[7] structural violence and problematic universals, even if this challenges its very foundations. Reversing the ontological negation of the 'Other' would help address the exclusion of non-white people and others who continue to be marginalized and recognize the full range of being human, or – as posthumanism suggests – being *tout court*. In other words, in a reconceptualized paradigm, which, it is worth recalling, is what the theorists from the margins call for, there would be no 'Other' who is erased or would have to assimilate. Furthermore, human rights might need to recognize not only different meanings associated with the concept of the human, but with other important concepts as well. Law can be created and lived in very different ways, as legal pluralism and Indigenous legal approaches highlight.[8] Another example are different conceptions not only of freedom but also of slavery. As Wynter has shown, in some African cultures, the "opposite to slave is not only being free: the opposite to slave is also *belonging* to a lineage".[9] Similarly, Western capitalist and racially imbued notions of ownership, property rights and belonging to a place[10] need to be transcended as they are at the basis of exclusive and exclusionary citizen-state relationships. They constitute the justification for recognizing the human rights of 'good citizens' but not of others, as is also captured by the figure of *migrating 'Others'*.

Moreover, since the human is never a *fait accompli*, and because suffering might take forms that cannot yet be known, there needs to be space not only for plurality and openness but also for change and fluidity to imagine and allow other forms of emancipation and alternative modalities of freedom to emerge or, since many already exist, be taken seriously.[11] Acting along these lines would open up new imaginaries, including with respect to the many ways of experiencing, thinking and being in the world. These insights are highly relevant for the international human rights system, as it will be further demonstrated in the next chapters by revealing its vision-centredness and the exclusions created through its limited sensorium.

6 Cohen, 183–4.
7 Gilroy, "Multiculture", 108.
8 See e.g. Macdonald & Sandomierski; Napoleon, "Thinking about Indigenous Legal Orders".
9 Wynter, "The Re-Enchantment of Humanism", 148.
10 Walcott, 103.
11 Weheliye, 15.

Part II

Towards more sensuous and inclusive international human rights

Informed by the previous theoretical discussions, Part II turns to the sensuous aspects of human rights to maintain that the current international human rights system is too limited, and hence exclusive, in its approach to subjectivity to be truly universal. The system relies heavily on a certain type of visual discourse and, more fundamentally, on the sense of vision to represent and construct its subject. As I will argue, the omnipresence and great influence of vision and the visual are detrimental to many individuals and groups that operate with a different sensorium than the one projected by the dominant Western approach.

The argument on the sensuous dimensions developed in this Part proceeds in two main steps. First, in Chapter 4, I offer a critical analysis of visual discourses in international human rights. This analysis focuses on images used by well-recognized international actors, such as United Nations agencies, and, in order to show that alternative discourses exist and are meaningful, on different forms of representation and self-representation, including by individuals who have experienced human rights violations. I demonstrate that it is not only the kind of visual discourse that is problematic and that accounts for various processes of 'othering', but also that vision has been constructed as the dominant and most rational sense in the Western world, and hence also in Western-rooted international human rights law. This entrenched focus on vision and visuality means that other ways of expressing oneself are precluded in and through international human rights.

In Chapter 5, I further develop the idea that the international human rights system is based on a rational and vision-centred sensorium and that the ideal subject of international human rights is conceived as largely devoid of emotions. I argue that, by ignoring the multifaceted role of the senses in the construction of subjectivity, the system discriminates against many, if not most, people, which is obviously contrary to the claim to universality professed by international human rights. Relying on numerous ethnographies that demonstrate a wide range and use of the senses beyond vision, and even beyond the Western 'classic five' sensorium, I suggest that the visiocracy in international

DOI: 10.4324/9781003427957-7

human rights must be transcended and that more attention should be given to other senses. I conclude that the international human rights system would benefit from recognizing a greater sensorial diversity and that it should be more attentive to other ways of sensing, feeling and understanding the world.

Chapter 4

Exposing the imagined subject of human rights through a visual discourse analysis

In this chapter, I expose how international human rights law, as an offspring of modern law, is heavily dependent on vision and on the influence of visual discourses, in particular in the context of the conceptualization of legal subjectivity. As I argue, the forms of exclusion of many human beings from law and the protection of human rights that I discussed in the previous chapters are reflected in and exacerbated through law's visual bias and dominant visual discourses, in other words the formation, expression and transfer of ideas through the visual. Indeed, vision has been considered the most important sense and an attribute of the modern Western rational subject for a long time,[1] and other senses have been ascribed, with depreciatory undertones, to other cultures.[2] Despite privileging vision, as law does, the power of images is rarely recognized in the context of modern law. The authority of the visual and the rich relationship between law and the aesthetics are seldom discussed and even less questioned in legal theory or practice.[3] An analysis of these dimensions is even more needed in international human rights law, whose visual aspects remain particularly understudied. Law's visual bias is especially relevant for international human rights precisely because of their claimed universality, which concerns their authority and applicability, in a spatial and in a moral sense, *and* their form and content.[4] I therefore suggest that it is crucial to better understand the ways in which – and reasons why – modern law was able to ascertain its power through the visual and a certain imagery, although – or rather because – not everyone would naturally or primarily rely on this mode of expression. In this sense, the focus on vision in the context of law, if not clearly constituting a cause of exclusion by itself, definitively exacerbates the processes of 'othering' I discussed in Part I. Exploring the more general relationship between law and the aesthetics can

---

1 Classen, "Foundations", 402.
2 Hsu, 434.
3 Goodrich, "Visiocracy", 500–1; Hibbitts, "Coming to Our Senses", 880.
4 For a discussion of universality in the context of international law more generally, see Aral, d'Aspremont & Scobbie.

DOI: 10.4324/9781003427957-8

also provide useful insights in this regard and helps seize what makes vision so influential in this context.

To pursue my analysis, I build on the insight that law not only uses the written word – notably in the form of statutes and judicial decisions – but relies on the visual in more complex and diverse ways. Through emblems, architecture, clothing, graffiti, stamps, films or other works of art, and digital media, law has always used the power of the visual to assert and maintain its authority.[5] I also draw on the claim that images play an especially important role in translating and further developing abstract legal concepts, such as justice, human rights and legal subjectivity. As Peter Goodrich has noted, law is constructed, transmitted and rendered accessible in sophisticated detail by images.[6] Analysing images hence allows transcending and questioning the alleged rationality of law that infuses written statutes and judicial decisions, which are key elements of law, its making and interpretation, and also the alleged rationality of the modern legal subject. Richard Sherwin has argued that images can convey more than text, or the written and spoken word, alone ever could, especially because they appeal to emotions, and because they are subjective and particularistic.[7] They can tap into the heart, into the otherwise hidden soul of law and the pursuit of justice, in a way that is not amenable to conscious reflection.[8] Costas Douzinas and Lynda Nead write that

> [i]mages are sensual and fleshy; they address the labile elements of the self, they speak to the emotions, and they organize the unconscious. They have the power to short-circuit reason and enter the soul without the interpolation or intervention of language or interpretation.[9]

Moreover, not only is the visual legal environment – from the actual courtroom to the legal culture in a metaphorical sense – full of meanings and values; these visual discourses also exercise great power. By way of example, the photographs used in the context of international human rights law can evoke a shared humanness but also difference, and provoke solidarity or fear,[10] which influences attitudes towards rights. Images are not neutral, and more generally, as I also discuss, relying on the sense of vision – as law does – is not a neutral endeavor either. These insights are useful to understand that, like other forms of communication, the visual can be used, whether consciously or unconsciously, as a tool to include and exclude, with images reflecting,

---

5 Manderson, "Introduction", 8.
6 Goodrich, "Visiocracy", 508, 520.
7 Sherwin, 38.
8 Goodrich, "Visiocracy"; Sherwin, 38; see also Rose, 153.
9 Douzinas & Nead, 7.
10 Wilke, 263.

constructing and entrenching existing forms of inequality, discrimination and injustice.

As I demonstrate in the first section of this chapter, considering the historical establishment of vision as the highest sense in the Western modern world, as well as exploring the relationship between law and the aesthetics, can shed light on how legal and visual discourses have influenced and constituted each other. In the second section, I conduct a critical visual discourse analysis of key moments in the history of human rights and of contemporary visual engagements with human rights to reveal some of the ways in which images have shaped legal ideology, consciousness and subjectivities. A telling example, as my analysis shows, consists in the visual representation of human rights, from a historical focus on texts to the contemporary emphasis on portraying victims of human rights violations. The analysis also echoes and builds on the insights from the critical theories discussed in the previous chapters. It shows, in particular, that the dominant approach, notably because of its vision-centredness, or ocularcentrism, has routinely excluded and denied the rights of certain individuals and groups – from non-citizens to other 'Others' who appear different to the dominant gaze. The inherent forms of exclusion in international human rights that I revealed by relying on the critique developed by Arendt (and other writers building on her), by posthumanist scholars and by theories from the margins are hence amplified through dominant visual discourses. Yet juxtaposing dominant visual discourses to other discourses, such as in the form of art, shows that there are alternative conceptions of the subject that human rights discourses could draw on. Finally, challenging the supremacy of vision in law and considering the relevance of other senses in the context of international human rights, as I suggest in the third section, responds to the call to deconstruct dominant frameworks and to imagine different approaches.

4.1   The powerful visiocracy of Western law

Vision clearly dominates Western law, including international human rights law, and the visual is omnipresent. Fundamentally, it is through visual representations and through images that the whole Western legal tradition operates. The metaphors that are used in the context of law are telling examples: law is a 'body', a 'text', a 'structure'. It is always something that can be looked at.[11] Another example is that visual evidence has long played a predominant role in the context of trials, to the detriment of evidence based on other senses. Although aurality has admittedly a long tradition and important presence in law, with the centrality of legal rhetoric in a trial being the most obvious example, it arguably still ranks only second in law's hierarchy

---

11 Hibbitts, "Senses of Difference".

of the senses.[12] Visual evidence is often considered more convincing than an oral argument,[13] and even in parts of a trial where aurality has always enjoyed some authority, in particular in the context of lawyers' opening and closing statements, more and more visual tools, such as digital re-enactments and visual documentaries, are used.[14] This is because aurality can only operate within a rigidly confined and regulated space; moreover, lawyers "are inclined to associate aural communication with fraud, carelessness, and lack of legal sophistication".[15]

It seems useful to recall that considering vision as a higher and more noble sense in the Western world has a long tradition that predates the era of human rights and has its roots in Greco-Roman antiquity, and the visual bias of modern law is arguably embedded in this tradition. The renewed importance given to vision emerged in Europe in the High Middle Ages, as Europeans embraced writing to preserve and disseminate information and maintain traditions.[16] Because letters, scrolls and manuscripts are relatively durable, they could easily travel between villages, cities and even countries, as well as across time, reaching distant people and future generations. As the authority of the written word became stronger, the sense of vision was privileged and other senses were sidelined; institutions and groups that still relied on sound, touch, taste and smell as main forms of expressions were denigrated, and their significance declined markedly.[17] The supremacy of vision in European thought consolidated itself with the development of modern science and the emphasis on reason in the 18th century, which relied heavily on this sense: with the rise of modernity, vision and knowledge became inseparable, including in the context of modern law, which has always been associated closely with both reason and vision.[18] The reign of science and its alleged rationality were established, along with its method relying almost exclusively on eye-centred techniques,[19] and have not been successfully challenged up to this day. Observing and measuring through visual tools even became the only acceptable way in European thought of judging the intelligence of human

12 As Howes and Classen argue, the "senses of sight and hearing dominate Western perception of justice". Howes & Classen, 94.
13 Sherwin, 39. The author suggests this when recounting the trial of Victor Harris before the United States Supreme Court and the particularly crushing video evidence in this case.
14 Sherwin, 14. The highly mediatized trial of Oscar Pistorius and the visual reconstitution of the crime through simulations and demonstrations during the trial is a telling example.
15 Hibbitts, "Coming to Our Senses", 896. The author refers particularly to Anglo-American lawyers.
16 For a seminal work on this development in England, see Clanchy.
17 Hibbitts, "Coming to Our Senses", 875. By way of example, Hibbitts associates the decline of rhetoric and theater with the rise of the visual. Ibid, 876.
18 Bently, 3; Dundes Renteln, 1575. For a study of the importance of vision in the context of contemporary international humanitarian law, see Wilke.
19 Flynn.

beings.[20] Quite obviously, this did not mean that the other senses became entirely irrelevant, but that vision was elevated as the highest – and most human – sense. Hearing followed vision quite closely in this hierarchy, but smell, taste and touch were relegated as lower or 'animal' senses and deemed central to non-European and allegedly uncivilized peoples, arguably paralleling some of the fundamental humanist beliefs discussed in the previous chapters. This was part of a broader process introduced by modernity that progressively suppressed the senses, their richness and diversity, and even erased memories and emotions based on the senses.[21] The same logic reflected and contributed to entrenching class difference within European society: vision, which was considered a noble sense that allowed aesthetic appreciation, was associated with the upper, educated classes, whereas the working masses were deemed to remain focused on tactility and sound.[22] In fact, the sensory experiences[23] of all those considered 'Others' were downplayed by the Western elite.[24] Common epistemological and methodological biases – not only in the natural sciences, but also in the humanities and social sciences, including law – led to the privileging of everything associated with vision and of written texts. Interestingly, 19th-century visitors from the Middle East describe Europe as a place of spectacle full of observing subjects, where everything is arranged to represent, as exemplified by museums, theatres, public gardens and zoos.[25] Europeans set up the world as an image, as "an object on display to be investigated and experienced by the dominating European gaze".[26]

A history of privileging vision and rationality in law

European modern thought and its emphasis on rationality, with vision considered the most rational and hence privileged sense, had significant consequences for the legal sphere: it arguably led to the imposition of the supremacy of vision – as opposed to other senses such as hearing or touch – and the visual in law, which also facilitated the claim to universality of Eurocentric international human rights law. Law was highly influenced by and also contributed to Western modernity's objective of establishing the legitimacy

---

20 Davis speaks of the paradoxical tendency of Western science to use the senses as instruments of measurement at the same time as "demanding a radical austerity of them". Davis, 66.
21 Seremetakis, 14.
22 Classen, "The Senses at the National Gallery", 86–7. The author explains that vision was "the avenue of spiritual enlightenment" in the context of museums opening their doors to the working classes. Ibid, 93.
23 For a discussion on the meaning of "experience" in anthropology and the understanding that there is a great variety of experiences that involve various levels of consciousness, see Pink, 42–6.
24 van Ede, 63.
25 Timothy Mitchell, 505.
26 Timothy Mitchell, 504.

of the rational, autonomous individual. In fact, law and justice have been presented as impartial and oblivious to feelings in the Western legal tradition; law developed a specialized "self-knowledge" and identified itself as a dispassionate science that could objectively manage society[27] and that could also be studied systematically, a belief that was particularly strong in the continental European tradition. Law's aesthetic dimensions were sidelined, and modern law evolved in isolation from art: "Art is assigned to imagination, creativity, and playfulness, law to control, discipline and sobriety".[28] According to Douzinas and Nead, a creator of art hence enjoys freedom, has desires and is an embodied subject whose past and social context are recognized; in contrast, the rational, seeing legal subject is limited to having rights and obligations and has no desires, history or gender.[29] The Western legal tradition has always presumed a strong – even if implicit – relationship between legal subjectivity and rationality, with the focus lying on the rational mind and the thinking subject. Since vision has been considered the highest and most – or even only – rational sense, the sense of vision and the visual became dominant in the legal sphere and a defining characteristic of legal subjectivity. The full meaning and potential of legal subjectivity have hence been curtailed, and the legal discipline has made great efforts to preserve the illusion that law is a rational and comprehensive normative regime.[30] In sum, law's form and content were disconnected from each other, and law was rationalized by modernity and emptied of its aesthetic dimensions. It is this alleged purification that allowed modern law to establish itself as a supposedly closed and coherent system, and that justified its reign over all other areas of life.

Modern thought also sanitized the aesthetics – what is considered beautiful, tasteful, or even just – and rendered it vision-centred, which, as will be discussed in more detail in the next chapter, is problematic in an international human rights context considering that many individuals and groups do not define themselves, and the world around them, primarily through vision. While *aisthetikos*, the original Greek word, referred to an inclusive and unbiased perception by all the senses,[31] with premodern aesthetic experiences possibly appealing to more than one sense simultaneously,[32] modernity attempted to separate the senses from each other and developed an artificial hierarchy of the senses in which vision and hearing were placed at the top, whereas touch, smell and taste were relegated to the bottom as lower senses not contributing to aesthetic experiences.[33] What can be considered beautiful

27 Santos, "Three Metaphors", 570.
28 Douzinas & Nead, 3.
29 Douzinas & Nead, 3.
30 Kleinhans & Macdonald, 28–9.
31 Online Etymology Dictionary.
32 Howes, "The Aesthetics of Mixing the Senses", 75.
33 Howes, "The Aesthetics of Mixing the Senses".

became associated almost exclusively with the visual. But, as Desmond Manderson has argued, the aesthetics cannot really be rationalized in this manner: it "appeals not to our judgment of truth and logic, but to our senses. It finds expression not in a judgment of goodness or rightness, but rather in a feeling of attraction or repulsion".[34] As such, the aesthetics continues to have considerable power. It generates influential sensorial discourses that can even "reify, overwhelm, and lay claim to a totalising authority".[35] Appealing to the senses may hence have positive and negative effects, such as social inclusion and exclusion of specific groups or individuals, which often determines whether or not human rights are granted and respected, as I explore in more detail in the next chapter.

Despite modernist attempts to keep things apart, it is an illusion to believe that law or justice do not have an aesthetic dimension. Law and the aesthetics are, indeed, thoroughly related, with the latter containing strong and specific normative claims about justice, and they interact with each other across the alleged rationality/non-rationality divide. As Manderson contends by recalling the inseparability of form and content, "[l]aw is one of the ways in which form is developed in society, and law expresses itself through form and structure and style and ritual".[36] It has even been claimed that if one was to destroy the aesthetics of law, law would lose its persuasiveness.[37] In other words, both the form and the content of a legal system are revealing of the values of such a system and the kind of justice one can expect to obtain. It is arguably because of law's legitimate forms that justice becomes possible.[38] Each legal tradition might have its own conceptions of what it considers just and beautiful, which may also change over time, but it is important to realize that these conceptions, that is the form of a legal system or its aesthetic dimensions, always matter. International human rights law is, of course, not an exception: its focus on the visual, the highly privileged form of representation and perception, influences conceptions of justice and subjectivity; it influences the creation, interpretation and application of rights and determines who can effectively claim rights.

While the visual legal environment, including the architecture of courtrooms, clothing of judges and the way in which legal documents are presented, is full of meanings and values, and exercises great power, the authority of visual governance, or the visiocracy of law, is rarely questioned: "The ceremonial, triumphal, and sartorial dimensions of law are generally assumed, taken somehow for granted, and thus overlooked or at best seen

---

34 Manderson, "Senses and Symbols", 200.
35 Manderson, "Senses and Symbols", 201.
36 Manderson, *Songs without Music*, 191.
37 Dahlberg, 4.
38 Goodrich, "Visiocracy", 517.

as something glimpsed, lateral to legal action".[39] Indeed, these dynamics have only been addressed and revealed quite recently in the scholarship.[40] However, the depth of the relationship between law and the visual, the most valued aesthetic dimension in this context, and, more specifically, the importance of visual discourses in international human rights have not yet entered the collective knowledge of human rights scholars, lawyers and advocates.

The power of the visual in the context of law and rights

It can be argued, drawing on scholarship on images more generally, that images are powerful in legal contexts both as material objects and as abstract entities. As Chiara Bottici has noted, images, as material objects, whether in physical or digital form, enter in direct, tangible contact with their surroundings; as abstract or conceptual representations, they are malleable carriers of messages, render visible what would otherwise remain hidden and reveal meaning and ideology.[41] This, I maintain, is also the case in the context of law and justice, and it is hence not surprising that images have become one of the principal media through which contemporary political and legal discourses are constructed and maintained.[42]

Images, and vision more generally, are important in the context of law and rights because they are a way of translating the idea of justice, which is an essential motivation of most legal systems but an abstract concept and very much "a matter of faith":[43] justice is arguably not a given that can be measured according to objective criteria but needs to be constantly developed and believed in. If the source of law is always abstract and even absent, the visual discourse used inside and outside the courtroom plays the crucial role of continuously alluding to its existence and power. Images hence do not simply reproduce something; they contribute to making and changing the world. Visual media, such as paintings, sculptures and photographs, contribute to the discursive creation and interpretation of law and other social structures. Put differently, images not only illustrate and reflect but also – and perhaps most importantly – determine questions of law and authority.[44] For instance, the architecture of most courts of justice and the choice of their location have always followed careful considerations in order to establish the authority of the law. In France, following the French Revolution, courthouses were built

---

39 Goodrich, "Visiocracy", 500–1.
40 In fact, as Hibbitts concluded in 1992, legal scholarship had largely been unaffected by academic insights regarding the meanings and implications of using different forms of communication. Hibbitts, "Coming to Our Senses", 880. See also Goodrich, "Visiocracy", 499.
41 Bottici, 12.
42 Bottici, chapter 1.
43 Goodrich, "Visiocracy", 516.
44 Bottici, 7.

like palaces to highlight the independence of the judiciary from the state's political apparatus.[45] *Palais de justice* are grandiose: their columns and high ceilings are meant to impress. The interior of the Western courtroom is also spatially organized to clearly and constantly remind all the parties of the authority of the law: judges typically sit higher, where they can oversee the proceedings, than the rest of the crowd; the witnesses' stand is up front, where everyone can see him or her; and the decoration is also consciously chosen, with visual symbols, such as the scale and the sword, and emblems carefully exhibited and placed where they will be seen most easily.[46] Even the dress code of judges and lawyers is meant to reflect their authority: wigs, gowns and expensive suits help the formal legal actor to be visible.[47] The idea of relying on the visual to establish power is well alive in the 21st century, where digital images have largely replaced official painted portraits of sovereign rulers and state-sponsored parades and fireworks that were meant to impress.[48]

Visual discourses, as I argue, also play a predominant role in constructing subjectivities, which is an important dimension of the quest for justice, since it is through visual discourses that the legal authority exercises its power to define. As it has been pointed out, with the rise of modernity, representation, and beliefs about representation, increasingly influence the ways in which the subject is conceived.[49] Leo Flynn claims that "[t]he sense of vision or, rather, particular versions of that sense, underlie the law's perception, the manner in which it obtains and structures knowledge about individuals, objectives and events".[50] It can even be argued that law, through a heavily vision-centred epistemology, determines legal subjects as well as their position and role in society, often with negative consequences. More specifically, the rational – and seeing – white man who makes law and enjoys rights was and still is the privileged subject of Western law; others are often represented, as in the context of contemporary visual human rights discourses, by highlighting and sometimes accentuating differences, or are sidelined or overlooked. Indeed, while the visual discourse is sometimes presented and perceived as natural and accessible to everyone, it has been developed and is often employed by dominant actors to sustain their influence and power.

---

45 Bottici, 3. The author highlights the fact that different jurisdictions have different visual features, and that the use of the visual to assert the authority of law is more pronounced in some jurisdictions than in others. While France would traditionally build grandiose palace-like courthouses, England and Sweden would privilege less marked architectural styles. This diversity illustrates the awareness of lawmakers *vis-à-vis* the power of the visual.

46 Bottici, 1. For a discussion of the history and meaning of legal emblems, see Goodrich, *Legal Emblems and the Art of Law*.

47 For the argument that "clothing is an image of law" and that "the nature of law as a social and cultural idea is expressed as well in clothing as in any written text", see Watt, 23.

48 Sherwin, 9.

49 Jones, 366.

50 Flynn, 139.

Visual discourses deployed in the context of international human rights could be conceived as a universal language that is part of a "legal system that speaks to everyone";[51] yet they are, as I suggest, inherently and necessarily biased and exclusionary. Visual representations are by themselves powerful tools to define, categorize and delineate legal subjectivity, and therefore contribute to the process of determining who can access human rights. In that sense, visual representations of subjects, because they express "power or weakness, amity or aggressivity, attractiveness or repulsion"[52] reflect and reinforce the common dynamics of exclusion in the human rights system. This is also illustrated by the strong tendency of the dominant system to focus on and to convey through its discourses – notably because of its limited forms of expression – certain types of violence and violations of human rights. What is difficult to see and to express visually remains invisible. This partly explains why violations of civil and political rights, such as in the form of physical violence, usually receive much more attention by the public and human rights organizations than violations of economic, social and cultural rights.[53] Similar cognitive biases have also been described in the context of digital evidence, such as videos posted on social media, used in international criminal investigations.[54] More generally, such biases mean that certain forms of violence, like economic exploitation, cultural violence and ongoing forms of coloniality are, relatively speaking, less noticed, which makes the provision of remedies less likely.

It is important to recall that every image is part of a specific social context and that it is created not only by certain individuals but thanks to collective knowledge.[55] This is why its meaning can resonate for a long time,[56] and why centuries-old representations, such as of Justice blindfolded and holding a balance, are still common and easily understood today. As Gillian Rose writes, "images do not exist in a vacuum, and looking at them for 'what they are' neglects the ways in which they are produced and interpreted through particular social practices".[57] As it has been noted in the context of photography, looking at and interpreting images is a social act. Every photograph is founded on a shared agreement on its meaning and the idea that it represents something in an objective manner.[58] But this is rarely recognized, and the common understanding of photography as a "self-evident" aspect of progress conceals its close relationship with the exercise of power.[59] Visual

51 Aral, d'Aspremont & Scobbie, 2.
52 Howes & Classen, 1.
53 On the difficulty defending economic, social and cultural rights in practice, see Roth.
54 McDermott, Koenig & Murray.
55 Dahlberg, 4.
56 Manderson, "Introduction", 3–4.
57 Rose, 55.
58 Azoulay, 41.
59 Azoulay, 41.

discourses are hence embedded within a particular context and are influ-enced by and sustain – but can also challenge – power relations and social difference.[60]

The effects that an image has are not only created by what is represented, and in which ways, but also by the way it is looked at. John Berger's work on *Ways of Seeing* is considered groundbreaking in this regard,[61] but, as noted in the previous chapter, Frantz Fanon already highlighted the crucial role of the viewer, in this case the "white gaze".[62] Feminist critiques have been crucial in further theorizing dominant "practices of looking".[63] Questioning a presum-ably objective gaze and well-established methods of interpreting images in Western art history, it has been argued that "[i]l n'existe pas de regard 'neu-tre' ni d'histoire de l'art qui détienne la 'vérité'".[64] Vision, as Donna Haraway notes, "is *always* a question of the power to see – and perhaps of the violence implicit in our visualizing practices".[65] In the West's enthusiastic embrace of images, it has been overlooked that the position of the viewers[66] and their background and *Weltanschauung* determine the meaning of what is seen.[67] Contrary to the Cartesian hyper-rational viewer – "a disembodied, ahistori-cal subject that refuses inter-subjectivity and stands outside the world which it claims to know only at a distance"[68] – the viewers transform what they see by the very act of seeing.[69] In other words, the visual is not a static one-way projection of authority; the viewers matter and play an active role in the meaning-making of images and the production and reproduction of power relations through visual discourses. By way of example, as it has been argued in the context of photography, there is an often underappreciated disconnect between the event and the representation of this event.[70] The spectator of a photograph "is required to reconstruct what has been there from out of the visible, as well as to reconstruct what is not immediately manifest, but which can – in principle – become visible in the exact same photograph".[71] It can

---

60 See Rose, 14–15.

61 Berger.

62 Fanon, *Peau noire, masques blancs*.

63 Sturken & Cartwright.

64 Adler, 83.

65 Haraway, 359. Haraway argues in this context that "[f]eminist objectivity is about limited location and situated knowledge, not about transcendence and splitting of subject and ob-ject. In this way we might become answerable for what we learn how to see". Ibid.

66 Flynn, 152. Or, as Stern argues more generally, "implicit in any measurement is the perspec-tive of the measurer. Both the choice of measurement and the exclusion of other forms of enquiry, and the interpretation of the data which it produces are dependent upon the percep-tions and preferences of the observer". Stern, 51.

67 Bottici, 28.

68 Flynn, 147.

69 Dahlberg, 4.

70 Azoulay, 43.

71 Azoulay, 43.

be concluded that an image does not only consist of what can be seen; the spectators themselves contribute, but in a subjective manner, with their personal and collective experiences, assumptions and aspirations, to what they see. What is often constructed as an objective world to be apprehended is, in fact, "permeated with bodily 'subjectivity'".[72]

'Othering' and the exercise of power through the visual

The non-neutrality of visual discourses in the context of human rights is particularly obvious when it comes to representational practices of difference and 'Otherness'. People who look different from the majority or dominant population are prone to stereotyping and, in Stuart Hall's words, often "seem to be represented through sharply opposed, polarized, binary extremes – good/bad, civilized/primitive, ugly/excessively attractive, repelling-because-different/compelling-because-strange-and-exotic. And they are often required to be *both things at the same time*!"[73] Reducing those represented to a few signifiers through stereotyping creates or reinforces inequalities and classifies "people according to a norm that constructs the excluded as 'other'".[74] In a Foucauldian approach, discourses are always related to power and knowledge, and representational practices can hence be understood as practices of power/knowledge, including the power to represent.[75] Photography, in particular, has been from its beginning a medium "that rudely and violently fixes anyone and anything" in a world that can be conquered as a picture.[76] As Ariella Azoulay argues, "[t]he gesture of identification – 'this is x' – frequently used in reference to photographs is made and unifies into a stable image, giving the illusion that we are facing a closed unit of visual information".[77]

The importance of visual discourses in the context of human rights has arguably increased over the past few decades, as television became a privileged and widespread media and digital technologies contributed to the proliferation of images, which, in turn, facilitated the reification of the dominant visual culture that lies beneath these developments.[78] While images have arguably always been used for ideological purposes, key events like the wars in Iraq and 9/11 have led to an "iconography of threat" that serves various political purposes.[79] Yet, easier access to digital technologies and the possibility of rapidly distributing images have also allowed victims of human rights violations to draw attention to their situation and experiences; the

72 Jones, 369.
73 Hall, "The Spectacle of the 'Other'", 229.
74 Hall, "The Spectacle of the 'Other'", 259.
75 Hall, "The Spectacle of the 'Other'", 259.
76 Azoulay, 41–2.
77 Azoulay, 44.
78 For an overview of approaches engaging with these developments, see Rose, 5–9.
79 Feldman, 163.

almost instant circulation of images via social media has even set off political movements, as first demonstrated particularly well by the Arab Spring. New technologies have, in fact, created further possibilities for representing violence and human rights violations for all actors involved, including victims, perpetrators, journalists and defenders of human rights. Striking examples across this range of actors include the live visual coverage of the first Gulf war, the circulation on social media of photographs and videos of horrific abuses at Guantanamo and Abu Ghraib and by Daesh, the wide coverage of migrants mainly from Africa and the Middle East desperately trying to reach Europe, and the staging of what has been called a border crisis at the United States–Mexican border, with migrants and those "facilitating" their journey being shown wearing surgical masks in the context of the COVID-19 pandemic.[80] The omnipresence of images, however, should not obscure the fact that not everything is represented, which may be accidental but is often intentional. The proliferation of images and the amplification of visual discourses actually mean that what is not represented is rendered more easily invisible, hidden, inexistent.[81]

It can even be argued that it has become normal in Western modernity to associate the exercise of power and the legitimation of political authority with the ability to control what is represented and visualized, and to impose this as the norm. The assumed power to visualize history and the claim to do so in an authoritative – even exclusive – way implies first being able to name and to define and hence to classify and, in a next step, to separate and to segregate. Crucially, such classification and separation are represented as normal, even as "right and hence aesthetic", which prevents those who are subjected to these processes from claiming and exercising genuine political subjectivity.[82] It should be noted that this power is constructed and more imaginary than actually perceptional through the eye.[83] Only the authority carrying out this visualization can escape visual scrutiny and even remain invisible, thus allowing this authority to maintain control unchecked.[84] As Nayrouz Abu Hatoum writes with reference to the state of Israel: "Visual dominance is manifested through differential power relations *vis-à-vis* state's visual superiority, through which dominant institutions maintain power over

---

80 Lakhani.
81 Feldman, 170.
82 Mirzoeff, 2–3.
83 Mirzoeff, 3.
84 Mirzoeff, 20. As Mirzoeff has argued, controlling the realm of the visual has enabled Western hegemony to establish itself in three stages, namely plantation slavery, imperialism and the ongoing "military-industrial complex". Direct forms of oversight and surveillance have yielded to "post-panoptic visuality" in contemporary politics, in which everyone and every site is considered a potential threat and is constantly and ubiquitously watched. In the current "industrial-military complex", the state and its institutions continue to exercise visual sovereignty and to dominate visual discourses in many ways. Ibid.

who can see what, who is being watched, and who is hidden".[85] "Visual rights" are not equally allocated and accessible,[86] and visual power is an important way to exercise domination.[87]

To contest this form of domination, Nicholas Mirzoeff claims what he calls the "right to look", which is, as he emphasizes, not simply about seeing, and therefore unidirectional, but involves being recognized as an autonomous other, through a mutual process of recognition.[88] It is a relational, not an individual right, as its exercise depends on the recognition of the person seeking to exercise it.[89] In other words, Mirzoeff links visuality to a claim to political subjectivity, to an existence that allows the contestation of what is visualized, and in which ways, by dominant institutions: it is the "picturing of the self or the collective that exceeds or proceeds that subjugation to centralized authority", with the objective of reconfiguring the dominant order.[90] This claim to political subjectivity is already exercised by those actors who seek to re-appropriate for themselves the authority to have a say in what is visualized and, because of the influence of visual discourses, what is considered normal. Indeed, visual discourses, by showing certain things and hiding others, shape collective imaginations as to what is possible or even existing, thus also legitimizing – or challenging – the exercise of authority. Politically engaged artists are perhaps among the most evident actors who produce a kind of countervisuality and who claim this right to look. Creative practices can indeed be particularly powerful as alternative discourses, as the visual discourse analysis below will further demonstrate, with art being "a crucial site for political subversion that cultivates and archives affective critiques of state violence".[91] In the context of Palestine, for instance, some visual artists forcefully contest and counter the visual dominance and violence exercised by the Israeli state, thus reclaiming visual sovereignty.[92] Importantly, these artists do not claim recognition through their art by the dominant system and its visuality; rather, they "operate through a politics of refusal" and, in this sense, offer alternative visualities and engage in the "subversion of dominant visual politics".[93] As Gil Z. Hochberg explains by drawing on a project initiated by a Palestinian art collective that turned an Israeli military water tower into an open-air cinema, the goal is to create new perspectives – including, as I would say, on human rights and their routine violation – and ways of looking, in

---

85 Abu Hatoum, 1062.
86 Hochberg, 3.
87 Abu Hatoum, 1062 (referring to Mirzoeff).
88 Mirzoeff, 1.
89 Mirzoeff, 25.
90 Mirzoeff, 23–4.
91 Abu Hatoum, 1066.
92 Abu Hatoum, 1062. Abu Hatoum argues that 'visual sovereignty' is considered more appropriate in a context of an occupying state than relying on a language of 'rights'. Ibid.
93 Abu Hatoum, 1063.

this instance by literally replacing the surveying gaze of the military with the look of cinema spectators.[94] Engaging in such countervisualities is of course a complex endeavour that entails different strategies and interventions, such as "physical interventions into the landscape, . . . the manipulation of visual positions, new settings for spectatorship, new modes of appearance, and at times new modes of *dis*appearance, concealment, or refusal to appear".[95] Moreover, recalling the crucial role and responsibility of the viewer, Hochberg notes that this process "also involves the ability to see one's own blindness and render visible one's failure to see".[96] The multilayered objectives of such countervisualities hence include making visible what usually remains hidden, as for instance in the dominant legal discourses, challenging dominant forms of representation and visual politics, and encouraging viewers to reflect on their own visual biases.

As I have discussed in this section, the modern Western world, including its legal realm, heavily relies on vision and visual discourses. Using (or not using) visual discourses in certain ways has become increasingly impactful in today's ocularcentric world, which makes it crucial to understand the power and biased nature of images in the context of law. Building on this discussion, I try in the next section to grasp the work that images do in the specific field of international human rights and in particular the exclusions that are created or entrenched by visual discourses.

4.2 A critical analysis of visual discourses in human rights

In this section, I analyse a few iconic images in the history of international human rights law and several contemporary examples of images used in the context of human rights by official organizations like the United Nations and media outlets, with a focus on representations of refugees and migrants. I then juxtapose these dominant visual discourses to alternative discourses by analysing selected works of creative photography, paying particular attention to representations of refugees and migrants to illustrate points made in the discussion in Part I and the proposed figure of *migrating 'Others'*. The purpose of pursuing a critical analysis of visual discourses in this field does not only consist in understanding how law and rights are expressed through images; it also entails exploring how law uses images, and how images shape legal ideology, consciousness and subjectivities.[97] Since my goal is to understand law's foundations and claim to authority as well as different conceptions of law, rights and subjectivity, I explore the roles of the visual in both dominant and alternative discourses.

94 Hochberg, 1–2.
95 Hochberg, 3.
96 Hochberg, 3.
97 Manderson, "Introduction", 8.

Inspired by a combination of methods that are commonly used in the social sciences and humanities to study various visual materials, the analysis is pursued at a formal and a contextual level. It considers visual elements, such as the colours, lines, space and composition of the images, and it also draws on knowledge about the social and political context and examines the ways in which images are put to work by different actors.[98] Contrary to a quantitative-oriented content analysis, which would follow strict selection criteria and coding of images,[99] the images I analyse here have been chosen because they are related to human rights in a general sense, because they are visually interesting, and because they are socially relevant since they address, implicitly or explicitly, exclusions.[100] Other images of course exist and could have been analysed too, but a selection is inevitable in the case of such a qualitative analysis.[101] Therefore, while it cannot be claimed that the images selected represent in a comprehensive way human rights' visual discourses, they exist, they tell a story, and they exert influence – as I would argue, even normative influence. They are influential, either because they are still used long after their creation, or because they are widely circulated; their creation is meaningful to those who produce them, as is particularly obvious in the case of self-representations; and they express in different ways what being a subject of human rights implies, which, in turn, impacts the meaning and reach of these rights. In sum, the images selected show how visual culture reflects and furthers underlying social relations of power, but also how images can reveal that there are other possibilities.

It should be noted again that there are, of course, several ways of interpreting a particular image.[102] An image can indeed have different plausible meaning, and its meaning(s) can be – or be rendered – ambiguous.[103] This is, among other reasons, because images are read within a broader context and also against other images.[104] Images "work", in other words they have the impact intended by the creator, if the viewers have the relevant references and codes implied in the image.[105] Moreover, images of law and authority evolve over time, as do conceptions of law and justice. In other words, images do not have a fixed meaning, but, as already mentioned above, meaning

98 This loosely follows Rose's distinction between different types of visual discourse analysis. Rose.
99 Rose; Bell.
100 Rose, 109.
101 Moreover, it would also be worthwhile to focus on the conditions of production and circulation of these images, including the role of technology, but this is beyond the scope of this analysis.
102 Rose, 150.
103 Hall, "The Spectacle of the 'Other'", 228.
104 Hall, "The Spectacle of the 'Other'", 232. Hall speaks of the regime of representation to designate "the whole repertoire of imagery and visual effects through which 'difference' is represented at any one historical moment". Ibid.
105 Hall, "The Spectacle of the 'Other'", 28–9.

is attributed to them, including by the viewer. More generally, things – that is all things, including but going far beyond images – are given meaning by the ways in which people and cultures represent them, whether this occurs through language, signs or images.[106] Highlighting the context and the fact that the meaning of images changes over time obviously diminishes the role and intentions of the producer of an image.[107] Nevertheless, even if an image can have different interpretations, there is usually a preferred meaning that is chosen by the producer of that image.[108] It is hence important to keep in mind that the creation and circulation of images are not neutral endeavours but often serve particular – political, ideological, economic or other – purposes. Furthermore, while photographs, like images more generally, have sometimes been promoted as a "universal language",[109] they can also be understood as a hegemonic language in the Gramscian sense, that is as the language used by dominant, ruling actors with the usually implicit consent of those subjected to this rule.[110] This is particularly problematic since photographs nowadays mediate close to all spheres of life.[111]

Making sense of iconic representations of key moments in the history of human rights

Images that were produced at key moments in the history of human rights and that are still looked upon today represent the essence of important changes in legal thought. Some of these key moments that have been depicted visually are the adoption of the 1789 *Déclaration des droits de l'homme et du citoyen* and the adoption of the *Universal Declaration of Human Rights* (UDHR) in 1948. While it should be remembered that the drafting of these declarations occurred, of course, within a complex context, carefully looking at the images produced at such decisive moments can nonetheless reveal much about the crystallization of particular concepts and norms. As Manderson writes: "Visual media provide us with critical representations that distil and illuminate with remarkable clarity transitions that took place very slowly".[112] In other words, analysing images and the context in which they were produced is one way to gain a critical perspective on longer processes, in this case the development of international human rights law.[113]

---

106 Hall, "The Spectacle of the 'Other'", 3.
107 Rose cites Roland Barthes' proclamation of "the death of the author" in this context. Rose, 26.
108 Hall, "The Spectacle of the 'Other'", 228.
109 Peter Hamilton, 144.
110 Gramsci.
111 Azoulay, 39.
112 Manderson, "Introduction", 9.
113 This is of course not how images, and in particular photographs, are usually understood, that is as "a neat slice of time". Sontag, 13.

One of the most famous images of the 1789 *Déclaration des droits de l'homme et du citoyen* (hereafter *Déclaration*) was painted, probably in 1789, by Jean-Jacques-François Le Barbier, an artist who was heavily involved in politics. Le Barbier was most likely a freemason and adhered to the ideas of the Revolution.[114] While different prints of the *Déclaration* were produced and distributed throughout France at the time, it seems that this painting served as the most important reference and inspired many printmakers.[115] The ongoing influence of this painting is revealed by the fact that the painting is now exposed in the musée Carnavalet, the museum dedicated to the history of Paris, and that electronic versions accompany important websites on the *Déclaration*, such as those of the French Presidency and the popular online encyclopedia Wikipedia.[116]

This painting consists of two horizontal sections: two female figures occupy the top third while the rest of the image is filled with written text in the form of a detailed list. The figure in the upper left corner, dressed in blue, red and white – the colours of France – represents the French people. She has just broken the chains of the old regime and absolute monarchy. The figure on the right side, the one with wings, is an angel that embodies Liberty and possibly the new *Assemblée nationale*. With her left arm, she directs the viewer's gaze to the text below, i.e. the new *Déclaration*. With a power-symbolizing sceptre in her right arm, she points to an eye, which stands for reason and consciousness and has even been described as "l'œil suprême de la raison".[117] The eye is the centre of a triangle that evokes the biblical trinity but arguably also symbolizes the French trinity (i.e. *liberté, égalité, fraternité*). In the lower and larger part of the painting, the rights and freedoms in the form of articles are listed on a support that evokes Moses' tables of law with the Ten Commandments. The pike – and not the sword of the king, previously a common symbol of power – between the two rows of rights and liberties represents the force of the law. This painting hence makes use of well-known and common symbols at the time (the tables of law, an angel, a scepter and an eye) to give authority to a groundbreaking new concept, namely a declaration of rights and freedoms that belong to the people. The image is trying to convince the viewer that these rights need to be codified and, despite certain references to democratic ideas, that they are handed down, or at least supported by, a higher authority. This also conveys the conviction that human rights are rooted in natural law. Indeed, elements like the shining light in the sky and the angel make it clear that god – not the king, as it was previously the case – gives the French people his benediction for declaring rights. The sculptured frame around the articles, evoking an ancient temple, also

114 Musée Carnavalet; Viroulaud, 80.
115 Viroulaud, 82.
116 Elysée; Wikipédia, "Déclaration des droits de l'homme et du citoyen 1789".
117 Viroulaud, 84.

Figure 4.1 Jean-Jacques-François Le Barbier's painting of the **1789** *Déclaration des droits de l'homme et du citoyen.*

Photo credit: Musée Carnavalet – Histoire de Paris, <www.carnavalet.paris.fr/en/collections/declaration-des-droits-de-lhomme-et-du-citoyen> (last accessed on February 12, 2024)

contributes to bestowing a sacred character to the *Déclaration.*[118] Finally, the symbols that are utilized, in particular the figure dressed in the colours of France and the triangle alluding to the French trinity, suggest that declaring

118 Viroulaud, 84.

rights require a political community, as discussed in Chapter 1 in the context of Arendt's critique of human rights.

The influence of this painting can perhaps be detected in another prominent image associated with human rights, namely a 1949 photograph of Eleanor Roosevelt, a distinguished human rights activist, holding and immersed in a printed version of the UDHR. This picture is one of a few that illustrate the United Nations webpage on the UDHR; it is also the image used by prominent non-governmental human rights organizations, such as

Figure 4.2 Eleanor Roosevelt holding a poster of the 1948 *Universal Declaration of Human Rights.*

Photo credit: Franklin D. Roosevelt Presidential Library and Museum, <www.fdrlibrary.org/eleanor-roosevelt> (last accessed on June 2, 2023)

Amnesty International, in their presentation of the UDHR, and also accompanies the UDHR entry on Wikipedia.[119]

In the tradition of European depictions of authority, and as it was the case in Le Barbier's painting, a figure is used to bestow authority. This time, it is not an allegorical figure, but a prominent member of the drafting committee of the UDHR, Eleanor Roosevelt. In this picture, the main lines consist of Roosevelt's arms that link her body to the poster, and thus create a circle that suggests a coherent or consistent whole. With this embrace, the first chairperson of the UN body that overlooked the coming together of the declaration, who was also a former first lady of the United States, arguably the strongest international power at the time, brings authority to the UDHR. This is underlined by the tight frame bringing the focus on Roosevelt and the poster; there is not much else in the picture that could divert the viewer's attention. At the same time, the main source of light comes from the poster itself, which, it can be argued, suggests that no higher or external authority, or even a particular political community in an Arendtian sense, is needed anymore: as the preamble of the UDHR stipulates, the authority comes from the "inherent dignity" of all members of the big human family. The most fundamental message to be conveyed by the photograph is precisely the importance and authority of this seminal text, and the tight composition and the soft shades of white and black create a sense of intimacy, which helps anyone looking at the photograph feel a connection to the figure, the text and the message.

In light of the traditional concept of the human, it is highly relevant that the UDHR is presented by a woman, namely the only female member of the drafting committee. While there is a long tradition of representing justice as a female figure in Western democracies, often with reference to Roman or Greek goddesses,[120] it is worth noting that the 1789 *Déclaration des droits de l'homme et du citoyen* had clearly been conceived in such a way as to restrict the concept of human to men, and hence imagined men as the only rights-bearers. This was highlighted by the rejection of Olympe de Gouges' 1791 attempt to broaden the meaning of the *Déclaration* by ironically re-naming it *Déclaration des droits de la femme et de la citoyenne*.[121] Given this historical bias of human rights as men's rights, the choice of having Eleanor Roosevelt in the 1949 photograph can be interpreted as an appeal to women (at least of the Western world), so that they too recognize the authority of human rights and embrace the values underlying the UDHR, such as equality. It is also interesting to remember that, at the time the picture was taken, the Cold War increasingly defined the international political context. Notwithstanding

119 United Nations, "Universal Declaration of Human Rights"; Amnesty International UK; Wikipedia, "Universal Declaration of Human Rights".
120 For a semiotic analysis of Justitia, see Sutherland-Smith.
121 Bottici, 163–4; Adami, 89.

Roosevelt's achievements as a human rights activist, it is worth noting that she was a wealthy woman, as her pearl necklace and sober yet elegant clothes remind the viewer; one could infer from this image that it is liberal democracy that brings about and guarantees human rights. She was, after all, a former first lady of the United States, the self-proclaimed champion of democracy and liberalism. In this sense, justice here is not only represented by a female figure, as in the earlier image; the figure, Roosevelt, has a particular identity that is relevant to the message to be conveyed by the image.

The same poster of the 1948 UDHR is used again by the United Nations, yet in a different context: taken in 1950, the photograph below celebrates the

Figure 4.3 A 1950 photograph of a group of children looking at a poster of the *Universal Declaration of Human Rights.*

Photo credit: UN Photo/United Nations Information Service Vienna, <https://unis.unvienna.org/unis/en/topics/human-rights.html> (last accessed on February 10, 2024)

second anniversary of the adoption of the UDHR. It illustrates the UN "History of the Declaration" webpage, which is indicative of its ongoing use by prominent actors in the field.[122]

A first reading of this picture shows a group of children from a UN nursery standing or sitting outside in a half circle around the poster of the UDHR. A little girl on the right side points to the declaration, with the gaze of all the children – not all of whom are white – following her finger. With the swing in the background and some clothes lying on the grass, it looks as if the children just stopped playing to gather around this poster. The UDHR – and its rights and freedoms – has been taken out of UN offices and animated and incorporated into everyday life.[123] Here again, the text itself is the main source of light, hinting at its self-referential authority. The rights and freedoms are no longer reserved for white people, but they are embraced by individuals from different ethnic backgrounds. The authority of the UDHR is now enhanced by it being accessible to all and by being a promise for future generations. Interestingly, a little girl is pointing to the declaration, in a similar manner as the angel in Le Barbier's painting, thus drawing the viewer's attention to the text. On a closer look, one wonders though: is the girl pointing to an article, a fleck or a blank spot? And what does the gaze of the other chil dren really say – are these children seriously concentrating on the UDHR, are they doubtful, or maybe just bored? In fact, only literate persons can read the UDHR, which, ironically, is probably not the case of most of these pre-school children, who are, moreover, "reading" the text upside down. As for universality, one can notice that only a couple of children are clearly non-white; the great majority still represents the dominant part of society. Moreover, as their clothes and overall appearance show, these children seem healthy and to come from middle-class or wealthy families. In short, in spite of the obvious efforts made to represent the UDHR as a document that is accessible to all, the image falls short of achieving this goal.[124] This illustrates the point that images, in all their meanings, are not only used by law; they are, as Manderson has argued, also "unruly" and reveal the "excessive and subconscious meaning" of legal culture.[125]

In both photographs of the UDHR – the one of Roosevelt and the one of the children – there is a certain indeterminacy and ambiguity. The title of the poster can easily be read and attracts attention, but the body of the text – the rights and freedoms themselves – is not readable. This could

122 United Nations, "History of the Declaration".
123 This draws on Goodrich, "Faces and Frames of Government", 65.
124 That the "imagined universality" of the UDHR has, from the outset, rested on exclusions is also visible in a travelling exhibition designed by UNESCO to explain the UDHR in the early 1950s, with the exhibition constructing "a universal history of human rights using a European lens". Charlesworth.
125 Manderson, "Introduction", 12.

be considered a weakness of the photograph, maybe resulting from a bad focus by the photographer. But, in fact, this ambiguity can be empowering by allowing human rights to be reinterpreted and appropriated in different contexts. In a way, hiding the text in such a way means that everyone can claim credit for and relate to the UDHR. The relative ambiguity in the representations of the UDHR was particularly useful in the context of the fundamental ideological divide between political and civil rights, which were promoted by Western, liberal countries, and economic, social and cultural rights, dear to the communist countries. In this sense, images are always more complex than they appear, and what matters is often what is not represented,[126] or not clearly represented. This representation of international human rights also reflects an important idea that draws on authors like Hannah Arendt, Seyla Benhabib and Ayten Gündoğdu discussed in Chapter 1, namely that rights, including new rights, are created through a continuous political practice; rights can be invented and reinterpreted, especially in the face of exclusions from existing rights, as the example of *sans-papiers* in France, who claim a right to a legal status, shows. The framing of the UDHR photographs is hence very different from Le Barbier's painting of the 1789 *Déclaration* and its easily readable list of rights and freedoms, presented in the form of rules reminiscent of the biblical Ten Commandments, which conveys a more straightforward message and leaves little room for different interpretations.

Yet it can be concluded with respect to both declarations that showing the text in some way was considered essential to affirm the legal authority and formal status of the declarations. A possible explanation is that the text matters more in the context of newly declared rights, which are not yet widely accepted or understood. Over time, this perceived necessity to strongly focus on the text to assert the authority of the respective legal instrument seems to diminish, which is reflected in visual human rights discourses.

Exposing emerging trends in contemporary official discourses

When considering contemporary visual discourses in human rights, an interesting shift from the earlier images analysed is noticeable.[127] The following two pictures, which have been selected because they are used by influential UN bodies in important documents and are hence arguably part of the

---

126 Goodrich, "Faces and Frames of Government", 71.
127 While the large number of photographs used nowadays by governmental and non-governmental organizations in the field makes it difficult to draw definite conclusions based on the analysis of a few images, and while the historical distance that would allow identifying certain images as iconic or as representing the essence of a key moment or change is lacking, it is nonetheless possible to identify what seems to be an emerging trend in the visual discourse in the field of international human rights.

Figure 4.4 The cover image of the 2013 Annual Report of the UN Office of the High Commissioner for Human Rights.

Photo credit: OHCHR/UNICEF/NYHQ2014–0349/Kate Holt, <www2.ohchr.org/english/OHCHRReport2013/WEB_version/index.html> (last accessed February 10, 2024)

Figure 4.5 The cover image of the 2016–2017 Global Appeal published by the UN
High Commissioner for Refugees.

Photo credit: UNHCR, <www.unhcr.org/ga16/index.xml> (accessed on 19 September 2016)

dominant visual discourse of international human rights, are revealing in
this regard.[128] The first one is the cover image of the 2013 Annual Report of
the UN Office of the High Commissioner for Human Rights; the second one
illustrates the 2016–2017 Global Appeal published by the UN High Commissioner for Refugees. These two documents are major publications that
have been widely shared to explain, justify and promote the work of these
UN bodies, which are among the most prominent actors in international human rights.

The people depicted in the first photograph, identified on the last page
of the report, in small print, as "[w]omen and children displaced by recent
fighting in South Sudan queuing to collect food",[129] look poor and mal-
nourished; those in the second picture, who are not identified in the report,
seem anxious and in some distress. In both pictures, they form, sitting or
standing, seemingly endless lines, probably waiting for further instructions

128 While it would be interesting to confirm the (strong) impression that such images dominate
    the official discourses of influential human rights actors through a quantitative-oriented
    content analysis, this is not the objective of the present analysis.
129 UN Office of the High Commissioner for Human Rights. *Annual Report 2013*, 200.

or for their turn. This conveys the idea that they are awaiting help or relief, and that they must be patient and "behave" in order for their rights claims to be heard – or one could even say for their rights to be given to them. This is reminiscent of the visual discourse used by the abolitionist movement that sought to end slavery. Commonly used images were meant to appeal

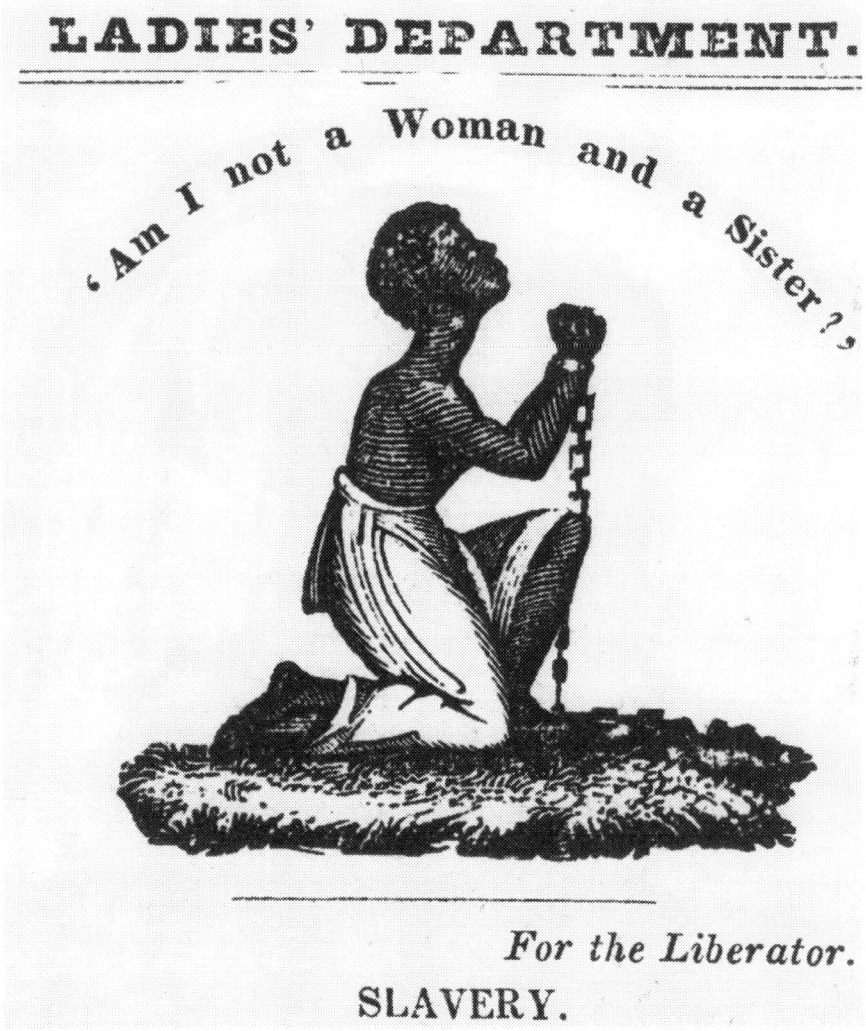

Figure 4.6 Anti-slavery campaign banner from the 1830s.

Photo credit: The Library Company of Philadelphia

to a shared humanness and accompanied slogans like "Are you not a man and brother?" and "Am I not a women and a sister?" However, Stuart Hall highlights how Black people in these representations were typically also represented as supplicants "kneeling to their white benefactors",[130] who by implication are imagined as superior and able to grant rights. This is exemplified by the image above taken from a campaign banner used in the 1830s.[131]

As explained above, images are always produced and viewed within a broader context that includes previous images, which is why historical images matter and can shed light on the creation and interpretation of more contemporary images. Both then and now, the persons represented in the pictures analysed here clearly do not correspond to the privileged subject of Western law, namely the white, rational man. The pictures define these people in a very restricted manner, one that fits with the image of the typical victim of human rights violations; they are portrayed as 'Others' – and will likely be considered as such by the viewers constituting the target readership of these reports – who lack agency and who cannot construct and take advantage of any kind of genuine legal subjectivity. In fact, there is a long history of racialized visual discourses in photography and other visual media, that operate with sets of binaries, like Black/white, savage/civilized, male/female, and express and reify the superiority and domination of one pole of the binary over the other, and that are rendered even more polarized through the image.[132] From the Black body being linked to 'nature' and imagined as savage and hence subjectable to white domination, as pointed out by Black studies authors and discussed in the previous chapter, to soap advertisements in the times of the British empire that suggested that black skin can be washed white,[133] historical representational practices continue to shape contemporary visual discourses and interpretations of images of difference. The long-standing tradition in visual discourses to rely on binaries and entrench difference explains why certain individuals and groups, such as visible minorities, Indigenous peoples and women, are still defined and

130 Hall, "The Spectacle of the 'Other'", 249.
131 A similar image is replicated on the website of the National Archives of the United Kingdom dedicated to the abolition of the slave trade. National Archives.
132 Hall, "The Spectacle of the 'Other'", 243. According to Stuart Hall, there are three key historical periods in the European "racialized regime of representation": the first period started in the 16th century with the European exploration of the African continent and the ensuing transatlantic slave trade; the second period consisted in the colonization of the African continent by European powers; and the third form of encounter began in the aftermath of World War II with the mounting migration of people from so-called developing countries to the Global North. Ibid, 239.
133 Hall, "The Spectacle of the 'Other'", 241–2.

entrapped by law and its visual discourse in their construction and representation as 'Others'.[134] More specifically, these developments also explain the significant shift in the representations of refugees and migrants; while writers like Arendt mostly had the Jewish people in mind when writing about refugees in the mid-20th century, the refugee has become increasingly racialized and is now typically represented as a racialized 'Other', as is also visible in the images analysed here.

Another striking example consists in a picture used by the UN High Commissioner for Refugees (UNHCR) for an awareness and fundraising campaign in the context of the persecution of members of the Rohingya community in Myanmar. The image appeared prominently on the main homepage of the agency in mid-2018, when the persecution of members of the Rohingya community intensified.[135] The image shows a close-up of the face of a dark-skinned child, looking directly at the viewer with wide-open eyes, as if pleading for help. The text next to the face, "Thousands of Rohingya children are fleeing violence. Send help now", suggests that this is a Rohingya child who is fleeing violence. On a closer look, one realizes that the child is separated from the viewer by a metal fence, which suggests that without help, it is stuck in a dangerous and hopeless situation. The dark colours in the upper two-thirds of the image can be viewed as alluding to the violence that Rohingyas experience and contrast with the white background in the lower third, from where help and relief can be expected, namely from the UN and from the viewer who can click on an icon "Help them survive" to make a donation. This icon is coloured in bright red, which contributes to creating a sense of urgency.[136]

These contemporary images produced and circulated by UN agencies illustrate that victims – and not legal instruments conveying a sense of hope, as in the previous iconic representations – have become the focus of the visual discourses in human rights, which is part of a larger shift that has occurred in international human rights in recent decades.[137] It is no longer the authority of human rights in a general sense that these images try to demonstrate

---

134 Flynn, 140.
135 The image is no longer available online and could, unfortunately, not be provided for publication in this book. It was, however, included in the author's PhD thesis, which is available here: <https://spectrum.library.concordia.ca/id/eprint/990630/> (see page 111).
136 It may be interesting to note in this context that UNHCR is funded almost entirely through voluntary contributions. The fact that most of these contributions come from countries in the Global North hints at the target viewership of such images. For more information, see UN High Commissioner for Refugees, "Budget and Expenditure". On the influence of semiotic choices, including the choice of words, in relation to visual discourse, see Machin & Mayr, chapter 3.
137 For instance, on the recent emphasis on victims' rights, see van Boven.

and establish. This authority now seems to be assumed, or even taken for granted; it is the protection of human rights in specific instances that is show-cased. Children and women are often represented as victims in these visual discourses, suggesting that human rights exist first and foremost for members of certain groups considered vulnerable, and conveying an image of an ideal victim of human rights violations who "deserves" the viewer's attention and reaction. The individuality of those represented, their history and aspirations are lost. Indeed, photographs of victims of human rights violations, which are usually taken by human rights organizations and defenders and by pho-tojournalists, and not by the victims themselves, construct and re-inscribe the identity of the victim in limited and predetermined ways. As Liisa H. Malkki argues with respect to refugees, they "stop being specific persons and become pure victims".[138] The ways in which refugees have been imagined in discur-sive and representational forms by governments, international organizations and also in the media have actually become standardized since the end of World War II.[139] The "ideal", "genuine" beneficiaries of international help, or rights, are represented and imagined as victims who have been affected by their experiences to such an extent that they cannot reason and think for themselves.[140] Since "[p]ictures of refugees are now a key vehicle in the elaboration of a transnational social imagination of refugeeness",[141] it can be said that certain ways of representing these "victims" serve as justification for the international community to carry out this task for them, notably via humanitarian actors.

Although visual discourses are now also present and extremely influen-tial on online platforms, and not only in traditional media, little seems to have changed over the years with respect to the kinds of images produced and circulated. When there are changes in the official discourses, they seem relatively minor, and they occur slowly. Recently, for instance, the images that have been chosen to illustrate the latest annual reports of the OHCHR are clearly meant to send a different, more positive signal than previously.

But the changes are arguably not fundamental: the agency of the smiling girl in Figure 4.7 is limited, as she almost certainly did not choose herself to be represented with this message; comparing this representation with the more complex and expressive forms of self-representation discussed below is telling. And the image that illustrates the main website of the UNHCR as late as 2023 is very much part of the conventional visual discourse that depicts people as generic victims awaiting relief.

138 Malkki, 378.
139 Malkki, 386.
140 Malkki, 384.
141 Malkki, 386.

Figure 4.7 Cover page of OHCHR's 2020 Annual Report.

Photo credit: OHCHR-Guinea, <www.ohchr.org/en/publications/annual-report/ohchr-report-2020> (last accessed on May 7, 2021)

Figure 4.8 UNHCR: "refugee response will need $445 million for rising numbers fleeing Sudan" (May 2023).

Photo credit: UNHCR/Colin Delfosse, <www.unhcr.org> (last accessed on May 11, 2023)

As I would conclude, the images analysed above seem to exemplify that recent visual discourses of influential actors in international human rights reflect and reinforce the idea that those in need of the protection of human rights lack agency and are helpless recipients of humanitarian assistance. The dominant visual discourse hence contributes to constructing (legal) subjects in certain, often limiting or even exclusionary ways.

It is also worth noting that efforts have been made, including by the UN-HCR, to give a greater voice – or visual presence – to refugees themselves. For instance, the "Refugee Storytelling Project" was launched in 2011. It consists of a series of YouTube videoclips in which refugees tell their own stories of migration.[142] Instead of being represented by an outsider, they are supposed to be given the opportunity to represent themselves. However, as it has been argued, the diversity of refugees' experiences is not really expressed in this initiative; rather, the UN agency controls the format, presentation and story, and even seems to impose a grand narrative, with the refugees who are featured in the project having been preselected to support a certain discourse and presented and celebrated as resilient victims.[143] This underlines that relying on or contributing to the creation of a particular visual discourse, as prominent actors in international human rights do, always risks creating exclusions, and that every representation, including self-representation, needs to be understood in its context and analysed critically.

Representing diversity and the legal subject through alternative visual discourses

While certain trends can be detected in the dominant visual discourse in international human rights, there are, of course, many different ways in which the subject of human rights and legal subjectivity can be represented. The following examples of photographs of refugees and migrants as well as of paintings and installations created by Indigenous artists reflect some of this diversity and help to contextualize the official, dominant discourse. The objective of analysing these images, as already noted when introducing the critical visual discourse analysis, is not to be comprehensive in any way or to suggest that these representations are more genuine or true than others. In fact, it would be impossible to do justice to the great diversity of visual discourses. With respect to Indigenous art – in this context, art that has been created by Aboriginal artists in the settler colonial state of Australia – it should also be highlighted that the works selected do not represent Indigenous art or Indigenous cosmovisions exhaustively, and the inclusion of these images here is not meant to contribute to the essentialization of Indigenous art or traditions.

142 See the YouTube channel UNHCR Story Telling.
143 Harsch.

Keeping these *caveats* in mind, I nevertheless suggest that the selected images show that alternative discourses are possible, and that these alternatives are important, meaningful and possibly inspiring.

The following picture, taken by a photographer of the news agency Reuters and published in 2015 in the Daily Mail, one of the largest newspapers in the United Kingdom, accompanies an article about migrants from the Middle East, especially Syria and Afghanistan, arriving on Greek islands and their subsequent journeys in Europe. It shows three young men, with relatively dark skin, posing for a selfie that one of them is taking with a cell phone. They stand on the shore of a pebble beach, in front of a rubber boat floating in the water, with another shoreline in the background. The three men have raised their index and middle fingers in a V-sign, and one of them is wearing a life vest, suggesting that they have recently disembarked from the boat and that they are celebrating their arrival. What would not be visible in the selfie but is shown by the photojournalist are orange life vests, a safety ring, a backpack and a few more items that are difficult to identify and that are scattered around the men, giving the impression of some random action or even disorder.

Self-representation, as it should be noted, has become increasingly accessible in recent years, among others thanks to the availability of technology,

Figure 4.9 A photograph of migrants accompanying a *Daily Mail* article in 2015.

Photo credit: Reuters/*Daily Mail* <www.dailymail.co.uk/news/article-3208849/We-just-Greece-Macedonia-Serbia-Hungary-Migrants-pose-selfies-second-reach-dry-land-completing-stage-trek-Europe.html> (last accessed on February 25, 2024)

such as smartphones and social media, and taking selfies has become popular also among refugees and migrants. Drawing on Jill Walker Rettberg's analysis of self-portraiture more generally, this can be understood as a reaction to feeling misrepresented in dominant visual discourses.[144] The subaltern, as Ella Shohat claims more specifically, because they have been denied "aesthetic representation" and historically been "spoken for", struggles to "speak for oneself".[145] With Roopika Risam, it can also be argued that migrants from the Global South, by engaging in self-representation, resist "commodification and appropriation for political ends of the Global North".[146] However, as demonstrated in a study of articles related to selfies of Syrian migrants published in major newspapers in the United States and the United Kingdom in 2015 and 2016, so-called refugee selfies remain marginal in the dominant discourse on human rights.[147] Moreover, they are not circulated by mainstream news media in the Global North in the way they were created; it is rather images taken by news photographers of refugees taking selfies of themselves, notably when reaching the shores of Europe, as illustrated above, or when posing with prominent politicians, that are circulated. As it is often the case with the images of refugees and migrants circulated by media in the Global North,[148] the image above is not the actual selfie taken by the migrants themselves; it is what Lilie Chouliaraki has called a "migrant-related selfie".[149] The fact that the original frame of the selfie represented above – without the scattered objects on the beach – and hence the selfie's intended message are not respected in the published image, and the fact that the migrants' names are never included in the captions accompanying these images – there are also no disclaimers that the migrants preferred not to share their real names – contribute to the objectification of the migrants represented.[150]

By controlling how self-representations of migrants are represented and circulated, dominant actors from the Global North hence continue to dominate the visual discourse and regulate its message. Risam usefully argues in this context that the act of taking selfies is co-opted by dominant discourses that represent the non-Western 'Other' in ways that are determined by those who represent, and not those who are represented.[151] This is achieved through a "well-worn colonialist trope: representation of the other from the Global South (here, Syrian refugees) as an object of knowledge for the Global

---

144 Rettberg, 29.
145 As Shohat has noted, this "struggle to 'speak for oneself' cannot be separated from a history of being spoken for, from the struggle to speak and be heard". Shohat, 173.
146 Risam, 68.
147 The author describes this methodology as "postcolonial digital humanities". Risam, 58.
148 Risam, 61.
149 Chouliaraki, 78.
150 Risam, 63.
151 Risam, 59 (drawing on Gayatri Chakravorty Spivak).

North (here, news media)".[152] It might be worth recalling that, as Edward Saïd already argued, the West has conceived the Orient as unable to represent itself, which means that the West allows itself to represent the Orient, "for the West, and . . . for the poor Orient".[153] From Dante to Shakespeare (and beyond), as demonstrated by Saïd, "the Orient and Islam are always represented as outsiders having a special role to play *inside* Europe".[154] Representations, such as "migrant-related selfies", always fulfill certain functions, including to justify power relations, in which the West actively studies and dominates the 'Other' that is constructed as a passive object of knowledge to be dominated;[155] ultimately, this also serves as a justification for colonialism and the construction of actual and symbolic borders.[156] In other words, even if self-representation, in particular through the use of selfies, has become common and accessible, the refugees' possibility of sovereign and impactful self-representation and agency are, again, denied or curtailed.

Creative photography is another way in which migrants have been visually represented and that often tries to reflect how they would like to present themselves. This can also be understood as a form of countervisuality, or even as an exercise of Mirzoeff's right to look as discussed above. Engaged fashion photography is an example, as illustrated by the work of Nigerian-born designer Walé Oyéjidé. In 2016, shortly after a significant increase in migration from African and Asian countries to Europe, this designer started to cast asylum seekers as models to showcase his latest collections, creating aesthetic and positive images of Black migrants purposefully set in fashion hotspots and appealing cities like Florence, Rome and New York. By circulating these images through the channels available to him as a successful designer, Oyéjidé seeks to challenge dominant discourses and to represent migrants, in close collaboration with these migrants, in a radically more positive light than what is common in mainstream media. His approach, as he himself describes it, consists in asking the migrants how they would like to be seen and photographed, and being cast as models for photoshoots reportedly felt gratifying for them.[157] While the fact that refugees and undocumented migrants, or their descendants, posed for Oyéjidé's photoshoots might be the most striking aspect of the following two photographs, there are several interesting visual aspects that are also worth mentioning.

This first image shows two Black models, a woman and a man, in colourful clothes, against a dark background. They look composed and elegant

152 Risam, 63.
153 Saïd, 21.
154 Saïd, 71.
155 Saïd, 308.
156 For a discussion of "symbolic bordering", see Chouliaraki.
157 Gharib.

Figure 4.10 A photograph features James Jean and Patrice Worthy, Haitian American and African American, respectively, in New York City.

Photo credit: Rog Walker for Walé Oyéjidé's label Ikiré Jones. A coloured, high-resolution version is available at <https://ikirejones.com/ss17-born-between-borders> (last accessed on February 25, 2024)

and gaze directly into the camera. The models stand side by side, as is common in the European tradition of portraits of wealthy couples.[158] The dark background and the light shining on the faces of the models are actually reminiscent of portraits made by Renaissance and Baroque artists like Raphaël, Rubens, and Rembrandt. Both wear clothes that seem to be made of high-quality fabrics and that are of contemporary creation, integrating

158 See for instance the 1434 portrait of Giovanni Arnolfini and his wife by Jan van Eyck.

different elements and styles. The man wears a suit of Western cut but in a colourful fabric that is evocative of African styles; a golden scarf, featuring motives of Renaissance paintings, is draped around half of his torso. A white symbol is painted on his face, reminiscent of traditional African symbols. The woman wears a sumptuous, bright red lace dress with a matching veil. Her posture, with her hands folded together, her veil covering her head and the opulence of her dress gathered below her chest, contribute to making her look like an aristocrat represented in the European tradition.[159] In other words, the artist seems to make direct reference to forms of representation in Western art history to convey a sense of pride, wealth and influence. All these elements, which have positive connotations and allow the subjects to be individuals with their own particularities – and not just a standardized representation of a migrant in need of assistance – are glaringly absent in the representation of refugees and migrants produced and circulated by human rights organizations analysed above.

In the next image, the venue and the images within the image are particularly striking. The model is a Black man with dreadlocks, standing in the middle of what looks like a church. The caption reveals that it is located in Rome. The sumptuous, spacious and well-lit church (or palace), with high, arched ceilings, is a setting that is familiar, and perhaps reassuring, to most Italian and many other Western viewers. It is also remarkable that sacral Renaissance paintings adorn the model's lavish dress and matching jacket and include representations of Black people with golden halos, next to details of grandiose buildings. While it may be stretched to argue that the model, Ousman Pa Manneh, originally from The Gambia, is meant to represent an angel or a saint – or perhaps even Jesus – the fact that he stands, by himself, in the middle of what looks like a church, in a warm light and under splendid candelabras, does hint at the idea of salvation. Here again, the intention of the designer and creator of this image is to convey the message that African migrants are not that different from Europeans. They are not dangerous people here, not poor and in need of help, as expressed in the examples of dominant visual human rights discourses discussed above. To build on the argument that I developed in the previous chapter by drawing on theories from the margins, it can even be said that the artist does not represent his African models as 'Others' against whom the modern Western subject historically defined itself.

The final products – both the designer's clothes and the photographs – are, of course, intended largely for consumers and other viewers in the Global North, and circulating them in the Global North potentially increases their

159 The representation of one of the founders of a Gothic cathedral in Germany, sculpted on the façade of the cathedral itself in exactly the same position, comes to mind. See the image of the founders of the 13th-century cathedral of Naumburg in Gombrich, 194.

Figure 4.11 Ousman Pa Manneh, originally from The Gambia, photographed in Rome in 2018.

Photo credit: 10 Leaves for Walé Oyéjidé's label Ikiré Jones. A coloured, high-resolution version is available at <https://ikirejones.com/after-migration2> (last accessed on February 25, 2024)

political impact. Yet, it is clear that representing migrants in a collaborative and celebratory mode, as in the two images above, sends a different message than the one of the dominant visual discourses illustrated with the images used by human rights organizations: suffering is not the main theme here, but pride and elegance are, and refugees and migrants are not portrayed as victims nor as a problem or threat, but as humans. This collaborative and artistic process is arguably also a way to respect the subjects' individuality and agency.

Making art is often conceived as an avenue to represent and express one's identity, subjecthood and suffering, including in relation to human rights violations. Different projects, such as workshops in refugee camps and host communities in Western cities, give refugees and migrants the chance to share their experiences through art.[160] Arguably building on the long-standing tradition of self-portraits in Western art,[161] self-representation through visual means seems to be a common avenue for such projects.[162] An example is a project titled "Self Portrait Refugee", which seeks to combat what researchers have found to be the typically negative press coverage of refugees in the United Kingdom[163] by encouraging refugees and asylum seekers to "make a creative statement about who they are, how they want to be seen and reveal their own experiences, hopes and dreams for the future".[164] The creations have been exhibited physically in public spaces, such as metro stations, as well as online. The next image is drawn from this collection.[165]

The collage was created by a woman identified as "Elisabeth" in the description at the bottom. It shows a young Black woman, possibly the creator herself, in black and white, standing in front of a wall of fire of various tones of red, orange and yellow. Her posture suggests she is tired yet calm and unmoved by the feeling of emergency and the risk of being engulfed by the threatening fire that occupies the entire background. Contrary to the standardized way of representing refugees and migrants, discussed above and exemplified in the photographs used in reports and campaigns of human rights organizations, the individuality of Elisabeth, her history and her aspirations are not lost. The impression that the viewer gets is that this young woman has seen and experienced a lot in her life, and that she will not allow herself to give up when facing a challenging situation. A flying bird of prey, probably a hawk, has been drawn above her, in the top right corner of the image. The hawk, which evokes freedom, strength and courage, reinforces

---

160 For the description of a project with Syrian and Palestinian refugees in Lebanon that involved women expressing themselves through art and an exhibition of their creations in Europe, see O'Brien.
161 For a history of self-portraiture, see James Hall.
162 One can wonder if the main reason is that many participants prefer this way of expressing themselves, or if it is that organizations facilitating these projects value and support this kind of expression.
163 For a comparative analysis of press coverage of refugees and migrants in five European countries, including the United Kingdom, see Berry, Garcia-Blanco & Moore.
164 Media 19.
165 See Media 19 for further examples.

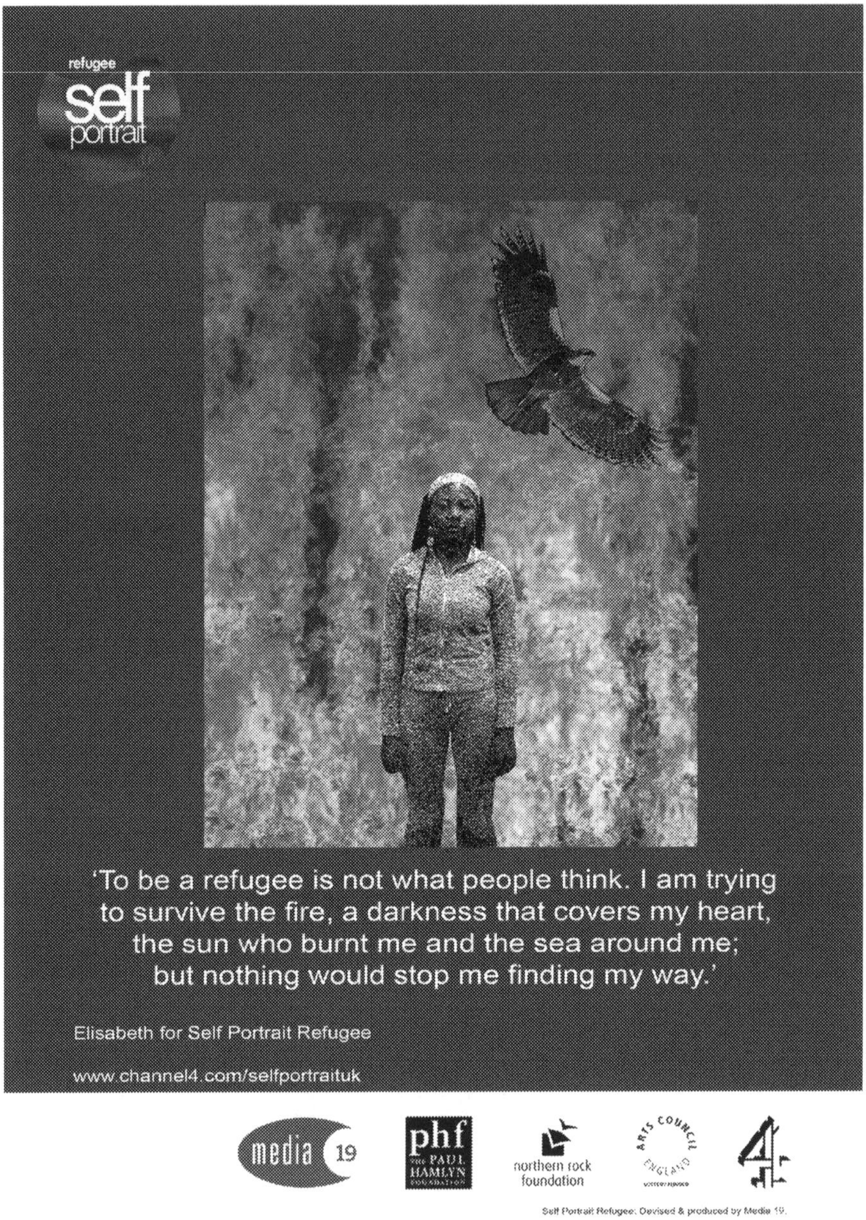
refugee
self
portrait
'To be a refugee is not what people think. I am trying to survive the fire, a darkness that covers my heart, the sun who burnt me and the sea around me; but nothing would stop me finding my way.'
Elisabeth for Self Portrait Refugee
www.channel4.com/selfportraituk
media 19
phf THE PAUL HAMLYN FOUNDATION
northern rock foundation
ARTS COUNCIL ENGLAND
Self Portrait Refugee: Devised & produced by Media 19.

Figure 4.12 A self-portrait of a refugee called Elisabeth, made as part of the UK-based project "Self Portrait Refugee".

Photo credit: Elisabeth for Self Portrait Refugee/Media 19, <www.media19.co.uk/projects/self-portrait-refugee/> (last accessed on August 28, 2023)

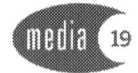

the perception of the woman's perseverance. A quote from the creator accompanies the image; it explains the difficulty of her situation but also affirms her resilience and individuality. At the same time, the symbols of the organization that hosted the project and of the institutions that financed it have been added – presumably by someone else at a later stage in the creation and publication process – at the top and bottom of the image, implicitly reminding the viewer that this image is part of a larger narrative influenced by different institutions and their objectives.

Other discourses in the context of refugees and migrants also challenge and question dominant representations. Atong Atem, an artist originally from South Sudan who moved to Australia as a refugee after having spent years in Ethiopia and Kenya to escape political tensions,[166] is a good example of such an alternative visual discourse, where she is in full control of her image and the message she wants to convey. She creates colourful photographs that seek to contribute to decolonizing the ways in which African people, and eventually migrants from Africa, have been represented by Europeans since the start of colonization to further colonial objectives. Through her art, she denounces the fact that early images of Africans "framed black bodies in such a potent way that socially those frames still exist today".[167] She explains that she seeks to both reclaim ownership of her own narrative, as Elisabeth does in the previous image, and contribute to the valorization of pre-existing visual modes of expression centred on Blackness.[168] Thus, Atem attempts to reshape visual discourses about the subjectivity of refugees and migrants from the Global South, and of colonized people more generally, through her art.

In this portrait, she depicts herself with exuberance and strength. She gazes directly into the camera, with determination and pride in her eyes, surrounded by vibrant colours. She wears artificial flowers of different colours in the form of a thick crown, from which a few strands of braided hair slip out; her eyes are heavily and brightly made-up; white dots are painted on her cheeks and nose; and green, yellow and reddish lines that evoke traditional facial paintings adorn her chin. Her shirt, or dress, which features small flowers on a dark textile, is fairly simple and seems to be of Western design. The close-up portrait leaves only some space for the backdrop, which is also colourful and is reminiscent of African fabrics and hence her origins. This format directs the viewer's attention to her face and gaze. All in all, the picture seems like an affirmation of the artist's subjectivity, expressing her diverse experiences and points of reference as a refugee and migrant, and a strong claim to self-representation.

166 The Pin, "Atong Atem".
167 Artist Profile, "Atong Atem".
168 The Design Files, "The Bright, Beautiful World of Atong Atem".

Figure 4.13 A self-portrait by Atong Atem.

Photo credit: Atong Atem, <www.atongatem.com/slf-prtrt> (last accessed on January 14, 2024)

A point worth emphasizing here is that many subjects photographed in the context of alternative discourses, as illustrated by the images analysed in this section, look directly into the camera, often with pride, sometimes with defiance. In this sense, they all confront the viewer and make a claim about their subjectivity that can hardly be ignored. They arguably assert ownership over the image, and over the way in which they are represented, which stands in stark contrast to the typical representation of refugees and migrants in dominant visual discourses.

The long European tradition of representing human figures, including through self-portraits, and its focus on humans' (assumed) particular subjectivity that underpins the idea of human rights contrasts with other ways of understanding the human through visual representation. The practice of many Australian Aboriginal artists, for instance, shows an emphasis on the strong relationship between human identity and the land.[169] This is particularly relevant for an analysis of the subject of human rights, because for many Indigenous peoples, human rights violations – if this language and logic are adopted in this context[170] – started with the loss of their land. As noted above, the following works have not been selected because they could supposedly represent Indigenous art or Indigenous cosmovisions. Yet it emerges that many Indigenous artists, rather than explicitly representing human beings as in the European tradition, have often conceived of humans as an integral part of the land, as "an interconnected feature of country".[171] As Jane Raffan writes, this is not a marginal phenomenon, but "Indigenous artists Australia wide demonstrate this concept of self in paintings of home/country".[172] In fact, they could be considered as "portraits", but portraits that, in Pamela McClusky's words, "reveal a person's identity in relation to others, to the land and to the creator ancestors".[173] By way of example, the artist Emily Kame Kngwarreye often said with respect to her paintings of her home country, Alhalkere, that she always painted the "whole lot", meaning that her own existence as a human being and her country could not be separated for her.[174]

Similarly, the Yulparija artist Weaver Jack has said the following about her own paintings: "This is me, this is mine, the whole lot is me . . . he is always here (clasping her heart). We are same one. My country is me".[175] In the following painting, she has painted sand dunes, waterholes, mudflats, trees

169 In fact, this relationship has even been described as a "major marker of identity" for Australian Aboriginal peoples. Caruana.
170 For a discussion of the limits of the dominant logic and language of human rights in the context of Indigenous peoples, see Corntassel.
171 Raffan. It is interesting to observe that some younger, especially urban-based Indigenous artists have taken a different artistic path and, for instance, do explicitly represent human beings, including through self-portraits. See for instance the work of the artist Christian Thompson, born in South Australia and of Bidjara heritage and of Badimaya First Nation artist Julie Dowling.
172 Raffan.
173 As cited in Raffan.
174 Schmidt. For examples of the artist's impressive work consisting of more than 3,000 paintings, such as *Emu Woman*, see the website of the National Museum of Australia, "Emily Kame Kngwarreye".
175 Raffan.

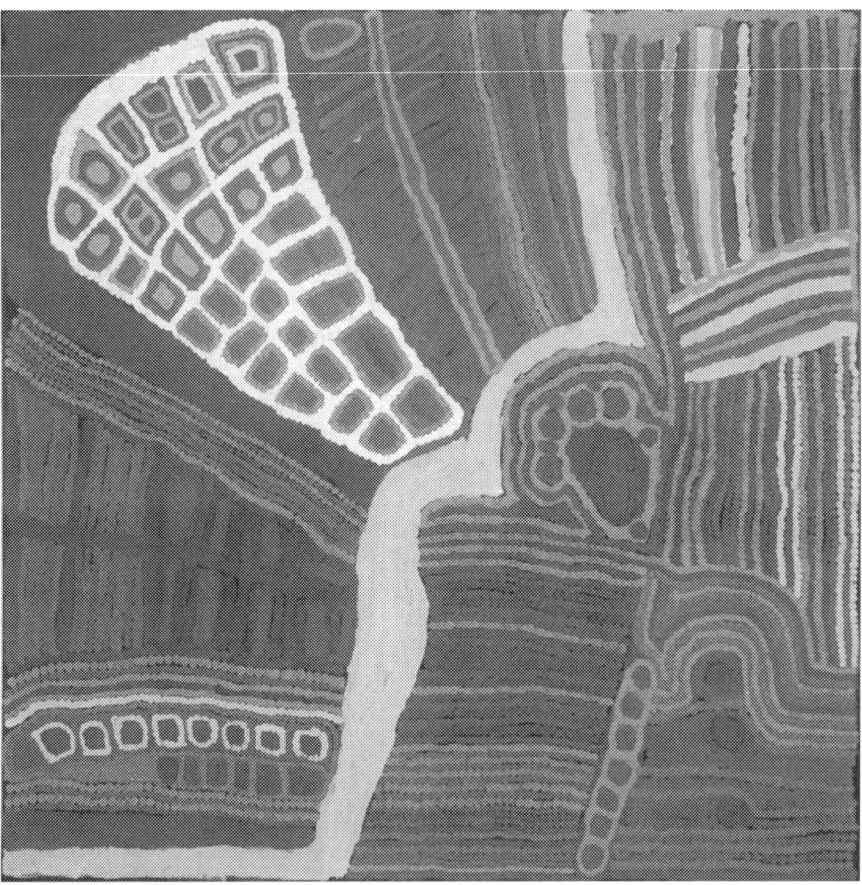

Figure 4.14 A painting, titled *Lungarung*, by Yulparija artist Weaver Jack.

Photo credit: Weaver Jack/Short St. Gallery, <www.shortstgallery.com.au/artworks/786559-weaver-jack-lungarung/> (last accessed on February 25, 2024)

as well as herself and other people.[176] In other words, the painting above is more than an abstract painting of a landscape, which is probably what most viewers would see in such artworks if they are not especially familiar with relevant Indigenous visual art and cosmovisions; Western art history and its dominant methods of interpreting art are obviously also influential in this context. However, as Raffan points out, non-figurative Aboriginal art does not mean an absence of representation.[177] As the artists Emily Kame Kngwarreye

176 Short St Gallery.
177 Raffan.

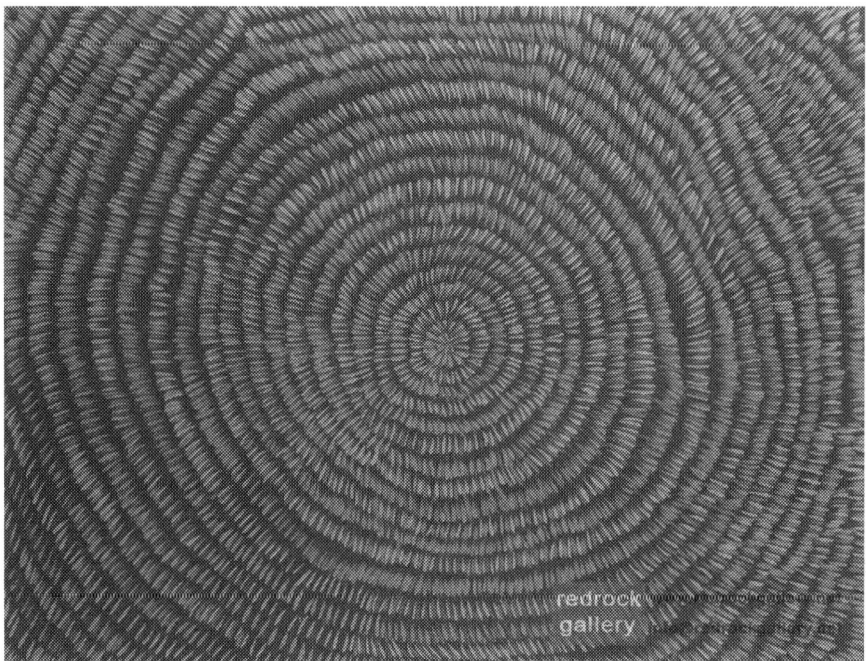

Figure 4.15 Bush Leaf Dreaming, a painting by Anmatyerre artist Gloria Tamerre Petyarre.

Photo credit: Gloria Tamerre Petyarre/Redrock Gallery, <www.redrockgallery.net/prod-ucts/Gloria-Petyarre%252dBush-Leaf-Dreaming%252dRRG223.html> (last accessed on January 14, 2024)

and Weaver Jack say, human beings are part of the "whole lot", which is what they choose to represent in their work.

The painting reproduced in Figure 4.15, titled *Bush Leaf Dreaming*, made by Gloria Tamerre Petyarre, an Anmatyerre woman from what Australians call the Northern Territories, is another example of a different way of representing the world without focusing on the human self.

As is visible in this painting, as in hundreds of other paintings by the artist, Gloria Tamerre Petyarre does not seem to be concerned with actual – or even abstract – representations of human beings, but rather with the metaphysical world.[178] According to the artist, the concentric pattern and the similar

---

178 As confirmed by a survey of 452 of her paintings shown on the art market website artnet. Similarly, not one of the almost 1,000 artworks by Emily Kame Kngwarreye, or of Weaver Jack's 27 paintings, shown on artnet depicts human figures in a Western sense.

shades of colour used in a repetitive manner evoke the rituals and ceremonies that are inherent to Aboriginal cosmology and an essential part of life for Aboriginal people. As she has said, "Aboriginal culture locates 'Dreamtime' as the beginning of all knowledge, from which came the laws of existence".[179] I should note again that developing a detailed and faithful analysis of Indigenous artwork would require a deeper understanding of and longer relationship with the respective tradition and work of the artist. However, in regard to the paintings made by this artist (and many others), it appears self-evident that the focus, approach and concerns are very different from the images that are part of the dominant visual human rights discourses. In this sense, the work of Gloria Tamerre Petyarre and of the other Indigenous artists included above echoes the critique made by non-dominant theories, like posthumanist approaches and obviously Indigenous approaches, that I discuss in Part I, according to which humans do not stand above other beings and entities, as in the dominant Western approach.

Interestingly, Judith Yinyika Chambers from the Warakurna community does depict human figures explicitly in her art, but these always seem to be one among other elements of the natural environment.[180] This inherent link of humans to nature that the European imagery tends to ignore or reject is illustrated in *Kunangurra Rockhole and Seven Sisters Dreaming*.[181] The warm and rich colours chosen by the artist closely follow those naturally occurring in the outback in Western Australia, where the artist comes from and lives, and contribute to a feeling of harmony between different beings and entities that are part of Country. Only the waterhole stands out to some extent through the bright tone used, which can be contextualized by the fact that waterholes occupy an important, sacred place in her culture; it is maybe for this specific reason that the composition of the painting is organized around the waterhole. The humans represented are roughly the same size as most of the trees and bushes scattered throughout the painting. The resulting impression, at least to me, is that they stand among other – equally important – beings; they do not try to transform or dominate nature and the land, as the European colonizers did and do, but are integrated in it. This representation of human beings as part of their environment is revealing and relevant in the context of human rights: whereas *Kunangurra Rockhole and Seven Sisters Dreaming* reflects a fundamental link to the land, it seems obvious that this link is not captured by dominant, anthropocentric visual human rights discourses. Moreover, as it has been noted, Judith Yinyika Chambers and other Warakurna artists seek

---

179 Redrock Gallery.
180 For further similar paintings by Judith Yinyika Chambers and by other Warakurna artists, see Darwin-based Outstation Gallery.
181 The image is no longer available online. It was included in the author's PhD thesis, which is available here: <https://spectrum.library.concordia.ca/id/eprint/990630/> (see page 124).

Figure 4.16 The Nullians by Sharyn Egan.

Photo credit: Sharyn Egan/*Garland Magazine*/Alessandro Bianchetti, <https://garlandmag. com/article/the-nullians/> (last accessed on December 12, 2023)

to "tell their own stories in their own way" through their paintings,[182] thus challenging dominant accounts of history.[183] This is also reminiscent of the reasons why migrants from the Global South started to represent themselves, as explained above.

The last example is an artwork by Noongar artist Sharyn Egan, which explicitly engages with an international law concept that heavily affected Indigenous peoples: *terra nullius*. The installation is made up of more than 200 pieces of dark wood, collected and assembled by the artist, that personify Aboriginal people. The items are made from the Balga tree, a plant that was particularly valuable and useful to the Noongar people before colonization, and hence before they had to abandon their traditional lifestyle, among others to make spears and other tools and also as medicine and food. White settlers often referred to Balga trees as "blackboys", because they apparently reminded them of Aboriginal people.[184] In contrast to its original use, Balga wood became popular among settlers and tourists as a material for various decorative objects.

Sharyn Egan's installation is titled *The Nullians*, which takes up, with irony, the notion of *terra nullius*, namely the legal fiction of the colonizers

182 National Museum of Australia, "Warakurna History Paintings".
183 National Museum of Australia, "Managing the Collection".
184 McCutcheon, 281.

that denied the existence of Indigenous peoples and allowed Europeans to claim, settle on and exploit the lands of Indigenous peoples. The artist criticizes the lack of legal status imposed by the colonizers to re-appropriate legal subjectivity for her people: "we, the Indigenous people, are the 'Nullians' of 'Terra Nullius'".[185] This meaning is conveyed by the bowls, vases, lamps, bookends and similar items assembled in the artwork, which form little groups of heterogenous yet harmonizing objects, reflecting both the diversity among Indigenous peoples and a sense of belonging to a larger group. The objects are compiled in a seemingly loose manner and can be re-arranged differently in another exhibition. In this sense, the artwork claims a fluid self-definition and self-representation of an Indigenous community and its members. This reflects the claim I make in Part I through the figure of *migrating 'Others'* with respect to the importance of recognizing the diversity of being in and experiencing the world, which is something that dominant visual human rights discourses do not tend to do. Subjects can be represented – or not explicitly represented – and hence also constructed in very different ways. Moreover, what emerges as fundamental is the striking contrast between generic representations, where an individual is (ab)used to precisely *represent* a whole group, such as refugees and migrants, and representations where the individuality of the person depicted is not lost but valued.

4.3   Concluding reflections: challenging the dominant paradigm

The above analysis shows that it is important to be conscious of the imagery that is produced and reproduced in the context of international human rights, and of the fact that human rights defenders and advocates are influenced by images and also utilize images to influence. Iconic historical representations of human rights, the common contemporary imagery of subjects of human rights circulated by UN agencies and the dominant representation of refugees and migrants in mainstream media, as instantiated by the representation of migrants taking selfies of themselves, all convey and reinforce certain messages that do not capture the complexity of subjectivities. These images contrast with alternative visual discourses, of which a few examples, created in different contexts, have been analysed to get a sense of the infinite possibilities of representing subjectivity. Paying closer attention to human rights' visual discourse and acquiring a higher level of visual literacy can hence be important tools in challenging law's conscious or unconscious (mis) representations and associated hegemonic tendencies, including in international human rights law. Although the visual discourse obviously does not

185 *Garland Magazine.* For an analysis of the installation and its relationship with the 1967 constitutional referendum on the status of Aboriginal peoples in Australia, see McCutcheon.

convey the whole story about law and human rights, and being critical about this discourse does not solve all related problems, I believe that examining visual discourses and their meanings may help understand the ways in which law relies on dogmas and presumed truths.[186]

Some individuals and groups currently marginalized by law have, in their quest for greater legal recognition and emancipation, chosen to engage with the predominance of vision in law and with problematic images. Such engagement is possible and potentially significant, because meaning can never be definitively fixed but can always be contested, re-appropriated and changed.[187] By way of example, some feminists claim that the deployment of law's authority, among others through its visual discourse, legitimizes patriarchal assumptions.[188] They have attempted to confront misrepresentations and to replace dominant visual discourses with alternative images that embrace their own understanding of the world,[189] which can certainly be empowering strategies. Stereotypes can be reversed, and negative images substituted with positive ones. The above-mentioned initiative of the Palestinian art collective and its creation of visual counternarratives as well as the photographs of refugees wearing designer clothes and self-representations that break with dominant narratives are further examples in this regard.

While focusing on the visual arsenal utilized by law and understanding its implications – as I have attempted to do with respect to international human rights – are important and revealing of fundamental biases, I would argue that such an approach only scratches the surface of a deeply rooted structural issue. Images typically operate on a monosensorial level that does not transcend the double centrality of vision and rationality in Western thought. The way in which images are usually perceived and analysed in the Western tradition is also problematic, for instance because of the overreliance on binary pairs,[190] a common feature of Western modernity that tends to oversimplify and cannot capture other ways of thinking about and seeing the world.[191] In other words, it is questionable whether pursuing a critical visual discourse analysis or offering alternative visual discourses can ever genuinely challenge or alter the dominant conception of law, including the allegedly universal yet inherently biased visual language of human rights. In fact, this critique, if it

---

186 Goodrich, *Legal Emblems and the Art of Law*, 248.
187 Hall, "The Spectacle of the 'Other'", 270. For arguments that the Cartesian subject, including its gaze, is, in fact, not necessarily disembodied or outside what is represented in an image, with Renaissance paintings already being "organized from within" and "*not* dominated from without by an external gaze", see Jones, 368 (discussing, among others, Joan Copjec's work).
188 Flynn, 139.
189 Flynn, 142.
190 D'Alleva, 34.
191 Moreover, every analysis, including the present one, is tainted by the background – education, ethnicity, gender, etc. – of the person pursuing it.

is not taken further, risks reinforcing, at least to some extent, modernity's rationalization of law as well as the separation and hierarchization of the senses.

A much more radical shift, I believe, would consist in overturning the supremacy of the visual in legal discourses, which would seem particularly important in international human rights, given their claim to universal authority and application. This does not imply abandoning the visual altogether, in a scopophobic move, since visual experiences obviously contribute to the creation of legal meaning and of subjectivities in important and not necessarily negative ways; it is the supremacy of the visual – in other words visiocracy – that must be challenged. This would also allow embracing the fact that law is embodied in different forms in different cultural and social contexts, and that it is experienced and lived in different ways by different individuals and groups. Therefore, in the following chapter, I further explore the relevance of the multisensorial dimensions of subjectivity in the context of law and human rights.

Bibliography

Abu Hatoum, Nayrouz. "Unsettling Visual Politics: Militarized Borders in the Work of Palestinian Artist Raeda Saaedh" (2019) 71:4 *American Quarterly* 1069.

Adami, Rebecca. *Women and the Universal Declaration of Human Rights* (New York: Routledge, 2019).

Adler, Laure. *Le corps des femmes: ce que les artistes ont voulu faire de nous* (Paris: Albin Michel, 2020).

Amnesty International UK. "What is the Universal Declaration of Human Rights?". <www.amnesty.org.uk/universal-declaration-human-rights-UDHR>.

Aral, Isil, Jean d'Aspremont & Iain Scobbie. "Universal and International Law: A Contestation Around Binaries" in I. Aral, J. d'Aspremont & I. Scobbie, eds, *International Law and Universality* (Oxford: Oxford University Press, 2023) 1.

Artist Profile. "Atong Atem", <www.artistprofile.com.au/atong-atem>.

Azoulay, Ariella. "The Ethics of the Spectator: The Citizenry of Photography" (2005) 33:2 *Afterimage* 38.

Bell, Philip. "Content Analysis of Visual Images" in Theo van Leeuwen & Carey Jewitt, eds, *The Handbook of Visual Analysis* (London: Sage, 2001) 10.

Bently, Lionel. "Introduction" in L. Bently & L. Flynn, eds, *Law and the Senses: Sensational Jurisprudence* (London: Pluto Press, 1996) 1.

Berger, John. *Ways of Seeing* (London: Penguin, 1972).

Berry, Mike, Inaki Garcia-Blanco & Kerry Moore. *Press Coverage of the Refugee and Migrant Crisis in the EU: A Content Analysis of Five European Countries, Report prepared for the United Nations High Commissioner for Refugees* (Cardiff: Cardiff University, 2016).

Bottici, Chiara. *Imaginal Politics – Images Beyond Imagination and the Imagery* (New York: Columbia University Press, 2014).

Bryans, John. "Masculinity Studies and the Senses", <www.lawandthesenses.org>.

Caruana, Wally. "The Bridge – A Brief History of Modern Aboriginal Art" in *Ancestral Modern: Australian Aboriginal Art*, <https://seattleartmuseum.org/Documents/Ancestral-Modern-Exhibition-Catalogue.pdf>.

Charlesworth, Hilary. "The Travels of Human Rights: The UNESCO Human Rights Exhibition 1950–1953" in Shane Chalmers & Sundhya Pahuja, eds, *Routledge Handbook of International Law and the Humanities* (New York: Routledge, 2023) 173.

Chouliaraki, Lilie. "Symbolic Bordering: The Self-Representation of Migrants and Refugees in Digital News" (2017) 15:2 *Popular Communication* 78.

Clanchy, Michael T. *From Memory to Written Record: England 1066–1307* (Hoboken: Wiley, 2012).

Classen, Constance. "Foundations of an Anthropology of the Senses" (1997) 49:153 *International Social Science Journal* 401.

———. "The Senses at the National Gallery: Art as Sensory Recreation and Regulation in Victorian England" (2020) 15:1 *The Senses and Society* 85.

Corntassel, John. "Towards Sustainable Self-Determination: Rethinking the Contemporary Indigenous-Rights Discourse" (2008) 33 *Alternatives* 105.

Dahlberg, Leif. "Introduction: Visualising Law and Authority" in Leif Dahlberg, ed, *Visualizing Law and Authority. Essays on Legal Aesthetics* (Berlin: Walter de Gruyter 2012) 4.

D'Alleva, Anne. *How to Write Art History* (London: Laurence King, 2006).

Davis, Elizabeth. "Structures of Seeing: Blindness, Race, and Gender in Visual Culture" (2019) 14:1 *The Senses and Society* 63.

The Design Files. "The Bright, Beautiful World of Atong Atem", <https://thedesign-files.net/2018/04/the-bright-beautiful-world-of-atong-atem>.

Douzinas, Costas & Lynda Nead. "Introduction" in Costas Douzinas & Lynda Nead, eds, *Law and the Image: The Authority of Art and the Aesthetics of Law* (Chicago: University of Chicago Press, 1999).

Dundes Renteln, Alison. "Visual Religious Symbols and the Law" (2004) 47:12 *American Behavioural Scientist* 1573.

Elysée. "Déclaration des droits de l'homme et du citoyen", <www.elysee.fr/la-presidence/la-declaration-des-droits-de-l-homme-et-du-citoyen>.

Fanon, Frantz. *Peau noire, masques blancs* (Paris: Les Éditions du Seuil, 1952).

Feldman, Allen. "On the Actuarial Gaze: From 9/11 to Abu Ghraib" in Nicholas Mirzoeff, ed, *The Visual Culture Reader*, 3rd ed (Abingdon, UK: Routledge, 2013) 163.

Flynn, Leo. "See What I Mean: The Authority of Law and Visions of Women" in L. Bently & L. Flynn, eds, *Law and the Senses: Sensational Jurisprudence* (London: Pluto Press, 1996) 139.

Garland Magazine. "The Nullians", <https://garlandmag.com/article/the-nullians/>.

Gharib, Malaka. "Stunning Photos Depict Migrants 'As They'd Rather Be Seen'" (7 October 2018), <www.npr.org/sections/goatsandsoda/2018/10/07/654492288/stunning-photos-depict-migrants-as-theyd-rather-be-seen>.

Gombrich, Ernst Hans. *Histoire de l'art* (Paris: Phaidon, 2002).

Goodrich, Peter. "Visiocracy: On the Futures of the Fingerpost" (2013) 39:3 *Critical Inquiry* 498.

———. *Legal Emblems and the Art of Law: Obiter Depicta as the Vision of Governance* (Cambridge: Cambridge University Press, 2014).

———. "Faces and Frames of Government" in Desmond Manderson, ed, *Law and the Visual: Representations, Technologies, and Critique* (Toronto: University of Toronto Press, 2018) 51.

Gramsci, Antonio. *Selections from the Prison Notebooks*, translated and edited by Q. Hoare & G. N. Smith (London: Lawrence & Wishart, 1971).

Hall, James. *The Self-Portrait: A Cultural History* (London: Thames & Hudson, 2014).

Hall, Stuart. "The Spectacle of the 'Other'" in Stuart Hall, ed, *Representation: Cultural Representations and Signifying Practices* (London: Sage, 1997) 223.

Hamilton, Peter. "Representing the Social: France and Frenchness in Post-War Humanist Photography" in Stuart Hall, ed, *Representation: Cultural Representations and Signifying Practices* (London: Sage, 1997) 76.

Haraway, Donna. "The Persistence of Vision" in Nicholas Mirzoeff, ed, *The Visual Culture Reader*, 3rd ed (New York: Routledge, 2013) 359.

Harsch, Leonie. "Giving Refugees a Voice? Looking Beyond 'Refugee Stories'" *Refugee Hosts* (8 January 2018), <https://refugeehosts.org/2018/01/08/giving-refugees-a-voice-looking-beyond-refugee-stories/>.

Hibbitts, Bernard J. "'Coming to Our Senses': Communication and Legal Expression in Performance Cultures" (1992) 41:4 *Emory Law Journal* 873.

———. "Senses of Difference: A Sociology of Metaphors in American Legal Discourse" in L. Bently & L. Flynn, eds, *Law and the Senses: Sensational Jurisprudence* (London: Pluto Press, 1996) 97.

Hochberg, Gil Z. *Visual Occupations: Violence and Visibility in a Conflict Zone* (Durham: Duke University Press, 2015).

Howes, David. "The Aesthetics of Mixing the Senses: Cross-Modal Aesthetics", <www.david-howes.com/senses/aestheticsofmixingthesenses.pdf> 75.

Howes, David & Constance Classen. *Ways of Sensing: Understanding the Senses in Society* (New York: Routledge, 2014).

Hsu, Elisabeth. "The Senses and the Social: An Introduction" (2008) 73:4 *Ethnos* 433.

Jones, Amelia. "The Body and/in Representation" in Nicholas Mirzoeff, ed, *The Visual Culture Reader*, 3rd ed (New York: Routledge, 2013) 369.

Kleinhans, Martha-Marie & Roderick A. Macdonald. "What Is a *Critical* Legal Pluralism?" (1997) 12 *Canadian Journal of Law and Society* 25.

Lakhani, Nina. "Is There a Crisis at the Border?" (19 March 2021) *The Guardian*, <www.theguardian.com/us-news/2021/mar/18/us-mexico-immigration-border-crisis>.

Machin, David & Andrea Mayr. *How to Do Critical Discourse Analysis: A Multimodal Introduction* (London: Sage, 2023).

Malkki, Liisa H. "Speechless Emissaries: Refugees, Humanitarianism, and Dehistoricization" (1996) 11:3 *Cultural Anthropology* 377.

Manderson, Desmond. "Senses and Symbols: The Construction of 'Drugs' in Historic and Aesthetic Perspective" in L. Bently & L. Flynn, eds, *Law and the Senses: Sensational Jurisprudence* (London: Pluto Press, 1996).

———. *Songs without Music – Aesthetic Dimensions of Law and Justice* (Berkeley: University of California Press, 2000).

———. "Introduction – Imaginal Law" in Desmond Manderson, ed, *Law and the Visual: Representations, Technologies, and Critique* (Toronto: University of Toronto Press, 2018).

McCutcheon, Jani. "On *the Nullians*" in Jani McCutcheon & Fiona McGaughey, eds, *Research Handbook on Art and Law* (Cheltenham: Edward Elgar, 2020).

McDermott, Yvonne, Alexa Koenig & Daragh Murray. "Open Source Information's Blind Spot: Human and Machine Bias in International Criminal Investigations" (2021) 19:1 *Journal of International Criminal Justice* 85.

Media 19. "Blog Archive Self Portrait Refugee", <www.media19.co.uk/projects/self-portrait-refugee/>.

Mirzoeff, Nicholas. *The Right to Look: A Counterhistory of Visuality* (Durham: Duke University Press, 2011).

Mitchell, Timothy. "Orientalism and the Exhibitionary Order" in Donald Preziosi & Claire Farago, eds, *Grasping the World: The Idea of the Museum* (New York: Routledge, 2004) 442.

Musée Carnavalet. "Déclaration des droits de l'homme et du citoyen", <www.carnavalet. paris.fr/fr/collections/declaration-des-droits-de-l-homme-et-du-citoyen>.

National Archives. "Abolition of the Slave Trade", <www.nationalarchives.gov.uk/pathways/blackhistory/rights/abolition.htm>.

National Museum of Australia. "Emily Kame Kngwarreye", <www.nma.gov.au/exhibitions/utopia/emily-kame-kngwarreye>.

———. "Managing the Collection", <www.nma.gov.au/about/corporate/annual-reports/annual-report-2011–2012/part-two-performance-reports/managing-the-collection>.

———. "Warakurna History Paintings", <www.nma.gov.au/explore/collection/highlights/warakurna-history-paintings>.

O'Brien, Jennifer. "Refugees Use art to Find a Little Freedom" *The Times* (22 October 2018).

Online Etymology Dictionary, <www.etymonline.com>.

Outstation Gallery. "Tjukurrpa Purtingkatja (History Paintings Part 2)", <www.outstation.com.au/exhibitions/2012/tjukurrpa-purtingkatja-history-paintings-part-2/>.

The Pin. "Atong Atem", <www.thepin.org/meet/atong-atem>.

Pink, Sarah. *The Future of Visual Anthropology: Engaging the Senses* (New York: Routledge, 2006).

Raffan, Jane. "The 'I' in Indigenous Art" (2013), <www.portrait.gov.au/magazines/46/indigenous-portraiture>.

Redrock Gallery. "Gloria Petyarre – Bush Leaf Dreaming", <www.redrockgallery.net/products/Gloria-Petyarre%252dBush-Leaf-Dreaming%252dRRG223.html>.

Rettberg, Jill Walker. *Seeing Ourselves Through Technology: How We Use Selfies, Blogs and Wearable Devices to See and Shape Ourselves* (New York: Palgrave, 2014).

Risam, Roopika. "Now You See Them: Self-Representation and the Refugee Selfie" (2018) 16:1 *Popular Communication* 58.

Rose, Gillian. *Visual Methodologist: An Introduction to Researching with Visual Materials*, 3rd ed (London: Sage, 2012).

Roth, Kenneth. "Defending Economic, Social and Cultural Rights: Practical Issues Faced by an International Human Rights Organization" (2004) 26 *Human Rights Quarterly* 63.

Saïd, Edward. *Orientalism* (New York: Vintage Books, 1978).

Santos, Boaventura de Sousa. "Three Metaphors for a New Conception of Law: The Frontier, the Baroque, and the South" (1995) 29:4 *Law & Society Review* 569.

Schmidt, Chrischona. "Utopia: The Genius of Emily Kame Kngwarreye" (2008) 4:1 *reCollections*, <https://recollections.nma.gov.au/issues/vol_4_no1/exhibition_reviews/utopia>.

Seremetakis, C. Nadia. "The Memory of the Senses: Historical Perception, Commensal Exchange and Modernity" (1993) 9:2 *Visual Anthropology Review* 2.

Sherwin, Richard K. *Visualizing Law in the Age of the Digital Baroque – Arabesques and Entanglements* (New York: Routledge, 2011).

Shohat, Ella. "The Struggle Over Representation: Casting, Coalitions, and Politics of Identification" in Román De La Campa, E Ann Kaplan & Michael Sprinkler, eds, *Late Imperial Culture* (London: Verso, 1995) 166.

Short St Gallery. "Weaver Jack", <www.shortstgallery.com.au/artworks/786559-weaver-jack-lungarung/>.

Sontag, Susan. *On Photography* (New York: Farrar, Straus and Giroux, 1977).

Stern, Kristina. "Law and the Lack of Sense" in L. Bently & L. Flynn, eds, *Law and the Senses: Sensational Jurisprudence* (London: Pluto Press, 1996) 42.

Sturken, Marita & Lisa Cartwright. *Practices of Looking: An Introduction to Visual Culture*, 2nd ed (Oxford: Oxford University Press, 2009).

Sutherland-Smith, Wendy. "Justice Unmasked: A Semiotic Analysis of Justitia" (2011) 185 *Semiotica* 213.

UNHCR Story Telling, <www.youtube.com/channel/UCjSP8f2bRQlE122zSiAJmIw>.

United Nations. "History of the Declaration", <www.un.org/en/sections/universal-declaration/history-document/index.html>.

———. "Universal Declaration of Human Rights", <www.un.org/en/universal-declaration-human-rights/index.html>.

United Nations High Commissioner for Refugees. "Budget and Expenditure", <https://reporting.unhcr.org/financial#tabs-financial-contributions>.

UN Office of the High Commissioner for Human Rights. *Annual Report 2013*, <www2.ohchr.org/english/OHCHRReport2013/WEB_version/allegati/downloads/1_The_whole_Report_2013.pdf>.

van Boven, Theo. "Reparative Justice: Focus on Victims" (2007) 25:4 *Netherlands Quarterly of Human Rights* 723.

van Ede, Yolanda. "Sensuous Anthropology: Sense and Sensibility and the Rehabilitation of Skill" (2009) 15:2 *Anthropological Notebooks* 61.

Viroulaud, Julie. "Jean-Jacques-François Le Barbier l'ainé et francs-maçons: autour d'une oeuvre d'inspiration maçonnique, La *Déclaration de l'homme et du citoyen*" (2011) 4 *Études* 80.

Watt, Gary. "Law Suits: Clothing as the Image of Law" in L. Dahlberg, ed, *Visualizing Law and Authority: Essays on Legal Aesthetics* (Berlin: Walter de Gruyter, 2012) 23.

Wikipédia. "Déclaration des droits de l'homme et du citoyen 1789", <https://fr.wikipedia.org/wiki/D%C3%A9claration_des_droits_de_l%27homme_et_du_citoyen_de_1789>.

Wikipedia. "Universal Declaration of Human Rights", <https://en.wikipedia.org/wiki/Universal_Declaration_of_Human_Rights>.

Wilke, Christiane. "The Optics of War: Seeing Civilians, Enacting Distinctions, and Visual Crisis in International Law" in Sheryl N. Hamilton et al., eds, *Sensing Law* (New York: Routledge, 2017) 257.

Chapter 5

Sensing the subject of international human rights

Informed by the insights gained from the critical discussion of the concept of the human, including its construction through visual discourses, I argue in this chapter that the international human rights system is not only based on a vision-centred sensorium but, as a field of law more generally, on allegedly rational processes of reasoning devoid of emotions and ignorant of the multiplicity of sensory experiences. This system, indeed, overlooks the senses and the multiple ways in which they influence the legal realm and, as a result, makes problematic assumptions about its subjects. Yet, emotions and the senses matter, precisely because they play a crucial role in constructing the identities and legal subjectivities of individuals and groups. It is particularly problematic that international human rights claim to be universal, given their homogenizing tendency that does not effectively acknowledge and embrace the diversity of being and sensing, with the result that many individuals and groups cannot – or not fully – access these rights.[1]

The engagement with anthropological scholarship on the senses supports my argument that the particular and biased normative sensorium in Western society – Elizabeth Davis speaks of a "politically charged" sensorium[2] – in which international human rights are implicitly embedded stands in stark contrast to their alleged universality. As a product of Western modernity, international human rights law draws on a limited number of sensory modes

---

1 It could be argued that attempts have been made in international human rights law to protect different sensory experiences and traditions, such as oral histories, via cultural rights. Yet this category of rights, while mentioned in important legal instruments, like the *Universal Declaration of Human Rights* and the *International Covenant on Economic, Social and Cultural Rights*, has traditionally received little attention within the international human rights system and has remained underdeveloped and, compared to other categories of rights, not well protected. Moreover, cultural rights were clearly not created with the objective to eliminate the sensory biases of international human rights, or to fundamentally expand the concept of the human through the recognition of different modes of sensing and being in the world.
2 Davis, 65, 76.

DOI: 10.4324/9781003427957-9

and codes,[3] which are heavily focused on vision. Vision is consistently privileged, whether with respect to rules of evidence and procedure, to the substantive law or to advocacy.[4] While meant to protect and empower, international human rights law also regulates behaviour and governs through the senses in particular ways. Like Western law more generally, it relies on vision to exercise and affirm its power. As Lionel Bently says, "law's use of the gaze is just that – a technique for the exertion of influence and control . . . to produce intersubjective relations where each person is either the empowered looker or disempowered object of the look".[5] Vision and envisioning, as part of an epistemological framework,[6] contribute to social and political oppression and, notably, produce a particular sensory subject in line with the Western liberal-rational-scientific tradition.[7] An important consequence is that non-Western sensory orders tend to be discriminated against. To take one example, this is illustrated by debates around banning the Islamic veil in some Western democracies. Indeed, in dominant Western discourses, it is sometimes overlooked that there exist different traditions concerning visual appearance, visibility and exposure – or non-exposure – to the gaze of others.[8] Moreover, the ways in which legal subjectivity or personality is conceived, metaphorically and in practice – with the legal subject (or human rights victim), for instance, physically standing before the law in a courtroom – are imbued with vision and, to a lesser degree, with sound.[9] As discussed in Chapter 4, courtrooms are full of visual symbols, but not all symbols are welcome. According to a common perception, those exhibited by ethnic and religious minorities should not be allowed in courtrooms, because they could influence the delivery of justice. This questions the traditional construction of justice as "blind", that is as unaffected by the visual appearance of its subjects that may reveal something about religious affiliation, social status, gender, and so on.[10]

Since little research has engaged specifically with the emotional or sensuous dimensions of international human rights,[11] I build on the existing scholarship on law and emotions and on anthropological studies on the senses that I apply to my object of study. It is interesting to note, however, that some

3 For the distinction between sensory modes and codes, see section 5.3.2 below.
4 Bently, 5.
5 Bently, 9.
6 Hamilton et al, 7.
7 Bently, 3; Davis, 64.
8 Thomas, "Contesting Allegations".
9 Antaki, 367. Bently has also argued that "the ordering of the senses informs law . . . [and] that ordering is constructed by, reflected in or reinforced by law". Bently, 1. Moreover, as Howes has noted, despite law's preference for vision, the "exercise of justice . . . depends on a complex orchestration of the senses". Howes, "Prologue: Introduction to Sensori-Legal Studies", 174.
10 Dundes Renteln, 1582.
11 For rare exceptions, see Barreto, "Human Rights and Emotions"; Rorty.

more specific research has considered the role of the senses, and in particular vision, in neighbouring fields of international human rights law. In international humanitarian law, vision arguably plays a particularly crucial role, notably for the fundamental distinction between combatants and civilians. Enshrined in the 1949 Geneva Conventions, this distinction is a routine visual exercise in the context of armed conflict.[12] As Christiane Wilke has noted, the ways in which NATO officers visually determine – typically from a great distance and without taking into consideration local knowledge – the status of Afghans before carrying out an air strike are part of "violent epistemologies".[13] She maintains that "the practices of sighting civilians and reading bodily performances are not incidental but central to the development of the law of armed conflict".[14] Vision and practices of visualizing can hence have dramatic consequences and determine if obligations arising under international human rights and humanitarian law are respected or violated. Certain forms of visualization also shape the field of international development, which arguably shares with international human rights some characteristics in terms of its concerns, biases and actors – especially but not only when framed through a human rights–based approach.[15] For instance, Christiana Abraham has shown how "difference" is produced through images by the Canadian International Development Agency, where photographs often present the world in a simple binary fashion: "the West as modern with science and technology and the rest as traditional and primitive", with the latter supposedly being able to achieve modernity by following a prescribed trajectory.[16]

It can even be argued that only certain ways of seeing and of (re)presentation are accepted as valid in the context of human rights. What Mark Antaki has noted with respect to Western law is also applicable in this context: "[s]i la vision sort souvent gagnante du concours des sens . . . ce ne sont pas toutes les formes de vision qui participent également à cette victoire".[17] In other words, there are dominant forms of seeing, such as the way in which subjects are envisioned by the state, whereas other forms of seeing may not even be recognized as such. The widespread and frequent use of images in the field of human rights, and the use of a particular type of images conveying a specific discourse, as analysed in Chapter 4, is a clear demonstration of this visual bias. Images, as it should be recalled, are not neutral, and what is not represented also matters: "Photographs . . . carry cultural messages by capturing certain scenes and leaving others unrecorded, or by portraying subjects so as

12 Wilke, 259.
13 Wilke, 260.
14 Wilke, 260–1.
15 See e.g. UN Sustainable Development Group.
16 Abraham, 13. On the importance of "seeing" and "framing" in the context of international law and development, see also Buchanan.
17 Antaki, 363.

to convey notions of power or weakness, amity or aggressivity, attractiveness or repulsion".[18] An interesting example concerns the visual representation of the act of touching. Given the latter's particularly significant meaning in India, visually capturing tactile gestures carries greater weight in this cultural context than in others and can have important socio-political implications.[19]

Considering the complex relationship between law, rationality and emotions, as I do in the first section of this chapter, helps understand the long-standing claim of Western law as to what constitutes proper legal reasoning and the ideal subject, which is rational, largely emotionless, disembodied and disconnected from the senses. As I argue, the sensuous dimensions of law are intertwined with its emotional dimensions,[20] and neglecting the role of emotions in law, including for the creation and expression of legal subjectivities, has facilitated law's estrangement from its sensuous dimensions and enabled numerous exclusions. Since vision has been conceived as the highest and most civilized sense that is equated with rationality and hence also closely associated with law, the ideal subject is supposed to be largely emotionless and only allowed to see in an Enlightened way; the other senses, along with the possibility of expressing oneself with or through emotions, have been dismissed or at times even suppressed. Although it is rarely recognized and discussed, there is a default position, with important sensuous biases rooted in the Western vision-centred sensorium, against which other experiences are assessed. This narrow construction of an ideal subject has arguably led to various forms of exclusion and discrimination based on assumed ontological differences, which explains why human rights are not a useful tool for many individuals and groups.

In the subsequent sections, I rely on anthropological scholarship on the senses to further explore the relevance of the senses for the construction of legal subjectivity and, more specifically, to underline the importance of the senses in the context of international human rights. Appreciating how the senses have been theorized reveal opportunities – so far mostly missed – for law to genuinely recognize the role and importance of the senses. It should be said that although the senses and different ways of experiencing the world were an understudied topic for a long time, even the legal discipline has, if somewhat timidly and only recently, started to turn to the senses. This change is significant and has great potential. As Antaki has put it, this

> tournant sensoriel . . . nous (r)amène à nos corps, et nous invite ainsi à (re)penser, à (res)sentir, à (ré)animer même, les corps du droit que nous

18 Howes & Classen, 1.

19 Alex, 538.

20 For the argument, made in relation to law, that there is no constructive difference between affective experiences, which are associated with emotions or, more generally, with "something internal", and sensory experiences usually associated with external stimuli, see Philippopoulos-Mihalopoulos.

visons – des *corpora iuris* qui sont ce qu'ils sont parce que nous sommes des êtres sensibles qui habitent et partagent un monde.[21]

I start my analysis of the senses in the context of legal subjectivity by briefly reviewing the growing attention given to the senses in the social sciences and the emergence of what has been called anthropology of the senses. Drawing on ethnographic studies concerned with the senses, I then demonstrate that, in addition to the assertion that cultures have different sensoria, there is also great variation in the ways in which the senses are categorized and hierarchized. Moreover, there can be several sensoria within a culture, and sensoria are dynamic: they can be influenced by the specific social context and the type of social interaction. Appreciating that sociality and identities, as well as different forms of inclusion and exclusion, are generated in interaction with others through the senses is particularly significant for an analysis of international human rights and my critique of their claim to universality. This will allow me to argue that the international human rights system, because it is based on a vision-centred sensorium, essentially ignores the ways in which identities, legal subjectivity and fundamentally also humanness are constructed and expressed through the senses. Claiming that the continued reliance on this biased sensorium and on the concept of a disembodied and emotionless subject constitutes an important obstacle to fulfilling the emancipatory potential of human rights, I conclude by suggesting that international human rights law should be more attentive to its emotional and sensuous dimensions.

5.1   Law's sense-less opposition between rationality and emotions

Western law claims that there is an opposition between reason and emotions[22] and considers a certain rationality devoid of emotions necessary for allegedly proper legal reasoning. This fundamental claim is problematic, among others because it sustains the exclusion from the realm of law of numerous individuals and groups who are associated with emotions and emotional decision-making. Whether or not this association is accurate, it is the basis for routinely excluding certain individuals and groups, like migrants

---

21 Antaki, 362.
22 I acknowledge that emotions are not easily defined and that several definitions exist in the literature. Without being overly preoccupied with the subtleties of these definitional aspects, I adopt Terry A Maroney's umbrella definition of emotion. The term emotion is hence used "in a broad sense to signify a spectrum of phenomena encompassing what might instead be called emotion, feelings, affect, and mood". Maroney, 124, n 19. For a discussion on the definition of emotions, see Bandes, "Introduction", 10–14. For the difference between emotions and feelings as understood in neurology, see Damasio, 143.

and Indigenous peoples, from the protection of human rights. It can even be argued, by relying on Upendra Baxi, that dominant human rights theory cannot take human suffering seriously, precisely because of its long history of adopting an abstract and disembodied stance on suffering and violence.[23] However, human rights violations are not an abstract or emotionless process that can be grasped in purely legal or intellectual terms. Rather, as José Manuel Barreto writes by building on subaltern studies,

> [f]or the victims, the violation of their rights does not mean first of all the breaching of constitutions or international treaties, nor the negation of political ideas or ethical principles. For the victims, violence has material consequences in the body and the mind, and is cause of immediate distress and physical or psychological pain.[24]

How human rights violations are experienced hence matters, but this experience may be very different for different subjects. This is why it would be important to consider the experience and position of those whose rights are violated, an observation that obviously resonates with the decolonial approaches explored in more detail in Chapter 3.

Based on the premise that the relationship between rationality, emotions and law is much more complex than traditionally assumed in Eurocentric legal thought, I build on the insight that emotions are omnipresent in the legal realm and play a crucial role, including for the construction of legal subjectivities. In fact, emotions are essential for human life. They are linked to many aspects, from individual creativity[25] to political and social life, as they highlight the interdependence of human beings.[26] It could even be argued that without emotions, the world would be deprived of meaning.[27] Law, as it is suggested here, contributes to this quest for meaning – and the meaning of being human – in various ways. It has been stated persuasively that "any conception of law in purely dispassionate terms threatens to be inhuman".[28]

The idea that there would be only one universal form of rationality that underpins legal reasoning and justifies the suppression of different rationalities is also flawed, and it has had major consequences for social justice in the world and can explain why many individuals and groups cannot genuinely benefit from the international human rights system;

---

23 Baxi, *The Future of Human Rights*, 14.
24 Barreto, "Human Rights and Emotions", 110.
25 For an analysis of the complex, culture-specific relationship between emotions and creativity, see Averill, Chon & Hahn.
26 Nussbaum, "Emotions and Women's Capabilities", 382, 386.
27 Nussbaum, "Emotions and Women's Capabilities", 380.
28 Solomon, 128.

undoing this domination starts with a critical examination of hegemonic positions. Since international human rights law stems from the Western legal tradition, it is imperative to investigate this tradition more generally and its conception of rationality. Moreover, since legal scholarship has only started to grasp, and in a limited way, the role of emotions in law,[29] considering recent insights from the humanities, social sciences and neuroscience is highly relevant. They reveal that emotions are involved in cognitive thinking and, therefore, cannot be separated from the kind of reasoning promoted by dominant legal thought. Delving into the complex relationship between law, rationality and emotions, as I do here, can help understand why law and its ideal subject have experienced a remarkable estrangement from the senses.[30]

Rational and emotionless: Western law imagines itself

Western legal thought has established an artificial, straightforward opposition between rationality and emotions.[31] It has attempted to hyper-rationalize legal decision-making, by highly valorizing predictability and finality, and to confine emotions to irrational, and hence extra-legal, processes as well as to reserve them for non-Western legal traditions. In this perspective, rationality, which is referred to as a way of thinking that gives primacy to human reason, has been a major characteristic of development, and especially of modernity, and believed to be intrinsic to the Western world. The common assumption has been that the more rational a society is, the better. Non-Western societies have been presented as devoid of reason and imbued with irrational emotions, a vestige of the past. This emphasis on rationality has its origins in early Greek philosophy (and maybe even earlier) and implies, since the 17th century, a particularly strong focus on the enlightened, disembodied and seeing individual.[32] This individual is supposed to reason logically and on the basis of scientific "facts", not intuitively or emotionally, nor by relying on perception through the other, presumably lower senses. Especially since René Descartes, rationality – and not emotions – is thought to allow the achievement of real knowledge and truth. It has even been said that rationality became the basis of secular authority that replaced religious authority, locating morality in "thoughtful reason".[33] The common stance of Western law

---

29 Abrams & Keren, 319–20. An often cited yet conceptually quite limited analysis of law and emotions from a law and economics perspective is offered by Posner. For a summary of legal scholarship on emotions, see Maroney.

30 For the argument that the affect, the senses and emotions are all closely entangled, see for instance Lamrani.

31 Solomon, 127–8.

32 Glenn, 2.

33 Marcus, 136.

vis-à-vis rationality and emotions has had significant consequences. It has led, among others, to the exclusion of numerous individuals and groups from the protection of law. These marginalized individuals and groups have been relegated to the sphere of emotions and irrationality and have been granted, at best, the status of passive victims. On a global level, a similar process occurred with the advent of Western modernity and colonialism: non-Western legal traditions, such as Indigenous and Islamic legal traditions, have been sidelined or even silenced.

Rationality, in this specific and problematic conception that constructs the subject in certain ways, which arguably also manifests itself in the context of human rights, has also been associated with a certain kind of stability rooted in universal rules.[34] This universality is supposedly made possible through rational reasoning, since it implies the ability to see the bigger picture and precludes consideration of the particularities of a situation.[35] In this sense, reasoning is "detached, cool and calculative".[36] This presumed universal rationality, in a Cartesian closure, puts forwards a "one-dimensional human personality".[37] This had important effects on various aspects of social life, and, by way of an interesting example, formed the basis of capitalism. As it has been argued with reference to capitalist interests, "men were expected or assumed to be steadfast, single-minded, and methodical, in total contrast to the stereotyped behaviour of men who are buffeted and blinded by their passions".[38] Certain emotions, such as avarice, were transformed into universal ones and hence valid interests that could presumably be pursued rationally. Subsequently, this model of rational thought and capitalist ideology mutually reinforced each other: the former was maintained and promoted precisely because it sustained the latter, and vice versa. Western law was of course not a neutral bystander in this process. Because of its association with and strong reliance on rational thought, it became a useful instrument to advance certain interests, and especially those of capitalism, which further entrenched the antagonism between rationality and emotions.

Given this importance attached to rationality, it is not surprising that the established discourse in Western thought postulates that its legal system is largely devoid of emotions, and certainly of emotionality, and that legal subjects are supposed to be, behave and feel in certain ways. In fact, emotions are undesirable elements associated with softness and weakness that

---

34 Santos, *Epistemologies of the South*, 63.
35 Young, 383. Young explains, drawing on Theodor Adorno, that "reason is *ratio*, the principled reduction of the objects of thought to a common measure, to universal laws". Ibid, 384.
36 Nussbaum, "Emotions and Women's Capabilities", 361.
37 Santos, *Epistemologies of the South*, 63.
38 Hirschman, 54.

must usually be suppressed or ignored when making or claiming rights.[39] Only certain emotions, in a simplified, one-size-fits-all version – like a highly moderated form of vengeance – have been allowed to occupy a limited and well-defined place, namely in criminal courts.[40] It is indeed in the context of criminal codes, from the 19th century onwards, that Western law started to contemplate emotions more consciously, in the form of motives or factors affecting intentionality. While emotions, such as jealousy and anger, have been treated as common to and understandable for everyone,[41] legal officials have been supposed to always be able to think and act in a purely cognitive and controlled manner. Thanks to their legal training, judges, in particular, can presumably make emotionless decisions, as if they, as individuals, felt no emotions and were not influenced by them. And while the notion that "[e]xcellent judging requires empathic excellence",[42] in other words the capacity to put oneself into another's position, was quite commonly accepted for some time during the 20th century, judges are now increasingly expected to apply the law with more objectivity, and hence less empathy.[43] In other words, it is typically considered desirable to be able to distance oneself from emotions in the context of Western law.

More generally, key concepts that are vital to the Western notion of the rule of law, such as impartiality and neutrality, seem to require such distancing from emotions,[44] and clear, predetermined categories are supposed to transcend individual cases and allow the application of general rules.[45] These

39 As Martha Nussbaum notes, emotions are often seen as "sources of softness, holes, so to speak, in the walls of the self". Nussbaum, "Emotions and Women's Capabilities", 367.

40 Bandes, "Introduction", 2.

41 The relationship of modern Western law, in particular of criminal law, with emotions has undergone important criticism since the 1990s. Critical approaches to law, including feminist approaches and critical race theory, have exposed the biases inherent in the typical "heat-of-passion" defenses. For a discussion in the context of so-called honour killings, see Frevert, 250.

42 West, "The Anti-Empathic Turn", 246.

43 West, "The Anti-Empathic Turn", 246. This presumed possibility of suppressing emotions is also illustrated by the common reminder made by judges to jury members not to let themselves be guided by emotions. Analysing the situation in the United States, with a particular focus on the Supreme Court, West also argues that the new standards of judicial decision-making are heavily influenced by economics and quantitative sociological tools in line with the scientific paradigm, in an attempt to predict the consequences of decisions. Ibid, 249–50.

44 Nedelsky, 93. It is important to recall that various philosophical traditions, not only in the West but also in the Chinese and Indian traditions, have objected to emotions on the basis that they lead to false judgments. As Nussbaum has summarized, personal judgments are often understood as false, "because they ascribe a very high value to external persons and events that are not fully controlled by the person's virtue or rational will". Nussbaum, "Emotions and Women's Capabilities", 367.

45 On the problematic implications of unitary categories in law, and especially the category of "women", see Spelman.

categories can only be upheld by making so-called rational abstraction from details that are deemed irrelevant. "Facts" related in judgments exemplify this narrowing of information; emotions will only play a role if and when they fit into a particular legal category, for instance as attenuating circumstances in sentencing proceedings. Otherwise, an impartial reasoning process, in its quest for universality, must ignore the specificities of the context, with reason standing above interests and desires.[46] Emotions, in contrast, expose the vast multiplicity and complexity of human life and human interaction, and are therefore sidelined.[47] They can even be said to threaten the law because they are, in dominant legal thought, considered to unduly interfere with the capacity to judge. For subjects, this means that, in order to benefit from the protection of the law, they must appear largely emotionless.

Embodied multiplicity: inspirations for transformation and emancipation

To re-imagine the relationship between law, rationality and emotions in a more constructive manner, it is useful to rely on Jennifer Nedelsky's concept of embodied multiplicity. Nedelsky has maintained that core concepts in legal thought are biased. The notion of impartiality, notably, which favours reason to the detriment of emotions, requires a universal condition that represses difference.[48] As already explained, reason and emotions have been separated in dominant thought, with emotions being associated with subordinated groups like women and people in the Global South, who are conceived as unable to engage in impartial and hence 'proper' reasoning. This, in turn, also explains why law, and society more broadly, continues to resist emotions and to favour rationality.

The analysis made by Nedelsky and other feminist authors with respect to the prevalent power dynamics based on gender can be extended to other hierarchies, with non-Western worldviews having been similarly reduced to emotional, irrational "traditions" by the dominant West, as I discuss below. Indeed, the existing standards routinely favour the Western, white, middle-class and rational man: "a society premised on disembodied rationality cannot be rendered 'equal' by attributing it to all",[49] because privileges are always based on a relationship of subordination. This is why it can be argued that emotions and the body should infuse notions like impartiality, subjectivity, and law more generally: emotions and bodily differences, such as sex, age, and mental and physical abilities, matter and are not simply pe-

46 Young, 383.
47 Nedelsky, 95.
48 Nedelsky, 10; Young, 385.
49 Nedelsky, 114.

ripheral, as is often assumed.[50] Similar to Boaventura de Sousa Santos, whose call for alternative epistemologies I discussed in Chapter 3, Nedelsky thus also proposes to turn to, seek inspiration from and embrace long-excluded elements and dimensions of humanity, and to include those individuals and groups that have typically been associated with emotions and the body.[51] Based on Nedelsky's claim that there is "equal moral worth on which to ground our new notion of impartiality and indeed all feminist and emancipatory projects",[52] the dominant conception of the legal subject can arguably transcend existing standards, which would allow greater openness and the recognition of the plurality of beings.

Emotions are everywhere, even in Western law

Contrary to the dominant legal narrative, law is, and has always been, inevitably impregnated and motivated by emotions. These emotions are often latent, perhaps precisely because they are deep-rooted, having evolved over a long time.[53] However, it can also be argued that law has always taken emotions into account, to some extent and in some form. As Terry A. Maroney has noted, "[t]he emotional aspects of our substantive and procedural law therefore have tended to develop *sub rosa*, consisting largely of unstated assumptions about human nature".[54] In this sense, emotions are present in the entire normative universe,[55] even if this is rarely obvious or acknowledged.

While both common perceptions and scholarship on Western law and emotions start (and usually end) with a consideration of the presence of emotions in criminal proceedings, in reality, emotions infuse all legal spheres. In fact, because law attempts to regulate human conduct and facilitate human interaction, it often triggers passionate responses.[56] As a human construction, law is also a vector of individual and collective emotions, such as fear and indignation,[57] as exemplified by criminal codes and immigration and citizenship laws. Moreover, the Western legal system is filled with and deals with not only the more obvious emotions, like anger and the desire for vengeance,

---

50 Nedelsky, 103.
51 Adopting such an approach would also break with a common assumption, held in Western and in some non-Western traditions, according to which, in Nussbaum's words, "[w]omen are emotional, emotions female", and reason is male. Nussbaum, "Emotions and Women's Capabilities", 360. Nussbaum argues that there is no valid reason to believe that women are naturally more emotional than men, and that such a distinction is rather the result of socialization. Ibid, 365–6.
52 Nedelsky, 114.
53 Bandes, "Introduction", 2.
54 Maroney, 121.
55 This language draws on Robert Cover.
56 Sanger, 41.
57 Solomon, 128.

but with many others too, such as shame, love and disgust.[58] If these emotions are obvious in criminal law, they are also present and influential in other, presumably less dramatic areas of law, such as family, inheritance and tax law. A good example is that a certain vision of love that privileges the heterosexual nuclear family is often articulated in these areas of law,[59] which arguably also explains the late development of women's rights in international human rights law and perhaps even more so the only recent recognition of discrimination based on sexual orientation as a human rights violation.

Emotions are also present during all stages, from the elaboration of laws to their application and enforcement, affecting all legal actors. Clearly, emotions do not only concern the legal subjects (who are, in orthodox legal thought, considered to be merely law-receivers); the law-makers, embodied in the legislator or the government, because they are also beings who have feelings, may have an emotional relationship with the legal issue at stake.[60] One can think of the heated debates, and even violent clashes, between parliamentarians, which are not uncommon in some countries.[61] Furthermore, legal professionals are not immune to emotions, although the idea that such professionals, especially judges, would be able to make perfect abstraction of their emotions is deeply entrenched. Even though the typical legal training attempts to craft people to 'think like lawyers', in other words in a presumably purely rational, analytic mode that factors out emotions, such reasoning is always indebted to emotions.

The 'Other' is not necessarily emotional

The West has sought to imagine itself as the only real rational system of thought, putting forward the idea of an opposition between rationality, as embodied by the West, and so-called traditions. A corollary of the Western claim to rationality, indeed, consists in the assumption that other legal traditions, and especially non-secular ones, are largely irrational and tainted by emotions, picturing Western law as the only one that is genuinely objective. However, as H. Patrick Glenn has usefully pointed out, the Western legal tradition is, in spite of its claims, a tradition like others: "[m]uch of western thought has tended to the rational, but the rest of the world sees this as the leading characteristic of

---

58 For a detailed analysis on the place of disgust in law, see Nussbaum, "Secret Sewers of Vice: Disgust, Bodies, and the Law".
59 See e.g. Leckey & Brooks.
60 Sanger, 41.
61 For a striking example, see "Ukraine Crisis: Violent Brawl at Kiev Parliament". Sanger argues that it is because of such possibilities that "precautions intended to modulate the role or at least the force of emotion have been incorporated into the very structure of legislatures and of law making". Sanger, 45.

the western . . . tradition".[62] This also implies that rationality and objectivity are subjective concepts and, as Santos has noted, that "the understanding of the world by far exceeds the West's understanding of the world".[63]

All traditions, in fact, contain elements of rationality; this can even be seen as one of the defining characteristics of the concept of tradition, because, as Glenn has said, without rationality, a tradition could not be maintained.[64] Information, on which a tradition is built, is never simply transmitted from the past, but is always processed: data is selected and reflected upon, whether through adherence, resistance or outright opposition, sometimes to the whole tradition.[65] While all traditions engage with such processes of rationality, these processes may, of course, play out very differently. Even the very meaning of rationality can vary; there are several ways of being rational;[66] and there is no inherent value attached to these different rationalities.[67]

Considering specific examples of different legal traditions and their respective logics is informative, as it reveals that rationality can take different forms and that the dominant Western, secular tradition does not have the exclusivity over rational thinking. In the Talmudic tradition, for instance, the role of emotions is very confined. An important distinction between rational rabbinic statements of legal reasoning and more "colourful" legal narratives can be made. As Barry Wimpfheimer argues, such narratives contextualize the rules of law and "create a dialogue between legal rules and other cultural contexts – be they sociological, psychological, political, or economic".[68] According to Wimpfheimer, "[w]here statements of legal reasoning aim to rationally justify positions of law in an imagined affectless world, legal narratives utilize surface and latent emotions to generate tone and nuance".[69] In other words, if emotions are banned, somewhat artificially, from official legal reasoning, they do have their place when Talmudic legal rules are contextualized through legal narratives. As for the Islamic legal tradition, god-given laws that require no further justification are sometimes believed to lie at the basis of arbitrary and unpredictable de-

---

62 Glenn, 2.
63 Santos, *Epistemologies of the South*, 164. It is worth recalling that even in the West, several models of Western modernity, including some in which rationality was not necessarily on a pedestal, were developed over its historical trajectory. But, as Santos puts it, "the disputes among them were [finally] decided on the basis of their adequacy for the historical objectives of capitalism and colonialism". Ibid, 164, n 1.
64 Glenn, 18.
65 Glenn, 18–20.
66 MacIntyre, 9.
67 Glenn, 4. It should also be kept in mind that analysing traditions that are based on other rationalities through the lens of Western rationality risks leading to biased results. Ibid.
68 Wimpfheimer, 164.
69 Wimpfheimer, 159.

cisions.[70] However, as John Makdisi demonstrates, and contrary to widely held beliefs in the West, "the method of legal reasoning in Islam is not arbitrary, discretionary or unsystematic".[71] It may, in fact, follow a logic that is not radically different from the one influencing legal reasoning in the West. By drawing on Western authors like Max Weber and Lawrence Friedman, Makdisi claims in his comparative analysis of rationality in Islamic law and the common law that "the exercise of a formally rational mode of thought may easily coexist with substantively rational and even irrational modes of thought in the solution of a legal problem".[72] Substantive rationality may, for instance, refer to moral or economic values that can influence judicial decision-makers in their deliberations. Moreover, irrationality, which takes the form of emotions in this analysis, can influence decision-makers, in particular in the context of reasoning by analogy through the perception of likeness.[73] Finally, it is worth mentioning that there are, of course, different ways even in Western philosophy in which rational inquiry has been pursued and rationality conceived.[74]

The variety of rationalities and its impact are well illustrated by the concept of time. It is a specific example, but an important one, because this concept facilitates the creation and legitimization of power relations in society and can arguably explain why it is possible to imagine a remedy, for instance through international human rights, for certain forms of violence and injustice but not for others, as argued with respect to colonial violence in Chapter 3. Fundamentally, time is conceived and appreciated differently in the world. Some cultures, as Santos has noted,

> control time, some live inside time; some are monochronous, some are polychromous; some concentrate on the necessary minimal time to carry out certain activities, some on the necessary activities to fill up time; some privilege schedule-time; some event-time . . .; some valorize continuity, some discontinuity; for some time is reversible, for some it is irreversible; some include themselves in a linear progression, some in a non-linear progression.[75]

Different logics and understandings of time determine whether there is a clear separation between the past, the present, and the future; whether, and to

---

70 For an overview of such arguments, see Makdisi, "Legal Logic and Equity in Islamic Law", 63.

71 Makdisi, "Legal Logic and Equity in Islamic Law", 92. For a list of further authors who have rebutted the claim that Islamic law is irrational, see ibid, 66, n 12.

72 Makdisi, "Formal Rationality", 104.

73 Makdisi, "Formal Rationality", 104.

74 As Alasdair MacIntyre has noted, the "concept of a kind of rational inquiry . . . is inseparable from the intellectual and social tradition in which it is embodied". MacIntyre, 8.

75 Santos, *Epistemologies of the South*, 176. See also Glenn, 4.

which extent, one influences the other; and whether there are actually such things as the past or the future. The dominant understanding of time today is that of a linear progression, which, as it has been remarked somewhat cynically, is "impersonal, rational, and extremely effective".[76] It was refined during the Western Enlightenment, when "history came to be viewed as a more reasoned or scientific understanding of the past".[77] Since then, time is divided into clear zones – the past, present and future – and is perceived as flowing in a single direction, always moving towards progress.[78] Such a linear conception of time permits the idea of change as we move forward;[79] at the same time, this conception implies that the past is inaccessible. Because of the distance that is introduced, the past cannot be influenced nor acted upon. This means, to take a grave example, that colonialism cannot be undone, for it occurred in the past, and that the potential for remediation, whether or not in the form of rights claims, is greatly limited. Associated with this linear conception of time are Western modernity's systems of classification that are based on binaries and hierarchies, which has facilitated important forms of domination and exclusion. According to the dominant conception, the present is also limited and short – Santos reveals, again, the important link to capitalist ideology, with those in dominant positions seeing no need for change – and this contracted moment can be repeated, over and over again, under the false promise of future progress and change.[80] In fact, capitalist ideology has impoverished the present, stripping the linear conception of time of its emancipatory potential. The dominant temporality – linear time as usurped by capitalism – excludes and marginalizes social experiences that are not understandable to itself because of a different conception of time.[81]

It is interesting to look beyond the Western model as other traditions that have different conceptions of time also have other perspectives on change.[82] For one thing, it is worth recalling that linear time is not the most commonly adopted conception and, even if it is a hallmark of Western modernity, it was never able – even within the West – to get totally rid of other conceptions.[83] This is illustrated by several traditions. Glenn highlights that for Indigenous peoples who have a close relationship with the land and their environment, time is

76 Smith, 55–6.

77 Smith, 55–6.

78 For more information on the origins of the Western concept of historical time, and more specifically for the role of the Greeks and of Christianity, see Glenn, 156–7.

79 Glenn specifies that this change occurs "more precisely at the frontier between the past and the present". Glenn, 26.

80 Santos, *Epistemologies of the South*, 73, 164–5.

81 Santos, *Epistemologies of the South*, 177.

82 And some traditions are simply not overly concerned with the question of time; time is not a major issue in their worldview.

83 Santos, *Epistemologies of the South*, 176.

not going anywhere; it surrounds all beings.[84] Communities are composed of multiple generations, where the ancestors that have passed away, the persons who are alive, and the yet to be born all engage and continuously interact with each other; those currently alive have obligations towards other generations: for instance, they must live in harmony with the world and must make sure they do not harm it in an irreversible manner, so that "there is no change in the life of the world".[85] Inter-generational obligations mean that change is not valued, but continuity is: "[t]he world must be recycled".[86] Glenn, moreover, points out that time is also cyclical in the Hindu tradition. Indeed, if the idea of change must be tolerated, since tolerance is fundamental within this tradition, it gives way to the "perpetuation of souls".[87] By way of example, Ruth Vanita recalls that while the caste system is a cornerstone of Indian society and usually prevents cross-caste marriages, marital unions in former lives may be drawn upon to legitimize otherwise unacceptable unions.[88] To take another example to illustrate the variety of conceptions of time, in the Confucian tradition, time is stable, and human beings live together with the dead and the yet to be born.[89] Here, too, there are obligations towards all generations – which can, for instance, explain the prominent place of elders – and the conception of change must take these obligations into account.[90]

In light of the above, it seems obvious that the 'Other', which here takes the form of non-Western traditions as conceptualized by Western thought, is not necessarily more or less influenced by emotions. Moreover, Western law clearly does not have the monopoly over rationality. Instead, as the example of various conceptions of time reveals, different rationalities exist and coexist with emotions in many ways.

No cognition without emotions

It is important to recognize that defining emotions in contrast to reason, as it is common in Western legal thought, is misleading. Emotions are not uncontrollable or simply based on instincts, and they are not entirely disconnected from reason.[91] There is, of course, a variety of emotions, and certain emotions are more easily associated with reason than others. Hope and pride, for instance, are sometimes considered to be more intellectual and cognitive in

---

84 Glenn, 79.
85 Glenn, 79–80.
86 Glenn, 80.
87 Glenn, 304–5.
88 Vanita, 125. Same-sex relations can also be legitimized on this basis. Ibid, 125–6.
89 Glenn, 340.
90 Interestingly, Confucian rationality focuses on social conduct and emphasizes social harmony; it is not a rationality that demands and facilitates enquiry. Glenn, 335.
91 Bandes, "Introduction", 14.

nature, whereas other emotions, like fear and fury, are more closely related to the body than the rational mind.[92] Vengeance, to give another example often cited as particularly relevant in the context of criminal law, is also understood as necessitating rational thought processes.[93] As I demonstrate in this section, not only are emotions related to reasoning, but constructive and emancipatory reasoning processes require emotions. Drawing on the insights from other disciplines, it is possible to put into perspective attempts to make sense of emotions through a legal lens and to obtain a more nuanced account.

Fundamentally, the opposition between emotions and reason that lies at the basis of dominant Western legal thought arguably rests on an inadequate philosophical and psychological understanding of emotions and their relation to judgment. In fact, emotions are part of so-called rational thinking. Nussbaum contends, from her philosophical perspective, that emotions "are not brutish irrational forces, but intelligent and discriminating elements of the personality, closely related to perception and judgement".[94] Said differently, emotions do not prevent but are rather necessary to make intelligent judgments, in law as in life more generally. Equally interesting is Antonio Damasio's argument, made from the point of view of neurology, that even if emotions are believed to be somewhat elusive and intangible, they are necessary to qualify our thoughts and cannot be left out of any concept of mind: "[e]motion and feeling, along with the covert physiological machinery underlying them, assist us with the daunting task of predicting an uncertain future and planning our actions accordingly".[95] Emotions emerge under the control of subcortical and neocortical structures, which means that they depend on "cerebral-cortex processing" and are therefore cognitive.[96] So-called somatic markers, or, in simplified terms, emotional responses,[97] do not reason for human beings, but they help with the crucial task of highlighting and discriminating between possible choices.[98] In other words, it is the alliance between cognitive processes and what is usually referred to as emotional processes that enables effective reasoning.[99] This is quite different from the conventional opposition between 'true' legal reasoning and emotions, which clearly proves to be flawed from a neurological perspective. Rather, it must be recognized that affective responses influence all decisions, including legal decisions, from law-making to judicial rulings and everyday decisions made by legal subjects *vis-à-vis* the law.

---

92 Averill, 25.
93 Indeed, the associated reflection may be "biased and narrow-minded", but it is still a reflection that "requires thinking, planning, and perspective". Solomon, 128–9.
94 Nussbaum, "Emotions and Women's Capabilities", 365.
95 Damasio, xiii. See also at 158–9.
96 Damasio, 159.
97 Nedelsky, 102.
98 Damasio, 174.
99 Damasio, 175.

The social construction of emotions

Notwithstanding their biological aspects, emotions are also socially constructed, and in this construction, law shapes, channels and is often expected to satisfy emotions.[100] As Susan A. Bandes claims, evaluating an emotion is a normative endeavour, since no emotion has an inherent, essential value.[101] Law hence contributes to deciding which emotions are recognized and dignified, and which ones are condemned or deemed inappropriate.[102]

Social constructivism highlights that emotions are complex, that they are socially scripted, and that norms influence emotional subjectivity. With respect to the first point, it is important to understand that an emotion is not a monolithic entity, which is one of the reasons why it cannot easily be defined.[103] There are many emotions, and each emotion can be understood and felt in various ways. Emotions are also influenced by culture and can play a completely different role in different parts of the world. They may, for instance, be considered remarkable and relevant in a certain cultural context, or trivial and not of much interest in another context.[104] Yet while emotions are shaped by culture in many aspects,[105] they should not be essentialized along cultural lines: two individuals from the same culture do not necessarily understand a particular emotion in exactly the same way.[106]

Furthermore, appropriate emotional behaviour is learned and, at least to some extent, dictated by society. As Chesire Calhoun argues, "[w]e learn emotions by learning emotional scripts. We assess the genuineness of our own emotions by comparing our own experiences to those scripts".[107] Emotions are commonly perceived as positive or negative, and this is not a trivial exercise: attributes of emotions and assumptions about who can have a particular emotion have consequences. By way of example, most societies do not

100 Solomon, 128–9; Sanger, 45.
101 Bandes, "Introduction", 13.
102 Nussbaum, "Emotions and Women's Capabilities", 365. By way of example, as Calhoun writes, "[a] liberal democratic theory of emotions would . . . be an account of the emotions that are sensitive to persons' freedom and equality". Calhoun, "Reliable Democratic Habits and Emotions", 220.
103 Bandes, "Introduction", 3.
104 As Averill, Chon and Hahn note, "if a Chinese villager is asked how he feels about a certain arrangement, the response might be, 'It doesn't matter how I feel'". Averill, Chon & Hahn, 171.
105 For instance, for a discussion on the differences between American and Korean conceptions of hope, see Averill.
106 Averill, Chon & Hahn, 169. Moreover, it would be important, in order to avoid ethnocentrism, "to define emotions in culturally neutral terms, to the extent that this is ever possible". Ibid, 166.
107 Calhoun, "Making Up Emotional People", 220. Moreover, these scripts vary over time. Ibid, 225. For an analysis of emotional group dynamics, see Bandes, "Emotion and Deliberation", 202.

understand or construct romantic love in the same way for heterosexual and homosexual couples: while romantic love is a way to transform the formers' primitive sexual desire "into the expression of the relational ideal of perfect unity", the latter are frequently presumed to be incapable of such feelings.[108]

Law, and its different subfields, plays a role with respect to emotional subjectivity in various ways. While law usually persists in pretending to uphold emotional neutrality, as previously discussed, it sometimes tries, even if this is rarely made explicit, to promote certain emotions and to suppress others. Law is, indeed, sometimes considered a means to cultivate so-called positive emotions.[109] The main objective, in this approach, is not necessarily to further compliance with legal rules, but to encourage, through legal rules and institutions, those emotions that are regarded as a social good, such as hope and compassion.[110] At the same time, it is also possible to suggest that law can channel negative emotions, like hatred, in a constructive way, rather than reproducing or aggravating them.[111] Legal responses to mass atrocities in times of radical political transitions, such as criminal trials of former government officials of a repressive regime or truth and reconciliation commissions, are particularly revealing of the role of individual and collective emotions. By way of example, the South African Truth and Reconciliation Commission was clearly influenced by and promoted the concept of *ubuntu*, which emphasizes communal well-being through the interconnectivity of the "basic humanity" of individual human beings,[112] as well as certain Christian values, such as redemption and forgiveness.[113] As this reconciliation process, which was supported by a legal institution, showed, certain emotions had to be triggered to be able to forgive, and others, like the desire for revenge, had to be suppressed.

Law and legal processes can be used both for the promotion of positive emotions and the suppression of negative emotions, but there are important

---

108 Calhoun, "Making Up Emotional People", 218.
109 For a discussion on law and the cultivation of hope, see Abrams & Keren.
110 Abrams & Keren, 321, 324.
111 Minow.
112 Mokgoro, "Ubuntu, the Constitution and the Rights of Non-Citizens", 225. For a discussion on the complexity of the concept ubuntu, and the relating difficulty to translate it, see Mokgoro, "*Ubuntu* and the Law in South Africa".
113 For a critical study of this process, see Wilson. It might be useful to draw on Peter Goldie's definition of emotion to understand forgiveness as an emotion: "An emotion . . . is a relatively complex state, involving past and present episodes of thoughts, feelings, and bodily changes, dynamically related in a narrative of part of a person's life, together with dispositions to experience further emotional episodes, and to act out of the emotion and to express that emotion. Your expression of emotion and the actions which spring from the emotion, whilst not part of the emotion itself, are none the less part of the narrative which runs through – and beyond – the emotion, mutually affecting and resonating in that emotion, and in further emotions, moods, and traits, and in further actions". Goldie, 144.

risks associated with such endeavours. Above all, emotions tend to be simplified in the legal context and are erroneously assumed to mean the same to everyone and to manifest themselves in the same way, which misses crucial nuances and can lead to exclusions. Moreover, as Calhoun recalls, social hierarchies are often preserved through emotional scripts, with certain groups being culturally devaluated, because they are considered to have "more emotional (and less rational) subjectivities".[114] Law, indeed, tends to assume that certain people, because of their gender, ethnicity, age or sexual orientation, are more or less emotionally competent and, as a result, deserve to be treated differently by the law.[115] The cultivation of presumably positive emotions may also follow political ideologies that are not shared by all. Particular concerns, as Carol Sanger claims, should be

> about *which* emotions are cultivated in the service of the social good . . . and about cultivating emotional states for the specific purpose of bringing about behavior that the law cannot otherwise legitimately regulate but that is likely to result once a person has been "emotionally cultivated" to feel a particular way.[116]

It emerges from the insights gained in this section that the relationship between law, rationality and emotions, as well as emotions themselves, are highly complex and, in particular, not as simple as typically assumed in the Western legal tradition. This is consequential for the way in which legal subjectivity is – and could be – conceptualized. As I have demonstrated, emotions are not necessarily opposed to rational thought; in fact, they are part of reasoning processes, including legal reasoning. And rationality may take different forms, as illustrated by different traditions having different conceptions of time. Taking into account other traditions and embracing different ways of being rational seems, indeed, crucial, in particular in the context of international human rights law, because certain forms of violence and injustice are otherwise not even grasped as human rights violations. Moreover, instead of trying to encourage particular emotions, law should perhaps attempt to develop its emancipatory potential by acknowledging the plurality and complexity of emotions. Core legal concepts, such as impartiality, need to be reconceptualized to reflect the multidimensional relationship between law, rationality and emotions as well as worldviews beyond the dominant Western one. Taking emotions seriously hence presents itself as an avenue to rehabilitate the body and also to develop a critique of the biased sensorium in law.

114 Calhoun, "Making Up Emotional People", 223.
115 Calhoun, "Making Up Emotional People", 218–19.
116 Sanger, 49.

5.2   Theorizing the senses: the basis for a sensori-legal approach to human rights

The senses and sensory experiences contribute to the construction of legal subjectivity and identities more generally in important ways; they are subjected to and shaped by different forms of regulation; and they can be used to regulate behaviour.[117] Law and authority, and the meanings of law and authority, are closely related to the senses.[118] Since the senses are greatly involved in power relations, any form of normative bias in this regard is potentially problematic and can lead to ontological imperialism – often in the form of "a rationalist, masculinist, and dualistic way of being-in-the-world"[119] – that suppresses other senses and sensations, and ways of being human.[120] The foundational and persistent claim of the international human rights system, with respect to both its conceptualization and application, to be universal and accessible to all human beings is contradicted by the denial of the great diversity of sensoria that make up humanity, as I discuss in this section. Arguably, the continued reliance on a biased and limited sensorium, although rarely recognized and discussed, constitutes an important obstacle to fulfilling the emancipatory potential of human rights.

As part of the long tradition in the West, established during Greco-Roman antiquity, in which vision has been and still is considered the most important sense,[121] other senses have been ascribed, with depreciatory undertones, to other cultures.[122] To recall the discussion in Chapter 4, the supremacy of vision in European thought consolidated itself with the development of modern science and the emphasis on reason in the 18th century, which relied heavily on this sense; similarly, law has always associated itself closely with both reason and vision.[123] Eye-centred techniques, such as observation and measuring, became the only acceptable ways in European thought of judging the intelligence of human beings.[124] Importantly, while hearing followed quite closely in this hierarchy, smell, taste and touch were relegated as

---

117 Sheryl N. Hamilton, 6.
118 Antaki, 365.
119 Geurts & Komabu-Pomeyie, 86.
120 Davis, 73.
121 Classen, "Foundations", 402. For a discussion of vision being a phenomenon with multiple dimensions, see Jay, 11.
122 Hsu, 434. At the same time, as Martin Jay has noted, relying on vision can, to some extent at least, be considered natural across all cultures, and hence a universal phenomenon. Moreover, "the threshold between what is 'natural' and what is 'cultural' is by no means easy to fix with any certainty". Jay, 3–4.
123 Bently, 3; Dundes Renteln, 1575.
124 Davis speaks of the paradoxical tendency of Western science to use the senses as instruments of measurement at the same time as "demanding a radical austerity of them". Davis, 66.

lower or 'animal' senses and deemed central to non-European and allegedly uncivilized peoples. This was part of a broader process introduced by modernity that progressively suppressed the senses, their richness and diversity, and even erased memories and emotions based on the senses.[125] The same logic reflected and contributed to entrenching class difference within European society: vision, which was considered a noble sense that allowed aesthetic appreciation, was associated with the upper, educated classes, whereas the working masses were thought to remain focused on tactility and sound.[126] In fact, the sensory experiences[127] of all those conceived as 'Others' were downplayed by the Western elite.[128] Common epistemological and methodological biases in favor of vision – not only in the natural sciences, but also in the humanities and social sciences, including law – led to the privileging of metaphors associated with vision and of written texts.

Early anthropologists also contributed to the promotion of the widespread belief that the senses had little to do with the mind but instead belonged to the body, that is to something irrational and less noble.[129] As David Howes has noted, it was thought, for instance, that one could determine the degree of 'savageness' of Indigenous people by relying on what was presented as modern and objective eye-centred techniques to measure their sensory capacities.[130] While such beliefs are certainly less prevalent or palpable among anthropologists today, vision and the visual continue to occupy a predominant place and to be primarily associated with the West.[131] Anthropology itself, and the way in which ethnographic research was conducted, did not escape this governance of vision for a long time. As Paul Stoller writes, "ethnographers have been participant *observers* who *reflect* on their *visual* experiences and then write *texts* that *represent* the Other's *patterns* of kindship, exchange, or religion".[132] This has obviously had important limitations for prevalent understandings of cultures and even discriminatory consequences *vis-à-vis* non-European cultures. As Constance Classen highlights, "to neglect to investigate such elaborations of the 'proximity' senses is often to practise reverse sensory discrimination by disregarding a body of symbolism

---

125 Seremetakis, 14.
126 Classen, "The Senses at the National Gallery", 86–7. The author explains that vision was "the avenue of spiritual enlightenment" in the context of museums opening their doors to the working classes. Ibid, 93.
127 For a discussion on the meaning of "experience" in anthropology and the understanding that there is a great variety of experiences that involve various levels of consciousness, see Pink, 42–6.
128 van Ede, 63.
129 Classen, "Foundations", 405. The author lists some of the scholars who documented the alleged 'animalistic' character of some senses in the 18th century.
130 Howes, "Charting the Sensorial Revolution", 120.
131 Hsu, 434.
132 Stoller, 55.

considered of prime importance by a society".[133] In the following, I explore and build on the argument developed by some anthropologists that a more careful engagement, and one less tainted by the traditional epistemological biases of the discipline, with the senses is needed.

A culture-specific and post-colonial perspective of the senses

Little attention was given to the senses in the social sciences until the 1960s, when new ideas on the topic emerged. One proposition that contributed to bringing the senses to the forefront was that there are significant differences in the ways in which cultures use and conceptualize the various senses.[134] Walter J. Ong, for instance, argued that people communicate with all their senses, but depending on their culture, in very different ways, and that studying and understanding the sensorium – defined by Ong as "the entire sensory apparatus as an operational complex"[135] – of a particular culture would expose almost all aspects of that culture.[136] Ong, together with Marshall McLuhan and Edmund Carpenter, established the basis for an approach that distances itself from the overreliance on text and instead integrates the senses.[137] Around the same time, Claude Lévi-Strauss suggested the very controversial yet influential notion that non-Europeans rely on "sensible properties" to interpret the world they inhabit and construct their cosmology;[138] in other words, native methods of observation, including for the purpose of myth-making, would involve using all the senses.[139] The growing interest, in the 1980s, in modes of knowing grounded in the body – as opposed to the idea that knowledge occurs only in the mind – further stimulated research on the senses from different social sciences perspectives.[140]

It is in the late 1980s and early 1990s that what has been called 'anthropology of the senses' took shape.[141] Among the main premises underlying this

---

133 Classen, "Foundations", 405. Howes highlights that there has been a shift from "participant observation" to "participant sensation" and speaks of "sensory ethnography". Howes, *Afterword*, 129.

134 Classen, "Foundations", 406.

135 Ong, 28. It is worth noting that Ong might have challenged the hegemony of sight, but the alternative he proposed was somewhat limited. Indeed, he suggested replacing the hegemony of sight with a model based on speech and aurality. His idea to speak of a 'world harmony' instead of a 'worldview' is telling. See Classen, "Foundations", 403.

136 Ong, 25–8.

137 Howes, "Introduction: 'To Summon All the Senses'", 8.

138 Lévi-Strauss, 268.

139 Lévi-Strauss, 54.

140 Howes, "Introduction: 'To Summon All the Senses'", 3–4.

141 Of particular importance were the contributions of Constance Classen, David Howes and Paul Stoller. For a fuller list of contributors, ideas and findings, see Classen, "Foundations", 406–9.

new field were that perception that occurs through the senses is not only a physical and psychological act, but importantly also a cultural process;[142] and that perception involves all the senses, not just vision. Ethnographic research revealed that different cultures place different emphases on different senses,[143] and that all the senses, including smell, touch, taste and hearing, contribute in important ways to the "metaphoric organization of experience".[144] Said differently, cultures "elaborate and extend the senses in different directions",[145] and values and norms are transmitted through the senses. Certain anthropologists thus advocated for and started to apply a sensory approach, that is an approach that recognizes the importance of the senses, to the study of culture.[146] It is worth noting that research in other disciplines, such as sociology and history, also contributed to a better understanding of the roles and importance of the senses in society.[147] The senses and perception through the senses were therefore no longer solely understood exclusively from a cognitive perspective, as it had been previously the case when psychology had a quasi-monopole on the study of the senses;[148] and their cultural dimension was recognized.[149] The senses have hence become a genuine object of inquiry in anthropology and the social sciences and humanities more generally, with significant theoretical and methodological implications.[150] It should be kept in mind that law, as a discipline, was comparatively slow to recognize the importance of the senses,[151] even if the progress made on the senses in other disciplines would already have offered great insights earlier, including for international human rights law.

Adopting a sensory approach is arguably not a neutral endeavour but has normative implications. In particular, anthropologists concerned with the senses have questioned the enduring claim that vision is associated with knowledge and rationality and is a characteristic of – and virtually exclusive to – the Western world. Some of the main objectives of scholars adopting this approach have been precisely to contest the supremacy of vision and to better understand the variations in the importance and meanings of all the senses,

---

142 Classen, "Foundations", 401; Howes, "Prologue: Introduction to Sensori-Legal Studies", 174.
143 Howes & Classen, 4.
144 Stoller, xvi.
145 Howes & Classen, 8.
146 Howes, "Introduction: 'To Summon All the Senses'", 7–8.
147 See e.g. Synnott; Porter; Gilman; Classen.
148 Howes, "Charting the Sensorial Revolution", 114. See also the discussion in Howes & Classen, 8–11.
149 Howes & Classen, 10.
150 Hamilton et al, 3.
151 Hamilton et al, 3. For a brief discussion of the beginnings of law's engagement with the senses, see ibid, 4–5.

and of cultures more generally.[152] In a way, this approach thus developed as a form of resistance to the dominant paradigm. As Howes explained in one of the early texts, "it is only by developing a rigorous awareness of the visual and textual biases of the Western episteme that we can hope to make sense of how life is lived in other cultural settings".[153] Moreover, studying and understanding all the senses, as it was hoped, also has the potential to contribute to liberating the West from its obsession with vision.[154] As Lionel Bently has noted, contesting the supremacy of vision and, more generally, the renewed interest in the senses are, in fact, part of a large critical discourse on the Western episteme.[155] Anthropology of the senses therefore suggested an alternative way of apprehending culture, one that goes beyond the habitual frame of vision and considers the wide range of meanings of different sensory experiences across cultures.[156] By encouraging ethnographic work that questioned and deconstructed the primacy of vision and that explored the roles of and values given to other senses, as discussed below, the development of anthropology of the senses can even be said, following Koen Stroeken, to be embedded within a post-colonial logic.[157]

Understanding vision beyond the West

The Western belief that relying on vision meant having a more developed form of intelligence, and the resulting appropriation of this sense by Western societies, can be challenged on various grounds. Intelligence can indeed take form and be expressed through other senses, and not only through vision, as commonly believed previously. For instance, while it is possible to reason and remember in visual forms, this can also occur through smell and taste.[158] Experiencing a particular taste or smell as an adult can bring back specific childhood memories that seemed to be forgotten. Moreover, many cultures prioritize one sense – not necessarily vision – and associate it with the intellect, and, by implication, tend to marginalize other senses.[159] Vision also does not guarantee unbiased observation or objective thinking.[160] It may be

152 Howes, "Law's Sensorium", 53.
153 Howes, "Introduction: 'To Summon All the Senses'", 3.
154 Howes, "Introduction: 'To Summon All the Senses'", 4.
155 Bently, 1. For an analysis of the "suspicion", or even "denigration", of vision in 20th-century thought, with a particular focus on French philosophers, social theorists, psychoanalysts, artists and cultural critics, see Jay.
156 Classen, "Foundations", 402; Howes, "Introduction: 'To Summon All the Senses'", 6.
157 Stroeken, 466; Potter, 445.
158 Howes, "Introduction: 'To Summon All the Senses'", 10–11. See also Seremetakis.
159 Howes, "Introduction: 'To Summon All the Senses'", 13.
160 Ingold, 246. Of note, Ingold relies on phenomenology to make this argument. Moreover, he focuses on the objectivity of the Western scientific gaze and also argues that perception via hearing might be more accurate or objective.

closely linked to rational thinking in the West, but it can have connotations of irrationality in other cultures; for some Indigenous peoples in Brazil, for instance, vision is even associated with witchcraft.[161] Therefore, different understandings of intelligence and rationality exist, without one understanding being superior to another one, and all the senses can potentially play a role in this context.

Even without questioning the veracity of the alleged vision-rationality-intelligence relationship, a sensory approach allows challenging the Western perspective for its exclusive appropriation of vision and the related justification of Western superiority. The fact that vision is considered the supreme sense in the West does not mean that it is not just as, or even more, important in some non-Western cultures. Vision is actually a prominent sense and constitutes a way of knowing in many cultures.[162] By way of example, in India, at least in the context of Hindu rituals, vision is deemed to be a superior sense, since it contributes to the communication with the divine: the worshipper looks at visual representations of deities, and is seen and recognized by these deities.[163] Moreover, seeing can be conceived in different ways, for example as intrusive and receptive; it can also involve other organs than the eyes.[164] In this respect, in some cultures, visual representations are not limited to their visual dimension, as it is usually the case in the West. The sand paintings made by the Navajo are not only representations to be seized by the eyes: as part of healing ceremonies, their pigments are pressed onto the bodies of patients, an act that transfers the power of the visual representation to the body of the participant.[165] Vision does not stand alone here; rather, vision and touch complement each other in this ritual. Finally, vision can have important aspects that are largely ignored or downplayed in the Western gaze. Colour is an interesting example: while it is often regarded as trivial in Western rational thought, it is said to be central for the Desena of the Amazon and their understanding of who they are. As Yolanda van Ede explains, "[c]olours define their ontology and epistemology, because every living being is surrounded by its personal field of colours, representing age, health, emotional state, and social status".[166] These examples thus confirm that the West does not have a monopoly on vision, and that vision can be conceptualized in very different ways.

Sensing beyond the 'classic five'

Individuals sense and understand the world in their own ways, and sensory models, with their sensory meaning(s) and value(s) that form the basis of

161 Classen, "Foundations", 404, 406.
162 Hsu, 435.
163 Alex, 525.
164 Stroeken, 467; Hsu, 436.
165 Classen, "Foundations", 403.
166 van Ede, 67.

conceptions of the world, are culturally specific. As Classen has pointed out, a culture's sensorium reveals this "society's aspirations and preoccupations, its divisions, hierarchies, and interrelationships".[167] Not only are the senses hence mediated by culture; cultures and their values are also moulded and transmitted in important ways by the senses.[168] This also implies that usually only those sensations that are supported by a society or culture are perceived as such; Elisabeth Hsu has highlighted that what has not undergone this process of socialization is not even considered a sensation.[169]

The great diversity in the conceptualization of the senses supports the argument that sensory models are culturally specific, which, in turn, explains that human rights, as a cultural system, also rely on a particular, vision-centred sensorium. Physiologically speaking, most human beings might have the same sensory capacities, but how these capacities are used varies greatly and is influenced by culture.[170] The fact that the senses are classified differently within the (admittedly large) cultural context of India, is a good illustration. Thinkers from the three great religions (i.e. Hinduism, Jainism and Buddhism) identify distinct orders of the senses, which reflects different concerns and motivations.[171] Of note, the concept of order is not equivalent to a hierarchy, which by itself suggests an important difference, namely that organizing the senses seems more important in this context than hierarchizing them from top to bottom, as it is the case in Western thought.[172] Another example is smell, which is at the centre of both Jain and Buddhist – but not Hindu – orders of the senses.[173] Yet another example of a very different categorization is the division of the senses into two main types of perception, visual and non-visual, among the Hausa in Nigeria.[174] Moreover, the use of the verb 'hearing' by the Sukuma people from northwestern Tanzania to refer to sensory experiences that also include smelling and touching suggests an evident emphasis on the sense of hearing, and hence a hierarchy that is markedly different from the Western one (and others).[175] If different cultures categorize and hierarchize the senses differently, it follows that the Western 'classic five' model of vision, hearing, smell, taste and touch – with vision, followed by hearing, believed to be the highest, most noble sense – cannot be universal.

167 Classen, "Foundations", 402.
168 Howes, "Introduction: 'To Summon All the Senses'", 3.
169 Hsu, 433.
170 A notable exception are persons living with certain disabilities.
171 McHugh, 414.
172 McHugh, 402.
173 McHugh, 407.
174 Classen, "Foundations", 401.
175 Stroeken, 468.

In addition to the senses being experienced and categorized in different ways across cultures, ethnographies have also shown the existence of senses and sensory experiences that are not even recognized by the dominant Western 'classic five' model. This, in fact, echoes what the theories from the margins that I discussed in Chapter 3 suggest, namely that fundamentally different ways of being, sensing and feeling exist and matter. Indeed, some senses are largely ignored – or not conceptualized as a sense – in the Western model: anthropologists have actually listed up to 33 senses.[176] In some cases, not recognizing a particular 'sense' can be explained by the assumption that this 'sense' does not disclose much about the external environment, but it is important to realize that such a 'sense' can nonetheless be socially significant in other cultures.[177] Such senses and sensations include pain, kinesthesia and balance, which are, for instance, particularly important for the Anlo-Ewe of Ghana.[178] Other interoceptive sensations, which relate to inner organs like the stomach and intestines, can also have social meanings.[179] By way of example, for the Sukuma, jealousy affects and is engraved in the liver, indicating a person's social isolation.[180] Arguably, a lot is lost in terms of understanding cultures and their sensoria if these senses are not even considered as such. These considerations hence bring additional depth to my argument that the dominant human rights system relies heavily on vision and on certain visual discourses. Because of its limited sensorium, the human rights system cannot comprehend how certain forms of violence and injustice are felt and articulated. The result is that what cannot be expressed in dominant language and through familiar terms usually remains overlooked.

There are also differences in how the senses relate to each other, with some cultures having a more genuinely plurisensorial understanding of the world that recognizes close connections between the senses.[181] Not unlike the above-mentioned perception of Navajo sand paintings, which involve more than vision, design-songs made by the Shipibo-Conibo, an Indigenous people in Peru, involve several senses. Seeing, hearing, speaking and smelling all come to play in the context of healing rituals: certain designs, which have healing powers, are transformed by the shaman into songs; when they reach the patient, they enter the body of this individual in the form of the designs and cure the disease; this process is, moreover, facilitated by the

---

176 Howes, *The Sixth Sense Reader*, 22.
177 Stroeken, 468. See also Geurts.
178 Geurts 2008. As it has also been shown by Potter, kinesthesia, which is related to the "ability to perceive the felt experience of movement within one's body", and heat are of particular importance to professional dancers in the West. Potter, 452–4.
179 Geurts & Komabu-Pomeyie, 87.
180 Stroeken, 468.
181 Howes, "Introduction: 'To Summon All the Senses'", 6.

'fragrance' of the design-songs.[182] It is worth noting that in several cultures, the mutual implications between several senses manifest themselves not only during special rituals but also in everyday life activities. For the Panará in Brazil, for instance, speaking, hearing and seeing are closely connected to each other, which is illustrated by the fact that the quality and value of a speech are evaluated both according to audible and visual criteria.[183] Another example is the Anlo-Ewe concept of *seselelame*, which can be translated as "feeling in the body" and which highlights even more clearly the interconnectedness of the senses for the Anlo-Ewe: it "spawns a fusion rather than atomization of the senses, an integration rather than splitting of mind-body communication".[184] Nadia Seremetakis' study of rural and urban Greek culture, which focuses on sensory memory, also points to the impossibility in some cultures of separating different sensory experiences in everyday life. The interconnectedness between the different senses is even articulated through common expressions in Greek: "'Listen to see' is the colloquial Greek phrase to demand attention in conversation"; another example is 'I can(not) hear it' when describing the taste of food.[185] With respect to remembering through the senses, Seremetakis also maintains that the "memory of one sense is stored in another: that of tactility in sound, of hearing in taste, of sight in sound".[186] This points to another limitation of the Western model and its neat separation of the five senses in grasping the interconnectedness of the senses and the richness of sensory experiences.

Another implication that results from the different ways in which cultures conceptualize and make use of the senses relates to the emphasis put on one or several senses. Such an emphasis can contribute to the development of certain physical abilities, like enhanced hearing or smelling capacities. It can also influence the development of certain values and norms. As Kathryn Linn Geurts argues, "in a cultural community's sensorium we find refracted some of the values that they hold so dear that they literally make these themes or motives into 'body'".[187] The example of kinesthesia among the Anlo-Ewe is insightful: here, the kinesthetic sense of balance is not only a matter of perception but also of thinking and knowing. Moreover, it suffuses their moral values and is closely linked to their idea of being human,[188] and it is believed that a flexible body enhances the flexibility of the mind, which is considered positive and desirable. Therefore, Anlo-Ewe children develop, as part of a largely unconscious process, bodily practices and skills, like the sense of bal-

---

182 Howes, "Introduction: 'To Summon All the Senses'", 5.
183 Ewart, 510.
184 Geurts & Komabu-Pomeyie, 88.
185 Seremetakis, 4.
186 Seremetakis, 4.
187 Geurts, 10.
188 Geurts, 50. This crucial point will be explored in more detail below.

ance, and thus carry their culture's sensory order and its priorities in their bodies.[189]

These theoretical insights and examples from different cultures underline that the senses and sensoria must be understood in all their diversity, and in particular beyond the Western classic five model. This is of great relevance to the international human rights system, which continues to operate with a particular, biased sensorium, certain forms of sensory regulation and ways of constructing its subject through the senses, as I further explore in the next sections.

5.3   Plurisensoriality and the relevance of the social context

Further aspects that appear particularly relevant for my discussion of the influence of the senses on legal subjectivity and human rights are the ideas that sensorial experiences also vary *within* a culture and according to the social context; that individual particularities matter; and that the senses and sensory models evolve over time.

Diversity within cultures

There is possibly not only great diversity of sensorial experiences across cultures but also within cultures.[190] No society or culture is characterized by a unique and uniform sensorium. Although common elements within a society may be identified and compared to those present or absent in another society, sensory realities are often quite complex, and there can be important variation within a given culture.[191]

A culture might, therefore, host several sensoria. Focusing on the case of the Western world is telling: while the dominant, mainstream sensorium that also underpins human rights relies heavily on vision, it can be argued that this sensorium is nonetheless only one among others and that it coexists with other sensoria that are marginalized to various degrees. One may think of the specific sensorium of musicians, for whom sound and hearing obviously play a predominant role in their life, and of perfumers and chefs, who spend their days focusing, respectively, on different smells and tastes. Moreover, persons with certain disabilities cannot access a particular sense (or senses), including the dominant one, in the same way as other people, and they compensate, at least to some extent, for the loss or diminution of a

---

189 Geurts, 50.
190 Howes, "Multisensory Anthropology", 23.
191 This is why Stroeken argues that sensory experiences, and cultures more generally, should not be essentialized. Stroeken, 473.

sense by further developing another or several other senses, thus forging for themselves a different sensorium. Clearly, these are not marginal instances of people finding themselves temporarily in a different sensory environment; rather, these persons live a great portion of their life relying on a sensorium that does not match the dominant one. The detailed study, carried out by Caroline Potter, of dance students' experiences within a Western modern dance school is interesting in this context.[192] During the extensive training that these students go through to become professionals, it is kinesthesia, a sense of motion, that is the leading sense. The students' sense of touch is also modified and further developed in this period through a heightened sense of kinaesthesia.[193] If one can rightly point to the fact that this institution is inaccessible to most other members of the same cultural group and hence not representative of the whole culture, it is nonetheless significant that these dancers, who live in a Western society, experience an important part of their life in a non–vision-centred environment. These dance students, similarly to other professionals, share a specific sensorium, which is distinct from the dominant one. Therefore, while a culture may have a dominant sensorium, these examples – from different professions like musicians, chefs and dancers to persons with disabilities – reinforce the claim that different sensoria can and do coexist within a culture.

The influence of both the social context and individual particularities

There is also variation in sensory experiences because the meaning attached to them can change with the social context.[194] To continue with the above-mentioned example, one can say that the dance students practice at school ways of touching that are different from and more refined than the ones common outside the studio. In fact, the students learn to navigate between different sensoria in their daily lives: a kinesthesia-centred one at school or at work, and the mainstream vision-centred one outside the school or work environment.[195] Moreover, what is accepted and expected in a certain situation would be considered awkward and intrusive in others.

To better analyse this type of variation, Stroeken has usefully distinguished between sensory modes and sensory codes.[196] Modes are more immediately related to the body: they stem from the stimulation of organs. Visual perception or experience, for instance, is a mode. Yet every sensory mode can be differently encoded. Codes are produced by society and allow activating sensory

192 Potter.
193 Potter, 458–9.
194 Hsu, 437.
195 Potter, 459.
196 Stroeken, 467.

modes in different ways, depending on and in line with what is deemed appropriate in this situation. Vision and touch, for example, can both be coded as intrusive or receptive, depending on the social context.[197] Making a distinction between modes and codes helps to recognize not only that there is a multiplicity of sensory codes, but also that shifting between these codes, consciously or unconsciously, can be socially acceptable and sometimes even expected.[198] To illustrate this with another example, in the context of crises or illness, sensory modes are encoded differently than in ordinary life: for the Sukuma, for instance, greeting one another by making eye contact is socially warranted and appreciated in normal times, but misfortune can transform the ordinary look into a suspicious act of witchcraft.[199] Moreover, while in some cultures, women's bodies are considered dirty because of menstruation, with men avoiding contact with women on that basis, there are obviously contexts and moments in which a woman's body and touch are coded differently, among others to allow procreation.[200] Finally, as highlighted by the COVID-19 pandemic, the spread of a contagious and dangerous virus radically alters the social acceptability of touching, or even approaching, other people, which can again be captured by the difference between sensory modes and (shifting) codes: while touching, embracing and being in physical proximity to others was previously normal in many instances, physical distancing becomes the norm in the time of a pandemic.

According to this reasoning, there is no direct or exclusive association between a specific sensory code and a certain sensory mode, even within the same cultural context. Looking and touching can be benign, acceptable and welcome; they can also be unwarranted and feared. Recognizing that shifts within a sensorium are at times socially acceptable and necessary avoids essentializing the senses, and cultures more generally.[201]

For the discussion of the role of the senses in the context of international human rights and their application, which is largely based on the rights of individuals, it seems especially important to keep in mind that individual particularities also influence a person's sensorium.[202] Indeed, the ways in which individuals apprehend their environment with their own bodies vary and contribute to shaping sensory experiences. Individuals are, of course, related to each other, but they are also autonomously sensing agents to some degree, which is why there is inevitably some variation in the way in which they express themselves socially through the senses. Individuals are hence responsible for some diversity in sensory engagements, even within the same

197 Stroeken, 467.
198 Stroeken, 466.
199 Stroeken, 477.
200 Stroeken, 470.
201 Stroeken, 473.
202 Hsu, 436. Howes and Classen also recognize this. Howes & Classen, 1.

culture.[203] While it has been rightly cautioned that the presence of certain individual idiosyncrasies should not be overemphasized nor lead to the conclusion that there is no shared sensorium in a given culture,[204] I would argue that the role of individuals should not be ignored either.

The interesting proposition, made by Adam Yuet Chau, of a "'sensory-production model' to highlight the active participatory role of human agents as makers of the social sensorium"[205] seems compatible with and does justice to both ideas: individuals do not create their own sensorium in isolation, but they certainly have some agency in constructing their own sensorium and consequently also the social one. Human beings, who have both individual and social facets, are not merely in this world; they also produce it.[206] This approach strongly resonates with some of the fundamental premises of a pluralistic understanding of law, which can usefully support socio-legal research on human rights and legal subjectivities. This understanding conceives every individual as a legal actor and emphasizes the role of this actor in the joint development and constant (re)negotiation of law.[207] In other words, law is shaped by sensing bodies that have specific characteristics.[208]

Evolution over time

It should also not be forgotten that categorizations and hierarchizations of the senses, and social meanings and values attached to the senses, are not necessarily stable but have evolved over time and will continue to evolve, which means that change is possible, including in the context of the dominant human rights system. Even the Western sensorium, while seemingly fixed to a contemporary observer, has of course undergone significant changes throughout history. There were times when the West acknowledged four, six or seven different senses. Taste and touch, for instance, were not always separated, but were at times considered to constitute one sense.[209] Moreover, in the Middle Ages and in early modern times, the senses were not separated from each other and did not have "autonomous faculties";[210] rather, they were all deemed to be interrelated. And before the enactment of extensive social regulations in Victorian England, the handling of objects, sculptures and paintings by visitors of museums was not uncommon: sometimes, as Classen

203 Chau, 487.
204 Classen, "Foundations", 410. See also Pink & Howes, 335.
205 Chau, 488 (emphasis omitted).
206 Chau, 490.
207 This relies on Roderick Macdonald's critical legal pluralism. See for instance Kleinhans & Macdonald.
208 Kilburn.
209 Classen, "Foundations", 401. See also Bently, 2.
210 Davis, 67.

has noted, "artworks were touched to assess their texture or materials, to enjoy the contrast between visual illusion and tactile reality, or to establish a sense of physical connection with the work and its creator".[211] There are also tendencies to standardize the senses over time. To refer to a non-Western context, for which the evolutionary dimension of the senses is obviously also relevant, the way in which smell is classified in the three great traditions in India has changed: probably out of a tacit understanding to ease inter-sectarian tensions, it has been increasingly harmonized.[212]

Changes over time occur, among other reasons, because sensoria are not fully immune to external influences and other ways of conceptualizing the senses. Indeed, sensoria do not exist in isolation but touch upon each other. They are dynamic, and they adjust as social and environmental transformations occur. Said differently, the senses are not fixed but contingent on the attention given and the value attached to them, whether explicitly or implicitly, in a specific social context and moment in time. These processes can take place over longer periods of time, thus appearing natural and going largely unnoticed; but in other cases, shifts in a culture's sensorium can appear to be imposed from the outside, for instance by a hegemonic culture and its values attached to the senses. A good example is again smell, which, at least in the modern West today, is associated with intuition and individual memories. However, previously, smell could also be a way of identifying essential truths, and it is still closely associated with the way justice is perceived in some non-Western cultures.[213]

Colonization, immigration and globalization have also contributed to changing and spreading sensory practices across cultures; as a result, different meanings are sometimes created in the receiving culture.[214] The spread of capitalism and consumerism, in particular, have affected taste and self-definition in many places. The recent changes to the ways in which Moroccan society engages with food reveal such changes and exemplify how the importance of the senses can gradually decline. Shopping for ingredients, traditionally at the local market, and preparing and sharing meals were multisensory activities – involving the senses of taste, smell, touch, vision and hearing, to use the Western classification – that have always had deep meaning for Moroccans.[215] As Myriam Lamrani argues, a sensorium can even be "the very ground for national identities".[216] But, as Western capitalism spread and

211 Classen, "The Senses at the National Gallery", 93.
212 McHugh, 413–14.
213 Howes & Classen, 96–7. James Parker offers an interesting account of why sound has an important relation to notions of justice and how it influences institutional outcomes. Parker.
214 Howes & Classen, 87.
215 Newcomb, 104, 114–15.
216 Lamrani, 2.

took root in Morocco over the past decades, Moroccans' food and shopping habits changed. Large supermarkets opened and more standardized and convenient, ready-to-eat types of food became available, inciting more and more families – especially wealthy ones – to adopt what was presented as a modern lifestyle based on consumer choice.[217] Instead of spending a significant part of the day preparing elaborate meals for the family and valuing the process of passing on this once highly praised knowledge to their daughters, many Moroccan women now affirm their identities through the products they buy in European-style supermarkets.[218] As Rachel Newcomb notes, the traditional, sense-rich cuisine has lost its importance in daily life and as a fundamental element of identity: "What it means to be a Moroccan citizen has become less about the ritual of local market banter, communal food preparation, and food sharing, and more about the consumption of products".[219] Said bluntly, what used to be a multisensorial experience became, in comparison, a relatively sense-less consumerist activity because of the hegemonic influence of another culture and its sensorium.

In sum, sensory models, like cultures, are dynamic, and they change over time, along with wider social transformations.[220] Individual particularities, as underlined by the role of sensing agents, and the social environment greatly matter, and often determine, the evolving construction of sensory experiences. It would therefore seem accurate to say that one sense or some senses are – consciously or not, arbitrarily or not – privileged in some parts of a society but not in others. A dominant sensorium might be identified in a given cultural group or society, with its members making sense of their world through and in relation to this sensorium; yet this sensorium always remains subject to some variation and may constitute only one of several sensoria that exist in a given context. In this sense, even if vision continued to dominate the sensorium of many actors in international human rights, there is definitely space for other sensoria in this context.

5.4   Grasping the relationship between human rights' biased sensorium and the construction of subjectivity

The vision-centredness of the international human rights system is problematic because it implies that the multiple ways in which identities, personhood and what it means to be human are constructed and expressed through the senses cannot be appreciated. I would even argue, based on the insights

217 Newcomb, 110–11. As Newcomb cautions, many Moroccans, especially from low-income families, still favour the local market. Ibid, 114–15. It could be argued that Western societies underwent a similar development a few decades earlier.
218 Newcomb, 102.
219 Newcomb, 116.
220 Classen, "Foundations", 409; Hsu, 437.

gained from the anthropological studies on the senses explored in the previous sections, that the many ways of understanding or experiencing the world, which rely on and operate with different sensory modes and codes, and in particular beyond vision as it is usually understood in the Western world, are discredited by the international human rights system. Contrary to the idea of genuine universality and accessibility, victims must adhere to and adopt the dominant sensorium for their claims to be successful; to have a chance to benefit from the protection of the law, they must first learn to see properly and to project the right image of themselves.

To better understand the consequences of the largely implicit sensorium of international human rights law, it is useful to consider how the senses are involved in constructing sociality, identities and related forms of inclusion and exclusion as well as the concept of personhood. This will help to demonstrate that, while rarely recognized, the senses and sensory models are highly relevant for the field of human rights and its construction of legal subjectivity. But first, I will briefly discuss a perhaps more obvious dimension of the relationship between law and the senses, namely how the senses are used to regulate behaviour.

Governance through the senses

As a socio-legal perspective emphasizes, activities involving the senses are defined and constrained through norms, and sensing is subjected to regulatory processes. This is a form of governance that is "embodied knowing, guiding and forming".[221] It determines which sensation is valued and which is dismissed, and it contributes to the social ordering of the senses and the regulation of social life more generally. As part of a civilizing endeavour, governance through and of the senses, as Sheryl N. Hamilton has argued, aims to produce compliant subjects, who are made to alter or adapt their everyday behaviours and to focus on certain sensory experiences, and to abandon others: subjects are made and remade "as within or outside of recognized norms" in relation to the senses.[222]

The concept of sensuous governance seeks to understand the multiple and complex processes of regulating sensing as part of this governance of social life.[223] In the words of Hamilton, we all partake in sensuous governance by "making and remaking our sensory experiences in language and legal consciousness, aligning our bodies with norms, measuring and being measured, and always, telling stories to make sense of it all".[224] For instance, museums

---

221 Sheryl N. Hamilton, 2.
222 Sheryl N. Hamilton, 1–2.
223 Sheryl N. Hamilton, 2.
224 Sheryl N. Hamilton, 6.

in Victorian England were created as "places for looking" and as "places for not touching", in line with the sensory preferences and values of the elite at the time.[225] Eventually allowing museums to be visited by the working class became a way to reaffirm this sensory model and to make sure that this model, along with the objects that were displayed and chosen to represent the elite, was respected. As instantiated by the mission of Victorian museums, working class visitors were induced to rely more on vision than on touch; "destructive sensuality" was to be transformed into "compliant sensitivity".[226] Applying the concept of sensuous governance to the changing food habits in Morocco also reveals the imposition of new values and associated rules pertaining to the senses, which have the effect of altering everyday life. As noted above, traditional cuisine was for a long time highly valued by Moroccans, and cooking and eating were used to differentiate themselves from neighboring countries. What used to best describe the identity and citizenship in Morocco was a "sensory engagement with food".[227] In recent decades, different forms of identity, such as gender and citizenship, have been influenced by Western ideas of modernity and economic liberalization, and the engagement with – and, as it could be added, governance of – the senses. As a result of the Western influence in the form of ready-to-eat products, traditional cuisine is increasingly disregarded, notably by younger generations. The identities and everyday life of Moroccans have been subjected to the hegemonic impact of Western culture and its sensorium, probably with enduring consequences. Behaviour can, in sum, be regulated through the senses in various ways, sometimes explicitly, but often implicitly. These important processes can be captured by the concept of sensuous governance, which suggests that the analysis of socio-political life must include the senses and sensoria.

Creating sociality through the senses

People engage their bodies in their relations with others and in their construction of the world, thus producing sociality through the senses.[228] As Sheryl N. Hamilton et al. have argued, "[t]he body and the senses are active agents as creators and disseminators of knowledge in a process that can transform the knowledge, the recipient of knowledge and, coming full circle, can transform the initial embodied source".[229] Social interaction is, in fact, impossible without sensory experiences and expressions, and sociality is created

---

225 Classen, "The Senses at the National Gallery", 93.
226 Classen, "The Senses at the National Gallery", 86.
227 Newcomb, 102, 114–15.
228 Chau, 500. See also Hsu, 441.
229 Hamilton et al, 20.

through very concrete physical experiences involving the senses: "[p]eople communicate not only through words and mental meaning making, but also in instances of simultaneously felt emotions, physically instantiated memories and sensations".[230] Recognizing these dimensions of social interaction contributes to challenging common, unhelpful assumptions, which confirms the fundamental importance of rethinking the role of emotions and the senses and also Nedelsky's notion of embodied multiplicity discussed above.

Interaction through bodily experiences occurs in various contexts. Chau provides a study of a particularly intense experience, namely of a major festival in Shaanbei, China, highlighting the active construction of the social environment through festivalgoers' bodies and their different and rich sensorial experiences. These experiences include the production and the perception of "noise, heat, taste, smell, spectacle, etc. (through speaking, shouting, singing, drumming, making music . . . sweating, getting hot, embracing, caressing, cooking, feasting, toasting, bathing".[231] There is hence an interpersonal dimension to sensory experience, which is made not primarily in the organs of individuals, but between these individuals.[232] In other words, it is a collectivity made up of individuals that creates a shared sensorium.[233] The effect of a rich, shared sensorial event like the festival in Shaanbei is felt both by the body of each participant and by the community of the participants.[234] Interestingly, there is even a specific term to describe the type of sociality produced during events like this festival, for which English (and other European languages) does not seem to have a precise equivalent: *honghuo*, which can be translated as 'social heat', is produced by the festivalgoers together, through their intense social engagement.[235]

The sensory interactions that can be observed during such particularly intense events also occur in more mundane situations. Indeed, the bodily interactions of everyday life – whether children play with each other, people greet or ignore one another on the street or dance together – also contribute to the creation of sociality and a sense of belonging. The feeling might start in an individual's body, such as the heat and sweat produced by the individual members of a dance group, but it is at the same time transmitted to others and therefore contributes to creating sociality.[236] Seeing, too, can be constructed as an interpersonal, social event, since it may also involve being seen. While

---

230 Hsu, 439.
231 Chau, 490.
232 Hsu, 437.
233 Chau, 490. While these exchanges are primarily understood as interpersonal events, it has also been argued that similar exchanges can take place between human beings and divinities as well as the environment. Alex, 526.
234 Chau, 488.
235 Chau, 495.
236 Potter, 455–6.

vision tends to be conceived as largely unidirectional in the modern Western worldview, it is more reciprocal in some other cosmologies. As discussed previously, in some Hindu rituals, for instance, an important reciprocal process of "[s]eeing the divine image and being seen by the deity" exists.[237] What matters here is not only what one sees, feels or smells as an individual but specifically the fact that this happens in relation with others, in other words being seen, touched or smelled by someone else.[238] With regard to sociality, embodied experience can arguably matter more than words: "intersubjective experience is possible not by sharing of meaning assigned to words, but by sharing of associative embodied experiences that make abstract concepts tangibly meaningful".[239] Even physical pain is not only felt individually but also fulfills important functions in contributing to social bonding and community building.[240]

The contribution of the senses to the construction of identity

The construction and expression of the self and social identities also occur through the senses and are, in this way, grounded in the body.[241] In many cultures, gender, age, class, caste and other categories that are closely related to one's identity are not just abstract ideas; they are lived and acknowledged through the body and the senses. As Hsu says, "through the senses we experience, enact, shape and express ourselves in social relations".[242] It is interesting to note that precisely because the senses play a fundamental role in the construction and expression of identities, resistance to political and social change can occur through the senses. The example of the way in which the abolition of the political category of 'untouchability' in India has been met is telling: despite the official abolition, touch (or the absence of touch) continues to fulfil important functions, such as the delineation of social boundaries.[243]

Touch, indeed, often plays a prominent role in the context of close relationships.[244] It is a way for individuals to convey feelings of love, through hugging and caressing, and, through physical violence or the absence of touch, feelings of anger and frustration. Touch is also an important way to embody one's belonging to a group in many cultures, and sharing the object

237 Alex, 525.
238 Hsu, 439.
239 Sekimoto, 85.
240 Hsu, 439.
241 Potter, 444.
242 Hsu, 441.
243 Alex, 526.
244 Alex, 523.

of touch "fosters identity with one's own cultural group".[245] In the case of the dance students discussed previously, it is above all touch that allows them to connect to one another, to sense the movement of others, and to create their identity as a group of dancers.[246] And it is precisely their shifted and shared sensorium, that is in particular their enhanced kinesthetic sense, which is related to touch, that makes the group and sets them apart from others.[247] Another example comes from South Asia, where the sense of touch is particularly relevant in mediating and constructing identities, as it "is believed to be capable of transmitting both polluting and purifying qualities".[248] The idea of 'untouchability' is probably the most obvious example of sensory regulation of social interactions, especially by determining rules of social proximity and distance, status and power, thus creating social identities based on touch.[249] While sharing the object of touch can lead to an enhanced cultural identity, the prohibition to touch – someone or something – that is present in one group also contributes to distinguishing this group from other groups.[250] It is through touch that simple distinctions between "own" and "other" are made, and children learn to differentiate between different types of relationships early on by observing and imitating tactile encounters.[251] These distinctions and tactile experiences obviously carry meaning, as touching someone from one's own group will usually be a positive experience imbued with love, while touching an individual from another community would be described as unpleasant and even painful.[252]

These examples suggest that rules around the senses contribute to processes of identification and embodied feelings of belonging and rejection. While inclusion and exclusion can be produced through all the senses, arguments and examples related to vision are particularly insightful, notably because of the hegemonic position of vision in Western cultures.

'Othering' through the senses

In the West, vision is clearly involved in ongoing processes of 'othering' in various forms and contexts, including in human rights. Identities of both individuals and groups are constructed in a vision-centred paradigm, which is embodied by an ideal subject, namely the Western white man, and therefore limited and discriminatory, as already discussed in the previous chapters. A

245 Potter, 457.
246 Potter, 453.
247 Potter, 459.
248 Alex, 526.
249 Alex, 524, 529–30.
250 Potter, 456–7.
251 Alex, 534–5.
252 Alex, 532–3.

sensuous approach that considers the role of the senses in these processes helps understand that forms of inclusion and exclusion, and 'Otherness', are not only abstract or symbolic constructions; rather, and similarly to identities, they are constructed of and through embodied sensory experiences, both individually and collectively. 'Otherness', such as based on the concept of race or gender, is recognized and entrenched through the senses, whether consciously or unconsciously, thus creating hegemonic and dominated body-subjects.[253]

The deployment, in the West, of images of people(s) and cultures to subjugate or exclude them arguably started with Western modernity,[254] and this process continues to operate today, even if in less explicit ways. As Uli Linke contends, "[t]he cultural logics of citizenship in Europe are founded on sensory regimes retrieved from the archives of race".[255] The Western world, as a legacy of colonialism, became a "hegemonic white space".[256] In this process of 'othering', 'whiteness' has come to be conceived and protected as an identity and lifestyle and is socially constructed in opposition to 'Blackness'; in turn, 'Blackness', also conceived as an important marker of identity, experiences visual marginalization in different ways, with those marked as 'Black', or non-white more generally, rendered vulnerable.[257] Racialization can be understood as a codified process that activates and validates only particular ways of seeing.[258] Whiteness becomes the standard sensory experience, with "black 'sensory otherness'" being constituted against the "normative senses of whiteness".[259] One of the socio-political consequences is that in Europe and other spaces that are politically constructed as 'white', people with non-European appearance are rendered out of place and risk being subjected to differential, possibly violent, treatment, including by the state.

Through imagined, enhanced and misinterpreted differences, race and racism – concepts based on visual markers – have permitted the white body to conceive foreign people as inhuman, and to justify control over them.[260] In other words, identity and subjectivity – or rather the recognition, or lack of recognition, of one's subjectivity – are dependent on skin colour, or one's appearance. This crucial point made by Black studies scholars can be rein-

---

253 Sekimoto, 88.
254 Panagia, 6.
255 Linke, 179. As Linke also argues, the visual discourse put forward by the European Community contributes to this: the visual record of Europe's population statistics shows photographs of white babies, thus participating in the statistical erasure of non-white people in Europe. Ibid, 185–6.
256 Linke, 179.
257 Linke, 191.
258 Sekimoto, 90.
259 Sekimoto, 94.
260 Mbembé, 17.

forced by a disability perspective, according to which the subject must also be able-bodied and, above all, capable to see.[261] In fact, it has been argued that the Western cultural imaginary, with its heavy focus on sight, has been constructed in opposition to – and hence based on – blindness.[262] Even in contemporary politics, the main subject, who is construed as a citizen, remains a viewing subject;[263] 'Others' are overlooked. Davis explains that "visual experience is constitutive of raced, gendered, and disabled difference, and (in)forms what differences are seen to matter".[264] Therefore, difference only counts when it can be seen, which explains the above-mentioned common privileging of more visible violations of certain civil and political rights, to the detriment of more structural and hence hidden forms of violations, often pertaining to economic, social and cultural rights.

Privileging rational vision in Western cultures is also related to the 'othering' of women. Historically, vision, a supposedly cleaner sense, could be accessed by and was reserved for men; women, and especially nursing mothers, because of their association with bodily fluids and odours, were considered "malodorous" and a threat to social stability.[265] As a result, women were, and sometimes still are, excluded from public spaces, in particular of those associated with the exercise of power. A telling example are museums and galleries, where most works exhibited constitute of visual art and are produced and owned by 'seeing' men. In 19th-century England, the possibility to even bar "leaky" persons, namely women and infants, from visiting museums was contemplated.[266]

Using sensory symbols in this way in order to identify and sideline groups that are perceived as jeopardizing the social order is arguably widespread and ongoing.[267] As Linke claims, dominant ways of visual representation, "with their phallocentric and violent technologies of sight", continue to produce and reproduce various forms of "exclusion, subordination, and fear".[268] The rational, heterosexual white man and his sensuous preferences are the default position against which other experiences are measured and compared.[269] It is worth highlighting that, whether in the context of access to public spaces

261 Davis, 68.
262 Davis, 65.
263 Panagia, 19. For the argument that vision and images play an important role in interpreting global politics, see Lamrani, 6.
264 Davis, 64. Processes of profiling and discrimination based on language and accent are often overlooked, yet frequent and consequential. For a succinct analysis, see Wang, "The Legal Paradox of Linguistic Profiling".
265 Classen, "The Senses at the National Gallery", 89.
266 Classen, "The Senses at the National Gallery", 89–90.
267 Howes & Classen, 7.
268 Linke, 181.
269 Bryans. The heterosexual white man's standard also determines how one should present oneself: as a study of women working in the traditionally masculine legal profession has

or with respect to the rules around practicing touch in relation with others, the prohibition to use certain senses is as important and consequential as social norms privileging specific sensory experiences.[270] Finally, the process of objectifying and excluding certain individuals and groups can be said to culminate in the questioning and denial of the subjective sensory experiences of these 'Others'.[271]

While vision plays a particularly prominent and obvious role, all the senses can participate in processes of 'othering'. The ways in which Muslim bodies have been framed in the post-9/11 era by United States authorities in their 'war against terror' is a stark example of how various forms of identity, including religious identity, can be ascribed to the body. Muslim bodies have been marked as ontologically different, with Muslim men embodying terrorist ideologies.[272] In this construction, Muslim bodies are identified not only through visible markers but also through smell. For instance, as law enforcement authorities were advised, in addition to suspicious behaviour, a particular smell or perfume, associated with Muslim men, can be used in the profiling to detect potential suicide bombers.[273] Even more concerning are so-called enhanced interrogation techniques that have been used on detainees in Guantanamo and that involve sensory overstimulation and deprivation, such as leaving detainees blindfolded in a soundproof room and wearing padded gloves to disorient them and provoke psychological distress.[274] Such violent techniques have fittingly been described as a "display of state power over object and objectified bodies".[275] The senses are undoubtedly a powerful political tool, and its use can have potentially drastic consequences.

The influence of the senses on 'personhood' and being human

The senses can also be linked to the very concept of personhood, or of being human, that is sustained within a particular culture, which is of obvious relevance to the way in which the subject of human rights is conceived. Different senses and sensory experiences are emphasized by different groups, and various forms of sensory regulation are relied upon. As the following examples highlight, it is notably through the senses that human beings experience and become part of their environment, and possibly any sense, or senses, can

---

highlighted, women must dress carefully in order to meet "expectations about visual aesthetics" associated with legitimacy and power. See Kilburn.

270 Howes & Classen, 5.
271 This relies on Sekimoto's argument which is focused on racism. Sekimoto, 94.
272 Rochelle, 215–16.
273 Rochelle, 217–18.
274 Rochelle, 219.
275 Rochelle, 219.

play a role in ascertaining humanness. Indeed, while there is great diversity across and within cultures in this regard, it is important to recognize that all cultures rely on the senses, explicitly or implicitly, to constitute and embody the human.[276] This highlights, once again, that the international human rights system, because of its vision-centredness and the resulting ideal subject, is seriously limited and even contributes to the exclusions of many individuals and groups.

Balance, as discussed above, is an important sense for the Anlo-Ewe in various respects, and it is held essential for their definition of being human. For them, "standing upright, balancing and moving on two legs" is precisely what defines them as humans and sets them apart from other animals.[277] Not unlike the importance attached to a highly developed sense of vision in Western cultures, vision is used by the Muinane of Colombia to distinguish human beings from animals and to determine what are genuine social relations between human beings.[278] Another sense lies at the core of the idea of being human for the Songhay people of Mali and Niger, who consider the stomach the site of human personality and agency.[279] In some cultures, it is touch that is a defining sense for the social persona. In India, people exchange through touch particles that carry meaning, which allows the touched person to absorb a part of the other person who has given out the substance. People do not exist by themselves, as individuals, but only when such exchanges take place; in other words, they only truly exist as human beings through the physical connection with others.[280] This is why a baby, which is not thought of as a full human or social person during its first months, will be held and carried around by family members extensively during this period.[281] By way of comparison, babies in the Western world are held and touched significantly less,[282] partly due to the belief that it is through the development of the higher senses of sight and hearing that they will become rational and full human beings. As part of a complex array of sensory regulation, which arguably "pervades most aspects of children's lives",[283] children in industrialized countries therefore grow up with the belief in the superiority of verbal communication and learn very early on the importance of sensory control.[284]

The sensory experiences that are often (co)constitutive of personhood are not necessarily of extraordinary or ceremonial nature; rather, and similar to

276 Sekimoto, 87.
277 Geurts, 50.
278 Ewart, 509.
279 Stoller, 7.
280 Alex, 527.
281 Alex, 531.
282 Thomas, "Growing Out of Touch".
283 Thomas, "Growing Out of Touch".
284 Thomas, "Growing Out of Touch".

sociality, they can be part of the everyday. For the Panará people in Brazil, it is "precisely the visibility of daily activities which testifies to their true human nature".[285] If speech and hearing are regarded as important elements in the development of an individual, the visibility of routine activities – like gardening and feeding children – carries more significant social connotations and determines the social relations within the group and, by extension, the idea of being human.[286] Vision is so important for social life that it even impacts the architecture of villages: the Panará people build round-shaped villages to allow individuals to see each other easily and to enhance the visibility of these everyday activities.[287] Yet, as it should be emphasized, sensory experiences do not seem sufficient by themselves to fully construct humanness; a moral or cognitive dimension always seems to be attached to these sensory experiences. In the case of the Muinane, for instance, the purely visual perception of another being must be accompanied with specific beliefs of the seer, with "properly human thoughts and emotions", to allow human beings to recognize themselves as such.[288]

5.5   Towards a more universal – and plurisensorial – human rights system

International human rights law, because it is a social and cultural phenomenon, "embedded *in* the social rather than somehow above society",[289] can – and, as I maintain, should – adopt a sensory approach that takes into consideration the importance of the senses. Fundamentally, it must be recognized that the emotions, the senses and, more generally, bodily experiences shape social reality, which includes law.[290] As Antaki writes, "l'essence du droit – les sens du droit – est une question sensorielle et sensuelle".[291] Law is inherently related to the senses; it is "a *sense-making activity*", with "sense" here being understood as both meaning and feeling.[292] I demonstrated earlier in this chapter that, although modern law has been perceived as being removed from the spheres of the emotions and the senses, both are greatly involved in the creation of law and its subject, and in the regulation of behaviour. Emotional and sensory experiences, which are closely related to each other, construct identities and even, at least in some cultures, define

---

285 Ewart, 519.
286 Ewart, 519.
287 Ewart, 513.
288 Ewart, 509.
289 Clifford Geertz, as cited by Howes, "Prologue: Introduction to Sensori-Legal Studies", 174 (referring to law more generally).
290 Alex, 540.
291 Antaki, 361.
292 Howes, "Prologue: Introduction to Sensori-Legal Studies", 175.

the human. With regard to international human rights law, its conception of emotions and the senses has a significant impact on who has agency and counts as a genuine subject and who can therefore access human rights. A sensory approach, I believe, could contribute to diffusing the unhelpful dichotomy of 'us' versus 'them' and various processes of 'othering' related to emotions and the senses.

I would argue that international human rights law should not only develop an awareness of its sensuous dimensions and biases but should take the next step and be more open to and embrace other ways of sensing and understanding the world, different ways of meaning-making and of belonging through the senses. Contemporary political life, as it should be remembered, is shaped by a diversity of political cultures and their respective sensoria, or "regimes of perceptions" that determine which experiences and motivations are considered valid.[293] Fundamentally, the senses and emotions are both fashioned by and intrinsic to politics.[294] Examining emotions and the senses exposes hierarchies, stereotypes, hegemonic influences and other biases that are significant – but often concealed – for the construction and expression of identities of both dominant and dominated groups and individuals and that are responsible for various forms of privilege and disadvantage, inclusion and exclusion. It is, therefore, important to acknowledge this inherent relationship between the exercise of authority, emotions and the senses as well as the consequences of relying on a particular, hegemonic sensorium. As I have argued, Western law's visiocracy – combined with modernity's conception of law as rational and emotionless – has resulted in the limitation of legal subjectivity and has afforded legal agency only to certain Western citizens, including in the context of international human rights. If visual discourses tend to become hegemonic, they are not – and can probably never be – truly universal. Since the system is focused on a certain type and a certain expression of subjectivity, many ways of being are currently not acknowledged or supported. Yet, different sensory practices – whether also primarily focused on vision or relying on other senses – are just as, or maybe even more, legitimate and effective ways of imagining law. In other words, relying solely on vision, that is on only one way of understanding the world, as the dominant international human rights system does, implies a subjective and limited self-referential understanding and the censoring of the diversity of ways of being and sensing the world.[295]

If Western law took its distance from – but not necessarily abandoned – vision to allow its sensorium to reflect greater diversity, a claim that can be supported by the theories from the margins discussed in Chapter 3, the

293 Panagia, 24.
294 Lamrani, 3.
295 Panagia, 50.

international human rights system could come closer to being universal, with the senses being an avenue for "navigating cross-cultural difference".[296] Indeed, legal subjectivity and agency, which are supposed to be recognized and enhanced through human rights, can take different forms. In India, to recall, subjectivity and agency are closely related to touch, which is a means to comply with the existing social order and social reforms, or to resist them, for instance by touching someone who should not be touched.[297] These are dimensions that can hardly be captured by the currently dominant sensorium of human rights. Justice begins "with an effort at comprehension",[298] and visual means alone cannot always enable this comprehension. Allowing and enabling legal subjects to construct themselves along the full – and, in fact, perhaps not yet fully recognized – sensorial spectrum can enhance legal agency and suggest novel avenues to achieve justice. As I have demonstrated in this chapter, all the senses and the interplay between them are involved in the forging of personal perspectives as well as of social expectations. They contribute to the construction of individual and group identities, including legal subjectivity, and to the pursuit of global justice. The multiple and plural identities in our worlds are constructed in various ways and through a variety and different *mélanges* of senses.[299] In addition to vision, the auditory, tactile, olfactory and gustatory – and other sensorial experiences – also play important communicative and educative roles. From socializing children into hygienic practices to transmitting conceptions of morality and acceptable postures, the senses are involved in the creation of perceptions of outsiders and serve to differentiate as markers of identities.[300] The senses also inform sentiments such as fear *vis-à-vis* 'Others', including in the supposedly more rational Western world, and different accents and allegedly bad smell have even been used explicitly as reasons for the exclusion of certain minority groups.[301] As such, honouring all the senses can give a greater variety of actors the possibility to experience the world according to their values and preferred modes of expression and perception. In other words, embracing plurisensoriality would contribute to rendering international human rights law and its subject more inclusive and dynamic, and thus also more empowering and emancipatory.

Furthermore, a commitment to plurisensoriality does not only imply being open to other sensoria, but possibly also learning to sense the world differently. As Sachi Sekimoto has maintained, our bodies can be rehabilitated and trained, at least to some extent, to enable different ways of sensing and being: "We must begin to collectively cultivate . . . bodily sensibilities, and inter-corporeal

296 Hamilton et al, 18.
297 Alex, 539.
298 Manderson, *Songs Without Music*, 198.
299 Howes, 'The Aesthetics of Mixing the Senses'.
300 Trnka, Dureau & Park, 5.
301 Trnka, Dureau & Park, 2–3, 5.

imaginations that affirm the humanities and lived experiences" of all subjects.[302] Or, in van Ede's words, "[s]ensuous investigations have to start with an open mind" and require the "courage and will to turn one's own body into a research tool".[303] Embodied and fluid approaches could, I feel, complement cognitive and presumably rational ways of thinking in international human rights.

Finally, I suggest that encouraging a diversity of metaphors in international human rights and legal discourses more generally to reflect the multiplicity of ways of sensing and being would be one way to bring about greater comprehension and tolerance for difference. The figure of the *migrating 'Others'*, proposed in Part I, with its embodiment of openness and fluidity, can also be relied upon here and further imagined as embracing plurisensoriality and the multifaceted emotional dimensions of the legal subject. Conceptualizing the subjects of international human rights not in the form of the historically dominant default position, that is as a seeing yet otherwise largely sense-less and disembodied human, but as *plurisensorial migrating 'Others'*, would be one way to render human rights more accessible.

Bibliography

Abraham, Christiana. "Race, Gender and 'Difference': Representations of 'Third World Women' in International Development" (2015) 2:2 *Journal of Critical Race Inquiry* 4.

Abrams, Kathryn & Hila Keren. "Law in the Cultivation of Hope" (2007) 95:2 *California Law Review* 319.

Alex, Gabriele. "A Sense of Belonging and Exclusion: 'Touchability' and 'Untouchability' in Tamil Nadu" (2008) 73:4 *Ethnos* 523.

Antaki, Mark. "Le tournant sensoriel en droit: vers un droit sensible et sensé?" (2019) 34:2 *Revue Canadienne Droit et Société* 361.

Averill, James R. "Vignette 2: Intellectual Emotions" in Rom Harre & W Gerrod Parrott, eds, *The Emotions: Social, Cultural and Biological Dimensions* (London: Sage, 1996) 24.

Averill, James R., Kyum Koo Chon & Doug Woong Hahn. "Emotions and Creativity, East and West" (2001) 4 *Asian Journal of Social Psychology* 165.

Bandes, Susan A. "Introduction" in Susan A Bandes, ed, *The Passions of Law* (New York: New York University Press, 1999) 1.

———. "Emotion and Deliberation: The Autonomous Citizen in the Social World" in James E. Fleming, ed, *Passions and Emotions* (New York: New York University Press, 2013) 189.

Barreto, José Manuel. "Human Rights and Emotions from the Perspective of the Colonised: Anthropofagi, Legal Surrealism and Subaltern Studies" (2013) 5:2 *Revista de Estudos Constitucionais, Hermenêutica e Teoria do Direito* 106.

Baxi, Upendra. *The Future of Human Rights* (Oxford: Oxford University Press, 2002).

Bently, Lionel. "Introduction" in L. Bently & L. Flynn, eds, *Law and the Senses: Sensational Jurisprudence* (London: Pluto Press, 1996) 1.

---

302 Sekimoto, 97. The author makes this argument in the context of racialization.
303 van Ede, 66, 70.

Buchanan, Ruth. "Looking into Law and Development: Pedagogies and Politics of the Frame" (2022) 59 *Osgoode Hall Law Journal* i.

Bryans, John. "Masculinity Studies and the Senses", <www.lawandthesenses.org>.

Calhoun, Cheshire. "Making Up Emotional People: The Case of Romantic Love" in Susan A Bandes, ed, *The Passions of Law* (New York: New York University Press, 1999) 217.

———. "Reliable Democratic Habits and Emotions" in James E. Fleming, ed, *Passions and Emotions* (New York: New York University Press, 2013) 212.

Chau, Adam Yuet. "The Sensorial Production of the Social" (2008) 73:4 *Ethnos* 484.

Classen, Constance. "Foundations of an Anthropology of the Senses" (1997) 49:153 *International Social Science Journal* 401.

———. "The Senses at the National Gallery: Art as Sensory Recreation and Regulation in Victorian England" (2020) 15:1 *The Senses and Society* 85.

Cover, Robert. "Foreword: Nomos and Narrative" (1983–1984) 97 *Harvard Law Review* 4.

Damasio, Antonio R. *Descartes' Error: Emotion, Reason, and the Human Brain* (New York: Putnam, 1994).

Davis, Elizabeth. "Structures of Seeing: Blindness, Race, and Gender in Visual Culture" (2019) 14:1 *The Senses and Society* 63.

Dundes Renteln, Alison. "Visual Religious Symbols and the Law" (2004) 47:12 *American Behavioural Scientist* 1573.

Ewart, Elizabeth. "Seeing, Hearing and Speaking: Morality and Sense among the Panará in Central Brazil" (2008) 73:4 *Ethnos* 505.

Frevert, Ute. "Honour and / or / as Passion: Historical Trajectories As Legal Defenses" (2014) 22 *Journal of the Max Planck Institute for European Legal History* 245.

Geurts, Kathryn Linn. *Culture and the Senses – Bodily Ways of Knowing in an African Community* (Berkeley: University of California Press, 2002).

Geurts, Kathryn Linn & Sekafor G.M.A. Komabu-Pomeyie. "From 'Sensing Disability' to Seselelame: Non-Dualistic Activist Orientations in Twenty-First-Century Accra" in Shaun Grech & Karen Soldatic, eds, *Disability in the Global South* (Cham: Springer, 2016) 85.

Gilman, Sander L. *Inscribing the Other* (Lincoln: University of Nebraska Press, 1991).

Glenn, H. Patrick. *Legal Traditions of the World: Sustainable Diversity in Law*, 5th ed (Oxford: Oxford University Press, 2014).

Goldie, Peter. *The Emotions: A Philosophical Exploration* (Oxford: Oxford University Press, 2002).

Hamilton, Sheryl N. "Introduction – Sensuous Governance" (2020) 15:1 *The Senses and Society* 1.

Hamilton, Sheryl N. et al. "Sensing Law – Introduction" in Sheryl N. Hamilton et al., eds, *Sensing Law* (New York: Routledge, 2017) 1.

Howes, David. "Introduction: 'To Summon All the Senses'" in David Howes, ed, *The Varieties of Sensory Experience: A Sourcebook in the Anthropology of the Senses* (Toronto: University of Toronto Press, 1991) 3.

———. "Introduction: Empire of the Senses" in David Howes, ed, *Empire of the Senses – the Sensual Culture Reader* (New York: Berg, 2005) 1.

———. "Charting the Sensorial Revolution" (2006) 1:1 *Senses and Society* 113.

———. *The Sixth Sense Reader* (Oxford: Berg, 2009).

———. "Law's Sensorium: On the Media of Law and the Evidence of the Senses in Historical and Cross-Cultural Perspective" in Sheryl N. Hamilton et al., eds, *Sensing Law* (New York: Routledge, 2017) 53.

———. "Multisensory Anthropology" (2019) 48 *Annual Review of Anthropology* 17.

———. "Prologue: Introduction to Sensori-Legal Studies" (2019) 34:2 *Canadian Journal of Law and Society* 173.

———. "Afterword – The Sensory Revolution Comes of Age" (2021) 39:2 *The Cambridge Journal of Anthropology* 128.

———. "The Aesthetics of Mixing the Senses: Cross-Modal Aesthetics", <www.david-howes.com/senses/aestheticsofmixingthesenses.pdf> 75.

Howes, David & Constance Classen. *Ways of Sensing: Understanding the Senses in Society* (New York: Routledge, 2014).

Hsu, Elisabeth. "The Senses and the Social: An Introduction" (2008) 73:4 *Ethnos* 433.

Ingold, Tim. *The Perception of the Environment: Essays on Livelihood, Dwelling and Skill* (London: Routledge, 2000).

Ingold, Tim & David Howes. "Worlds of Sense and Sensing the World: A Response to Sarah Pink and David Howes" (2011) 19:3 *Social Anthropology/Anthropologie Sociale* 313.

Jay, Martin. *Downcast Eyes: The Denigration of Vision in Twentieth-Century French Thought* (Berkeley: University of California Press, 1993).

Kilburn, Jessye. "A Lawyer and a Lady? Visual Aesthetics of Femininity and Professionalism in Law", <www.lawandthesenses.org>.

Kleinhans, Martha-Marie & Roderick A. Macdonald. "What Is a *Critical* Legal Pluralism?" (1997) 12 *Canadian Journal of Law and Society* 25.

Lamrani, Myriam. "Introduction – Beyond Revolution: Reshaping Nationhood through Senses and Affects" (2021) 39:2 *The Cambridge Journal of Anthropology* 1.

Leckey, Robert & Kim Brooks, eds. *Queer Theory: Law, Culture, Empire* (New York: Routledge, 2010).

Lévi-Strauss, Claude. *The Savage Mind* (London: Weidenfeld and Nicolson, 1962).

Linke, Uli. "Off the Edge of Europe – Border Regimes, Visual Culture, and the Politics of Race" in Sheryl N. Hamilton et al., eds, *Sensing Law* (New York: Routledge, 2017) 178.

MacIntyre, Alasdair. *Whose Justice? Which Rationality?* (Notre Dame, IN: University of Notre Dame Press, 2020).

Makdisi, John. "Formal Rationality in Islamic Law and the Common Law" (1985) 34 *Cleveland State Law Review* 97.

———. "Legal Logic and Equity in Islamic Law" (1985) 33:1 *American Journal of Comparative Law* 63.

Manderson, Desmond. *Songs without Music – Aesthetic Dimensions of Law and Justice* (Berkeley: University of California Press, 2000).

Marcus, George E. "Reason, Passion, and Democratic Politics: Old Conceptions – New Understandings – New Possibilities" in James E. Fleming, ed, *Passions and Emotions* (New York: New York University Press, 2013) 127.

Maroney, Terry A. "Law and Emotion: A Proposed Taxonomy of an Emerging Field" (2006) 30:2 *Law and Human Behavior* 119.

McHugh, James. "The Classification of Smells and the Order of the Senses in Indian Religious Traditions" (2007) 54:4 *Religion through the Senses* 374.

Minow, Martha. "Institutions and Emotions: Redressing Mass Violence" in Susan A Bandes, ed, *The Passions of Law* (New York: New York University Press, 1999) 265.

Mokgoro, Yvonne. "Ubuntu and the Law in South Africa" (1998) 4 *Buffalo Human Rights Law Review* 115.

———. "Ubuntu, the Constitution and the Rights of Non-Citizens" (2010) 21 *Stellenbosch Law Review* 221.

Nedelsky, Jennifer. "Embodied Diversity and the Challenges to Law" (1997) 42 *McGill Law Journal* 91.

Newcomb, Rachel. "Modern Citizens, Modern Food: Taste and the Rise of the Moroccan Citizen-Consumer" in S. Trnka, C. Dureau & J. Park, eds, *Senses and Citizenships: Embodying Political Life* (New York: Routledge, 2013) 147.

Nussbaum, Martha. "Emotions and Women's Capabilities" in Martha Nussbaum & Jonathan Glover, eds, *Women, Culture and Development: A Study of Human Capabilities* (Oxford: Clarendon Press, 1995) 360.

———. "Secret Sewers of Vice: Disgust, Bodies, and the Law" in Susan A Bandes, ed, *The Passions of Law* (New York: New York University Press, 1999) 19.

Ong, Walter J. "The Shifting Sensorium" in David Howes, ed, *The Varieties of Sensory Experience* (Toronto: University of Toronto Press, 1991) 25.

Panagia, Davide. *The Political Life of Sensation* (London: Duke University Press, 2009).

Parker, James. "The Soundscape of Justice" (2011) 4 *Griffith Law Review* 962.

Philippopoulos-Mihalopoulos, Andreas. "Atmospheres of Law: Senses, Affects, Lawscapes" (2013) 7 *Emotion, Space and Society* 35.

Pink, Sarah. *The Future of Visual Anthropology: Engaging the Senses* (New York: Routledge, 2006).

Pink, Sarah & David Howes. "The Future of Sensory Anthropology/the Anthropology of the Senses" (2010) 18:3 *Social Anthropology/Anthropologie Sociale* 331.

Porter, Roy. "Barely Touching: A Social Perspective on Mind and Body" in G.S. Rousseau, ed, *The Languages of Psyche* (Berkeley, CA: University of California Press, 1990) 45.

Posner, Richard, A. "Emotion versus Emotionalism in Law" in Susan Bandes, ed, *The Passions of Law* (New York: New York University Press, 1999) 309.

Potter, Caroline. "Sense of Motion, Senses of Self: Becoming a Dancer" (2008) 73:4 *Ethnos* 444.

Rochelle, Safiyah. "Encountering the 'Muslim': Guantanamo Bay, Detainees, and Apprehensions of Violence" (2019) 34:2 *Canadian Journal of Law and Society* 209.

Rorty, Richard. "Human Rights, Rationality and Sentimentality" in Obrad Savić, ed, *The Politics of Human Rights* (New York: Verso, 1999) 67.

Sanger, Carol. "Legislation with Affect: Emotion and Legislative Law Making" in James E. Fleming, ed, *Passions and Emotions* (New York: New York University Press, 2013) 38.

Santos, Boaventura de Sousa. *Epistemologies of the South – Justice against Epistemicide* (Boulder, CO: Paradigm Publishers, 2014).

Sekimoto, Sachi. "Race and the Senses – Toward Articulating the Sensory Apparatus of Race" (2018) 6:1 *Critical Philosophy of Race* 82.

Seremetakis, C. Nadia. "The Memory of the Senses: Historical Perception, Commensal Exchange and Modernity" (1993) 9:2 *Visual Anthropology Review* 2.

Smith, Linda Tuhiwai. *Decolonizing Methodologies: Research and Indigenous Peoples* (London: Zed Books, 1995).

Solomon, Robert C. "Justice v. Vengeance: On Law and the Satisfaction of Emotions" in Susan A Bandes, ed, *The Passions of Law* (New York: New York University Press, 1999) 123.

Spelman, Elizabeth V. *Inessential Woman: Problems of Exclusion in Feminist Thought* (Boston: Beacon Press, 1988).

Stoller, Paul. *Sensuous Scholarship* (Philadelphia: University of Pennsylvania Press, 1997).

Stroeken, Koen. "Sensory Shifts and 'Synaesthetics' in Sukuma Healing" (2008) 73:4 *Ethnos* 466.

Synnott, Anthony. *The Body Social: Symbolism, Self and Society* (New York: Routledge, 1993).

Thomas, Sarah-Michelle. "Contesting Allegations: The Islamic Veil and Gender In/ Equality", <www.lawandthesenses.org>.

———. "Growing Out of Touch: The Social and Sensory Regulation of Childhood", <www.lawandthesenses.org>.

Trnka, Susanna, Christine Dureau & Julie Park. "Introduction: Senses and Citizenships" in S. Trnka, C. Dureau & J. Park, eds, *Senses and Citizenships: Embodying Political Life* (New York: Routledge, 2013) 1.

"Ukraine Crisis: Violent Brawl at Kiev Parliament" (8 April 2014) *BBC News*, <www.bbc.com/news/world-europe-26933905>.

UN Sustainable Development Group. "Human Rights-Based Approach", <https://unsdg.un.org/2030-agenda/universal-values/human-rights-based-approach>.

van Ede, Yolanda. "Sensuous Anthropology: Sense and Sensibility and the Rehabilitation of Skill" (2009) 15:2 *Anthropological Notebooks* 61.

Vanita, Ruth, "'Wedding of Two Souls': Same-Sex Marriage and Hindu Traditions" (2004) 20:2 *Journal of Feminist Studies in Religion* 119.

Wang, Lily Maya. "The Legal Paradox of Linguistic Profiling", <www.lawandthesenses.org>.

———. "A Sensory Exploration of the Tsuu T'ina Court", <www.lawandthesenses.org>.

West, Robin. "The Anti-Empathic Turn" in James E. Fleming, ed, *Passions and Emotions* (New York: New York University Press, 2013) 243.

Wilke, Christiane. "The Optics of War: Seeing Civilians, Enacting Distinctions, and Visual Crisis in International Law" in Sheryl N. Hamilton et al., eds, *Sensing Law* (New York: Routledge, 2017) 257.

Wilson, Richard A. *The Politics of Truth and Reconciliation in South Africa: Legitimizing the Post-Apartheid State* (Cambridge: Cambridge University Press, 2001).

Wimpfheimer, Barry. "Talmudic Legal Narrative: Broadening the Discourse of Jewish Law" (2007) 24 *Diné Yisrael* 157.

Young, Iris Marion. "Impartiality and the Civic Public: Some Implications of Feminist Critiques of Moral and Political Theory" (1986) 5:4 *Praxis International* 381.

Concluding thoughts and feelings

I have sought to explain in this book some of the paradoxical tendencies in international human rights to create exclusions. There is notably a well-entrenched but tacit assumption that there exists an ideal subject that has historically been defined against 'Others'. This ideal subject must be a citizen of a state and, more fundamentally, human in a specific way, in line with the dominant Western notion of an enlightened, male, rational and seeing subject. Yet belonging to a group can take different forms. Moreover, whether a fundamentally human identity – if this actually exists – is based on such markers as nationality or ethnicity, it is inherently problematic if rights are dependent on group identities that are constructed in opposition to different 'Others'.

Bringing together several critical theories, including non-Western critical theories that are rarely considered together, I suggested *migrating 'Others'* as a useful figure to explain these complex and varied processes of 'othering'. The exploratory study of dominant and alternative visual discourses in international human rights allowed me to test and illustrate the theoretical arguments. Informed by this, I demonstrated that the focus on rationality and vision in international human rights and their highly limited engagement with emotions and other senses, which result from the Western origins of human rights, explain the undue and problematic influence of certain dominant visual discourses in this context. These inherent biases explain, in turn, why international human rights remain largely inaccessible and an ineffective tool for many individuals and groups. This is why I believe that imagining the subjects of human rights as *plurisensorial migrating 'Others'* could render human rights more effective.

In line with Boaventura de Sousa Santos' invitation to embrace alternative epistemologies, and I would add alternative ontologies, which includes different ways of sensing, it would be important that international human rights respect and seek inspiration from different conceptions of knowing, being and sensing. While the main objectives of international human rights certainly include respecting the dignity and equality of all human beings,[1]

---

1 All major human rights instruments link human rights to dignity. See, for instance, the preambles of the *Universal Declaration of Human Rights* and the *International Covenant on*

DOI: 10.4324/9781003427957-10

difference and diverse ways of knowing and being have not been sufficiently taken into account. Transcending purported universals, which tend to essentialize, to suppress diversity and to exclude,[2] would allow welcoming, and possibly being transformed by, the variety of social experiences that exist in the world.[3] As I have argued, international human rights could contribute to this endeavour through a reconfigured understanding of legal subjectivity along these lines. Decentring the dominant subject could be valuable for all beings that do not correspond to the norms associated with this ideal. This would be a way for law to contribute to empowering currently marginalized individuals and groups, instead of being an instrument of oppression, as it has historically often been.[4] In other words, to be more just and inclusive, and therefore also more legitimate and effective, international human rights would benefit from recognizing and cherishing alternative views and from being open to radical approaches that may actually challenge the foundations on which these rights rest.[5]

It is useful to keep in mind that because the Western world takes for granted the relevance and supremacy of the current paradigm, it can only provide limited and weak answers to crucial contemporary questions.[6] The understanding of the world is not limited to Western worldviews, and so-called modernization and progress in the Global South do not necessarily result from Westernization.[7] Western law, for instance, privileges what is perceptible to the eye, knowable and measurable, and therefore "ignores the unknowable, spiritual, and less tangible aspects of human experience".[8] The importance of dreaming in some Indigenous traditions, and its direct relevance for decision-making in everyday life, is a good example of what dominant Western thought and law have chosen to disregard as something that cannot be grasped.[9] Moreover, the Western world cannot be explained

---

Civil and Political Rights as well as article 5 of the *African Charter on Human and Peoples' Rights*.

2 Calarco, 9.

3 Santos, *Epistemologies of the South*, 165.

4 See e.g. Anghie.

5 The risk that a legal system could temporarily become ineffective or paralyzed if radical approaches are adopted, for instance if emotions are recognized as being integral to the legal system, is not negligible but should not be overstated. The smooth functioning of a particular legal system seems to be a secondary concern to its inclusiveness, which has the potential to bring about greater justice in the long run.

6 Santos, *Epistemologies of the South*, 20.

7 Santos, *Epistemologies of the South*, viii; Comaroff & Comaroff, 119. It is worth recalling that in the West, or the Global North, the concept of modernity as "a vision of history as a progressive, man-made construction" has been equated with Enlightenment and its application limited to Europe and North America. Comaroff & Comaroff, 9.

8 Stern, 43.

9 Povinelli, "Do Rocks Listen?", 509.

and could arguably not have developed without other traditions. Imperialism and globalization, to take crucial factors in the so-called development of the West, could obviously not have happened without the Global South.[10] The same is true of whatever fate the entire world will face: there will always be a variety of inputs from people from the Global North and South (and from those who feel that they are not captured by this dichotomy).[11]

Once the pervasive Western paradigm is transcended, alternative conceptions of law and of legal subjectivity, which form alternative conceptions of rationality and of law's relationship with emotions and the senses, will be able to develop and thrive. The desire and means for change and social emancipation can come from different loci and voices, and especially from those that have been suppressed and that are not part of the dominant discourse.[12] In fact, those who have long been excluded can – and already do – suggest solutions to current problems of injustice in the world. Indeed, although this has long been ignored by the North, the South produces theory and can offer explanations for historical events that have influenced the world, including modernity: as Jean Comaroff and John L. Comaroff have noted, modernity can be and is narrated from "ex-centric" positions as well as from "self-proclaimed centers", precisely because it resulted from a process in which both the South and the North were involved and influenced.[13] The South, as I have argued, might understand the world through different kinds of knowledges and also *feel* the world differently, notably beyond rationality and cognition, and through different sensorial experiences. In other words, the experiences and theories in and from the South, and the exchanges between those who have been traditionally dominant and marginalized, are significant and potentially valuable for all. While this does not imply that the North should stop producing theory altogether, it must be recognized that the North does not hold a monopoly over theory-making. Diversity and difference matter.

It emerges that in order to enhance justice at a global level, it would be important to try to attain real equity between different epistemologies and ontologies, including in international human rights. As it stands, even progressive societies that claim to be committed to recognizing different traditions and worldviews, such as Indigenous legal traditions, allocate themselves the right to recognize this alterity, with genuine recognition, that is on its own terms, always being extremely limited. Even in groundbreaking judgments, the courts of settler colonial societies, for instance, clearly do not consider Indigenous law to be on an equal footing with Western law.[14] For international

---

10 Comaroff & Comaroff, 117.
11 Queer theory radically questions the use of such categories. For a discussion in reference to law, see e.g. Leckey & Brooks; Otto.
12 Santos, *Epistemologies of the South*, 63.
13 Comaroff & Comaroff, 3, 7.
14 For a discussion in the context of Australia, see Povinelli, "The Cunning of Recognition", 22.

human rights law, trying to realize epistemological and ontological equity would imply, among others, recognizing its visual biases as well as considering other, non-hegemonic ways of knowing, being and sensing as equally valid. This would help appreciate that subjectivity can be conceptualized differently than in its currently dominant form.

Since the 'human' in human rights has arguably always been characterized by a high degree of indeterminacy, the idea that the subject of human rights can be reconfigured by drawing on different epistemologies and ontologies is conceptually coherent. As Jean L. Cohen has argued,

> it is precisely the indeterminacy of the concept of man as the subject of human rights, the impossibility of deciding once and for all the content of human rights . . . that gives to human rights discourses their "groundless ground" and their political, creative trust. The indeterminacy of the discourse of human rights is its greatest advantage.[15]

I would add that this non-essentialist approach also implies a commitment to some degree of non-prescriptivism: if one is honest about valorizing different understandings and experiences in the context of law and rights, then there can be no legal solutions, and no law at all, outside and apart from legal and sensing subjects.[16] Non-prescriptivism, as I conceive it, involves an openness, including to the unknown and to change. Subjectivities are not static; they are constantly in flux,[17] and existing tools might simply not allow to properly grasp different or new forms of political and legal subjectivities.[18] Similarly, the senses and sensorial experiences are subject to changing epistemologies and can therefore be understood as processes themselves.[19] Furthermore, since law is a matter of dynamic social relations, there is no reason to try to predetermine or to permanently fix it. International human rights can and do evolve through these relations, and through the initiative of relevant actors, as the example of refugees and migrants shows. Such an openness can shift the dominant perspective and contribute to the realization of emancipatory projects.[20] In other words, everyone needs to learn to live with plurality, complexity and uncertainty.

While the major shift in the conception of legal subjectivity and in the relationship between law, emotions and the senses that I have suggested

---

15 Cohen, 183–4 (footnote omitted). Or, in Ben Golder's words, because there is "no human as such, no abstract set of guidelines to guide us", human rights actually bear the "the possibility for contestation and subversive renewal of the human". Golder, 156.
16 This draws on Kleinhans & Macdonald, 40–1; see also Antaki, 366.
17 Panagia, 4; Hamilton et al, 23.
18 Panagia, 11.
19 Howes & Classen, 5; Stoller, 91.
20 Nedelsky, 113.

would certainly imply major challenges for orthodox law and legal theory as well as society as a whole, effectively pluralizing legal subjectivities and law would constitute a meaningful attempt to recognize and value difference – in terms of different ways of knowing, being and sensing – and to foster mutual understanding. Moreover, if this suggestion may be considered particularly difficult to implement in the case of Western law, which is usually associated with such notions as stability, predictability and uniformity, being open to change and the unknown may not be, after all, a radical idea. As I discussed, the currently dominant understanding of legal subjectivity is a historical construction;[21] it evolved in the past, and it can continue to do so. In fact, the struggle for human rights arguably involves a constant rearticulation of the human.[22] Furthermore, and perhaps more fundamentally, it is possible to build on non-dominant approaches to law and to legal subjectivity in order to apprehend plurality and uncertainty. There are understandings of law – notably Indigenous approaches, as captured by legal pluralism and other critical theories – that can be useful allies in this open-ended, multisensory-legal endeavour. Finally, I submit that embracing plurality and flexibility is not equivalent to a "naive epistemological relativism";[23] rather, it is part of an argument for greater creativity and understanding. It is possible to understand, sense and be in the world in different ways, including, as I believe – and feel – in the context of international human rights.

Bibliography

African Charter on Human and Peoples' Rights (adopted on 27 June 1981, entered into force 21 October 1986) 1520 UNTS 217.

Anghie, Anthony. *Imperialism, Sovereignty and the Making of International Law* (Cambridge: Cambridge University Press, 2005).

Antaki, Mark. "Le tournant sensoriel en droit: vers un droit sensible et sensé?" (2019) 34:2 *Revue Canadienne Droit et Société* 361.

Butler, Judith. *Undoing Gender* (New York: Routledge, 2004).

Calarco, Matthew. *Zoographies: The Question of the Animal from Heidegger to Derrida* (New York: Columbia University Press, 2008).

Cohen, Jean L. "Rights, Citizenship and the Modern Form of the Social: Dilemmas of Arendtian Republicanism" (1996) 3(2) *Constellations* 164.

Comaroff, Jean & John L. Comaroff. *Theories from the South: Or, How Euro-America Is Evolving toward Africa* (Boulder, CO: Paradigm Publishers, 2012).

Davis, Elizabeth. "Structures of Seeing: Blindness, Race, and Gender in Visual Culture" (2019) 14:1 *The Senses and Society* 63.

Golder, Ben. "Critical Humanities and the Human of International Human Rights Law" in Shane Chalmers & Sundhya Pahuja, eds, *Routledge Handbook of International Law and the Humanities* (New York: Routledge, 2023) 148.

21 See also Davis, 68.
22 Butler, *Undoing Gender*, 33.
23 Stoller, 91.

Hamilton, Sheryl N. et al. "Sensing Law – Introduction" in Sheryl N. Hamilton et al, eds, *Sensing Law* (New York: Routledge, 2017) 1.

Howes, David & Constance Classen. *Ways of Sensing: Understanding the Senses in Society* (New York: Routledge, 2014).

International Covenant on Civil and Political Rights (adopted on 16 December 1966, entered into force 23 March 1976) 999 UNTS 171.

Kleinhans, Martha-Marie & Roderick A. Macdonald. "What Is a *Critical* Legal Pluralism?" (1997) 12 *Canadian Journal of Law and Society* 25.

Leckey, Robert & Kim Brooks, eds. *Queer Theory: Law, Culture, Empire* (New York: Routledge, 2010).

Nedelsky, Jennifer. "Embodied Diversity and the Challenges to Law" (1997) 42 *McGill Law Journal* 91.

Otto, Dianne. "International Human Rights Law: Towards Rethinking Sex/Gender Dualism" in Vanessa E. Munro and Margaret Davies, eds, *The Ashgate Research Companion to Feminist Legal Theory* (New York: Routledge, 2013) 197.

Panagia, Davide. *The Political Life of Sensation* (London: Duke University Press, 2009).

Povinelli, Elizabeth A. "Do Rocks Listen? The Cultural Politics of Apprehending Australian Aboriginal Labor" (1995) 97:3 *American Anthropologist* 505.

———. "The Cunning of Recognition: Real Being and Aboriginal Recognition in Settler Australia" (1998) 11:1 *Australian Feminist Law Journal* 3.

Santos, Boaventura de Sousa. *Epistemologies of the South – Justice against Epistemicide* (Boulder, CO: Paradigm Publishers, 2014).

Stern, Kristina. "Law and the Lack of Sense" in L. Bently and L. Flynn, eds, *Law and the Senses: Sensational Jurisprudence* (London: Pluto Press, 1996) 42.

Stoller, Paul. *Sensuous Scholarship* (Philadelphia: University of Pennsylvania Press, 1997).

Universal Declaration of Human Rights (adopted on 10 December 1948), UNGA Res 217A (III), UN Doc A/810 (1948) 71.

Bibliography

Legal documents

African Charter on Human and Peoples' Rights (adopted on 27 June 1981, entered into force 21 October 1986) 1520 UNTS 217.

American Declaration of Independence (4 July 1776).

Convention on the Elimination of All Forms of Discrimination against Women (adopted on 18 December 1979, entered into force 3 September 1981) 1249 UNTS 13.

Convention Relating to the Status of Refugees (adopted on 28 July 1951, entered into force 22 April 1951) 189 UNTS 150.

Déclaration des droits de l'homme et du citoyen (1789).

International Covenant on Civil and Political Rights (adopted on 16 December 1966, entered into force 23 March 1976) 999 UNTS 171.

Report of the Special Rapporteur on Contemporary Forms of Racism, Racial Discrimination, Xenophobia and Related Intolerance, UN Doc A/HRC/38/52 (25 April 2018).

Report of the Special Rapporteur on Contemporary Forms of Racism, Racial Discrimination, Xenophobia and Related Intolerance, UN Doc A/74/321 (21 August 2019).

Report of the Special Rapporteur on Contemporary Forms of Racism, Racial Discrimination, Xenophobia and Related Intolerance: Global Extractivism and Racial Equality, UN Doc A/HRC/41/54 (14 May 2019).

Universal Declaration of Human Rights (adopted on 10 December 1948), UNGA Res 217A (III), UN Doc A/810 (1948) 71.

Vienna Declaration and Programme of Action (adopted on 12 July 1993), UNGA Res 48/121 (20 December 1993).

Scholarly books and articles

Abraham, Christiana. "Race, Gender and 'Difference': Representations of 'Third World Women' in International Development" (2015) 2:2 *Journal of Critical Race Inquiry* 4.

Abrams, Kathryn & Hila Keren. "Law in the Cultivation of Hope" (2007) 95:2 *California Law Review* 319.

Abu Hatoum, Nayrouz. "Unsettling Visual Politics: Militarized Borders in the Work of Palestinian Artist Raeda Saaedh" (2019) 71:4 *American Quarterly* 1069.

Adami, Rebecca. *Women and the Universal Declaration of Human Rights* (New York: Routledge, 2019).

Adler, Laure. *Le corps des femmes: ce que les artistes ont voulu faire de nous* (Paris: Albin Michel, 2020).

Agamben, Giorgio. "We Refugees" (1995) 49:2 *Symposium: A Quarterly Journal in Modern Literatures* 114.

——. *Homo Sacer: Sovereign Power and Bare Life* (Stanford: Stanford University Press, 1998).

——. *The Open: Man and Animal* (Stanford: Stanford University Press, 2004).

——. *State of Exception* (Chicago: University of Chicago Press, 2005).

——. "Beyond Human Rights" (2008) 15 *Social Engineering* 90.

Alex, Gabriele. "A Sense of Belonging and Exclusion: 'Touchability' and 'Untouchability' in Tamil Nadu" (2008) 73:4 *Ethnos* 523.

Alston, Philip. "Making Space for a New Human Rights: The Case of the Right to Development" (1988) 1 *Harvard Human Rights Yearbook* 3.

Amparo Alves, Jaime. "Neither Humans Nor Rights: Some Notes on the Double Negation of Black Life in Brazil" (2014) 45:2 *Journal of Black Studies* 143.

Anaya, James. *Indigenous Peoples in International Law* (Oxford: Oxford University Press, 2004).

Anderson, Kay. *Race and the Crisis of Humanism* (London: Routledge, 2007).

——. "Mind over Matter? On Decentring the Human in Human Geography" (2014) 21:1 *Cultural Geographies* 3.

Anghie, Anthony. *Imperialism, Sovereignty and the Making of International Law* (Cambridge: Cambridge University Press, 2005).

An-Na'im, Abdullahi A. "Toward a Cross-Cultural Approach to Defining International Standards of Human Rights: The Meaning of Cruel, Inhuman, or Degrading Treatment or Punishment" in Abdullahi A. An-Na'im, ed, *Human Rights in Cross-Cultural Perspectives: A Quest for Consensus* (Philadelphia: University of Pennsylvania Press, 1992).

Antaki, Mark. "Le tournant sensorial en droit: vers un droit sensible et sensé?" (2019) 34:2 *Revue Canadienne Droit et Société* 361.

Aral, Isil, Jean d'Aspremont & Iain Scobbie. "Universal and International Law: A Contestation Around Binaries" in I. Aral, J. d'Aspremont & I. Scobbie, eds, *International Law and Universality* (Oxford: Oxford University Press, 2023) 1.

Araújo, Marta & Silvia R. Maeso. "The Power of Racism in Academia: Knowledge Production and Political Disputes" in Boaventura de Sousa Santos & Bruno Sena Martins, eds, *The Pluriverse of Human Rights: The Diversity of Struggles for Dignity* (New York: Routledge, 2021) 186.

Arendt, Hannah. *The Human Condition* (Chicago: Chicago University Press, 1958).

——. *The Origins of Totalitarianism* (Cleveland: Meridian Books, 1958).

——. "We Refugees" in Marc Robinson, ed, *Altogether Elsewhere* (London: Faber and Faber, 1994) 111.

——. *Elemente und Ursprünge totaler Herrschaft* (München: Piper, 2011).

Averill, James R. "Vignette 2: Intellectual Emotions" in Rom Harre & W Gerrod Parrott, eds, *The Emotions: Social, Cultural and Biological Dimensions* (London: Sage, 1996) 24.

Averill, James R., Kyum Koo Chon & Doug Woong Hahn. "Emotions and Creativity, East and West" (2001) 4 *Asian Journal of Social Psychology* 165.

Azoulay, Ariella. "The Ethics of the Spectator: The Citizenry of Photography" (2005) 33:2 *Afterimage* 38.

Badmington, Neil. "Mapping Posthumanism" (2006) 7:4 *Social & Cultural Geography* 1344.

Balibar, Etienne. *We, thePeople of Europe?*, translated by James Swenson (Princeton, NJ: Princeton University Press, 2004).

——. "(De)Constructing the Human as Human Institution: A Reflection on the Coherence of Hannah Arendt's Practical Philosophy" (2007) 74:3 *Social Research* 727.

Balkin, J.M. "Understanding Legal Understanding: The Legal Subject and the Problem of Legal Coherence" (1993) 103:1 *Yale Law Journal* 105.

Bandes, Susan A. "Introduction" in Susan A. Bandes, ed, *The Passions of Law* (New York: New York University Press, 1999) 1.

———. "Emotion and Deliberation: The Autonomous Citizen in the Social World" in James E. Fleming, ed, *Passions and Emotions* (New York: New York University Press, 2013) 189.

Barreto, José Manuel. "Human Rights and Emotions from the Perspective of the Colonised: Anthropofagi, Legal Surrealism and Subaltern Studies" (2013) 5:2 *Revista de Estudos Constitucionais, Hermenêutica e Teoria do Direito* 106.

———. "Decolonial Thinking and the Quest for Decolonising Human Rights" (2018) 46 *Asian Journal of Social Science* 484.

Barthes, Roland. *Éléments de sémiologie* (Paris: Éditions du Seuil, 1964).

Bauman, Zygmunt. *Wasted Lives – Modernity and Its Outcasts* (Oxford: Wiley, 2013).

Bawaka Country. "Working with and Learning from Country: Decentring Human Authority" (2015) 22:2 *Cultural Geography* 269.

———. "Co-Becoming Bawaka: Towards a Relational Understanding of Place/Space" (2016) 40:4 *Progress in Human Geography* 455.

Baxi, Upendra. "From Human Rights to the Right to Be Human: Some Heresies" (1986) 13:3/4 *India International Centre Quarterly* 185.

———. *The Future of Human Rights* (Oxford: Oxford University Press, 2002).

Beck, Colin J., Gili S. Drori & John W. Meyer. "World Influences on Human Rights Language in Constitutions: A Cross-National Study" (2012) 27:4 *International Sociology* 483.

Bell, Philip. "Content Analysis of Visual Images" in Theo van Leeuwen & Carey Jewitt, eds, *The Handbook of Visual Analysis* (London: Sage, 2001) 10.

Benhabib, Seyla. *The Reluctant Modernism of Hannah Arendt* (London: Sage, 1996).

———. *The Rights of Others: Aliens, Residents, and Citizens* (Cambridge: Cambridge University Press, 2004).

Bentham, Jeremy. *Introduction to the Principles of Morals and Legislation* (Oxford: Clarendon Press, 1879).

Bently, Lionel. "Introduction" in L. Bently and L. Flynn, eds, *Law and the Senses: Sensational Jurisprudence* (London: Pluto Press, 1996) 1.

Berger, John. *Ways of Seeing* (London: Penguin, 1972).

Bernstein, Richard. *Hannah Arendt and the Jewish Question* (Cambridge: Polity Press, 1996).

Blaser, Mario. "Life Projects: Indigenous Peoples' Agency and Development" in Mario Blaser, Harvey A. Feit & Glenn McRea, eds, *In the Way of Development: Indigenous Peoples, Life Projects, and Globalization* (New York: Zed Books, 2004) 26.

———. "'Way of Life' or 'Who Decides': Development, Paraguayan Indigenism and the Yshiro People's Life Projects" in Mario Blaser, Harvey A. Feit & Glenn McRea, eds, *In the Way of Development: Indigenous Peoples, Life Projects, and Globalization* (New York: Zed Books, 2004) 52.

———. "Ontology and Indigeneity: On the Political Ontology of Heterogeneous Assemblages" (2014) 21:1 *Cultural Geographies* 49.

Bobo, Jacqueline, Cynthia Hudley & Claudine Michel. "Introduction" in Jacqueline Bobo, Cynthia Hudley & Claudine Michel, eds, *The Black Studies Reader* (New York: Routledge, 2004) 1.

Borrows, John. "Uncertain Citizens: Aboriginal Peoples and the Supreme Court" (2001) 80 *Canadian Bar Review* 15.

———. "Indigenous Constitutionalism: Pre-Existing Legal Genealogies in Canada" in Peter Oliver, Patrick Macklem & Nathalie Des Rosiers, eds, *The Oxford Handbook of the Canadian Constitution* (Oxford: Oxford University Press, 2017).

Bottici, Chiara. *Imaginal Politics – Images Beyond Imagination and the Imagery* (New York: Columbia University Press, 2014).

Boyle, James. "Is Subjectivity Possible? The Postmodern Subject in Legal Theory" (1991) 62 *University of Colorado Law Review* 489.

Braun, Bruce. "Modalities of Posthumanism" (2006) 7:4 *Social & Cultural Geography* 1352.

Broeck, Sabine. "Legacies of Enslavism and White Abjectorship" in Sabine Broeck & Carsten Junker, eds, *Postcoloniality – Decoloniality – Black Critique – Joints and Fissures* (Frankfurt: Campus Verlag, 2014) 109.

Brown, Chris. "The Only Thinkable Figure? Ethical and Normative Approaches to Refugees in International Relations" in Alexander Betts and Gil Loescher, eds, *Refugees in International Relations* (Oxford: Oxford University Press, 2011) 151.

Buchanan, Ruth. "Looking into Law and Development: Pedagogies and Politics of the Frame" (2022) 59 *Osgoode Hall Law Journal* i.

Bunch, Charlotte. "Women's Rights as Human Rights: Toward a Re-Vision of Human Rights" (1990) 12 *Human Rights Quarterly* 486.

Butler, Judith. *Precarious Life* (London: Verso, 2004).

———. *Undoing Gender* (New York: Routledge, 2004).

Calarco, Matthew. *Zoographies: The Question of the Animal from Heidegger to Derrida* (New York: Columbia University Press, 2008).

Calhoun, Cheshire. "Making Up Emotional People: The Case of Romantic Love" in Susan A. Bandes, ed, *The Passions of Law* (New York: New York University Press, 1999) 217.

———. "Reliable Democratic Habits and Emotions" in James E. Fleming, ed, *Passions and Emotions* (New York: New York University Press, 2013) 212.

Cameron, Emilie, Sarah de Leeuw & Caroline Desbiens. "Indigeneity and Ontology" (2014) 21:1 *Cultural Geographies* 19.

Castree, Noel & Catherine Nash. "Introduction: Posthumanism in Question" (2004) 36:8 *Environment and Planning A* 1341.

———. "Editorial: Posthuman Geographies" (2006) 7:4 *Social & Cultural Geography* 501.

Césaire, Aimé. *Discours sur le colonialisme* (Paris: Présence africaine, 1955).

———. "Discours sur la Négritude" in Aimé Césaire, *Discours sur le colonialisme, Suivi de Discours sur la Négritude* (Paris: Présence africaine, 2000).

Charlesworth, Hilary. "The Travels of Human Rights: The UNESCO Human Rights Exhibition 1950–1953" in Shane Chalmers & Sundhya Pahuja, eds, *Routledge Handbook of International Law and the Humanities* (New York: Routledge, 2023) 173.

Charlesworth, Hilary, Christine Chinkin & Shelley Wright. "Feminist Approaches to International Law" (1991) 85:4 *American Journal of International Law* 613.

Chau, Adam Yuet. "The Sensorial Production of the Social" (2008) 73:4 *Ethnos* 484.

Chouliaraki, Lilie. "Symbolic Bordering: The Self-Representation of Migrants and Refugees in Digital News" (2017) 15:2 *Popular Communication* 78.

Clanchy, Michael T. *From Memory to Written Record: England 1066–1307* (Hoboken: Wiley, 2012).

Classen, Constance. "Foundations of an Anthropology of the Senses" (1997) 49:153 *International Social Science Journal* 401.

———. "The Senses at the National Gallery: Art as Sensory Recreation and Regulation in Victorian England" (2020) 15:1 *The Senses and Society* 85.

Cohen, Jean L. "Rights, Citizenship and the Modern Form of the Social: Dilemmas of Arendtian Republicanism" (1996) 3:2 *Constellations* 164.

Comaroff, Jean & John L. Comaroff. *Theories from the South: Or, How Euro-America Is Evolving toward Africa* (Boulder, CO: Paradigm Publishers, 2012).

Corntassel, John. "Towards Sustainable Self-Determination: Rethinking the Contemporary Indigenous-Rights Discourse" (2008) 33 *Alternatives* 105.

Cotter, Bridget. "Hannah Arendt and 'the Right to Have Rights'" in Anthony F. Lang, Jr. & John Williams, eds, *Hannah Arendt and International Relations: Readings Across the Lines* (New York: Palgrave Macmillan, 2005) 95.

Cover, Robert. "Foreword: Nomos and Narrative" (1983–1984) 97 *Harvard Law Review* 4.

Cox, Rupert. "Senses, Anthropology of" in H. Callan, ed, *The International Encyclopedia of Anthropology* (Wiley, 2018).

Dahlberg, Leif. "Introduction: Visualising Law and Authority" in Leif Dahlberg, ed, *Visualizing Law and Authority: Essays on Legal Aesthetics* (Berlin: Walter de Gruyter, 2012) 4.

D'Alleva, Anne. *How to Write Art History* (London: Laurence King, 2006).

Damasio, Antonio R. *Descartes' Error: Emotion, Reason, and the Human Brain* (New York: Putnam, 1994).

Davis, Elizabeth. "Structures of Seeing: Blindness, Race, and Gender in Visual Culture" (2019) 14:1 *The Senses and Society* 63.

Dayan, Colin. *The Law Is a White Dog: How Legal Rituals Make and Unmake Persons* (Princeton, NJ: Princeton University Press, 2011).

de Leeuw, Sarah. "State of Care: The Ontologies of Child Welfare in British Columbia" (2014) 21:1 *Cultural Geographies* 59.

DeLyser, Dydia & Harriet Hawkins. "Introduction: Writing Creatively – Process, Practice, and Product" (2014) 21:1 *Cultural Geographies* 131.

Dembour, Marie-Bénédicte. "What Are Human Rights? Four Schools of Thought" (2010) 32 *Human Rights Quarterly* 1.

Derrida, Jacques. "The Ends of Man" (1969) 30:1 *Philosophy and Phenomenological Research* 31.

———. "The Animal That Therefore I Am (More to Follow)" (2002) 28:2 *Critical Inquiry* 369.

Derrida, Jacques & Elisabeth Roudinesco. *For What Tomorrow . . .: A Dialogue*, translated by Jeff Fort (Stanford: Stanford University Press, 2004).

Desbiens, Caroline & Étienne Rivard. "From Passive to Active Dialogue? Aboriginal Lands, Development and *métissage* in Québec, Canada" (2014) 21:1 *Cultural Geographies* 99.

Disch, Lisa J. "More Truth Than Fact: Storytelling as Critical Understanding in the Writings of Hannah Arendt" (1993) 21(4) *Political Theory* 665.

Douzinas, Costas. "The Paradoxes of Human Rights" (2013) 20:1 *Constellations* 51.

Douzinas, Costas & Lynda Nead. "Introduction" in Costas Douzinas & Lynda Nead, eds, *Law and the Image: The Authority of Art and the Aesthetics of Law* (Chicago: University of Chicago Press, 1999).

Dowling, Robyn, Kate Loyd & Sandra Suchet-Pearson. "Qualitative Methods II: 'More-Than-Human' Methodologies and/in Praxis" (2017) 41:6 *Progress in Human Geography* 823.

Dubal, Sam. *Against Humanity: Lessons from the Lord's Resistance Army* (Oakland, CA: University of California Press, 2018).

Dundes Renteln, Alison. "Visual Religious Symbols and the Law" (2004) 47:12 *American Behavioural Scientist* 1573.

Engle, Karen. "Female Subjects of Public International Law: Human Rights and the Exotic Other Female" (1991) 26 *New England Law Review* 1509.

Escobar, Arturo. "Worlds and Knowledges Otherwise – The Latin American Modernity/Coloniality Research Program" (2007) 21:2–3 *Cultural Studies* 179.

———. *Encountering Development: The Making and Unmaking of the Third World* (Princeton, NJ: Princeton University Press, 2012).

Ewart, Elizabeth. "Seeing, Hearing and Speaking: Morality and Sense among the Panará in Central Brazil" (2008) 73:4 *Ethnos* 505.

Fagundes, David. "What We Talk about When We Talk about Persons: The Language of Legal Fiction" (2001) 114:6 *Harvard Law Review* 1745.

Fanon, Frantz. *Peau noire, masques blancs* (Paris: Les Éditions du Seuil, 1952).

———. *Les damnés de la terre* (Paris: La Découverte, 2002).

Feldman, Allen. "On the Actuarial Gaze: From 9/11 to Abu Ghraib" in Nicholas Mirzoeff, ed, *The Visual Culture Reader*, 3rd ed (New York: Routledge, 2013) 163.

Fischer-Lescano, Andreas & Tillmann Löhr. *Legal Opinion: Border Controls at Sea: Requirements under International Human Rights and Refugee Law* (European Center for Constitutional and Human Rights, 2007).

Flynn, Leo. "See What I Mean: The Authority of Law and Visions of Women" in L. Bently & L. Flynn, eds, *Law and the Senses: Sensational Jurisprudence* (London: Pluto Press, 1996) 139.

Foucault, Michel. *The Order of Things: An Archaeology of the Human Sciences* (London: Routledge, 1970).

Frevert, Ute. "Honour and / or / as Passion: Historical Trajectories as Legal Defenses" (2014) 22 *Journal of the Max Planck Institute for European Legal History* 245.

Geurts, Kathryn Linn. *Culture and the Senses – Bodily Ways of Knowing in an African Community* (Berkeley: University of California Press, 2002).

Geurts, Kathryn Linn & Sekafor G.M.A. Komabu-Pomeyie. "From 'Sensing Disability' to Seselelame: Non-Dualistic Activist Orientations in Twenty-First-Century Accra" in Shaun Grech & Karen Soldatic, eds, *Disability in the Global South* (Cham: Springer, 2016) 85.

Gilman, Sander L. *Inscribing the Other* (Lincoln: University of Nebraska Press, 1991).

Gilroy, Paul. *Against Race: Imagining Political Culture beyond the Color Line* (Cambridge, MA: Harvard University Press, 2000).

———. "Multiculture and the Negative Dialectics of Conviviality" in Rebecka Rutledge Fisher & Jay Garcia, eds, *Retrieving the Human: Reading Paul Gilroy* (Albany, NY: SUNY Press, 2014).

Glendinning, Simon. "From Animal Life to City Life" (2000) 5:3 *Angelaki: Journal of the Theoretical Humanities* 19.

Glenn, H. Patrick. *Legal Traditions of the World: Sustainable Diversity in Law*, 5th ed (Oxford: Oxford University Press, 2014).

Golder, Ben. "Critical Humanities and the Human of International Human Rights Law" in Shane Chalmers & Sundhya Pahuja, eds, *Routledge Handbook of International Law and the Humanities* (New York: Routledge, 2023) 148.

Goldie, Peter. *The Emotions: A Philosophical Exploration* (Oxford: Oxford University Press, 2002).

Gombrich, Ernst Hans. *Histoire de l'art* (Paris: Phaidon, 2002).

Goodrich, Peter. *Oedipus Lex: Psychology, History, Law* (Berkeley, CA: University of California Press, 1995).

———. "Visiocracy: On the Futures of the Fingerpost" (2013) 39:3 *Critical Inquiry* 498.

———. *Legal Emblems and the Art of Law: Obiter Depicta as the Vision of Governance* (Cambridge: Cambridge University Press, 2014).

———. "Faces and Frames of Government" in Desmond Manderson, ed, *Law and the Visual: Representations, Technologies, and Critique* (Toronto: University of Toronto Press, 2018) 51.

Gramsci, Antonio. *Selections from the Prison Notebooks*, translated and edited by Q. Hoare & G. N. Smith (London: Lawrence & Wishart, 1971).

Grear, Anna. "Human Rights – Human Bodies? Some Reflections on Corporate Human Rights Distortion, the Legal Subject, Embodiment and Human Rights Theory" (2006) 17:2 *Law and Critique* 171.

Griffiths, John. "What Is Legal Pluralism?" (1986) 24 *Journal of Legal Pluralism* 1.

Grosfoguel, Ramón. "The Epistemic Decolonial Turn – Beyond Political-Economy Paradigms" (2007) 21:2–3 *Cultural Studies* 211.

Grove, Kevin. *Resilience* (London: Routledge, 2018).

Gündoğdu, Ayten. *Rightlessness in an Age of Rights: Hannah Arendt and the Contemporary Struggles of Migrants* (Oxford: Oxford University Press, 2015).

Haddad, Emma. *The Refugee in International Society: Between Sovereigns* (Cambridge: Cambridge University Press, 2008).

Hall, James. *The Self-Portrait: A Cultural History* (London: Thames & Hudson, 2014).

Hall, Stuart. "The Spectacle of the 'Other'" in Stuart Hall, ed, *Representation: Cultural Representations and Signifying Practices* (London: Sage, 1997) 223.

Hamilton, Peter. "Representing the Social: France and Frenchness in Post-War Humanist Photography" in Stuart Hall, ed, *Representation: Cultural Representations and Signifying Practices* (London: Sage, 1997) 76.

Hamilton, Sheryl N. "Introduction – Sensuous Governance" (2020) 15:1 *The Senses and Society* 1.

Hamilton, Sheryl N. et al. "Sensing Law – Introduction" in Sheryl N. Hamilton et al, eds, *Sensing Law* (New York: Routledge, 2017) 1.

Haraway, Donna. "The Persistence of Vision" in Nicholas Mirzoeff, ed, *The Visual Culture Reader*, 3rd ed (New York: Routledge, 2013) 359.

Harris, Cheryl I. "Whiteness as Property" (1993) 106:8 *Harvard Law Review* 1707.

Hartman, Saidita V. *Scenes of Subjection – Terror, Slavery, and Self-Making in Nineteenth-Century America* (New York: Oxford University Press, 1997).

Hayden, Patrick. "From Exclusion to Containment: Arendt, Sovereign, Power, and Statelessness" (2008) 3 *Societies without Borders* 248.

Hegarty, Paul. "Giorgio Agamben (1942-)" in Jon Simons, ed, *Contemporary Critical Theorists* (Edinburgh: Edinburgh University Press, 2010) 14.

Hibbitts, Bernard J. "'Coming to Our Senses': Communication and Legal Expression in Performance Cultures" (1992) 41:4 *Emory Law Journal* 873.

———. "Senses of Difference: A Sociology of Metaphors in American Legal Discourse" in L. Bently & L. Flynn, eds, *Law and the Senses: Sensational Jurisprudence* (London: Pluto Press, 1996) 97.

Hirschman, Albert O. *The Passions and the Interests: Political Arguments for Capitalism before Its Triumph* (Princeton, NJ: Princeton University Press, 1977).

Hochberg, Gil Z. *Visual Occupations: Violence and Visibility in a Conflict Zone* (Durham: Duke University Press, 2015).

Holder, Cindy L. & Jeff J. Corntassel. "Indigenous Peoples and Multicultural Citizenship: Bridging Collective and Individual Rights" (2002) 24:1 *Human Rights Quarterly* 126.

Howes, David. "Introduction: 'To Summon All the Senses'" in David Howes, ed, *The Varieties of Sensory Experience: A Sourcebook in the Anthropology of the Senses* (Toronto: University of Toronto Press, 1991) 3.

———. "Introduction: Empire of the Senses" in David Howes, ed, *Empire of the Senses – the Sensual Culture Reader* (New York: Berg, 2005) 1.

———. "Charting the Sensorial Revolution" (2006) 1:1 *Senses and Society* 113.

———. *The Sixth Sense Reader* (Oxford: Berg, 2009).

———. "Law's Sensorium: On the Media of Law and the Evidence of the Senses in Historical and Cross-Cultural Perspective" in Sheryl N. Hamilton et al, eds, *Sensing Law* (New York: Routledge, 2017) 53.

———. "Multisensory Anthropology" (2019) 48 *Annual Review of Anthropology* 17.

———. "Prologue: Introduction to Sensori-Legal Studies" (2019) 34:2 *Canadian Journal of Law and Society* 173.

———. "Afterword – The Sensory Revolution Comes of Age" (2021) 39:2 *The Cambridge Journal of Anthropology* 128.

———. "The Aesthetics of Mixing the Senses: Cross-Modal Aesthetics", <www.david-howes.com/senses/aestheticsofmixingthesenses.pdf> 75.

Howes, David & Constance Classen. *Ways of Sensing: Understanding the Senses in Society* (New York: Routledge, 2014).

Howitt, Richard & Sandra Suchet-Pearson. "Rethinking the Building Blocks: Ontological Pluralism and the Idea of 'Management'" (2006) 88:3 *Geografiska Annaler: Series B, Human Geography* 323.

Hsu, Elisabeth. "The Senses and the Social: An Introduction" (2008) 73:4 *Ethnos* 433.

Hudson, Laura. "A Species of Thought: Bare Life and Animal Being" (2011) 43:5 *Antipode* 1659.

Hunt, Sarah. "Ontologies of Indigeneity: The Politics of Embodying a Concept" (2014) 21:1 *Cultural Geographies* 27.

Ingold, Tim. *The Perception of the Environment: Essays on Livelihood, Dwelling and Skill* (London: Routledge, 2000).

Ingold, Tim & David Howes. "Worlds of Sense and Sensing the World: A Response to Sarah Pink and David Howes" (2011) 19:3 *Social Anthropology/Anthropologie Sociale* 313.

Jackson, Mark, ed. *Postcolonialism, Posthumanism and Political Ontology* (London: Routledge, 2017).

Jackson, Zakiyyah Iman. "Animal: New Directions in the Theorization of Race and Posthumanism" (2013) 39:3 *Feminist Studies* 669.

———. "Outer Worlds: The Persistence of Race in Movement 'Beyond the Human'" (2015) 21:2–3 *Gay and Lesbian Quarterly* 215.

Jay, Martin. *Downcast Eyes: The Denigration of Vision in Twentieth-Century French Thought* (Berkeley: University of California Press, 1993).

Jones, Amelia. "The Body and/in Representation" in Nicholas Mirzoeff, ed, *The Visual Culture Reader*, 3rd ed (New York: Routledge, 2013) 369.

Joseph, Jonathan. "Resilience as Embedded Neoliberalism: A Governmentality Approach" (2013) 1:1 *Resilience: International Policies, Practices and Discourses* 38.

Kennedy, David. "Spring Break" (1984) 63 *Texas Law Review* 1377.

———. "International Human Rights Movement: Part of the Problem?" (2002) 15 *Harvard Human Rights Journal* 101.

King, Barbara J. "The Orca's Sorrow" (2019) 320:3 *Scientific American* 30.

Kleinhans, Martha-Marie & Roderick A. Macdonald. "What Is a Critical Legal Pluralism?" (1997) 12 *Canadian Journal of Law and Society* 25.

Koch, Grace & Alexandra Crowe. "Song, Land and Ceremony: Interpreting the Place of Songs as Evidence for Australian Aboriginal and Torres Strait Islander Land Claims" (2013) 6 *Collaborative Anthropologies* 373.

Krause, Monika. "Undocumented Migrants: An Arendtian Perspective" (2008) 7(3) *European Journal of Political Theory* 331.

Kuokkanen, Rauna. "What Is Hospitality in the Academy? Epistemic Ignorance and the (Im)Possible Gift" (2008) 30:1 *Review of Education, Pedagogy, and Cultural Studies* 60.

Lamrani, Myriam. "Introduction – Beyond Revolution: Reshaping Nationhood through Senses and Affects" (2021) 39:2 *The Cambridge Journal of Anthropology* 1.

Law, Stephen. "Humanism" in Stephen Bullivant & Michael Ruse, eds, *The Oxford Handbook of Atheism* (Oxford: Oxford University Press, 2013) 263.

Lechte, John & Saul Newman. "Agamben, Arendt and Human Rights – Bearing Witness to the Human" (2012) 15:4 *European Journal of Social Theory* 522.

Leckey, Robert & Kim Brooks, eds. *Queer Theory: Law, Culture, Empire* (New York: Routledge, 2010).

Lévi-Strauss, Claude. *The Savage Mind* (London: Weidenfeld and Nicolson, 1962).

Lewis, Hope. "Reflections on 'BlackCrit' Theory: Human Rights" (2000) 45 *Villanova Law Review* 1975.

Linke, Uli. "Off the Edge of Europe – Border Regimes, Visual Culture, and the Politics of Race" in Sheryl N. Hamilton et al, eds, *Sensing Law* (New York: Routledge, 2017) 178.

Macdonald, Roderick A. "Pour la reconnaissance d'une normativité juridique implicite et 'inférentielle'" (1986) 18:1 *Sociologie et sociétés* 47.

———. "Metaphors of Multiplicity" (1998) 15:1 *Arizona Journal of International and Comparative Law* 69.

Macdonald, Roderick A. & David Sandomierski. "Against Nomopolies" (2006) 57 *Northern Ireland Legal Quarterly* 610.

Machin, David & Andrea Mayr. *How to Do Critical Discourse Analysis: A Multimodal Introduction* (London: Sage, 2023).

MacIntyre, Alasdair. *Whose Justice? Which Rationality?* (Notre Dame, IN: University of Notre Dame Press, 2020).

Makdisi, John. "Formal Rationality in Islamic Law and the Common Law" (1985) 34 *Cleveland State Law Review* 97.

———. "Legal Logic and Equity in Islamic Law" (1985) 33:1 *American Journal of Comparative Law* 63.

Maldonado-Torres, Nelson. "On the Coloniality of Being – Contributions to the Development of a Concept" (2007) 21:2–3 *Cultural Studies* 240.

Malkki, Liisa H. "Speechless Emissaries: Refugees, Humanitarianism, and Dehistoricization" (1996) 11:3 *Cultural Anthropology* 377.

Manderson, Desmond. "Senses and Symbols: The Construction of 'Drugs' in Historic and Aesthetic Perspective" in L. Bently and L. Flynn, eds, *Law and the Senses: Sensational Jurisprudence* (London: Pluto Press, 1996).

———. *Songs without Music – Aesthetic Dimensions of Law and Justice* (Berkeley: University of California Press, 2000).

———. "Introduction – Imaginal Law" in Desmond Manderson, ed, *Law and the Visual: Representations, Technologies, and Critique* (Toronto: University of Toronto Press, 2018).

Marable, Manning. "Black Studies and the Racial Mountain" (2000) 2:3 *Souls: Critical Journal of Black Politics & Culture* 17.

Marcus, George E. "Reason, Passion, and Democratic Politics: Old Conceptions – New Understandings – New Possibilities" in James E. Fleming, ed, *Passions and Emotions* (New York: New York University Press, 2013) 127.

Marks, Stephen. "The Human Right to Development: Between Rhetoric and Reality" (2004) 17 *Harvard Human Rights Journal* 137.

Marks, Susan. "Human Rights and Root Causes" (2011) 74:1 *Modern Law Review* 57.

Maroney, Terry A. "Law and Emotion: A Proposed Taxonomy of an Emerging Field" (2006) 30:2 *Law and Human Behavior* 119.

Marshall, Stephen H. "The Political Life of Fungibility" (2012) 15:3 *Theory and Event* (no page).

Martin, John Jeffries. "The Myth of Renaissance Individualism" in Guido Ruggiero ed, *A Companion to the Worlds of the Renaissance* (Malden, MA: Blackwell, 2007) 208.

Mbembé, Achille. "Necropolitics" (2003) 15:1 *Public Culture* 11.

McCrudden, Christopher, ed. *Understanding Human Dignity* (Oxford: Oxford University Press, 2013).

McCutcheon, Jani. "On *The Nullians*" in Jani McCutcheon & Fiona McGaughey, eds, *Research Handbook on Art and Law* (Cheltenham: Edward Elgar, 2020) 278.

McDermott, Yvonne, Alexa Koenig & Daragh Murray. "Open Source Information's Blind Spot: Human and Machine Bias in International Criminal Investigations" (2021) 19:1 *Journal of International Criminal Justice* 85.

McGoldrick, Dominic. "The Development and Status of Sexual Orientation Discrimination under International Human Rights Law" (2016) 16:4 *Human Rights Law Review* 613.

McGregor, Deborah. "Traditional Ecological Knowledge and Sustainable Development: Towards Coexistence" in Mario Blaser, Harvey A. Feit & Glenn McRea, eds, *In the Way of Development: Indigenous Peoples, Life Projects, and Globalization* (New York: Zed Books, 2004) 72.

McHugh, James. "The Classification of Smells and the Order of the Senses in Indian Religious Traditions" (2007) 54:4 *Religion through the Senses* 374.

McPherson, Annika. "Rastafari and/as Decoloniality" in Sabine Broeck & Carsten Junker, eds, *Postcoloniality – Decoloniality – Black Critique – Joints and Fissures* (Frankfurt: Campus Verlag, 2014) 353.

Melissaris, Emmanuel. "The More the Merrier? A New Take on Legal Pluralism" (2004) 13:1 *Social and Legal Studies* 57.

Menke, Christoph, Birgit Kaiser & Kathrin Thiele. "The 'Aporias of Human Rights' and the 'One Human Right': Regarding the Coherence of Hannah Arendt's Argument" (2007) 74(3) *Social Research* 739.

Merry, Sally Engle. "Legal Pluralism" (1988) 22 *Law & Society Review* 869.

Mignolo, Walter D. "Introduction – Coloniality of Power and De-Colonial Thinking" (2007) 21:2–3 *Cultural Studies* 155.

———. *The Darker Side of Western Modernity: Global Futures, Decolonial Options* (Durham: Duke University Press, 2011).

———. "Further Thought on (De)Coloniality" in Sabine Broeck & Carsten Junker, eds, *Postcoloniality – Decoloniality – Black Critique – Joints and Fissures* (Frankfurt: Campus Verlag, 2014) 21.

Minow, Martha. "Institutions and Emotions: Redressing Mass Violence" in Susan A. Bandes, ed, *The Passions of Law* (New York: New York University Press, 1999) 265.

Mirzoeff, Nicholas. *The Right to Look: A Counterhistory of Visuality* (Durham, NC: Duke University Press, 2011).

Mitchell, Timothy. "Orientalism and the Exhibitionary Order" in Donald Preziosi & Claire Farago, eds, *Grasping the World: The Idea of the Museum* (New York: Routledge, 2004) 442.

Mitchell, W.J.T. "Foreword: The Rights of Things" in Cary Wolfe, ed, *Animal Rites – American Culture, the Discourse of Species, and Posthumanist Theory* (Chicago: University of Chicago Press, 2003) ix.

Mokgoro, Yvonne. "*Ubuntu* and the Law in South Africa" (1998) 4 *Buffalo Human Rights Law Review* 115.

———. "Ubuntu, the Constitution and the Rights of Non-Citizens" (2010) 21 *Stellenbosch Law Review* 221.

Morton, Stephen. "Gayatri Chakravorty Spivak (1942-)" in Jon Simons, ed, *Contemporary Critical Theorists* (Edinburgh: Edinburgh University Press, 2010) 210.

Moten, Fred. "The Case of Blackness" (2009) 50:2 *Criticism* 177.

Murdoch, Jonathan. "Humanising Posthumanism" (2006) 7:4 *Social & Cultural Geography* 1356.

Napoleon, Val. "Extinction by Number: Colonialism Made Easy" (2001) 16:1 *Canadian Journal of Law and Society* 113.

———. "Aboriginal Self-Determination: Individual Self and Collective Selves" (2005) 29:2 *Atlantis* 31.

———. "Thinking about Indigenous Legal Orders" in René Provost & Colleen Sheppard, eds, *Dialogues on Human Rights and Legal Pluralism* (Dordrecht: Springer, 2013) 229.

Ndlovu-Gatsheni, Sabelo J. *Empire, Global Coloniality and African Subjectivity* (New York: Berghahn Books, 2013).

Nedelsky, Jennifer. "Embodied Diversity and the Challenges to Law" (1997) 42 *McGill Law Journal* 91.

Nékám, Alexander. *The Personality Conception of the Legal Entity* (Cambridge: Harvard University Press, 1938).

Newcomb, Rachel. "Modern Citizens, Modern Food: Taste and the Rise of the Moroccan Citizen-Consumer" in S. Trnka, C. Dureau & J. Park, eds, *Senses and Citizenships: Embodying Political Life* (New York: Routledge, 2013) 147.

Niezen, Ronald. "Culture and the Judiciary: The Meaning of the Culture Concept as a Source of Aboriginal Rights in Canada" (2003) 18:2 *Canadian Journal of Law and Society* 1.

Nimako, Kwame. "Location and Social Thought in the Black: A Testimony to Africana Intellectual Tradition" in S. Broeck & C. Junker, eds, *Postcoloniality – Decoloniality – Black Critique* (Frankfurt: Campus Verlag, 2014) 53.

Nussbaum, Martha. "Emotions and Women's Capabilities" in Martha Nussbaum & Jonathan Glover, eds, *Women, Culture and Development: A Study of Human Capabilities* (Oxford: Clarendon Press, 1995) 360.

———. "Secret Sewers of Vice: Disgust, Bodies, and the Law" in Susan A Bandes, ed, *The Passions of Law* (New York: New York University Press, 1999) 19.

Ong, Walter J. "The Shifting Sensorium" in David Howes, ed, *The Varieties of Sensory Experience* (Toronto: University of Toronto Press, 1991) 25.

Otto, Dianne. "International Human Rights Law: Towards Rethinking Sex/Gender Dualism" in Vanessa E. Munro & Margaret Davies, eds, *The Ashgate Research Companion to Feminist Legal Theory* (New York: Routledge, 2013) 197.

Outram, Dorinda. *The Enlightenment* (Cambridge: Cambridge University Press, 2011).

Owens, Patricia. "Reclaiming 'Bare Life'? Against Agamben on Refugees" (2009) 23:4 *International Relations* 567.

———. "Beyond 'Bare Life': Refugees and the 'Right to Have Rights'" in Alexander Betts & Gil Loescher, eds, *Refugees in International Relations* (Oxford: Oxford University Press, 2011) 133.

Pager, Devah & Hana Shepherd. "The Sociology of Discrimination: Racial Discrimination in Employment, Housing, Credit, and Consumer Markets" (2008) 34 *Annual Review of Sociology* 181.

Panagia, Davide. *The Political Life of Sensation* (London: Duke University Press, 2009).

Parker, James. "The Soundscape of Justice" (2011) 4 *Griffith Law Review* 962.

Pastoureau, Michel. *Noir: histoire d'une couleur* (Paris: Seuil, 2008).

Patterson, Orlando. *Slavery and Social Death: A Comparative Study* (Cambridge: Harvard University Press, 2000).

Pavlich, George. *Law and Society Redefined* (Oxford: Oxford University Press, 2010).

Petrarca, Francesco. *Petrarch's Secret or the Soul's Conflict with Passion: Three Dialogues between Himself and S. Augustine*, translated by William H. Draper (London: Chatto & Windus, 1911).

Philippopoulos-Mihalopoulos, Andreas. "Atmospheres of Law: Senses, Affects, Lawscapes" (2013) 7 *Emotion, Space and Society* 35.

Pico della Mirandola, Giovanni. *Oration on the Dignity of Man*, translated by A. Robert Caponigri (Chicago: Henry Regnery, 1956).

Pink, Sarah. *The Future of Visual Anthropology: Engaging the Senses* (New York: Routledge, 2006).

Pink, Sarah & David Howes. "The Future of Sensory Anthropology/the Anthropology of the Senses" (2010) 18:3 *Social Anthropology/Anthropologie Sociale* 331.

Porter, Roy. "Barely Touching: A Social Perspective on Mind and Body" in G. S. Rousseau, ed, *The Languages of Psyche* (Berkeley, CA: University of California Press, 1990) 45.

Posner, Richard, A. "Emotion versus Emotionalism in Law" in Susan Bandes, ed, *The Passions of Law* (New York: New York University Press, 1999) 309.

Potter, Caroline. "Sense of Motion, Senses of Self: Becoming a Dancer" (2008) 73:4 *Ethnos* 444.

Povinelli, Elizabeth A. "Do Rocks Listen? The Cultural Politics of Apprehending Australian Aboriginal Labor" (1995) 97:3 *American Anthropologist* 505.

———. "The Cunning of Recognition: Real Being and Aboriginal Recognition in Settler Australia" (1998) 11:1 *Australian Feminist Law Journal* 3.

Quijano, Aníbal. "Coloniality and Modernity/Rationality" (2007) 21:2–3 *Cultural Studies* 168.

Rabinow, Paul, ed. *The Foucault Reader* (New York: Pantheon, 1984).

Radcliffe, Sarah A. "Geography and Indigeneity I: Indigeneity, Coloniality and Knowledge" (2017) 41:2 *Progress in Human Geography* 220.

———. "Geography and Indigeneity II: Critical Geographies of Indigenous Bodily Politics" (2017) 42:3 *Progress in Human Geography* 436.

Rajagopal, Balakrishnan. "Counter-Hegemonic International Law: Rethinking Human Rights and Development as a Third World Strategy" (2006) 27 *Third World Quarterly* 767.

Rancière, Jacques. "Who is the Subject of the Rights of Man?" (2004) 103:2 *The South Atlantic Quarterly* 297.

Reid, Papaarangi, Donna Cormack & Sarah-Jane Paine. "Colonial Histories, Racism and Health – The Experience of Māori and Indigenous People" (2018) 28 *European Journal of Public Health (Supplement 1)* 3.

Rettberg, Jill Walker. *Seeing Ourselves Through Technology: How We Use Selfies, Blogs and Wearable Devices to See and Shape Ourselves* (New York: Palgrave, 2014).

Risam, Roopika. "Now You See Them: Self-Representation and the Refugee Selfie" (2018) 16:1 *Popular Communication* 58.

Roberts, Mark S. *The Mark of the Beast: Animality and Human Oppression* (West Lafayette, IN: Purdue University Press, 2008).

Rochelle, Safiyah. "Encountering the 'Muslim': Guantanamo Bay, Detainees, and Apprehensions of Violence" (2019) 34:2 *Canadian Journal of Law and Society* 209.

Rorty, Richard. "Human Rights, Rationality and Sentimentality" in Obrad Savić, ed, *The Politics of Human Rights* (New York: Verso, 1999) 67.

Rose, Gillian. *Visual Methodologist: An Introduction to Researching with Visual Materials*, 3rd ed (London: Sage, 2012).

Roth, Kenneth. "Defending Economic, Social and Cultural Rights: Practical Issues Faced by an International Human Rights Organization" (2004) 26 *Human Rights Quarterly* 63.

Saïd, Edward. *Orientalism* (New York: Vintage Books, 1978).

Sanders, Douglas. "Collective Rights" (1991) 13 *Human Rights Quarterly* 368.

Sanger, Carol. "Legislation with Affect: Emotion and Legislative Law Making" in James E. Fleming, ed, *Passions and Emotions* (New York: New York University Press, 2013) 38.

Santos, Boaventura de Sousa. "Three Metaphors for a New Conception of Law: The Frontier, the Baroque, and the South" (1995) 29:4 *Law & Society Review* 569.

———. "A Non-Occidentalist West? Learned Ignorance and Ecology of Knowledge" (2009) 26:7–8 *Theory, Culture & Society* 103.

———. *Epistemologies of the South – Justice against Epistemicide* (Boulder, CO: Paradigm Publishers, 2014).

———. "Epilogue: A New Vision of Europe: Learning from the South" in G. Bhambra & J. Narayan, eds, *European Cosmopolitanism: Colonial Histories and Postcolonial Societies* (New York: Routledge, 2017) 172.

———. "Human Rights, Democracy and Development" in Boaventura de Sousa Santos & Bruno Sena Martins, eds, *The Pluriverse of Human Rights: The Diversity of Struggles for Dignity* (New York: Routledge, 2021) 21.

Santos, Boaventura de Sousa & Bruno Sena Martins. "Introduction" in Boaventura de Sousa Santos & Bruno Sena Martins, eds, *The Pluriverse of Human Rights: The Diversity of Struggles for Dignity* (New York: Routledge, 2021) 1.

———, eds. *The Pluriverse of Human Rights: The Diversity of Struggles for Dignity* (New York: Routledge, 2021).

Schoolman, Morton. "Series Editor's Introduction" in Seyla Benhabib, ed, *The Reluctant Modernism of Hannah Arendt* (London: Sage, 1996) xxiii.

Schulze Wessel, Julia. "On Border Subjects: Rethinking the Figure of the Refugee and the Undocumented Migrant" (2016) 23:1 *Constellations* 46.

Schwartz, Andi. "Radical Vulnerability: Selfies as a Femme-Inine Mode of Resistance" (2022) 13:1 *Psychology and Sexuality* 43.

Sekimoto, Sachi. "Race and the Senses – Toward Articulating the Sensory Apparatus of Race" (2018) 6:1 *Critical Philosophy of Race* 82.

Seremetakis, C. Nadia. "The Memory of the Senses: Historical Perception, Commensal Exchange and Modernity" (1993) 9:2 *Visual Anthropology Review* 2.

Sexton, Jared. "People-of-Color-Blindness: Notes on the Afterlife of Slavery" (2010) 28:2 *Social Text* 31.

Sheehan, Paul. "Introduction – Contingencies of Humanness" in Paul Sheehan, ed, *Becoming Human: New Perspectives on the Inhuman Condition* (Westport, CT: Praeger, 2003) 1.

Sherwin, Richard K. *Visualizing Law in the Age of the Digital Baroque – Arabesques and Entanglements* (New York: Routledge, 2011).

Shohat, Ella. "The Struggle Over Representation: Casting, Coalitions, and Politics of Identification" in Román De La Campa, E Ann Kaplan & Michael Sprinkler, eds, *Late Imperial Culture* (London: Verso, 1995) 166.

Simm, Gabrielle. "Queering CEDAW? Sexual Orientation, Gender Identity and Expression and Sex Characteristics (SOGIESC) in International Human Rights Law" (2020) 29:3 *Griffith Law Review* 374.

Simpson, Audra. "Paths Toward a Mohawk Nation: Narratives of Citizenship and Nationhood in Kahnawake" in Duncan Ivison, Paul Patton & Will Sanders, eds,

Political Theory and the Rights of Indigenous Peoples (Cambridge: Cambridge University Press, 2000) 113.

Singer, Peter. "Prologue: Ethics and the New Animal Liberation Movement" in Peter Singer, ed, *In Defense of Animals* (New York: Blackwell, 1985) 1.

Sithole, Tendayi. "The Concept of the Black Subject in Fanon" (2016) 47:1 *Journal of Black Studies* 24.

Slobodchikoff, C. N. et al. "Semantic Information Distinguishing Individual Predators in the Alarm Calls of Gunnison's Prairie Dogs" (1991) 42 *Animal Behavior* 713.

———. "Prairie Dog Alarm Calls Encode Labels about Predator Colors" (2009) 12:3 *Animal Cognition* 435.

Smith, Linda Tuhiwai. *Decolonizing Methodologies: Research and Indigenous Peoples* (London: Zed Books, 1995).

Solomon, Robert C. "Justice v. Vengeance: On Law and the Satisfaction of Emotions" in Susan A Bandes, ed, *The Passions of Law* (New York: New York University Press, 1999) 123.

Sontag, Susan. *On Photography* (New York: Farrar, Straus and Giroux, 1977).

Spelman, Elizabeth V. *Inessential Woman: Problems of Exclusion in Feminist Thought* (Boston: Beacon Press, 1988).

Spillers, Hortence. *Black, White, and in Colour: Essays on American Literature and Culture* (Chicago: Chicago University Press, 2003).

Spivak, Gayatri Chakravorty. "Criticism, Feminism, and the Institution" in Sarah Harasym, ed, *Gayatri Chakravorty Spivak: The Post-Colonial Critic* (New York: Routledge, 1990) 1.

———. "Subaltern Talk: Interview with the Editors" in Donna Landry & Gerald MacLean, eds, *The Spivak Reader: Selected Works of Gayatri Chakravorty Spivak* (New York: Routledge, 1996) 287.

———. *A Critique of Postcolonial Reason: Toward a History of the Vanishing Present* (Cambridge, MA: Harvard University Press, 1999).

Stern, Kristina. "Law and the Lack of Sense" in L. Bently & L. Flynn, eds, *Law and the Senses: Sensational Jurisprudence* (London: Pluto Press, 1996) 42.

Stoller, Paul. *Sensuous Scholarship* (Philadelphia: University of Pennsylvania Press, 1997).

Stroeken, Koen. "Sensory Shifts and 'Synaesthetics' in Sukuma Healing" (2008) 73:4 *Ethnos* 466.

Sturken, Marita & Lisa Cartwright. *Practices of Looking: An Introduction to Visual Culture*, 2nd ed (Oxford: Oxford University Press, 2009).

Sundberg, Juanita. "Decolonizing Posthumanist Geographies" (2014) 21:1 *Cultural Geographies* 33.

Sutherland-Smith, Wendy. "Justice Unmasked: A Semiotic Analysis of Justitia" (2011) 185 *Semiotica* 213.

Swiffen, Amy. *Law, Ethics and the Biopolitical* (New York: Routledge, 2010).

———. "Giorgio Agamben: Thought between Two Revolutions" in Charles Barbour & George Pavlich, eds, *After Sovereignty – On the Question of Political Beginnings* (New York: Routledge, 2010) 166.

———. "Derrida Contra Agamben: Sovereignty, Biopower, History" (2012) 2 *Societies* 345.

Synnott, Anthony. *The Body Social: Symbolism, Self and Society* (New York: Routledge, 1993).

Tamanaha, Brian. "A Non-Essentialist Version of Legal Pluralism" (2000) 27 *Journal of Law & Society* 296.

Tlostanova, Madina. "The Imperial-Colonial Chronotope – Istanbul-Baku-Khurramabad" (2007) 21 *Cultural Studies* 406.

Trnka, Susanna, Christine Dureau & Julie Park. "Introduction: Senses and Citizen-ships" in S. Trnka, C. Dureau & J. Park, eds, *Senses and Citizenships: Embodying Political Life* (New York: Routledge, 2013) 1.

van Boven, Theo. "Reparative Justice: Focus on Victims" (2007) 25:4 *Netherlands Quarterly of Human Rights* 723.

van Ede, Yolanda. "Sensuous Anthropology: Sense and Sensibility and the Rehabilita-tion of Skill" (2009) 15:2 *Anthropological Notebooks* 61.

Vanita, Ruth, "'Wedding of Two Souls': Same-Sex Marriage and Hindu Traditions" (2004) 20:2 *Journal of Feminist Studies in Religion* 119.

van Leeuwen, Theo. "Semiotics and Iconography" in Theo van Leeuwen & Carey Jewitt, eds, *The Handbook of Visual Analysis* (London: Sage, 2001) 92.

van Leeuwen, Theo & Carey Jewitt, eds. *The Handbook of Visual Analysis* (London: Sage, 2020).

Vaughan-Williams, Nick. "We are *Not* Animals! Humanitarian Border Security and Zoopolitical Spaces in EUrope" (2015) 45 *Political Geography* 1.

Viroulaud, Julie. "Jean-Jacques-François Le Barbier l'aîné et francs-maçons: autour d'une oeuvre d'inspiration maçonnique, La *Déclaration de l'homme et du citoyen*" (2011) 4 *Études* 80.

Walcott, Rinaldo. "The Problem of the Human: Black Ontologies and 'the Coloniality of Our Being'" in Sabine Broeck & Carsten Junker, eds, *Postcoloniality – Decoloniality – Black Critique – Joints and Fissures* (Frankfurt: Campus Verlag, 2014) 93.

Watt, Gary. "Law Suits: Clothing as the Image of Law" in L. Dahlberg, ed, *Visualizing Law and Authority. Essays on Legal Aesthetics* (Berlin: Walter de Gruyter, 2012) 23.

Weheliye, Alexander G. *Habeas Viscus: Racializing Assemblages, Biopolitics, and Black Feminist Theories of the Human* (Durham: Duke University Press, 2014).

West, Robin. "Disciplines, Subjectivity, and Law" in Austin Sarat & Thomas Kearns, eds., *The Fate of Law* (Ann Arbour: University of Michigan Press, 1991) 119.

———. "The Anti-Empathic Turn" in James E. Fleming, ed, *Passions and Emotions* (New York: New York University Press, 2013) 243.

Whatmore, Sarah. *Hybrid Geographies* (London: Sage, 2002).

———. "Humanism's Excess: Some Thoughts on the 'Post-Human/ist' Agenda" (2006) 7:4 *Social & Cultural Geography* 1360.

———. "Materialist Returns: Practicing Cultural Geography in and For a More-Than-Human World" (2006) 13 *Cultural Geographies* 600.

Wilderson III, Frank B. *Red, White & Black – Cinema and the Structure of U.S. An-tagonisms* (Durham: Duke University Press, 2010).

Wilke, Christiane. "The Optics of War: Seeing Civilians, Enacting Distinctions, and Visual Crisis in International Law" in Sheryl N. Hamilton et al., eds, *Sensing Law* (New York: Routledge, 2017) 257.

Williams, John & Anthony F. Lang, Jr. "Introduction" in Anthony F. Lang, Jr & John Williams, eds, *Hannah Arendt and International Relations: Readings Across the Lines* (New York: Palgrave Macmillan, 2005) 1.

Williams, Robert A. *Savage Anxieties: The Invention of Western Civilization* (New York: Palgrave Macmillan, 2012).

Wilner, Isaiah Lorado. "A Global Potlatch: Identifying the Indigenous Influence on Western Thought" (2013) 37:2 *American Indian Culture and Research Journal* 87.

Wilson, Richard A. *The Politics of Truth and Reconciliation in South Africa: Legiti-mizing the Post-Apartheid State* (Cambridge: Cambridge University Press, 2001).

Wimpfheimer, Barry. "Talmudic Legal Narrative: Broadening the Discourse of Jewish Law" (2007) 24 *Diné Yisrael* 157.

Wolfe, Cary. *Animal Rites – American Culture, the Discourse of Species, and Posthu-manist Theory* (Chicago: University of Chicago Press, 2003).

———. *What is Posthumanism?* (Minneapolis: University of Minnesota Press, 2010).

Wynter, Sylvia. "1492: A New Worldview" in V Hyatt & R Nettleford, eds, *Race, Discourse, and the Origin of the Americas* (Washington, DC: Smithsonian Institution Press, 1995) 5.

———. "The Re-Enchantment of Humanism: An Interview with Sylvia Wynter" (2000) 8 *Small Axe* 119.

Young, Iris Marion. "Impartiality and the Civic Public: Some Implications of Feminist Critiques of Moral and Political Theory" (1986) 5:4 *Praxis International* 381.

Young-Bruehl, Elisabeth. "Hannah Arendt's Storytelling" (1977) 44:1 *Social Research* 183.

Reports, websites and other resources

Amnesty International UK. "What is the Universal Declaration of Human Rights?", <www.amnesty.org.uk/universal-declaration-human-rights-UDHR>.

Artist Profile. "Atong Atem", <www.artistprofile.com.au/atong-atem>.

Artnet, "Emily Kame Kngwarreye", <www.artnet.com/artists/emily-kame-kngwarreye/>.

———. "Petyarre Gloria Tamerre", <www.artnet.com/artists/petyarre-gloria-tamerre/>.

———. "Weaver Jack", <www.artnet.com/artists/weaver-jack/>.

Berry, Mike, Inaki Garcia-Blanco & Kerry Moore. *Press Coverage of the Refugee and Migrant Crisis in the EU: A Content Analysis of Five European Countries, Report prepared for the United Nations High Commissioner for Refugees* (Cardiff: Cardiff University, 2016).

Bryans, John. "Masculinity Studies and the Senses", <www.lawandthesenses.org>.

Caruana, Wally. "The Bridge – A Brief History of Modern Aboriginal Art" in *Ancestral Modern: Australian Aboriginal Art*, <https://seattleartmuseum.org/Documents/Ancestral-Modern-Exhibition-Catalogue.pdf>.

The Design Files. "The Bright, Beautiful World of Atong Atem", <https://thedesignfiles.net/2018/04/the-bright-beautiful-world-of-atong-atem>.

El-Hadi, Nehal. "Harlem on the Prairies: How Blackness Is Harmfully Used as Shorthand" (15 April 2021) *CBC News*, <www.cbc.ca/news/canada/saskatchewan/black-on-the-prairies-harlem-1.5986189>.

Elysée. "Déclaration des droits de l'homme et du citoyen", <www.elysee.fr/la-presidence/la-declaration-des-droits-de-l-homme-et-du-citoyen>.

European Court of Human Rights. "Factsheet – Migrants in Detention" (March 2021), <www.echr.coe.int/Documents/FS_Migrants_detention_ENG.pdf>.

Farbota, Kim. "Black Crime Rates: What Happens When Numbers Aren't Neutral" (9 February 2015) *Huffington Post*, <www.huffingtonpost.com/kim-farbota/black-crime-rates-your-st_b_8078586.html>.

Garland Magazine. "The Nullians", <https://garlandmag.com/article/the-nullians/>.

Gharib, Malaka. "Stunning Photos Depict Migrants 'As They'd Rather Be Seen'" (7 October 2018), <www.npr.org/sections/goatsandsoda/2018/10/07/654492288/stunning-photos-depict-migrants-as-theyd-rather-be-seen>.

Guterres, António. "The World Faces a Pandemic of Human Rights Abuses in the Wake of Covid-19" (22 February 2021) *The Guardian*, <www.theguardian.com/global-development/2021/feb/22/world-faces-pandemic-human-rights-abuses-covid-19-antonio-guterres>.

Hamilton, Rebecca. "The Hidden Danger of User-Generated Evidence for International Criminal Justice" (23 January 2019) *Just Security*, <www.justsecurity.org/62339/hidden-danger-user-generated-evidence-international-criminal-justice/>.

Harsch, Leonie. "Giving Refugees a Voice? Looking Beyond 'Refugee Stories'" (8 January 2018) *Refugee Hosts*, <https://refugeehosts.org/2018/01/08/giving-refugees-a-voice-looking-beyond-refugee-stories/>.

Human Rights Watch. "Greece: Camp Conditions Endanger Women, Girls" (4 December 2019), <www.hrw.org/news/2019/12/04/greece-camp-conditions-endanger-women-girls>.

———. "Covid-19 Triggers Wave of Free Speech Abuse" (11 February 2021), <www.hrw.org/news/2021/02/11/covid-19-triggers-wave-free-speech-abuse>.

———. "Saudi Arabia: Mass Killings of Migrants at Yemen Border" (21 August 2023), <www.hrw.org/news/2023/08/21/saudi-arabia-mass-killings-migrants-yemen-border>.

International Organization for Migration. *World Migration Report 2015 – Migrants and Cities: New Partnerships to Manage Mobility*, <http://publications.iom.int/system/files/wmr2015_en.pdf>.

———. *World Migration Report 2020*, <https://publications.iom.int/system/files/pdf/wmr_2020.pdf>.

"Jacques Derrida and the Question of 'The Animal', Interview with Jacques Derrida", <www.youtube.com/watch?v=Ry49Jr0TFjk>.

Julie Dowling, <www.juliedowling.net/solo-shows.html>.

Khazam, Olivia. "The Senses on Trial", <www.lawandthesenses.org>.

Kilburn, Jessye. "A Lawyer and a Lady? Visual Aesthetics of Femininity and Professionalism in Law", <www.lawandthesenses.org>.

Lakhani, Nina. "Is There a Crisis at the Border?" (19 March 2021) *The Guardian*, <www.theguardian.com/us-news/2021/mar/18/us-mexico-immigration-border-crisis>.

Media 19. "Blog Archive Self Portrait Refugee", <www.media19.co.uk/projects/self-portrait-refugee/>.

Musée Carnavalet. "Déclaration des droits de l'homme et du citoyen", <www.carnavalet.paris.fr/fr/collections/declaration-des-droits-de-l-homme-et-du-citoyen>.

National Archives. "Abolition of the Slave Trade", <www.nationalarchives.gov.uk/pathways/blackhistory/rights/abolition.htm>.

National Inquiry into Missing and Murdered Indigenous Women and Girls. "Executive Summary of the Final Report" (2019), <www.mmiwg-ffada.ca/wp-content/uploads/2019/06/Executive_Summary.pdf>.

National Museum of Australia. "Emily Kame Kngwarreye", <www.nma.gov.au/exhibitions/utopia/emily-kame-kngwarreye>.

———. "Managing the Collection", <www.nma.gov.au/about/corporate/annual-reports/annual-report-2011–2012/part-two-performance-reports/managing-the-collection>.

———. "Warakurna History Paintings", <www.nma.gov.au/explore/collection/highlights/warakurna-history-paintings>.

O'Brien, Jennifer. "Refugees Use Art to Find a Little Freedom" (22 October 2018) *The Times*.

The Observer France. "The Observer View on the Riots in France: A Grim Tale of the Growing Gulf between Haves and Have-Nots" (2 July 2023), <www.theguardian.com/commentisfree/2023/jul/02/observer-view-riots-france-nahel-merzouk>.

Office of the Auditor General of Canada. "Access to Safe Drinking Water in First Nations Communities – Indigenous Services Canada" (2021), <https://opencanada.blob.core.windows.net/opengovprod/resources/7445c056-703f-4dee-85a0-886102794011/parl_oag_202102_03_e.pdf?sr=b&sp=r&sig=VgNsS5jGt9UlRw7CzKntUUT8z5%2B/qkFwaOM/HlspiAE%3D&sv=2015-07-08&se=2021-10-04T21%3A02%3A24Z>.

Online Etymology Dictionary, <www.etymonline.com>.

Outstation Gallery. "Tjukurrpa Purtingkatja (History Paintings Part 2)", <www.outstation.com.au/exhibitions/2012/tjukurrpa-purtingkatja-history-paintings-part-2/>.

The Pin. "Atong Atem", <www.thepin.org/meet/atong-atem>.

Pro Asyl. *Walls of Shame: Accounts from the Inside: The Detention Centers of Evros* (2012), <www.proasyl.de/fileadmin/fm-dam/q_PUBLIKATIONEN/2012/Evros-Bericht_12_04_10_BHP.pdf>.

———. *Pushed back: systematic human rights violations against refugees in the aegean sea and the greek-turkish land border* (2013), <www.proasyl.de/wp-content/uploads/2015/12/PRO_ASYL_Report_Pushed_Back_english_November_2013.pdf>.

Raffan, Jane. "The 'I' in Indigenous Art" (2013), <www.portrait.gov.au/magazines/46/indigenous-portraiture>.

Redrock Gallery. "Gloria Petyarre – Bush Leaf Dreaming", <www.redrockgallery.net/products/Gloria-Petyarre%252dBush-Leaf-Dreaming%252dRRG223.html>.

Schmidt, Chrischona. "Utopia: The Genius of Emily Kame Kngwarreye" (2008) 4:1 *re-Collections*, <https://recollections.nma.gov.au/issues/vol_4_no1/exhibition_reviews/utopia>.

Short St Gallery. "Weaver Jack", <www.shortstgallery.com.au/artworks/786559-weaver-jack-lungarung/>.

Statistics Canada. "Suicide among First Nations People, Métis and Inuit" (2011–2016), <www150.statcan.gc.ca/n1/pub/99–011-x/99–011-x2019001-eng.htm>.

Thomas, Sarah-Michelle. "Contesting Allegations: The Islamic Veil and Gender In/Equality", <www.lawandthesenses.org>.

———. "Growing Out of Touch: The Social and Sensory Regulation of Childhood", <www.lawandthesenses.org>.

Thompson, Christian, <www.christianthompson.net/all/australian-graffiti-series-2007>.

Trans-Atlantic Slave Trade Database (hosted by Emory University), <www.slavevoyages.org>.

Treaties and Historical Research Centre, P.R.E. Group, Indian and Northern Affairs. "Historical Development of the Indian Act" (1978).

"Ukraine Crisis: Violent Brawl at Kiev Parliament" (8 April 2014) *BBC News*, <www.bbc.com/news/world-europe-26933905>.

UNHCR Story Telling, <www.youtube.com/channel/UCjSP8f2bRQlE122zSiAJmIw>.

United Nations. "Global Issues: Migration", <www.un.org/en/global-issues/migration>.

———. "History of the Declaration", <www.un.org/en/sections/universal-declaration/history-document/index.html>.

———. *International Migration 2013*, <www.un.org/en/development/desa/population/migration/publications/wallchart/docs/wallchart2013.pdf>.

———. "Universal Declaration of Human Rights", <www.un.org/en/universal-declaration-human-rights/index.html>.

United Nations High Commissioner for Refugees. "Budget and Expenditure", <https://reporting.unhcr.org/financial#tabs-financial-contributions>.

United States Sentencing Commission. *Booker Report2012*, <www.ussc.gov/sites/default/files/pdf/news/congressional-testimony-and-reports/booker-reports/2012-booker/Part_A.pdf#page=55>.

University of British Columbia. "First Nations & Indigenous Studies", <http://indigenousfoundations.arts.ubc.ca/the_indian_act/#potlatch>.

UN Office of the High Commissioner for Human Rights. "About Indigenous Peoples and Human Rights", <www.ohchr.org/EN/Issues/IPeoples/Pages/AboutIndigenousPeoples.aspx>.

———. *Annual Report 2013*, <www2.ohchr.org/english/OHCHRReport2013/WEB_version/allegati/downloads/1_The_whole_Report_2013.pdf>.

———. "Indigenous Peoples Have Been Disproportionately Affected by COVID-19 – Senior United Nations Official Tells Human Rights Council" (28 September 2021), <www.ohchr.org/EN/NewsEvents/Pages/DisplayNews.aspx?NewsID=27556&LangID=E>.

———. "Millennium Development Goals and Human Rights Standards", <www.ohchr.org/EN/Issues/SDGS/Pages/MDGsStandards.aspx>.

UN Special Rapporteur on the Human Rights of Migrants, <https://ohchr.org/EN/Issues/Migration/SRMigrants/Pages/SRMigrantsIndex.aspx>.

UN Sustainable Development Group. "Human Rights-Based Approach", <https://unsdg.un.org/2030-agenda/universal-values/human-rights-based-approach>.

Walfish, Simcha. "Credibility and Immediacy in Refugee Hearings", <www.lawandthesenses.org>.

Wang, Lily Maya. "The Legal Paradox of Linguistic Profiling", <www.lawandthesenses.org>.

———. "A Sensory Exploration of the Tsuu T'ina Court", <www.lawandthesenses.org>.

Wikipédia. "Déclaration des droits de l'homme et du citoyen 1789", <https://fr.wikipedia.org/wiki/D%C3%A9claration_des_droits_de_l%27homme_et_du_citoyen_de_1789>.

Wikipedia. "Universal Declaration of Human Rights", <https://en.wikipedia.org/wiki/Universal_Declaration_of_Human_Rights>.

Zouev, Alexandre. "COVID and the Rule of Law: A Dangerous Balancing Act", <www.un.org/en/coronavirus/covid-and-rule-law-dangerous-balancing-act>.

Index

Printed in the United States
by Baker & Taylor Publisher Services